THE PEERS® CURRICULUM FOR SCHOOL-BASED PROFESSIONALS

The PEERS® Curriculum for School-Based Professionals brings UCLA's highly acclaimed and widely popular PEERS® program into the school setting. This 16-week program, clinically proven to significantly improve social skills and social interactions among teens with Autism Spectrum Disorder (ASD), is now customized for the needs of psychologists, counselors, speech pathologists, administrators, and teachers. The manual is broken down into clearly divided lesson plans, each of which have concrete rules and steps, corresponding homework assignments, plans for review, and unique, fun activities to ensure that teens are comfortable incorporating what they've learned. The curriculum also includes parent handouts, tips for preparing for each lesson, strategies for overcoming potential pitfalls, and the research underlying this transformative program.

Elizabeth A. Laugeson, PsyD, is a licensed clinical psychologist and an assistant clinical professor in the department of psychiatry and biobehavioral sciences at the UCLA Semel Institute for Neuroscience and Human Behavior. Dr. Laugeson is the director of The Help Group – UCLA Autism Research Alliance, a collaborative research initiative dedicated to developing and expanding applied clinical research in the treatment of children and adolescents with ASD. She is also the founder and director of the UCLA PEERS® Clinic, an outpatient hospital-based program providing parent-assisted social skills training for adolescents and young adults with ASD, as well as youths with ADHD, depression, anxiety, and other social impairments.

THE PEERS® CURRICULUM FOR SCHOOL-BASED PROFESSIONALS

Social Skills Training for Adolescents with Autism Spectrum Disorder

Elizabeth A. Laugeson

Routledge
Taylor & Francis Group

NEW YORK AND LONDON

First published 2014
by Routledge
711 Third Avenue, New York, NY 10017

and by Routledge
27 Church Road, Hove, East Sussex BN3 2FA

© 2014 Taylor & Francis

Routledge is an imprint of the Taylor & Francis Group, an informa business

Library of Congress Cataloging in Publication Data
A catalog record for this book has been requested

ISBN: 978–0–415–70576–9 (hbk)
ISBN: 978–0–415–62696–5 (pbk)
ISBN: 978–0–203–10237–4 (ebk)

Typeset in Stone Serif by Refinecatch Limited, Bungay, Suffolk

Printed and bound in the United States of America by Publishers Graphics,
LLC on sustainably sourced paper.

This book is dedicated to the educators who work tirelessly to help their students, both academically and socially.

CONTENTS

TABLES

ABOUT THE AUTHOR

Dr. Elizabeth Laugeson is a licensed clinical psychologist and an assistant clinical professor in the Department of Psychiatry and Biobehavioral Sciences at the UCLA Semel Institute for Neuroscience and Human Behavior. Laugeson is the founder and director of the UCLA PEERS® Clinic, which is an outpatient hospital-based program providing parent-assisted social skills training for teens and young adults with Autism Spectrum Disorder (ASD), Attention-Deficit/Hyperactivity Disorder (ADHD), depression, anxiety, and other social impairments. She is also the director of The Help Group – UCLA Autism Research Alliance, which is a collaborative research initiative dedicated to developing and expanding applied clinical research in the treatment of children and adolescents with ASD.

As a principal investigator and collaborator on a number of research studies, she has investigated the effectiveness of social skills training for youth from preschool to early adulthood, and is the co-developer of the *Program for the Education and Enrichment of Relational Skills (PEERS®)*, an evidence-based social skills intervention for teens and young adults. This program has been translated and disseminated in over a dozen countries to date. The author of two additional books, *Social Skills for Teenagers with Developmental and Autism Spectrum Disorders: The PEERS Treatment Manual* (Laugeson & Frankel, 2010) and *The Science of Making Friends: Helping Socially Challenged Teens and Young Adults* (Laugeson, 2013), she is considered one of the world's leading experts in evidence-based social skills training.

Laugeson received her doctorate in clinical psychology from Pepperdine University in 2004, and completed a pre-doctoral psychology internship and a post-doctoral research fellowship at UCLA in 2004 and 2007, respectively. She regularly conducts national and international training seminars for educators and mental health professionals on her evidence-based social skills programs, and has presented her research at conferences throughout the world. Her work has been featured on national and international media outlets such as *People Magazine, Los Angeles Times, New York Times, Washington Post, USA Today*, CBS, NBC, and Channel 4 in the United Kingdom.

In this current work, Laugeson shares her research-supported strategies for teaching social skills to adolescents with ASD in the school setting.

PREFACE

This manual is based upon the original work, *Social Skills for Teenagers with Developmental and Autism Spectrum Disorders: The PEERS Treatment Manual*, which is a parent-assisted social skills program for adolescents with Autism Spectrum Disorder (ASD) and other social challenges. The research upon which the original work was conducted was funded through a Ruth L. Kirschstein National Research Service Award, through the National Institutes of Health Training Grant NIH T32-MH17140 (Andrew Leuchter, Principal Investigator). The research upon which this derivative work was conducted was funded through grants from the Nathan and Lily Shapell Foundation, the Shapell and Guerin Family Foundation, and The Friends of the Semel Institute at UCLA.

This manual includes several adaptations of the original *PEERS Treatment Manual*, replacing the original parent-assisted outpatient model with a teacher-facilitated school-based model. Using the new curriculum, social skills groups that were once facilitated by mental health professionals in clinical settings are now taught in the classroom by school personnel, much like we would teach math or science. One benefit of the current approach is that we teach social skills in one of the most natural adolescent social settings of all: the school. Parents are provided with Parent Handouts outlining the lessons and corresponding homework assignments each week, but concurrent parent groups are not offered in this manual. School personnel wishing to include parent groups as part of their program are encouraged to do so by using the Parent Therapist Guides found in the original *PEERS Treatment Manual*.

Another departure from the original manual is that this curriculum utilizes a daily lesson format rather than a once weekly format. School personnel present the curriculum daily in the classroom for 30–60 minutes at a time, 4–5 days per week, as opposed to once a week for 90 minutes. School personnel wishing to conduct weekly 90-minute groups should use the suggestions for modifying this curriculum described in Chapter 1 or refer to the original *PEERS Treatment Manual*.

This manual is also different from the original manual in that it includes 16 weeks of lessons, as opposed to the 14 weeks offered in the parent-assisted program. The supplement of two additional weeks of material includes an added lesson on strategies for handling cyber bullying, as well as the separation of didactic lessons on handling physical bullying and changing a reputation, which were combined into one lesson in the original manual. The additional didactic lesson on cyber bullying was developed as an outgrowth of greater research in this area since the publication of the original manual in 2010. The separation of lessons on handling physical bullying and changing a reputation was the result of feedback from teachers involved with the implementation of the PEERS® curriculum in the school setting during two large research trials.

In an effort to stay current with the evolving research in social skills, this manual also includes additional lesson content above and beyond handling cyber bullying. New ecologically valid social skills have been added to nearly every lesson, including new lessons on **starting individual conversations** and **exchanging contact information**, for example. Dozens of additional rules, steps, and buzz phrases of social behavior have also been added to the lessons, such as **don't police** others during conversations, **use a prop** when **entering group conversations**, and **stay near an adult when the bully is around**, to name a few.

Just as the didactic content for PEERS® has evolved, so too have the role-play demonstrations, which highlight the targeted skills. New and updated role-play demonstrations of appropriate and inappropriate social behavior are offered in this manual to help facilitators provide a means for teaching the skills. New role-play demonstrations include humorous examples of **policing** and **getting too personal** during conversations, inappropriate use of **eye contact** and **body boundaries**, and tactics for **handling rumors and gossip**, just to highlight a few. New and revised role-play demonstrations will provide facilitators with additional tools for providing fun and engaging delivery of the lesson content.

Another significant addition to this manual includes the use of **Perspective Taking Questions** throughout the lessons. The UCLA PEERS® Clinic (the place in which this curriculum was originally developed and tested) uses **Perspective Taking Questions** as a matter of standard practice in our research and clinical groups for teens and adults. These questions follow good and bad role-play demonstrations of targeted social skills in order to improve social cognition. **Perspective Taking Questions** include, *"What do you think that was like for that person?" "What do you think they thought of the other person?"* and *"Do you think they'll want to talk to the other person again?"* Appropriate responses are provided at the end of each series of **Perspective Taking Questions** to enhance teaching and promote discussion. These questions have been added to this manual given research findings suggesting improved social cognition following treatment, in addition to overall improvements in social skills and friendships.

While the overarching content of this curriculum is based upon the original *PEERS® Treatment Manual*, it is expected that the change in format from weekly lessons to daily lessons, the supplement of new lessons and didactic content, as well as the addition of new role-play demonstrations and perspective taking questions, will provide new users and even seasoned experts of the PEERS® curriculum with useful new strategies for teaching social skills in the school setting.

ACKNOWLEDGEMENTS

The research and clinical work upon which this manual is based is a huge collaborative effort. I wish to thank our amazing team of clinicians, researchers, and graduate students for their hard work and dedication to what we fondly call Team PEERS®. Most particularly, a special thanks to my clinical team: Shannon Bates, Mina Park, Jennifer Sanderson, Jessica Hopkins, and Enjey Lin—your clinical gifts are the backbone of our program and your dedication to our families is truly inspiring. To my research team: most especially Lara Tucci, Yasamine Bolourian, Ruth Ellingsen, Josh Mandelberg, and Ashley Dillon—thank you for giving credence to our work and allowing me to *geek out* with you on the data. To my editorial team: Jason Tinero, Melissa Wasserman, Lyndsay Brooks, Meagan Cronin, and Rohini Bagrodia, most of whom masquerade as graduate students when they're not busy copy-editing social skills treatment manuals—thank you for always going the extra mile. To our *friendly army* of research assistants and behavioral coaches: thank you for being the legs on which we stand—without your contributions, we would not get far.

To my friends and colleagues at UCLA: I wish to thank Peter Whybrow and Jim McCracken for their support of this work and my research; Fred Frankel, Mary O'Connor, and Blair Paley for introducing me to the wonderful world of social skills research; and Andy Leuchter for being the kind of inspirational and supportive mentor I aspire to be.

A special thanks to my colleagues and collaborators at The Help Group. I am most particularly indebted to Barbara Firestone, Susan Berman, Philip Levin, Pamela Clark, and all of the amazing teachers at Village Glen School for their steadfast support of our research efforts. Thank you for giving PEERS® a welcome home in your schools and allowing us to do this important research.

I also wish to thank our generous donors and funders for making possible the research on which this manual is founded. To my dear friends Vicky Goodman, Patty Evans and Sally Weil at The Friends of the Semel Institute at UCLA, thank you for your continual support of our research program—it's nice to be a friend of The Friends. To Vera Guerin and the Shapell and Guerin Family Foundation, thank you for your unwavering support of our research with PEERS® in the school setting. Without your generosity, we would not be where we are today.

No list of thanks would be complete without acknowledging the love and support of my family and friends. To my husband, Lance Orozco, thank you for your constant encouragement and patience through the endless writing retreats. To my mother, Janet Tate, thank you for giving my creativity a home and for helping me become who I am. To my besties, Jennifer Wilkerson, Carrie Raia, and Dan Oakley, thank you for your friendship. In PEERS®, we often say *friendship is a choice*— I'm glad we chose each other.

Finally, to the amazing families we have had the privilege and pleasure of working with, thank you for inspiring this work and giving meaning to all we do. You have touched our hearts, challenged our minds, and made us better for knowing you—you are the *gift* in the giving.

GETTING STARTED

Use of the PEERS® Curriculum

The Program for the Education and Enrichment of Relational Skills (PEERS®) was originally developed as a parent-assisted intervention focusing on teens in middle school and high school who were having difficulty making and keeping friends. The program has been field-tested extensively with teens and young adults with Autism Spectrum Disorder (ASD), and to a lesser extent with teens diagnosed with Intellectual Disabilities (ID), Fetal Alcohol Spectrum Disorders (FASD), and Attention-Deficit/Hyperactivity Disorder (ADHD). PEERS® is also used clinically with teens and young adults with depression, anxiety, and other social challenges.

The curriculum is intended for higher functioning adolescents without significant intellectual disabilities, focusing on skills related to making and keeping friends and managing peer conflict and rejection. Lessons include having two-way conversations, entering and exiting conversations, electronic forms of communication, choosing appropriate friends, using humor appropriately, being a good sport, having successful get-togethers, managing arguments with friends, and handling teasing, physical bullying, and other forms of social rejection. Rules and steps of social behavior are created from research evidence regarding: (1) the common social errors often committed by those with ASD, (2) the core social skills needed to make and keep friends, and (3) the ecologically valid ways in which socially accepted teens handle peer conflict and rejection.

The PEERS® curriculum is meant to be used as a complete program in its entirety. Lessons are intended to be delivered in the order they are presented, as each skill builds upon the last. The orientation of the manual is cognitive-behavioral in the sense that material is presented as a series of rules or steps to be followed by teens. Didactic lessons are based upon ecologically valid social skills known to be used by socially successful teens. The techniques used, such as role-play demonstrations, behavioral rehearsal exercises, and homework assignments have been shown to improve social skills outcomes through research.

The curriculum has been used in public and nonpublic schools, as well as outpatient mental health programs and residential programs, both in North America and abroad. The effectiveness of the curriculum was initially established through our research at the UCLA PEERS® Clinic, where we have conducted multiple research trials and social skills groups in the school and hospital settings with over 700 adolescents. The effectiveness of the program has been further validated through multiple studies conducted inside and outside of the United States by research teams unaffiliated with UCLA. At present, the PEERS® intervention has been translated and used in over a dozen countries around the world.

Delivery methods for instruction have been modified over the past eight years, based upon therapist and educator feedback. The current school-based curriculum and techniques reflect many years of research, and clinical and educational practice with teens with social skills challenges. School personnel need not have much experience running social skills groups in order to use the curriculum effectively, but they should have background knowledge in working with teens with ASD.

Organization of the Manual

PEERS® is conducted as a structured class focused on teaching teens the social skills necessary to make and keep friends and improve their reputation among peers®. An overview of the curriculum is presented in Table 1.1.

This manual is intended to serve as a step-by-step outline for each lesson. Through our work with educators, we have found that an outline rather than a narrative script facilitates a more spontaneous-sounding presentation of the material, and is easier to follow as it allows the instructor to ad-lib with material consistent with each lesson. This manual is meant to be used at the time of each class. Memorization of the curriculum is neither required nor encouraged. Students seem comfortable with instructors having the manual open in front of them as they guide the class through the skills. The rationale for following the manual closely is that the instructor needs to be sure to cover all the necessary elements of the skills being taught.

Chapter 1 provides an introduction to the curriculum and includes information about the organization of the manual, composition of classes, required personnel, teaching methods, and behavioral management techniques. Chapter 1 also includes information about what you can expect and how to track progress. Chapters 2–17 include daily lesson guides highlighting the 16-week PEERS® curriculum. The material includes information about preparing for the lessons, how to conduct homework reviews, how to present didactic lessons, role-play demonstrations, and behavioral rehearsal exercises, as well as guidelines for conducting teen activities.

Daily Lesson Format

In Chapters 2–17 of the manual, the curriculum is presented using a daily lesson format such that lessons are taught daily in the classroom for 30–60 minutes at a time, 4–5 days per week, over a 16-week period. The first day of the week generally includes a review of the socialization homework assignments from the previous week (with the exception of week one, which includes an introduction to the class). Day two of the week involves the presentation of a didactic lesson, sometimes including role-playing exercises to be demonstrated by the instructors. Day three involves a brief review of the lesson from the previous day and a behavioral rehearsal exercise in which the teens practice the newly learned skill. Days four and five involve a teen activity in which students practice newly learned social skills through a socialization activity. Skills presented in the daily lesson format are identical to those taught in the weekly lesson format found in the original PEERS® Treatment Manual.

Table 1.1 Overview of Curriculum

Week	Didactic	Homework Review	Teen Activity	Materials Needed	Homework Assignment
1	Introduction and Trading Information	None	Jeopardy	Board, markers, Jeopardy answer sheets, scissors, pens	1. In-class call 2. Practice trading info with parent
2	Two-Way Conversations	1. In-class call 2. Practice trading info with parent	Jeopardy	Board, markers, Jeopardy answer sheets, scissors, pens	1. In-class call 2. Practice trading info with parent
3	Electronic Communication	1. In-class call 2. Practice trading info with parent	Jeopardy	Board, markers, Jeopardy answer sheets, scissors, pens	1. In-class call 2. Practice phone call with parent 3. Personal item
4	Choosing Appropriate Friends	1. In-class call 2. Practice phone call with parent 3. Personal item	Trading information about personal items	Board, markers	1. In-class call 2. Out-of-class call 3. Extracurricular activities 4. Personal item
5	Appropriate Use of Humor	1. In-class call 2. Out-of-class call 3. Extracurricular activities 4. Personal item	Trading information about personal items	Board, markers	1. In-class call 2. Out-of-class call 3. Extracurricular activities 4. Humor feedback 5. Personal item
6	Starting and Joining Conversations	1. In-class call 2. Out-of-class call 3. Extracurricular activities 4. Humor feedback 5. Personal item	Entering conversations	Board, markers	1. Join a conversation 2. In-class call 3. Out-of-class call 4. Extracurricular activities 5. Humor feedback 6. Personal item
7	Exiting Conversations	1. Join a conversation 2. In-class call 3. Out-of-class call 4. Extracurricular activities 5. Humor feedback 6. Personal item	Entering and exiting conversations	Board, markers	1. Join a conversation 2. Out-of-class call 3. Extracurricular activities 4. Inside game
8	Good Sportsmanship	1. Join a conversation 2. Out-of-class call 3. Extracurricular activities 4. Inside game	Good sportsmanship with inside games	Board, markers, inside games	1. Be a good sport 2. Join a conversation 3. Out-of-class call 4. Extracurricular activities 5. Inside game
9	Get-Togethers	1. Be a good sport 2. Join a conversation 3. Out-of-class call 4. Extracurricular activities 5. Inside game	Get-togethers and good sportsmanship	Board, markers, inside games	1. Get-together 2. Be a good sport 3. Join a conversation 4. Inside game

(Continued overleaf)

Table 1.1 Overview of Curriculum (continued)

Week	Didactic	Homework Review	Teen Activity	Materials Needed	Homework Assignment
10	Handling Arguments	1. Get-together 2. Be a good sport 3. Join a conversation 4. Inside game	Get-togethers and good sportsmanship	Board, markers, inside games	1. Get-together 2. Be a good sport 3. Handle an argument 4. Inside game
11	Changing Reputations	1. Get-together 2. Be a good sport 3. Handle an argument 4. Inside game	Get-togethers and good sportsmanship	Board, markers, inside games	1. Get-together 2. Be a good sport 3. Steps to change a reputation 4. Handle an argument 5. Outdoor sports equipment
12	Handling Teasing and Embarrassing Feedback	1. Get-together 2. Be a good sport 3. Steps to change a reputation 4. Handle an argument 5. Outdoor sports equipment	Good sportsmanship and outdoor activities	Board, markers, outdoor sports equipment, outdoor play area or gymnasium	1. Get-together 2. Using teasing comebacks 3. Steps to change a reputation 4. Handle an argument 5. Outdoor sports equipment
13	Handling Physical Bullying	1. Get-together 2. Using teasing comebacks 3. Steps to change a reputation 4. Handle an argument 5. Outdoor sports equipment	Good sportsmanship and outdoor activities	Board, markers, outdoor sports equipment, outdoor play area or gymnasium	1. Get-together 2. Handle physical bullying 3. Using teasing comebacks 4. Steps to change a reputation 5. Outdoor sports equipment
14	Handling Cyber Bullying	1. Get-together 2. Handle physical bullying 3. Using teasing comebacks 4. Steps to change a reputation 5. Outdoor sports equipment	Good sportsmanship and outdoor activities	Board, markers, outdoor sports equipment, outdoor play area or gymnasium	1. Get-together 2. Handle cyber bullying 3. Handle physical bullying 4. Using teasing comebacks 5. Steps to change a reputation 6. Outdoor sports equipment
15	Minimizing Rumors and Gossip	1. Get-together 2. Handle cyber bullying 3. Handle physical bullying 4. Using teasing comebacks 5. Steps to change a reputation 6. Outdoor sports equipment	Good Sportsmanship and Outdoor Activities	Board, markers, outdoor sports equipment, outdoor play area or gymnasium	1. Get-together 2. Handle rumors and gossip 3. Handle cyber bullying 4. Handle physical bullying 5. Steps to change a reputation
16	Final Review, Post-Test Assessment, and Graduation	1. Get-together 2. Handle rumors and gossip 3. Handle cyber bullying 4. Handle physical bullying 5. Steps to change a reputation	Graduation party and ceremony	Post-test measures, graduation diplomas, food, beverages, plates, napkins, cups, silverware, decorations, TV, DVD player, PG-rated DVDs	None

Classes must be highly structured to maintain the focus of the lessons and the skills being taught. Each of the daily lesson guides (with the exception of Weeks 1 and 16) are broken down to include the following:

- **Preparing for the Lesson**. The rationale for each lesson is presented in this section to help instructors place appropriate emphasis on the most important material. Possible issues that may arise during the lesson are discussed and suggestions for how to overcome these issues are provided.

- **Homework Review (Day One)**. Reviewing the homework at the beginning of the week underscores the importance of homework completion and allows sufficient time to troubleshoot homework problems, thereby individualizing the curriculum to the specific needs of each student.

- **Didactic Lesson (Day Two)**. The didactic material is usually presented using a Socratic method and/or through the use of role-play demonstrations. These methods of instruction keep the teens engaged and give them a feeling of competence that they (at least collectively) are generating the rules or steps themselves.

- **Lesson Review and Behavioral Rehearsal (Day Three)**. One way for teens to begin to translate the material into their daily lives is to practice newly learned skills in school while receiving performance feedback from instructors. This occurs on day three during the Behavioral Rehearsal. Teens engage in a brief overview of the lesson, in some cases observe a role-play demonstration, and then practice the newly learned skills. Skills must also be used outside of the classroom in order to be useful, which is why homework assignments are also given on day three. By assigning weekly homework corresponding to new and previous lessons, the instructor establishes a formal way in which the teens will begin to generalize the newly learned skills outside of the classroom.

- **Teen Activity (Days Four and Five)**. If teens do not find the lessons fun and rewarding, they will be less likely to use the skills being taught. The Teen Activity is not only a fun part of the class, but also affords additional opportunities to practice newly learned skills. The Teen Activity section helps instructors effectively facilitate relevant socialization activities and includes the following:

  - **Lesson Review**. Days Four and Five begin with a brief lesson review in which teens regenerate the rules and/or steps from the lesson. This is followed by some socialization activity in which teens practice newly learned skills while receiving coaching with performance feedback.
  - **Materials Needed**. A list of materials needed for the activity is presented in the Teen Activity section. Items should be secured prior to the start of the class when possible.
  - **Rules**. Specific instructions on how to facilitate the activity are provided in this section, including how to coach and give points during the activity.

- **Parent Handout**. Parent handouts appear at the end of every chapter of the corresponding week. The handouts are suitable for photocopying purposes and should be distributed to parents at the beginning of the week for each lesson. Handouts are provided to keep parents abreast of the skills being taught, and to provide useful tips about how to help teens generalize the skills to the home and community setting through the completion of weekly socialization homework assignments. The current curriculum does not include a parent component beyond these handouts; however, in our research through the UCLA PEERS® Clinic we have found the participation of parents in this program to be significantly beneficial. School personnel interested in conducting concurrent parent social coaching groups should utilize our parent-assisted manual, *Social Skills for Teenagers with Developmental and Autism Spectrum Disorders: The PEERS Treatment Manual* (Laugeson & Frankel, 2010), which includes structured lessons for weekly 90-minute teen groups and parent groups.

Weekly Lesson Format

School personnel interested in conducting weekly social skills classes might consider using this manual in the following manner, once a week during 90-minute classes:

- **Homework Review (30 minutes).** Review the homework at the beginning of the class following the guidelines in Day One of the daily lesson guides.

- **Didactic Lesson and Role-Play Demonstrations (40 minutes).** Present the didactic lesson, including role-play demonstrations, found in Day Two of the daily lesson guides.

- **Teen Activity (15 minutes).** Have teens practice newly learned skills through behavioral rehearsal exercises outlined in the Teen Activity section, found in Days four–five of the daily lesson guides.

- **Homework Assignment (5 minutes).** Provide an overview of the homework assignments for the coming week as described in the Teen Activity section, found in Days four–five of the daily lesson guides.

- **Parent Handout.** Distribute Parent Handouts to interested family members each week. Parent Handouts appear at the end of each chapter and are meant to be photocopied.

Alternatively, *Social Skills for Teenagers with Developmental and Autism Spectrum Disorders: The PEERS Treatment Manual* (Laugeson & Frankel, 2010) includes structured lessons for weekly 90-minute groups. This alternative manual includes separate teen and parent sessions, although school personnel could choose to implement the teen group alone if parent groups are not feasible.

Composition of the Class

Social Motivation

One of the most important deciding factors about who should be included in your class relates to social motivation. Only teens expressing an interest in making and keeping friends should be included in the class. Including those who do not want to be there is a recipe for disaster and will likely result in attrition and/or a negative contagion.

Class Size

The recommended PEERS® class size is between 7–10 students, although we have tested the program in classes comprised of as many as 15 students. More than 15 students per class could be difficult, but not impossible, with some adaptations. For example, time allotted for homework review and behavioral rehearsal would have to be adjusted accordingly.

Age Distribution of the Class

Classes may have a wide range in age providing there is more than one teen around the same grade level. Ideally, middle school and high school groups should be separate, but this is not absolutely necessary.

Gender Distribution of the Class

Girls and boys are easily mixed in PEERS® without problems. Historically, boys are more likely to present for social skills treatment, so it is likely that classes will be composed of fewer girls. It is recommended that classes with only one female member be avoided, unless the girl agrees.

Including Students Without ASD

It has been repeatedly observed that teens with ASD are often most comfortable and appear to thrive more successfully in social skills groups with other teens with ASD. Therefore, homogenous PEERS® classes for teens with ASD are encouraged. However, teens with ADHD, depression, anxiety, and other social behavioral problems, who are accepting of the unique challenges of teens with ASD, might also be included. Although the curriculum was developed for teens with ASD, we have seen lasting benefits for other teens as well. Since PEERS® targets skill development through instruction of *ecologically valid social skills* (those behaviors exhibited by socially accepted teens), PEERS® may have widespread applicability, regardless of the diagnosis of the teen. We suspect that any teen who does not know the rules for developing and maintaining friendship could benefit from this curriculum.

Required Personnel

School-based PEERS® instructors typically include teachers, school counselors, school psychologists, speech and language therapists, occupational therapists, recreational therapists, school nurses, teacher aides, and teaching assistants. Whatever the professional background, instructors should have previous experience working with high-functioning teens with ASD and be fully trained on all aspects of the PEERS® curriculum, either by reading this manual beforehand or attending a PEERS® Training Seminar.

In addition to having one primary instructor, it will be essential to have 1–2 behavioral coaches to assist with the class. Behavioral coaches often include teacher aides, teaching assistants, or other school personnel. Some schools have even included neurotypical peer mentors as coaches in PEERS® classes, although the effectiveness of this approach has yet to be tested. Coaches should be trained on all aspects of the PEERS® curriculum and have a good understanding of behavior management strategies. Behavioral coaches are often responsible for conducting role-play demonstrations, providing performance feedback through coaching during behavioral rehearsal exercises and teen activities, and assisting the primary instructor with reinforcement and behavior management.

Physical Facilities

The PEERS® curriculum should be presented much like any class, particularly during the homework review and didactic portions of the lessons. The classroom should have a whiteboard and markers, with tables/desks and chairs for students to sit facing the board. Smartboards may be used, but rules and steps from the lesson should not be created prior to the class, as the lesson should appear to be generated by the students using a Socratic method. Sufficient space should be available in the classroom to break the class into smaller dyads or groups during behavioral rehearsal exercises. Teen activities during Weeks 12–15 are conducted on an outside play area or in an indoor gymnasium in order to practice good sportsmanship during sports activities. Access to sports equipment such as a basketball hoop, soccer net, and/or volleyball net is preferable if possible. In the event that such outdoor accommodations are not possible, teen activities for Weeks 12–15 will need to be modified for indoor games as described in Weeks 8–11.

Materials Needed

The following materials will need to be available for the class:

- **Phone Roster.** A roster including each student's name and number, where they can be easily reached for in-class phone assignments, is needed for Weeks 1–6 to practice conversational skills. This roster should be distributed to teens during the first week of the class (see Appendix C). Depending on the policies of the school, consent from parents to release this information to other students may be needed.

- **In-Class Call Assignment Log.** This sheet is needed to track in-class call assignments during Weeks 1–6, while teens are practicing conversational skills with one another. Keeping careful track of which teens are assigned to call one another will enable instructors to switch the order of "caller" and "receiver" for these phone calls and video chats, while ensuring that teens call different classmates throughout this process (see Appendix D).

- **Daily Point Log.** The Daily Point Log is used to track the individual points earned during each day of the class. This log should include the name of each teen, along with individual points used toward the distribution of graduation prizes (see Appendix E).

- **Good Sportsmanship Point Log.** A few copies of the Good Sportsmanship Point Log will be needed in Weeks 8–15 to track teens' attempts at good sportsmanship during both indoor games and outdoor sports activities. The number of point logs needed will be determined by the number of instructors and behavioral coaches in the class (see Appendix F).

- **Homework Compliance Sheets.** These sheets are highly recommended to track weekly progress and completion of homework assignments. The Homework Compliance Sheets may be completed by a behavioral coach during the Homework Review on Day One of each week. These sheets might be filed for future reference and used to track program compliance (see Appendix G).

- **Certificates of Completion.** These certificates are given at the graduation ceremony on the last day of the class. It is strongly encouraged that certificates be awarded as a way of honoring the accomplishments of the students and celebrating their achievements (see Appendix H).

- **Dry Erase Board and Markers**. A dry erase board and markers used for keeping track of teens' points and writing the rules or steps from the lessons will be an essential tool for the class.

- **Teen Activity Materials**. Additional materials needed for the teen activities are provided in the "Teen Activity" section of the weekly lesson guides (typically Days 4–5).

Teaching Methods

Didactic Lessons using Concrete Rules and Steps

Many teens with ASD have a penchant for rules and are likely to follow them. This may be due to the fact that the world is generally unpredictable, and rules provide a stable means of understanding social surroundings. Those with ASD are also known for thinking in very concrete and literal ways. Taking into account this preference for rules, and the tendency to think in black-and-white terms, PEERS® teaches social skills using concrete rules and steps of social behavior. Sophisticated and sometimes complex social behaviors are deconstructed into smaller rules and steps in order to aid comprehension during didactic lessons.

Ecologically Valid Social Skills

One aspect of PEERS® that is unique from other social skills programs is the use of ecologically valid social skills. This essentially involves teaching social behaviors that are naturally used by teens that are socially accepted. In other words, this includes not teaching what adults often tell teens to do in social situations, but what actually works according to research.

Socratic Method

Another important teaching method utilized through PEERS® includes the use of the Socratic method. This involves asking certain questions, or demonstrating certain behaviors through role-play exercises, that elicit specific responses from teens. This method essentially feeds students the answers without actually giving them the answers. The power in this approach is that it gives teens the sense that they or their peers® are generating the rules and steps of social behavior. Rather than lecturing, having the teens generate elements of the lessons using the Socratic method ensures that they are more likely to believe what is taught and remember what is learned.

Role-Play Demonstrations

The modeling of appropriate and inappropriate social behavior is a critical ingredient to understanding social skills. Role-play demonstrations are used throughout the PEERS® manual to illustrate specific rules and steps of social etiquette. Examples of role-play demonstrations are provided in a scripted format in the lesson guides to assist instructors and behavioral coaches in understanding how to demonstrate certain behaviors. These scripts are not intended to be read verbatim, but instead serve as an example of what a role-play demonstration might look like.

Perspective Taking Questions

In order to promote better social cognition, perspective taking questions are provided following role-play demonstrations. These questions will help facilitate discussion with students about appropriate and inappropriate social behavior, while assisting teens with reading social cues and understanding the perspectives of others.

Use of Buzzwords

Another unique aspect of the PEERS® curriculum is the use of ***buzzwords***. Terms that are ***bold and italicized*** in the manual are buzzwords and represent important concepts from the curriculum. The buzzwords represent complex social behaviors that can be identified in just a few simple words. Using the buzzwords as much as possible will help to develop a common language between instructors, behavioral coaches, teens, and parents. When instructors come across the first instances of buzzwords in the lesson guide, they should emphasize the words when speaking and write them down on the board.

Behavioral Rehearsal Exercises

In order to fully comprehend a particular set of social skills, it is necessary to actually use them through practice and repetition. The use of behavioral rehearsal exercises occurs in Days 3–5 of the daily lessons, and during the teen activity portion of the weekly lessons. Behavioral rehearsal exercises are often labeled as such, but also include the socialization activities described in the Teen Activity sections of the manual.

Coaching with Performance Feedback

To receive the full benefit of behavioral rehearsal opportunities, it is also critical that instructors and behavioral coaches provide performance feedback through coaching. Parents are also encouraged to provide coaching in the home and community, as described in the Parent Handouts. Coaching is an important component of PEERS® because not all students will perfect these skills immediately, and will instead need additional assistance in mastering and generalizing the skills being taught.

Homework Assignments

Each lesson includes homework assignments to promote the use of skills in more natural settings. Some of the assignments are intended to be completed by teens and parents, although the degree to which parents will be involved with these assignments varies greatly. Either way, instructors and behavioral coaches should strongly encourage the practicing of newly learned skills outside of the classroom. Our research suggests that when teens do not complete their homework assignments, the program is less effective.

Behavioral Management Techniques

Some teens may be disruptive during the class and will require behavioral management techniques to modify these disruptions. Three particular types of behaviors that will require attention include: (1) inattention (e.g., trouble focusing or maintaining attention); (2) disruption (e.g., engaging in behaviors that distract or disturb the lesson); and (3) disrespect (e.g., teasing, bullying, making rude or inappropriate comments). Suggestions for how to handle these behaviors are listed below.

Verbal Praise

One of the most powerful behavioral management techniques you have with socially motivated teens is the use of verbal praise. Periodically praising the class or individual students for behaviors you want to see will probably increase their frequency. For example, saying, *"You guys are doing a great job listening,"* or *"I like how you're raising your hand before you speak,"* are nice ways to encourage teens to act in a socially appropriate manner.

Reinforcement Using Points

In each class, teens should be earning points for completing homework assignments, through class participation, and the following of rules. During the first class, teens are told that they will be earning points toward a graduation party with graduation prizes. However, these incentives do not hold the power of the points. The true power in using points comes from social comparison. Teens' names should be listed on the whiteboard in the front of the room tracking points during every class. You will observe teens watching their points very closely. They may even begin to count them, or remind you if you have forgotten to give them a point for something. In fact, we have observed that teens that are known to speak very little in class will begin to participate more just to get points. Again, this is probably just a simple case of social comparison or competition. Regardless of the reason, this behavioral management strategy works, so be sure to use the point system. If points are not visible on the board and are tallied separately by behavioral coaches, they will not be effective.

Using Names to Redirect Attention

It is fairly common for teens to appear to drift off during lessons. They will sometimes appear distracted when in fact they are attending perfectly, although it is difficult to know for sure. If you suspect a teen is having trouble paying attention, rather than interrupting the lesson to bring them back to task, simply use their name as you're presenting the lesson. For example, you might say, *"So Jimmy, one of the rules for trading information is . . ."* or *"So the goal of trading information is to find common interests, right Jimmy?"* (nodding your head to prompt him). Using names to redirect attention is a nice way to bring your students back to task without embarrassing them or seeming punitive.

Using Peer Pressure

Teens will invariably make inappropriate comments or behave improperly from time to time. Rather than scold teens in front of their peers®, causing defensiveness or hurt feelings, apply a little peer pressure and utilize the situation as a teachable moment. You can do this by using the very handy sentence stem, *"What could be the problem with . . .?"* followed by responses from students uninvolved with the inappropriate behavior. Never ask the student who is engaging in the inappropriate behavior what the problem with their behavior is, as that will not work. Instead, ask the other teens what is wrong with a certain behavior, and they will be happy to answer your question. Avoid asking questions like, *"What was wrong with Jimmy's behavior?"* since this is too personal. The question should be vague and general. The vast majority of teens will not argue with their peers® over these points and you can simply move on. Here are some common examples of how it works:

- When a teen talks out of turn, you might say, *"We need to raise our hands. What could be the problem with not raising our hands in this class?"*

- When a teen inappropriately laughs at someone else's comment, you might say, *"We need to be respectful. What could be the problem with laughing at people?"*

- When a teen tries to make jokes during the class, you might say, *"We need to be serious. What could be the problem with making jokes in class?"*

- When a teen points out another teen's mistake, you might say, *"We don't police people. What could be the problem with policing?"*

These comments will help redirect the teens toward the behavioral expectations you have established, while avoiding being too punitive at first. By using this method, you are applying peer pressure without directly calling out the misbehaving teen. It will be natural for teens to test limits initially. If you address these situations with respect, you will be able to minimize the negative effects.

Stating Your Expectations

One helpful way to redirect inappropriate behavior from the class is to state your expectations. Using the examples above, comments include saying things like, *"We need to raise our hands,"* *"We need to be respectful,"* or *"We need to be serious."* After stating your expectations, you quickly move on as if you fully expect them to comply. If you wait for your students to agree, you may find yourself in a standoff. Interestingly, when you state your expectations to a group of socially motivated teens, and you expect them to comply, they usually do. You should also use the pronoun *"we"* rather than *"I"* when stating your expectations. This gives the impression that you are speaking on behalf of the class, which applies a bit of healthy peer pressure.

Giving Warnings

If a teen misbehaves during the class, you may need to give a warning by saying what the teen is doing wrong, what the consequence will be for continuing that behavior, and what you expect him or her to do differently. For example, you might say, *"Jimmy, this is a warning. If you continue to make jokes, I'm going to have to send you out of class. We need you to be serious."* It is acceptable to give a few warnings before enforcing the consequence, so long as the teen gives some appropriate response to each warning. If the teen continues to misbehave after repeated warnings, give one final warning. For example, you might say, *"Jimmy, this is your final warning. If you continue to make jokes, we're going to have to send you out of class."* If the behavior does not improve, follow through on the consequence.

Enforcing Consequences

When removing the teen from class:

- Find a neutral location where no other students are present if possible.

- Briefly explain the behavioral problem.

- Say what you expect him or her to do differently.

- Explain that he or she is welcome to come back to the class when ready to behave appropriately.

  ○ Example: *"You were getting pretty silly in there. I'm going to give you some time to think. When you're ready to be more serious, you're free to come back to the class."*

- Once the teen returns to class, wipe the slate clean and do not bring up the inappropriate behavior from before.

Handling Verbal or Physical Threats

Two types of misbehavior that should receive immediate consequences involve verbal or physical attacks. This includes simulated or pretend fighting. It is never acceptable for a teen to be teased, bullied, or physically threatened in any form during the class. These rare instances should result in immediate removal of the teen from the class. Depending on school policies, the teen may return to the class once the matter has been adequately addressed. It is critical for all teens to feel safe in the class and for these types of incidents to be addressed immediately. It is important to have behavioral coaches who are trained to handle these issues while the instructor continues with the rest of the class.

Including Parents as Social Coaches

Although this manual does not include a parent-assisted component, apart from providing parents with weekly handouts highlighting the lessons and corresponding homework assignments, it is highly recommended that school personnel include parents and other family members in the program as much as possible.

The simplest and most straightforward way to include parents is by distributing PEERS® Parent Handouts each week. These handouts may be found at the end of each weekly lesson guide and should be photocopied and sent home. In previous school-based programs using PEERS®, facilitators have chosen to send these handouts home via student delivery methods, communication logs, or through the mail. Many school personnel have also opted to scan Parent Handouts and send them as electronic documents directly to parents over email.

Another option for including parents in this program would be to offer weekly 90-minute parent groups during the duration of the class. Although this option may not be feasible for some schools, inclusion of parent groups is anticipated to enhance outcome. For school personnel interested in providing weekly parent groups, please refer to the original work, *Social Skills for Teenagers with Developmental and Autism Spectrum Disorders: The PEERS Treatment Manual* (Laugeson & Frankel, 2010), which includes lesson guides for parent groups.

Whatever the method of inclusion, involvement of parents and other family members will likely improve the effectiveness and generalizability of your school-based program through the use of social coaching outside of the school setting.

Using this Curriculum with Young Adults

PEERS® also uses a caregiver-assisted model to teach young adults with ASD how to develop and maintain meaningful relationships. This 16-week program utilizes a separate manual known as the *PEERS® for Young Adults Treatment Manual*, which includes modified lessons adapted from the original manual, as well as four new lessons related to dating etiquette. New didactic material on dating etiquette includes ecologically valid strategies for letting someone know you like them, assessing interest, asking someone on a date, accepting rejection, organizing and having successful dates, and general dating do's and don'ts. Social coaching is provided by caregivers close to young adults with ASD, including parents, adult siblings, peer mentors, job coaches, life coaches, or other family members. Although the *PEERS® for Young Adults Treatment Manual* is anticipated to follow the publication of this manual by 1–2 years, educators and practitioners interested in using the program sooner might use the existing manuals as an alternative tool in the interim, as approximately 65 percent of the young adult manual is derived from the original PEERS® manual.

Tracking Progress

Tracking progress is an essential part of determining whether your program is working. It is how a program maintains quality control. Below are the tests we have used in our published studies with PEERS®. Several standardized assessments of social functioning are included. These measures are widely available and have shown substantial change following the program. They also impose few demands upon teachers, teens, and parents to complete. Teachers and teens should complete the pre- and post-test assessments before and after the program. The forms can easily be administered as a packet sent to parents to complete before the class begins and again after the class ends.

Social Responsiveness Scale, Second Edition (SRS-2; Constantino & Gruber, 2012)

The SRS-2 consists of 65 items assessing the presence and severity of social deficits (i.e., social awareness, social cognition, social communication, social motivation, and restricted interests and repetitive behaviors) associated with ASD as they occur in natural social settings. The SRS-2 can be completed by teachers and parents. It was normed on a representative national sample and has good internal consistency ($a = .95$), interrater agreement reliability ($r = .61$), and convergent validity (Constantino & Gruber, 2012).

Social Skills Improvement System (SSIS; Gresham & Elliot, 2008)

The SSIS is a standardized, 75-item measure that assesses social skills (communication, cooperation, assertion, responsibility, empathy, engagement, self-control) and problem behaviors (externalizing and internalizing behaviors, bullying, hyperactivity and inattention, ASD-related behaviors) for adolescents between the ages of 13 and 18 years. Using a four-point rating system, teachers, parents, and students rate the frequency and relative importance of various social skills and problem behaviors.

Social Anxiety Scale (SAS; La Greca & Lopez, 1998)

The SAS was developed to assess perceptions of children's and adolescent's feelings of social anxiety in the context of their peer relations. The SAS can be administered to parents and teens and has been found to have good convergent validity with the Social Phobia and Anxiety Inventory for Children (SPAI-C) in a sample of 1,147 adolescents aged 13–17 years. The fit indices of confirmatory factor analyses were comparable to those obtained in prior studies and supported the hypothesized models of the SAS-P and SPAI-C. The internal consistency was good, and 12-month test–retest reliability was modest for both measures. A significant, positive correlation was found between the SAS-P and SPAI-C, showing that these measures assess related, but relatively independent, constructs of social anxiety and phobia.

Friendship Qualities Scale (FQS; Bukowski, Hoza & Boivin, 1994)

The FQS is a teen self-report measure that assesses the quality of best friendships. It consists of 23 Likert scale items, ranging from 1–5, from five different subscales (Companionship, Closeness, Helpfulness, Security, and Conflict) and takes approximately five minutes to complete. Teens are instructed to identify their best friend and keep this friendship in mind while completing this measure. For example, items include, "My friend and I spend all of our free time together." The total score ranges from 23–115, with higher scores reflecting better-quality friendships. According to the authors, coefficient alphas for subscales range from .71 to .86. Confirmatory factor analysis supported the factor structure of the subscales and comparisons between ratings by reciprocated versus non-reciprocated friends supported the discriminant validity of the scales (Bukowski et al., 1994).

Test of Adolescent Social Skills Knowledge (TASSK; Appendix A)

The TASSK is a 26-item criterion-referenced test developed for PEERS® to assess teens' knowledge about the specific social skills taught during the intervention. Items are derived from key elements from the didactic lessons. Teens are presented with sentence stems and asked to choose the best option from two possible answers. Scores range from 0–26, with higher scores reflecting greater knowledge of teen social skills. The coefficient alpha for the TASSK was .56. This moderate level of internal consistency was acceptable, given the large domain of questions on the scale. The TASSK takes approximately five minutes to complete and can be found in Appendix A.

Quality of Socialization Questionnaire (QSQ; Appendix B; adapted from Quality of Play Questionnaire, Frankel & Mintz, 2011)

The QSQ consists of 12 items administered to parents and teens independently to assess the frequency of get-togethers with peers® over the previous month and the level of conflict during these get-togethers. The QSQ takes approximately 2–3 minutes to complete. The ten items which make up the Conflict Scale ask for individual parent and teen ratings of peer conflict, (e.g., "criticized or teased each other"). The other two items ask parents and teens to individually estimate the number of invited and hosted get-togethers the teen has had over the previous month.

The QSQ was adapted for teens from the Quality of Play Questionnaire (QPQ; Frankel & Mintz, 2011), which was developed through factor analysis of 175 boys and girls. The coefficient alpha was .87 for the Conflict Scale. This scale also demonstrated convergent validity with the SSRS Problem Behaviors scale (rho = .35, $p < .05$) and significantly discriminated community from clinic-referred samples ($p < .05$). The reported frequency of hosted and invited get-togethers also significantly discriminated community-referred from clinic samples ($p's < .005$). Spearman correlation between teen and parent ratings at baseline for the first randomized controlled trial of PEERS® was .55 for the Conflict Scale, .99 for the frequency of hosted get-togethers, and .99 for the frequency of invited get-togethers (deleting reports of "0" get-togethers resulted in correlations of .97 and .94, respectively, all $p's < .001$). The adolescent and parent versions (QSQ-A and QSQ-P) are presented in Appendix B.

What You Can Expect: The Research Evidence

While teaching social skills is an important priority in many schools, much of the research literature on social skills training for those with ASD has focused on interventions with younger children in the lower ranges of social functioning. Few social skills interventions have been devoted to investigating the efficacy of social skills training for teens that are less intellectually impaired. Even among the social skills intervention studies conducted with this population, most have not been formally tested in terms of improving social competence or the development of close friendships, nor have they assessed the benefit of including educators and/or parents in training in order to promote social functioning. The lack of evidence-based social skills instruction to improve social competence and promote the formation of friendships for adolescents with ASD is what inspired the development of this manual.

Social Skills Training in the School Setting

One method for teaching social skills to teens with ASD involves instruction in the school setting. In this case, social skills are taught in the classroom, much in the way we might teach math or science. In the first school-based clinical trial using the PEERS® curriculum in the classroom, 73 middle school students with ASD and their parents participated in a study conducted through Village Glen School, a non-public school for students with ASD. Thirty-eight participants were assigned to the PEERS® treatment condition, while 35 participants were assigned to an alternative social skills curriculum.

Participants received daily social skills instruction in the classroom for 20–30 minutes, five days per week, for 14 weeks. Instruction was provided by classroom teachers and teaching assistants. Students in the active treatment control group received the customary social skills scope and sequence curriculum taught at the Village Glen School following the same timeframe.

Results revealed improvement in social functioning along multiple domains for the PEERS® treatment group in comparison to the active treatment control group. Teacher-reports revealed significant decreases in problem behaviors, particularly with regard to decreased internalizing. Improvement in teacher-reported overall social responsiveness was also observed in the areas of improved social awareness, social cognition, social communication, social motivation, and decreased autistic mannerisms. Results further suggest improved social cognition according to parent-report. Teen self-reports of social functioning revealed improved knowledge of social skills, improved friendship quality in the areas of helpfulness and security, and increased frequency of hosted get-togethers with friends.

In a second large clinical trial testing the effectiveness of the PEERS® curriculum in the classroom, 146 middle and high school students with ASD participated in a school-based study with their parents and teachers. Changes in skills related to developing friendships were measured for high-functioning students with ASD attending a non-public school for adolescents with autism and other social communication disorders. Adolescent self-report, teacher-report, and parent-report were examined to detect changes in social functioning following the implementation of PEERS® in the classroom.

Adolescent participants received daily social skills instruction in the classroom for 20–30 minutes, five days per week, for 14 weeks. Instruction was provided by 22 classroom teachers and 21 teacher aides trained and supervised during the intervention. Skills were taught through didactic instruction using concrete rules and steps of social etiquette in conjunction with role-play demonstrations. Students practiced newly learned social skills during behavioral rehearsal exercises in the classroom and weekly socialization homework assignments in the community, while parents were invited to attend weekly group sessions instructing them on key strategies for helping their teens make and keep friends.

Results of pre- to post-test comparisons reveal significant treatment effects. Teen self-reports revealed significant improvements in self-esteem and knowledge of social skills. Teacher-reports revealed a significant decrease in internalizing behavior. Parent-reports of social functioning indicated improvement in overall social skills, decreased social anxiety, overall improvement in social responsiveness, and increased frequency of get-togethers with friends.

These combined results suggest that the use of PEERS® as a manualized school-based teacher-facilitated curriculum is effective in improving the social functioning of adolescents with ASD. This research represents two of only a few treatment intervention studies aimed at improving the friendship skills of adolescents with ASD in the classroom.

Parent-Assisted Social Skills Training

Another method for teaching social skills to teens with ASD includes parent assistance. In this case, parents are included in the intervention, attending separate but concurrent group sessions in which they are taught to be social coaches for their teens. The first randomized controlled trial of PEERS® using parent assistance was published in the *Journal of Autism and Developmental Disorders* in 2009 (Laugeson, Frankel, Mogil, & Dillon, 2009). This study compared 17 teens receiving a parent-assisted version of the PEERS® intervention with a delayed treatment control group of 16 teens 13–17 years of age with ASD. Results revealed, in comparison with the control group, that the treatment group significantly improved their knowledge of social skills, increased their frequency of hosted get-togethers, showed changes in friendship quality, and improved in overall social skills as reported by parents. Social skills improvement reported by teachers also showed a strong trend toward improvement. To date, this study comprises the largest number of subjects reported in the social skills treatment outcome literature for older adolescents with ASD.

In a second clinical trial using the parent-assisted version of PEERS®, published in the *Journal of Autism and Developmental Disorders* in 2012 (Laugeson, Frankel, Gantman, Dillon, & Mogil, 2012), original findings were replicated for a different group of 28 teens with ASD. Results revealed improvements in parent-reported social skills, specifically in the areas of improved cooperation, assertion, and responsibility for those receiving the PEERS® intervention, in comparison to those waiting for treatment. Results further showed a significant decrease in autism symptoms related to social responsiveness in the areas of improved social motivation, social communication, social cognition, and social awareness, as well as a decrease in autistic mannerisms for treatment participants. Increases in teen-reports of frequency of hosted get-togethers and improved knowledge of social etiquette were also observed.

These treatment gains were generally maintained at the end of a 14-week follow-up assessment period, and in some cases improved even more. Furthermore, the 14-week follow-up assessment revealed significant improvements in overall social functioning, particularly in the area of assertion, according to teacher-reports. This latter finding is of particular import as teachers in this study were blind to the conditions under investigation, noticing demonstrable improvements in teens' social functioning, yet unaware these teens had participated in a social skills treatment group.

Social Skills Training for Young Adults with ASD

In addition to school-based and parent-assisted social skills training, PEERS® has also utilized a caregiver-assisted model in working with young adults with ASD. In this case, social coaching is provided by caregivers close to young adults with ASD, such as parents, adult siblings, peer mentors, job coaches, life coaches, or other family members.

In the first clinical trial of its kind, using a randomized controlled trial design, 17 young adult participants ranging from 18–23 years of age participated in a study with their caregivers testing the effectiveness of an intervention known as *PEERS® for Young Adults*. Participants were randomly assigned to a treatment or a delayed treatment control group. Treatment included weekly 90-minute small group sessions delivered over a 16-week period. Skills were taught through didactic instruction and role-playing demonstrations using concrete rules and steps of social etiquette from the *PEERS® for Young Adults* curriculum, which focuses on developing and maintaining friendships and romantic relationships. Young adults practiced newly learned skills during in-session behavioral rehearsal exercises and caregiver-assisted weekly socialization homework assignments.

Results revealed that the treatment group improved significantly more than the delayed treatment control group at post-test, in young adult self-reported social and emotional loneliness and social skills knowledge. Caregiver reports of social functioning also showed significant improvement for the treatment group in social responsiveness, in the areas of social communication and decreased autistic mannerisms. Improved social skills in the areas of cooperation, self control, and assertion, as well as improved empathy and increased frequency of invited get-togethers and hosted get-togethers, were also reported by caregivers.

Conclusion

These combined research findings suggest that the use of PEERS® as a teacher-facilitated or parent/caregiver-assisted social skills intervention leads to improvement in friendship skills for adolescents and young adults with ASD.

WEEK 1

INTRODUCTION AND TRADING INFORMATION

Preparing for the Lesson

The primary goal of the first week is to orient the teens to the structure of the class and establish group cohesion through a brief didactic lesson and behavioral rehearsal exercise. It will be very important for you to establish clear expectations in the first lesson and to minimize any misbehavior. For assistance with misbehavior, see the Behavioral Management Techniques section in Chapter 1 of this manual.

In the very early stages of the class, it is common for teens to exhibit the "too cool for school syndrome." They may act as if they do not need help and as if they do not belong in the class as a means to "save face." It is common for one or two students to behave in this way, particularly older teens. It is recommended that you do not attempt to engage in a debate with these teens about why they should participate in the program. This will only serve to embarrass other teens who were eager to participate. Instead, in an attempt to normalize the experience, you should speak generally about the benefits of improving friendships by explaining that making and keeping friends can be difficult, and that everyone can stand to learn more about the process. If the "too cool for school syndrome" is disruptive to the class, you may need to meet with the teen outside of the class and make sure he or she wants to be there. Remember that social motivation is critical to success in PEERS®. If you have a student that does not want to be there, he or she should not be. It may create a negative contagion in the class and will probably do very little good for the oppositional teen.

A controlled classroom environment is important to ensure that the teens get the maximum benefit from the didactic portion of the lesson. Students should have to raise their hands in order to speak, and teens should not be allowed to talk over one another or engage in long or overly personal stories. Establish these expectations by presenting the rules for the class, as indicated in the lesson guide. In order to ensure that the teens are compliant with these rules, it will be helpful to present the rules by having the teens generate explanations for why each of these rules is important. This discussion will help them be more compliant with the rules.

If a teen launches into an unrelated discussion, you should avoid allowing the teen to get too far off track by redirecting him or her by saying, *"Is this on topic?"* You should also not hesitate to redirect tangential teens who give overly lengthy responses to questions, as this also takes away from the class. In such cases, it can be helpful to say, *"Okay, we're going to have to move on. We have a lot to cover."* If the teen persists, you might say, *"If we have time later, we can talk about that."* However, it is not advisable to revisit the topic, as this only reinforces tangential comments.

It is very important for you to establish a fun environment for the class. Creating a fun environment involves getting the teens actively engaged in the process of generating the rules for the lessons. PEERS® uses a very specific curriculum involving concrete rules and steps for social behavior. The process by which these rules and steps are generated is through a Socratic method of questioning, and through role-playing demonstrations. The former involves asking specific questions in such a way that you elicit the response you were seeking. The latter involves specific demonstrations of both appropriate and inappropriate behaviors, in order to generate the rules for a more complex series of social behavior (e.g., demonstrating what it looks like to be a *conversation hog*, and then asking, *"What did I do WRONG in that conversation?"*).

These techniques of instruction are used to keep the teens' attention during the didactic lessons and help them to more readily buy into the skills being taught. Teens are far more likely to believe what you have to teach them if they believe they or their peers are generating the rules. They are also more likely to remember these rules and steps if they or their peers are engaged in the process of creating them.

When presenting the rules and steps for social behavior, avoid asking *open-ended questions* like, *"Does anyone have any ideas about how to have a good conversation?"* Questions like this are too broad and often result in inappropriate responses from the teens who do not know the rules of social etiquette yet. Instead, stick to the questions outlined in the didactic portion of this manual.

You will be conducting a series of inappropriate and appropriate role-play demonstrations in conjunction with the didactic lesson this week. The scripts provided in the manual are *not meant to be read verbatim*. They simply serve as a guide for what you might say. You should feel free to make up your own inappropriate and appropriate role-play scenarios to demonstrate the skills. Inappropriate role-play demonstrations generally represent common social errors committed by teens with Autism Spectrum Disorder (ASD) and other social challenges. Appropriate role-play demonstrations represent *ecologically valid social skills* used by socially accepted teens. The social errors demonstrated in the inappropriate role-plays should be quite obvious to the teens and somewhat over-the-top (for instructive as well as entertainment value). However, for groups of older teens, you may want to be less dramatic with your demonstrations as they may think you are talking down to them.

The inappropriate role-plays are often very humorous and will help to engage the teens in the class. Some teens will use this as an opportunity to act silly and make jokes. It is important you remain serious when eliciting feedback from the teens about what went wrong in the role-play to avoid losing control of the class. If a teen provides an inappropriate comment about the role-play in an effort to make a joke, rather than engaging in a debate about why this was an inappropriate response, you should *open this comment up to the class* by asking in a general way why the suggestion might be inappropriate. For example, if a teen made the comment that a particular role-play was inappropriate because the coach should have told the instructor to *"mind her own business,"* rather than getting into a debate, it is more advisable to generally say to the group, *"What could be the problem with telling someone to 'mind their own business'?"* Using the sentence stem, *"What could be the problem with . . ."* as a means of handling inappropriate behavior from teens is far more effective in defusing the situation and makes it far less likely that other teens will follow in this inappropriate behavior. The goal is not to embarrass the teen, which is why it is important for you to remain serious and respectful, but rather to provide just enough peer pressure to make the behavior less reinforcing. Most teens will back down from any oppositional behavior if you *open up their comments to the class*. Once this has been done, it is critical to move on to a more appropriate topic immediately.

Inappropriate role-play demonstrations generally lead to the formulation of specific rules and steps of social etiquette. As you are generating these rules and steps, be sure to write them on the board where the teens can easily view the material. This includes all of the bullet points and buzz-words from the lessons, which are easily identified in the manual as they are ***bold and italicized***. Remember that it is important to stress these buzzwords and use them frequently since they are the common language used between you, the teens, and their parents.

Buzzwords are helpful because they allow you to refer to sophisticated social behavior in only a few words and help you to avoid lecturing during coaching. Consequently, all buzzwords should be listed on the board along with the other rules and steps. Do not write the buzzwords or the rules and steps on the board before the class begins, as that would defeat the purpose of having the teens help generate the rules through the Socratic method. The same is true if you are using a smart-board. Avoid having any material pre-programmed into screens, as this would give the impression that the teens are not generating the rules and steps.

Finally, although PEERS® should be treated as a class, it should be fun and lively for the teens. That does not mean that you should be silly and make a lot of jokes with the teens, as this may result in a loss of control and difficulty staying on track. Each instructor will bring his or her own style to the class, so you should feel free to be yourself. Do not try to act cool for the teens; they will see right through that. Just be yourself, and if there are things they bring up that you do not know, feel free to ask them if it is relevant. They are usually very happy to talk about the latest videogames, comic books, and so on, if you are unfamiliar with them. You do not have to know every little detail about their personal interests right away. There will be plenty of time to learn more as the class progresses.

Day One: Introduction

Set Up and Opening Remarks

At the start of the class, write the teens' names on the board and leave room for awarding points after each name. Points will be given for homework completion and participation. This will be the same procedure each week of the class. Given that teens have different learning styles, it is suggested that when presenting the rules of social behavior, buzzwords and bullet points relating to rules and steps be written on the board. This is recommended for lesson reviews on days 3–5 throughout the program. These rules and steps should remain on the board for the entire class (not to be erased), as the teens may need to rely on them for their behavioral rehearsal exercises. You will need to allot room on the board for both the lesson and the distributing of points. Be sure teens remain seated throughout the class, and raise their hands to make statements or ask questions, otherwise the class could get out of control.

Introductions

[List the name of each teen on the board and start giving points right away for following directions and participation. If the teens ask about the points, tell them you will explain later.]

- If the teens don't already know each other, go around the room and have them say their name and grade

- Instructors and behavioral coaches should also introduce themselves

Rules for the Class

Present the following rules and ask, *"Why is this a good rule to have?"* after each rule:

1. Listen to the others (no talking when others are speaking)

2. Follow directions

3. Raise your hand

4. Be respectful (no teasing or making fun of others, no swearing)

5. No touching (no hitting, kicking, pushing, hugging, etc.)

Overview of PEERS®

Reason for the Class

Explain the following:

- Tell the teens that the name of the class is PEERS®

- Ask them, *"What is a peer?"*

  - Answer: Someone else your age, a friend, a classmate

- PEERS® is a social skills class to help teens make and keep friends

- The class will be held every day for the next 16 weeks

- At the end of the 16 weeks, there will be a graduation party and ceremony

Structure of the Classes

Explain the following:

- Day One (Mondays)

  - The class begins each week with a review of the homework

    - You will be given homework assignments each week to practice the skills you learn in PEERS®
    - These are FUN assignments—so don't worry
    - Your parents will receive weekly parent handouts to help you

      - Your parents may or may not be helping you with these assignments
      - We encourage you to discuss your homework with your parents using the buzzwords

        - Explain, *"Buzzwords are words that we use to describe some type of social skill. We use them so we can have a common language when we're talking about the rules or steps of making and keeping friends."*

- Day Two (Tuesdays)

  - On the second day, we will go over the lesson for the week

    - This may involve role-playing demonstrations

- Day Three (Wednesdays)

  - On the third day, we will review the lesson and practice the newly learned skills
  - You will also receive your homework assignments for the coming week on this day

- Days Four and Five (Thursdays and Fridays)

  - On the fourth and fifth days, we will practice the skills during organized activities like games or sports

Earning Points

- Explain that teens will receive points for the following:

- ○ Following the rules (e.g., listening, being respectful, following directions)
- ○ Completing homework assignments
- ○ Participation in the class
- ○ Practicing newly learned skills in the class

- Points are calculated at the end of every class

- Group points are earned for a graduation party at the end of the intervention

  - ○ The more points earned, the bigger and better the party

- Individual points are earned for graduation prizes

  - ○ The individuals with the most points get to choose from the prizes first
  - ○ The prizes may include (depending on the resources of the school):

    - ■ Basketballs, footballs, volleyballs, soccer balls, baseball equipment, Frisbees
    - ■ Board games, card games
    - ■ [Note: prizes are intended to be interactive and promote social engagement with peers]

- Ask the question, *"So when you earn points are you helping yourself, helping the group, or both?"*

  - ○ Answer: Both

Discussion Questions

- Explain, *"The name of this class is PEERS®. Peers are sometimes also friends or potential friends. The purpose of this class is for us to learn how to make and keep friends. Which means it's important for us all to agree on what makes a good friend."*

- Ask the following questions and allow them to briefly discuss:

  - ○ *"What is a friend?"*

  - ○ *"How do you know when you have a friend?"*

  - ○ *"What do friends have in common?"*

  - ○ *"What is a best friend?"*

[Use this as a brainstorming activity, in which you write their good responses on the board. Try to fit the answers the teens provide into the language described in the *Characteristics of Good Friendship*s section below until all bullet points are covered.]

Characteristics of Good Friendships

After the teens brainstorm, briefly review the basic characteristic of good friendships:

- Common interests

  - ○ Similar interests, likes, hobbies (e.g., you have things in common)

- Self-disclosure/share secrets
  - Feel comfortable sharing private thoughts, feelings, stories (e.g. you feel comfortable sharing your secrets)
- Understanding
  - Mutual understanding (e.g., you get one another)
- Shared/equal
  - An equal friendship is shared and reciprocal (e.g., you're equals; you both share the friendship; no one dominates the other person)
- Mutual affection/care
  - A friendship based on fondness, warmth, and mutual caring for one another (e.g., you both care about the other person)
- Commitment/loyalty/trust
  - A friendship based on loyalty, allegiance, and trust (e.g., you're loyal to each other; you trust each other; you're committed to the friendship)
- Conflict resolution
  - Can solve potential arguments without hurting the friendship (e.g., if you argue or disagree, you can make up and still be friends)

Wrap Up

Say, *"So now we're all clear about what makes a good friend. For the next 16 weeks we're going to be talking about how to make and keep friends, so I wanted to make sure we're all in agreement. Tomorrow we'll be talking about some specific ways we can make friends and how to have good conversations."*

Calculate Points

Calculate the number of points earned by each teen (see Appendix E for the Daily Point Log):

- Do not publicly disclose the individual number of points
- Discourage attempts to compare number of points earned between teens
  - Remind them that they are working as a team to earn a bigger and better graduation party

Day Two: Didactic Lesson—Trading Information

Didactic Lesson: Trading Information

- Explain, *"Each week in PEERS® we focus on a different social skill. This week we're going to be talking about how to have a conversation with someone. One of the most important parts of making and keeping friends when you're a teen is being able to have good conversations. We call this trading information."*

[Present the rules for **trading information** by writing the following bullet points (**bold and italicized**) on the board. Do not erase the rules until the end of the lesson.]

- *Ask the other person about him or herself* (e.g., their interests, hobbies, weekend activities)
  - Say, *"One of the first rules for trading information is to ask the other person about him or herself. You might ask them about their interests, their hobbies, or what they like to do on the weekend."*
  - Ask, *"Why is it important to ask the person about him or herself?"*
    - Answer: Because this is how you discover their interests, hobbies, and likes; it helps you discover if you have **common interests**

- *Answer your own question*
  - Say, *"Another rule for trading information is that we need to answer our own questions and share something related about ourselves. This includes sharing our own interests, likes, or hobbies. Sometimes the person will ask you the same questions back, but if they don't, you can answer your own question."*
  - Ask, *"Why is it important to answer your own question?"*
    - Answer: Because they may not ask you the same question, and in order to *trade information* you need to tell them about you too
  - Explain, *"After the other person finishes, share something related about yourself that relates to the topic."*

- *Find common interests*
  - Say, *"The most important goal of trading information is to find common interests. We need to find common interests so that we have things to talk about and things to do together. It's also helpful to pay attention to what people don't like, so we can avoid doing those things when we're together."*
  - Ask, *"Why is it so important to find common interests?"*
    - Answer: Because they give you things to talk about and things to do together, they keep the conversation interesting
  - Explain the following:
    - *Common interests are the foundation of friendships*
    - *Our goal when trading information is to find common interests*
    - Identify things you can talk about and you can do together
    - Pay attention to what they do not like so you can avoid doing those things together

- *Share the conversation*

  ○ Say, *"Another rule for trading information is to share the conversation."*
  ○ Ask, *"Why is it important to share the conversation?"*

    ■ Answer: This is how we **trade information** and get to know one another

  ○ Explain the following:

    ■ Give the person a chance to ask you a question or make a comment
    ■ Pause occasionally to let the other person direct the conversation

- *Don't be a conversation hog*

  [The instructor and behavioral coach should do an INAPPROPRIATE role-play with the instructor being a conversation hog.]

  ○ Begin by saying, *"Watch this and tell me what I'm doing WRONG."*

        Example of an INAPPROPRIATE role-play:

    ■ Instructor: *"Hi (insert name). What have you been up to?"*
    ■ Coach: *"Not much. Just going to school and hanging out. What about you?"*
    ■ Instructor: *"Well, I had a really fun weekend. I went to the movies and we saw that new sci-fi movie."*
    ■ Coach: *"Oh, I heard that was good . . ."*
    ■ Instructor: (Interrupts) *"Yeah, it was. And then we went out to eat at my favorite restaurant and I ate a whole pizza on my own. And then the next day I went to the mall and we went to this really good gaming store and played videogames all day . . ."*
    ■ Coach: *"Oh, you like videogames . . ."*
    ■ Instructor: (Interrupts) *"Yeah, and then we went home and watched some movies and I didn't go to sleep until really late and I'm so tired today. I thought I'd fall asleep . . ."*
    ■ Coach: (Looks bored)
    ■ Instructor: *". . . and tomorrow I have so much work to do, so I'm going to have to stay up really late again . . ."*
    ■ Coach: (Looking around, appears bored)

  ○ End by saying, *"Okay, so time out on that. So what did I do WRONG in that conversation?"*

    ■ Answer: You were not letting the other person talk, you were being rude

  ○ Ask the following *Perspective Taking Questions*:

    ■ *"What was that like for (name of coach)?"*

      • Answers: Annoying; frustrating; boring

    ■ *"What do you think (name of coach) thought of me?"*

      • Answers: Selfish; boring; obnoxious; self-centered

- *"Is (name of coach) going to want to talk to me again?"*

  - Answer: No; too obnoxious; too self-centered

- Ask the behavioral coach the same *Perspective Taking Questions*:

  - *"What was that like for you?"*
  - *"What did you think of me?"*
  - *"Would you want to talk to me again?"*

- Explain, *"One of the rules for trading information is don't be a conversation hog."*

  - Do not monopolize the conversation
  - Do not brag about yourself
  - Try not to interrupt
  - Let the other person talk
  - Ask the person what they like

- ***Don't be an interviewer***

  [The instructor and behavioral coach should do an INAPPROPRIATE role-play with the instructor being an interviewer.]

  - Begin by saying, *"Watch this and tell me what I'm doing WRONG."*

    Example of an INAPPROPRIATE role-play:

    - Instructor: *"Hi (insert name). How are you doing?"*
    - Coach: *"Fine. How are you?"*
    - Instructor: *"I'm good. Hey, I was wondering, what kind of movies do you like?"*
    - Coach: *"Oh, I like action adventure movies and comedies. What about you?"*
    - Instructor: *"Yeah, and what's your favorite movie?"*
    - Coach: *"I guess my favorite is (insert current movie). What's your favorite?"*
    - Instructor: *"Yeah, that was good. What about TV shows? What kind of TV shows do you watch?"*
    - Coach: *"I like sit-coms. What about you?"*
    - Instructor: *"Well, what's your favorite TV show?"*
    - Coach: (Looks annoyed) *"I guess (insert current TV sit-com) is my favorite."*
    - Instructor: *"So what kind of music do you like?"*
    - Coach: (Looking around, appears bored) *"I guess I like (insert genre of music)."*

  - End by saying, *"Okay, time-out on that. So what did I do WRONG in that conversation?"*

    - Answer: You were asking question after question, you never shared anything about yourself

  - Ask the following *Perspective Taking Questions*:

- ■ *"What was that like for (name of coach)?"*
  - • Answers: Annoying; exhausting; a lot of work; frustrating; boring
- ■ *"What do you think (name of coach) thought of me?"*
  - • Answers: Like a drill sergeant; interrogator; nosy; annoying; weird
- ■ *"Is (name of coach) going to want to talk to me again?"*
  - • Answer: No; too exhausting; too much work

- ○ Ask the behavioral coach the same *Perspective Taking Questions*:
  - ■ *"What was that like for you?"*
  - ■ *"What did you think of me?"*
  - ■ *"Would you want to talk to me again?"*

- ○ Explain, *"One of the rules for trading information is don't be an interviewer."*
  - ■ Don't ask question after question
  - ■ Ask the other person questions and then share things about yourself
  - ■ Make sure all of your questions and comments are related to the topic

- • **Don't get too personal at first**

  [The instructor and behavioral coach should do an INAPPROPRIATE role-play with the instructor getting too personal.]

  - ○ Begin by saying, *"Watch this and tell me what I'm doing WRONG."*

    Example of an INAPPROPRIATE role-play:

    - ■ Instructor: *"Hey (insert name). What are you doing this weekend?"*
    - ■ Coach: *"I'm going to my dad and step-mom's house."*
    - ■ Instructor: *"Your step-mom? Are your parents divorced?"*
    - ■ Coach: (Surprised) *"Yeah."*
    - ■ Instructor: *"When did that happen?"*
    - ■ Coach: (Confused) *"When I was twelve."*
    - ■ Instructor: *"Why?"*
    - ■ Coach: (Uncomfortable) *"I don't know."*
    - ■ Instructor: *"Was that hard on you?"*
    - ■ Coach: (Uncomfortable) *"I don't know."*
    - ■ Instructor: *"Did they tell you why?"*
    - ■ Coach: *"Can we talk about something else?"*
    - ■ Instructor: *"Do you see one of them more than the other? Do they get jealous?"*
    - ■ Coach: (Uncomfortable) *"I don't know."*
    - ■ Instructor: *"Do they fight over you? Is it awkward?"*
    - ■ Coach: (Looks uncomfortable)

- ○ End by saying, *"Okay, time-out on that. So what did I do WRONG in that conversation?"*
  - ■ Answer: You were asking really personal questions
- ○ Ask the following *Perspective Taking Questions*:
  - ■ *"What was that like for (name of coach)?"*
    - • Answers: Uncomfortable; awkward; embarrassing; creepy; weird
  - ■ *"What do you think (name of coach) thought of me?"*
    - • Answers: Creepy; stalker; nosy; weird
  - ■ *"Is (name of coach) going to want to talk to me again?"*
    - • Answer: No; too uncomfortable; too creepy
- ○ Ask the behavioral coach the same *Perspective Taking Questions*:
  - ■ *"What was that like for you?"*
  - ■ *"What did you think of me?"*
  - ■ *"Would you want to talk to me again?"*
- ○ Explain, *"One of the rules for trading information is don't get too personal at first."*
  - ■ When we are first getting to know someone we should avoid getting too personal
  - ■ Avoid sharing private thoughts and feelings or asking personal questions
  - ■ You might make the other person feel uncomfortable
  - ■ As you become closer friends it may be okay to get more personal

- • *Assess their interest*
  - ○ You also need to make sure the other person is interested in the conversation
  - ○ Questions you can ask yourself to *assess their interest*:
    - ■ *Are they talking to you?*
    - ■ *Are they looking at you?*
    - ■ *Are they facing you?*
  - ○ If they do not seem interested in talking to you, then you may need to *move on* and find someone else to talk to

Role-Play: Trading Information

[The instructor and behavioral coach should do an APPROPRIATE role-play of trading information]

- • Begin by saying, *"Now that we know the rules for trading information, watch this and tell me what we're doing RIGHT."*

Example of an APPROPRIATE role-play:

- ○ Instructor: *"Hey (insert name)! How are you doing?"*
- ○ Coach: *"I'm fine. How are you?"*
- ○ Instructor: *"I'm great. So how was your weekend?"*
- ○ Coach: *"It was good. I went to the movies with some friends."*
- ○ Instructor: *"That sounds fun. What did you see?"*
- ○ Coach: *"We saw that new sci-fi movie everyone's been talking about."*
- ○ Instructor: *"How cool! I've been wanting to see that. Was it good?"*
- ○ Coach: *"Yeah, it was really good. I might see it again. Do you like sci-fi movies?"*
- ○ Instructor: *"Yeah, I love them! I like reading sci-fi books, too."*
- ○ Coach: *"Me too. I read them all the time."*
- ○ Instructor: *"Same here."*

- Say, *"Time-out on that. Who can tell me what we did RIGHT in that conversation?"*

  - ○ Answer: ***Traded information; asked each other questions; answered your own questions; found common interests; shared the conversation; was not a conversation hog; was not an interviewer; didn't get too personal***

- Ask, *"Did it seem like we wanted to talk to each other?"*

  - ○ Answer: Yes

- Ask, *"How could you tell?"*

  - ○ Answers: ***Talking to each other; looking at each other; facing each other***

- Ask the following *Perspective Taking Questions*:

  - ○ *"What was that like for (name of coach)?"*

    - ■ Answers: Nice, pleasant

  - ○ *"What do you think (name of coach) thought of me?"*

    - ■ Answers: Nice; interesting; pretty cool

  - ○ *"Is (name of coach) going to want to talk to me again?"*

    - ■ Answer: Yes

- Ask the behavioral coach the same *Perspective Taking Questions*:

  - ○ *"What was that like for you?"*
  - ○ *"What did you think of me?"*
  - ○ *"Would you want to talk to me again?"*

Wrap Up

Say, *"So that's what it looks like to trade information. Tomorrow we'll continue our discussion about trading information and having good conversations. We'll be reviewing the rules, practicing trading information, and finding common interests with our classmates."*

Calculate Points

Calculate the number of points earned by each teen (see Appendix E for the Daily Point Log):

- Do not publicly disclose the individual number of points

- Discourage attempts to compare number of points earned between teens

    ○ Remind them that they are working as a team to earn a bigger and better graduation party

Day Three: Lesson Review and Behavioral Rehearsal

Lesson Review: Trading Information

- Say, *"Yesterday we learned how to trade information. Who can tell us what some of the rules are for trading information?"*

[Have teens generate all of the rules. Be prepared to give prompts if necessary. Write the following buzzwords (**bold and italicized**) on the board and do not erase until the end of the lesson.]

  - ***Ask the other person about him or herself***

  - ***Answer your own questions***

  - ***Find common interests***

  - ***Share the conversation***

  - ***Don't be a conversation hog***

  - ***Don't be an interviewer***

  - ***Don't get too personal at first***

- Ask, "What questions can you ask yourself to tell if someone wants to talk to you?"

  - ***"Are they talking to me?"***

  - ***"Are they looking at me?"***

  - ***"Are they facing me?"***

Role-Play: Trading Information

[The instructor and behavioral coach should do an APPROPRIATE role-play of trading information]

- Begin by saying, *"Now that we know the rules for trading information, watch this and tell me what we're doing RIGHT."*

    Example of an APPROPRIATE role-play:

  - Instructor: *"Hey (insert name)! How are you doing?"*
  - Coach: *"I'm fine. How are you?"*
  - Instructor: *"I'm good. So what have you been up to lately?"*
  - Coach: *"Not much. I went to a football game last night."*
  - Instructor: *"Oh, you went to the game! That sounds fun."*

- ○ Coach: *"Yeah it was. Did you go?"*
- ○ Instructor: *"No, I couldn't make it. Was it a good game?"*
- ○ Coach: *"Yeah, it was a great game. You should've been there. Do you like football?"*
- ○ Instructor: *"Yeah, I love football! How about you?"*
- ○ Coach: *"Me too. I go to games all the time."*

- Say, *"time-out on that. Who can tell me what we did RIGHT in that conversation?"*

  - ○ Answer: **Traded information; asked each other questions; answered your own questions; found common interests; shared the conversation; was not a conversation hog; was not an interviewer; didn't get too personal**

- Ask, *"Did it seem like we wanted to talk to each other?"*

  - ○ Answer: Yes

- Ask, *"How could you tell?"*

  - ○ Answers: **Talking to each other; looking at each other; facing each other**

- Ask the following *Perspective Taking Questions*:

  - ○ *"What was that like for (name of coach)?"*

    - ■ Answers: Nice; pleasant

  - ○ *"What do you think (name of coach) thought of me?"*

    - ■ Answers: Nice; interesting; pretty cool

  - ○ *"Is (name of coach) going to want to talk to me again?"*

    - ■ Answer: Yes

- Ask the behavioral coach the same *Perspective Taking Questions*:

  - ○ *"What was that like for you?"*
  - ○ *"What did you think of me?"*
  - ○ *"Would you want to talk to me again?"*

Behavioral Rehearsal: Trading Information

- Say, *"Now that we know the rules for trading information and we've seen what it looks like, we're going to have each of you practice trading information with someone else in the class. Remember, the goal is to find a common interest."*

- Assign teens to practice **trading information** with someone else in the class

  - ○ Assign pairs and move teens around to create appropriate dyads
  - ○ If there is an uneven number of teens, create one triad

- Help facilitate the exercise when necessary by providing *prompting* and *feedback*; troubleshoot when problems arise

  ○ Examples of *prompting*:

    - *"You could ask each other about your interests or hobbies."*
    - *"You could talk about your favorite books, movies, or television programs."*
    - *"You could find out what the other person likes to do on the weekend."*

  ○ Examples of *feedback*:

    - *"Remember not to get too personal at first."*
    - *"Be sure to share the conversation."*
    - *"You may need to answer your own question."*

- Spend about five minutes on each dyad or triad

- If there is time, switch dyads/triads for an additional five minutes

- Then briefly have teens identify whether they were able to find a *common interest* by saying, *"It's time to wrap up your conversations. I heard lots of good trading information. Let's go around the room and find out what common interests you found."*

  ○ Have teens identify *common interests*
  ○ Follow up *common interests* by asking, *"What could you do with that information if you were going to hang out?"*
  ○ Praise teens for their efforts and reward points accordingly

Homework Assignments

- [Assign the *in-class calls* for the week and write this on the In-Class Call Assignment Log (Appendix D) for future reference. If there is an uneven number of teens, assign someone *double duty*. This person will have two *in-class calls* (one as a caller and the other as a receiver) and will receive extra points for completing the extra call. If the teens are uncomfortable with making phone calls, video chat is an alternative.]

- [Distribute the Parent Handout (found in the last section of this chapter), and inform teens that they should give this handout to their parents immediately. You may choose to email these handouts to parents as an alternative, but you will need to notify them of the day and time of their teen's *in-class call*.]

- [Distribute the Phone Roster (Appendix C) to the teens and have them confirm that the information is correct. Be prepared to have the teens coordinate a day and time to make the *in-class call*, and then have each teen write the day and time of the call on the Phone Roster and Parent Handout.]

- Briefly explain the homework for the week by saying, *"We're going to continue to have you practice trading information this week. Remember that each week you're going to have some homework assignments related to the lessons you're learning in PEERS®."*

- Present the homework assignment for the coming week:

    1. Teens should practice **trading information** with their parent this week
        a. Teens should go over the rules for **trading information** from the Parent Handout with their parent before practicing
        b. Find one **common interest** to share with the class

    2. ***In-class call or video chat***

        a. Before the call:
            i. Before the class ends, teens should arrange to call another member of the class to practice **trading information**
            ii. Set up a day and time to make the call
            iii. Write the day and time of the call on the Phone Roster and the Parent Handout

        b. During the call:
            i. Teens should **trade information** on this call
            ii. Find a **common interest** to report back to the class

        c. After the call:
            i. Teens should discuss the call with their parent, identify **common interests**, and **troubleshoot** any problems

Wrap Up

Say, *"So those are your homework assignments for this week. Be sure to start working on these assignments right away. We'll be reviewing how they went at the beginning of next week. Tomorrow we'll continue our discussion about trading information. We'll be reviewing the rules for trading information, practicing having good conversations, and finding common interests with our classmates."*

Calculate Points

Calculate the number of points earned by each teen (see Appendix E for the Daily Point Log):

- Do not publicly disclose the individual number of points
- Discourage attempts to compare number of points earned between teens

    ○ Remind them that they are working as a team to earn a bigger and better graduation party

Days Four and Five: Teen Activity—Jeopardy

Lesson Review: Trading Information

- Say, *"This week we've been talking about how to trade information. Who can tell us what some of the rules are for trading information?"*

[Have teens generate all of the rules. Be prepared to give prompts if necessary. Write the following buzzwords (**bold and italicized**) on the board and do not erase until the end of the lesson.]

- ○ *Ask the other person about him or herself*

- ○ *Answer your own questions*

- ○ *Find common interests*

- ○ *Share the conversation*

- ○ *Don't be a conversation hog*

- ○ *Don't be an interviewer*

- ○ *Don't get too personal at first*

- Ask, *"What questions can you ask yourself to tell if someone wants to talk to you?"*

- ○ *"Are they talking to me?"*

- ○ *"Are they looking at me?"*

- ○ *"Are they facing me?"*

Teen Activity: Jeopardy

Materials Needed

- Whiteboard and markers

- *Jeopardy Answer Sheets* for each teen

- Pens

- Scissors

Rules

- Teens will compete in this game of ***trading information***

- Like the television show *Jeopardy*, teens will be given answers and asked to respond in the form of a question

  ○ Example:

    ▪ Instructor: *"The answer is Jimmy's favorite sport."*
    ▪ Teen: *"What is baseball?"*

  ○ The teen does not have to answer in the form of a question (most do not)

- To promote interest and cooperation, points will be given for correct responses

- The purpose of *Jeopardy* is not to practice *trading information* perfectly, since the teens will sound like they are *interviewing* when asking the questions

- The true purpose of *Jeopardy* is to improve:

  ○ *Topic initiation*

    ▪ Talking about a variety of topics, rather than only those of restricted interest

  ○ *Listening skills*

    ▪ Listening and remembering what people share about themselves

How to Play

- Pass out *Jeopardy Answer Sheets* (found at the end of this lesson guide)

- Have teens fill in responses and return to the instructor

- Write the *Jeopardy Topics* on the board where teens can see them

  ○ *Favorite music*
  ○ *Favorite weekend activity*
  ○ *Favorite sport*
  ○ *Favorite game*
  ○ *Favorite movie*
  ○ *Favorite television show*
  ○ *Favorite book*
  ○ *Eye color* [Note: this is NOT to be asked, but noticed by using good eye contact]

- Have teens practice *trading information* about the *Jeopardy Topics* in small groups for 2–3 minutes each

  ○ Change groups a few times (depending on time)
  ○ Prompt teens to ask relevant questions to the Jeopardy topics when necessary

- While teens are *trading information*:

  ○ Cut the *Jeopardy Answer Sheets* into individual questions along the lines provided
  ○ Separate the *Jeopardy Answer Sheets* according to category and mix the order of the answer sheets
  ○ Write the names of the Jeopardy categories on the board

- Once the teens have finished trading information, reconvene as a group and begin the **Jeopardy Challenge**

  - Begin by having the teen with the most points that week pick the first category
  - Notify the class that if they raise their hand before the question has been asked fully, they are disqualified from answering that question
  - The person who raises their hand first gets to take the first guess
  - If they provide the wrong answer, the person who raised their hand second has a chance to answer, and so on
  - The teens get only one guess per question
  - Do not give teens clues

- You may need to enforce a time limit if teens take a long time to answer

- Do not correct the teens if they answer the questions in the incorrect format (i.e., instead of saying *"What is baseball?"* they say *"Baseball"*)

  - All that matters is that they remembered the information they obtained through **trading information**

- The person who answers the question correctly gets a point and gets to choose the next category

- If no one answers correctly, the person about which the last question relates gets to pick the next category

- Encourage the teens to clap and cheer for each other during the game

- Give points for correct responses

- Keep track of the points on the board using a different colored marker (to differentiate from points earned during the lesson review)

- At the end of the game, the person with the most points is the **Jeopardy Challenge Winner**

- SAVE TEEN ANSWER SHEETS FOR NEXT WEEK

Homework Assignments

- [Be prepared to read off the **in-class call** assignments for the week as a reminder of the homework. This should be written on the In-Class Call Assignment Log (Appendix D). Make sure the teens have scheduled the **in-class call** and have the correct phone number.]

- Briefly remind teens of the homework for the week by saying, *"Remember, we're going to continue to have you practice trading information this week through simple and fun homework assignments."*

- Present the homework assignments for the coming week:

  1. Teens should practice **trading information** with their parent this week
     a. Teens should go over the rules for **trading information** from the Parent Handout with their parent before practicing
     b. Find one **common interest** to share with the class

2. ***In-class call or video chat***

    a. Before the call:

        i. Before the class ends, teens should arrange to call another member of the class to practice ***trading information***

        ii. Set up a day and time to make the call

        iii. Write the day and time of the call on the Phone Roster and the Parent Handout

    b. During the call:

        i. Teens should ***trade information*** on this call

        ii. Find a ***common interest*** to report back to the class

    c. After the call:

        i. Teens should discuss the call with their parent, identify ***common interests***, and ***troubleshoot*** any problems

Wrap Up

Say, *"So those are your homework assignments for this week. Be sure to start working on these assignments right away. We'll be reviewing how they went at the beginning of next week."*

Calculate Points

Calculate the number of points earned by each teen (see Appendix E for the Daily Point Log):

- Do not publicly disclose the individual number of points

- Discourage attempts to compare number of points earned between teens

    ■ Remind them that they are working as a team to earn a bigger and better graduation party

Jeopardy Answer Sheets

"Music" to Your Ears	TGIF
The answer is: _____'s favorite band. (Name) The question is: What is_____? (Favorite band)	The answer is: _____'s favorite weekend activity. (Name) The question is: What is_____? (Favorite weekend activity)
Sports & Leisure	**"Game" Time**
The answer is: _____'s favorite sport. (Name) The question is: What is_____? (Favorite sport)	The answer is: _____'s favorite game. (Name) The question is: What is_____? (Favorite game)
Movies, Movies, Movies	**"TV" Time**
The answer is: _____'s favorite movie. (Name) The question is: What is_____? (Favorite movie)	The answer is: _____'s favorite TV show. (Name) The question is: What is_____? (Favorite TV show)
Bestseller List	**The "Eyes" Have It**
The answer is: _____'s favorite book. (Name) The question is: What is_____? (Favorite book)	The answer is: The color of _____'s eyes. (Name) The question is: What is_____? (Your eye color)

Parent Handout 1

PEERS® *Program for the Education and Enrichment of Relational Skills*

Introduction and Trading Information

Welcome to PEERS®! For the next 16 weeks, you will be receiving a parent handout informing you about the social skills lessons your teen is receiving in the classroom. These handouts are meant to keep you up to date on what your teens are learning about making and keeping friends, and how you might best support your teen in his or her efforts to make friends.

Parent handouts will be comprised of a brief review of the didactic lesson for the week, along with an overview of your teen's homework assignment. **We encourage you to engage in regular conversations with your teen about these social skills and the assignments. Research shows that your teen will be more likely to succeed in the program with your help and support!**

Goal of the PEERS® Class

1. To help your teen learn how to make and keep friends.

2. To help parents more effectively support their teen's efforts at finding suitable friends.

3. To help your teen foster independence with his or her social relationships.

Teaching Methods

1. Each week teens will receive brief instruction about how to handle challenging social situations.

2. Parents will be briefed about each teen lesson in the parent handout.

   a. Key elements from the lessons are included in the handouts.
   b. Pay close attention to buzzwords; these terms are **bold and italicized** and will help you create a common language between you, your teens, and their instructors.

3. Each week, your teen will rehearse the skills being taught in the class.

4. Your teen will be given homework assignments every week in order to practice the skills being taught outside of the classroom setting.

5. Teens will review homework assignments in class at the beginning of each week.

6. The most important jobs parents have are to:

   a. Practice these skills with your teen and provide feedback and social coaching.
   b. Encourage your teen to complete the weekly homework assignments.
   c. Involve your teen in activities where he or she can meet other teens.
   d. Help your teen arrange get-togethers with friends to practice newly learned skills.

Didactic Lesson: Trading Information

This week your teen will be learning how to trade information in a conversation in order to find common interests and develop close friendships. The rules for trading information are:

- *Ask the other person about him or herself* (e.g., their likes, interests, hobbies)
- After the other person finishes, *answer your own question*
  - *Share something related about yourself* (e.g., your likes, interests, hobbies)
- *Find common interests*
  - *The goal of trading information is to find common interests*
  - *Friendships are based on common interests*
  - Identify things you can talk about and you can do together
  - Find out what the other person does not like so you can avoid doing these things together
- *Share the conversation*
  - Give the person a chance to ask you a question or make a comment
  - Pause occasionally to let the other person direct the conversation
- *Don't be a conversation hog*
  - Don't monopolize the conversation
  - Don't brag about yourself
  - Try not to interrupt
  - Let the other person talk
  - Ask the person what they like
- *Don't be an interviewer*
  - Don't ask question after question
  - Ask the other person questions and then share things about yourself
  - Make sure all of your questions and comments are related to the topic
- *Don't get too personal at first*
  - This may make the other person uncomfortable
  - They may be less willing to talk to you in the future
- *Assess interest*
  - You may need to make sure the person is interested in the conversation
  - Ask yourself these questions to *assess interest*:
    - *Are they talking to me?*
    - *Are they looking at me?*
    - *Are they facing me?*

Homework Assignments

Every week your teen will have homework assignments to practice new and previously learned social skills. It is extremely helpful if parents assist teens in completing these assignments. The homework assignments for this week include the following:

1. Teens should practice **trading information** with their parent this week

    a. Teens should go over the rules for **trading information** from the Parent Handout with their parent before practicing

    b. Find one **common interest** to share with the class

    c. After identifying **common interests**, parents should ask, *"What could we do with that information if we were going to hang out?"*

2. **In-class call or video chat**

    a. Before the call:

        i. Teens should have arranged to call another member of the class to practice **trading information** (instructor has assigned the calls)

        ii. Teens should have set up a day and time to make the call (this information should be listed below and on your teen's Phone Roster)

    b. During the call:

        i. Teens should **trade information** on this call

        ii. Find a **common interest** to report back to the class

    c. After the call:

        i. Teens should discuss the call with their parent, identify **common interests**, and **troubleshoot** any problems

        ii. After identifying **common interests**, parents should ask, *"What could you do with that information if you were going to hang out?"*

How to Help Your Teen Do Homework

- *Troubleshoot problems*

    ○ Do not expect your teen to master these skills immediately

    ○ Be prepared to **troubleshoot problems** when they come up

    ○ Provide social coaching during teachable moments

- *Offer suggestions* when your teen is struggling with a new skill

    ○ Suggestions can often be given with statements that start with, *"How about if . . ."*

    ○ Good example: *"How about if next time you're trading information, you ask your friend what he likes to do, too?"*

- Do not overtly tell your teen that he or she did something wrong

- ○ This may be discouraging and embarrassing
- ○ Bad example: *"You didn't trade information the right way!"*

IN-CLASS CALL ASSIGNMENT

Your teen has been assigned to be the **caller/receiver** (circle one) with:

Name:

Phone Number:

Day:

Time:

TWO-WAY CONVERSATIONS

Preparing for the Lesson

This lesson addresses the nuances of conversational skills. The first task for anyone first meeting someone with whom they would like to be friends is to search for **common interests**. This skill is crucial for beginning and maintaining friendships. Becoming friends is a continuous process; however, from a pragmatic point of view it is easier to understand this process as occurring in discrete stages. The first stage is turning a stranger into a friendly acquaintance. The next stage is the beginning of closer friendships. The third stage is turning these closer friendships into best friendships if mutually desired. Each stage calls for different conversational rules.

Teens should regulate how intimate their exchanges are depending upon the phase of their relationships. Effective regulation involves greater disclosure only with repeated contact and receptivity by the partner. At first meetings, teens need to focus on information exchange of superficial aspects by describing what they like and dislike. They need to avoid evaluating each other, especially in a negative light, and avoid telling each other what to do.

The focus of the didactic lesson this week is on the rules for having a **two-way conversation**. It will be critical to engage the teens in this lesson and win over any teens that may be ambivalent about the class at this point. This session involves a number of role-play demonstrations, which will afford a wonderful opportunity to engage and entertain the teens. Perhaps the best method of engaging the teens in the class is to have them generate the rules for the lesson. Use a Socratic method of instruction in combination with role-play demonstrations of inappropriate methods of conversation.

This method of showing bad examples (i.e., what not to do) has been found to be highly effective in encouraging teens to generate rules of social etiquette, thereby making them more likely to believe what you are teaching them. Inappropriate role-plays should be introduced by saying, *"Watch this and tell me what I'm doing WRONG?"* At the end of the role-play ask the question, *"So what did I do WRONG in that conversation?"* The demonstrations should be overdramatized and obvious to the teens, which they will find amusing and easy to decode.

Of course, following the presentation of the didactic lesson should be the demonstration of an appropriate role-play of good methods of conversation. Appropriate role-plays of good social behavior are also critical to success in the program, in that they will demonstrate the **ecologically valid social skills** that the teens should actually be following. The appropriate role-plays are often demonstrated at the end of the didactic lesson, preceded by the question, *"Watch this and tell me what I'm doing RIGHT"* and followed by the question, *"So what did I do RIGHT in that conversation?"*

All role-play demonstrations, whether inappropriate or appropriate, should be followed with ***Perspective Taking Questions***. These questions are intended to improve social cognition and assist teens in reading social cues while understanding the perspectives of others. The ***Perspective Taking Questions*** are always the same and include: (1) *"What do you think that was like for that person?"* (2) *"What do you think that person thought of me?"* and (3) *"Do you think that person will want to talk to me again?"* The questions remain the same because when asked repetitively throughout the program, teens are more likely to begin to ask themselves the same questions when they are interacting with others.

Some of the rules for having a ***two-way conversation*** do not involve role-play demonstrations. In these cases, it is helpful to begin by presenting the rule and immediately asking, *"Why is it important to. . .(state the rule)?"* or *"What could be the problem with. . . (state the rule?)"* These are very effective methods of rule generating, in that teens are being asked to generate rationales for the rules, thereby making it more likely that they will believe what they are being taught. Teens are more likely to believe what you have to teach them if they and their classmates imagine that they are generating the ideas themselves.

Finally, because people have different types of learning styles, it will be helpful to present the material in each lesson in multiple formats. This should not only include verbal instruction and behavioral demonstration, but also writing the bullet points and buzzwords (***bold and italicized***) on the board. These bullet points and buzzwords should be visually accessible to the teens during behavioral rehearsal exercises, and should not be erased until the end of the class.

Day One: Homework Review

Homework Review

[Start with completed homework first. If you have time, you can inquire as to why others were unable to complete the assignment and try to **troubleshoot** how they might get it done for the coming week. When reviewing homework, be sure to use the buzzwords (**bold and italicized**) and **troubleshoot** issues that come up. Spend the majority of the homework review on the **in-class call**, as this is the most important assignment.]

[Note: Give multiple points for homework parts—not just one point per assignment.]

1. Practice ***trading information*** with parents

   a. Say, *"One of your assignments this week was to practice trading information with a parent. Raise your hand if you practiced trading information with one of your parents this week."*

      i. Ask the following questions:

         1. *"Who did you practice trading information with (mom, dad, etc.)?"*
         2. *"Did you find a common interest?"*

            a. When they identify **common interests** ask, *"What could you do with that information if you were going to hang out with your parent?"*

2. ***In-class call or video chat***

   a. Say, *"The other assignment you had this week was to have a phone or video chat conversation with someone in the class in order to practice trading information and finding common interests. Raise your hand if you did the in-class call."*

      i. Ask the following questions:

         1. *"Who did you talk to?"*
         2. *"Who called who?"*
         3. *"Did you trade information?"*
         4. *"Did you find a common interest?"*

            a. When they identify **common interests** ask, *"What could you do with that information if you were going to hang out?"*

         5. Avoid general questions like, *"How did it go?"*

      ii. Do not allow teens to talk about mistakes the other person made
      iii. Have the other person who participated in the call give their account immediately after, but not at the same time

Wrap Up

Say, *"Good work for those of you who completed your homework assignments. Tomorrow we will be talking about the rules for having a two way conversation."*

Calculate Points

Calculate the number of points earned by each teen (see Appendix E for the Daily Point Log):

- Do not publicly disclose the individual number of points
- Discourage attempts to compare number of points earned between teens
    - Remind them that they are working as a team to earn a bigger and better graduation party

Day Two: Didactic Lesson—Two-Way Conversations

Discussion Questions

- Begin by saying, *"Today we're going to continue our discussion about having good conversations. In particular, we're going to talk about how to have a two-way conversation with someone. Before we get into the rules of having a two-way conversation, it might be helpful to brainstorm what kinds of things to talk about."*

- Ask the question, *"What do teenagers talk about?"*

- Have the class brainstorm common topics of conversation for teens

- Mention the topics in Table 3.1 if the class does not think of them on their own

Table 3.1 Common Conversational Topics among Teens

School gossip	Videogames/Computer games	Classes
Problems with friends	Computers/Technology	Exams
Problems with family	Comic books/Anime/Manga	Teachers
Boyfriends/Girlfriends	Movies	Applying to college
Dating	TV shows	Sports
Parties/Get-togethers	Youtube/Viral videos	Cars/Motorcycles/Bikes
Weekend activities	Internet websites	Celebrities
Extra-curricular activities	Music/Concerts	Fashion/Clothes
Social clubs/Activities	Books	Shopping
Hobbies/Interests	News/Media/Politics	Make-up/Hair

Didactic Lesson: Two-Way Conversations

- Explain, *"So now that we have some ideas about WHAT to talk about, we need to figure out HOW to talk to our friends and have good conversations. We can do this by trading information and having two-way conversations."*

[Present the rules for having a **two-way conversation** by writing the following bullet points and buzzwords (**bold and italicized**) on the board. Do not erase the rules until the end of the lesson.]

- ***Trade information***

  - Explain, *"Last week we talked about the rules for trading information. Who can remember what the rules for trading information are?"*

    - Answers:

      - ***Ask the other person about him or herself***
      - ***Answer your own questions***

- *Find common interests*
- *Share the conversation*
- *Don't be a conversation hog*
- *Don't be an interviewer*
- *Don't get too personal at first*

   ○ Say, *"The rules for having a two-way conversation also include the rules for trading information and vice versa. They're both parts of having good conversations."*

- *Ask open-ended questions*

   ○ Explain, *"Another rule for trading information and having a two-way conversation is to ask open-ended questions. Open-ended questions are ones where the answers are longer and can lead to more conversation. Closed-ended questions are ones that only require a short response, like yes or no answers. This doesn't mean you can't ask closed-ended questions, but you should try not to ask too many or you'll sound like you're being an interviewer."*

   ○ Say, *"For example, if the closed-ended question were, 'What's your favorite movie?' the open-ended question might be 'What kind of movies do you like?' The open-ended question could lead to a longer answer and more conversation."*

   ○ Go around the room and have each teen generate an ***open-ended question*** from the stem of a ***closed-ended question*** (use ***Jeopardy Topics*** to keep it simple)

      ■ Ask for example: *"If the closed-ended question were, 'What is your favorite movie?'; what would the open-ended question be?"*

         • Answer: *"What kind of movies do you like?"*

      ■ Ask for example: *"If the closed-ended question were, 'What is your favorite TV show?'; what would the open-ended question be?"*

         • Answer: *"What kind of TV shows do you like?"*

      ■ Ask for example: *"If the closed-ended question were, 'What is your favorite band?'; what would the open-ended question be?"*

         • Answer: *"What kind of music do you like?"*

- *Ask follow-up questions*

   ○ Explain, *"Another rule for trading information and having a two-way conversation is to ask follow-up questions. Follow-up questions are questions we ask on a specific topic to keep the conversation going. For example, if you asked someone what kind of movies they like and they tell you they like comedies, a good follow-up question might be 'Have you seen any good comedies lately?' "*

   ○ Ask, *"Why is it important to ask follow-up questions?"*

      ■ Answer: Because it keeps us on a topic for a little longer and prevents us from switching topics too much

   ○ Go around the room and have each teen come up with THREE ***follow-up questions*** to the following topics of conversation:

      ■ *"What kind of TV shows do you like?"*
      ■ *"What kind of movies do you like?"*

- *"What kind of music do you like?"*
- *"What kind of books do you like?"*
- *"What kind of food do you like?"*
- *"What sports do you like?"*
- *"What games do you like?"*
- *"What videogames do you like?"*
- *"What do you like to do on the weekends?"*
- *"What classes are you taking?"*

- **Don't be repetitive**

  - Explain, *"Another rule for trading information and having a two-way conversation is don't be repetitive. That means we don't talk about the same thing over and over."*
  - Ask, *"Just because you find a common interest with someone, does that mean that's the only thing you should talk about?"*

    - Answer: No, you should talk about a variety of things

  - Ask, *"What could be the problem with being repetitive?"*

    - Answer: It is boring for the other person, even if the topic is a **common interest**

  - Explain the following:

    - If your goal is to make and keep friends, **don't be repetitive**
    - Find different topics to talk about now and then to keep it interesting
    - It will be boring if you talk about the same thing all the time

- **Listen to your friend**

  - Explain, *"Another rule for trading information and having a two-way conversation is that we need to listen to our friends."*
  - Ask, *"If you ask your friend a question, do you think you should listen to the answer?"*

    - Answer: Yes

  - Ask, *"What could be the problem with not listening to the answer?"*

    - Answer: Your friend will think you don't care about what they have to say

  - Explain the following:

    - If you ask a question, you need to listen to the answer
    - You're supposed to know the answer once you have asked the question
    - You should not ask the same question again
    - When you listen, it shows that you are interested in your friend

- **Don't police**

  [The instructor and behavioral coach should do an INAPPROPRIATE role-play with the instructor policing]

  - Begin by saying, *"Watch this and tell me what I'm doing WRONG."*

Example of an INAPPROPRIATE role-play:

- Instructor: *"Hey (insert name). How's it going?"*
- Coach: *"I'm doing good."*
- Instructor: *"Actually, it's 'I'm doing well.' 'Well' is an adverb and 'good' is an adjective and in this situation you actually want to use the adverb 'well.'"*
- Coach: *(Annoyed) "Okay, sorry. I'm doing well."*
- Instructor: *"Well, you know it's for your benefit."*
- Coach: *(Annoyed) "Yeah right."*
- Instructor: *"So, what did you do this weekend?"*
- Coach: *(Looking around, planning an escape) "I don't know."*
- (Long awkward pause)

 ○ End by saying, *"Okay, time-out on that. So what did I do WRONG in that conversation?"*

  ■ Answer: You were correcting the person's grammar, you were being a know-it-all

 ○ Ask the following *Perspective Taking Questions*:

  ■ *"What was that like for (name of coach)?"*

   • Answers: Annoying; obnoxious; embarrassing

  ■ *"What do you think (name of coach) thought of me?"*

   • Answers: Rude; arrogant; know-it-all

  ■ *"Is (name of coach) going to want to talk to me again?"*

   • Answers: No; too annoying; too rude

 ○ Ask the behavioral coach the same *Perspective Taking Questions*:

  ■ *"What was that like for you?"*
  ■ *"What did you think of me?"*
  ■ *"Would you want to talk to me again?"*

 ○ Explain, *"One of the rules for trading information and having a two-way conversation is don't police others."*

  ■ Do not criticize or point out other people's mistakes
  ■ Policing others is annoying and will make you look like a know-it-all

- **Don't Tease**

[The instructor and behavioral coach should do an INAPPROPRIATE role-play with the instructor teasing]

 ○ Begin by saying, *"Watch this and tell me what I'm doing WRONG."*

Example of an INAPPROPRIATE role-play:

- Instructor: *"Hey (insert name). What did you do this weekend?"*
- Coach: *"I actually hung out with my parents."*
- Instructor: (Teasing) *"You hung out with you parents?! Who hangs out with their parents on a weekend?!"*
- Coach: (Uncomfortable) *"I don't know."*
- Instructor: (Teasing) *"Does your mom lay out your clothes on your bed too?"*
- Coach: (Uncomfortable) *"No."*
- Instructor: (Teasing) *"Does she know where you are right now? Maybe you should text her. She might be worried."*
- Coach: (Embarrassed, looking away)
- Instructor: (Teasing) *"Make sure she knows where you are. She's your mommy."*
- Coach: (Looking around for an escape)

○ End by saying, *"Okay, time-out on that. So what did I do WRONG in that conversation?"*

- Answer: You were teasing the other person, you were being mean

○ Ask the following ***Perspective Taking Questions***:

- *"What was that like for (name of coach)?"*
  - Answers: Irritating; annoying; hurtful; embarrassing
- *"What do you think (name of coach) thought of me?"*
  - Answers: Mean; unfriendly; unkind; rude; annoying
- *"Is (name of coach) going to want to talk to me again?"*
  - Answers: No; too mean

○ Ask the behavioral coach the same ***Perspective Taking Questions***:

- *"What was that like for you?"*
- *"What did you think of me?"*
- *"Would you want to talk to me again?"*

○ Explain, *"One of the rules for trading information and having a two-way conversation is don't tease others."*

- ***Teasing*** or ***bantering*** is risky behavior if you're trying to make and keep friends
- Boys in particular like to ***tease*** or ***banter***, but this is very risky if your goal is to make and keep friends
- Even if you think you are being funny, it may upset other people or hurt their feelings
- This is especially true when you are FIRST getting to know someone and they don't know your sense of humor yet

- *Be a little more serious when you're first getting to know someone*

  - Explain, *"Another rule for trading information and having a two-way conversation is that you should be a little more serious when you're FIRST getting to know someone."*
  - Ask, *"What could be the problem with acting silly and cracking lots of jokes when you're FIRST getting to know someone?"*

    - Answer: They may think you are strange, they may not understand your humor, they may think you are making fun of them

  - Explain, *"So don't act silly or try to be funny when you're FIRST getting to know someone."*

    - You might make the other person uncomfortable
    - They might not understand your sense of humor and they might think you're making fun of them
    - *Humor is one of the fastest ways to push people away* if used inappropriately

- *Use good volume control*

  [The instructor and behavioral coach should do an INAPPROPRIATE role-play with the instructor speaking too quietly]

  - Begin by saying, *"Watch this and tell me what I'm doing WRONG."*

    Example of an INAPPROPRIATE role-play:

    - Instructor: (Whispering) *"Hi (insert name). How's it going?"*
    - Coach: (Straining to hear) *"What?"*
    - Instructor: (Whispering) *"How's it going?"*
    - Coach: (Looking confused) *"Oh, fine thanks."*
    - Instructor: (Whispering) *"So what have you been up to?"*
    - Coach: (Straining to hear, moving closer) *"What?"*
    - Instructor: (Whispering) *"What have you been up to?"*
    - Coach: (Looking around, appears bored) *"What have I been up to? Oh, not much."*
    - (Long awkward pause)

  - End by saying, *"Okay, time-out on that. So what did I do WRONG in that conversation?"*

    - Answer: You were speaking too quietly

  - Ask the following *Perspective Taking Questions*:

    - *"What was that like for (name of coach)?"*

      - Answers: Confusing; annoying; exhausting; a lot of work

    - *"What do you think (name of coach) thought of me?"*

      - Answers: Weird; maybe a little shy; maybe depressed

    - *"Is (name of coach) going to want to talk to me again?"*

      - Answers: Probably not; too much work

- Ask the behavioral coach the same *Perspective Taking Questions*:

  - *"What was that like for you?"*
  - *"What did you think of me?"*
  - *"Would you want to talk to me again?"*

- Explain, *"One of the rules for trading information and having a two-way conversation is to use good volume control."*

  - Do not speak too quietly because the person may not hear you
  - If the person cannot hear you, they may avoid speaking to you in the future

[The instructor and behavioral coach should do an INAPPROPRIATE role-play with the instructor speaking too loudly]

- Begin by saying, *"Watch this and tell me what I'm doing WRONG."*

  Example of an INAPPROPRIATE role-play:

  - Instructor: (Speaking very loudly) *"Hi (insert name). How's it going?"*
  - Coach: (Startled, moves back) *"Oh, it's going well."*
  - Instructor: (Speaking very loudly) *"What have you been up to?"*
  - Coach: (Embarrassed, moving further away) *"Oh, not much."*
  - Instructor: (Speaking very loudly) *"So what did you do over the weekend?"*
  - Coach: (Looking around, trying to escape) *"I don't know."*
  - (Long awkward pause)

- End by saying, *"Okay, time-out on that. So what did I do WRONG in that conversation?"*

  - Answer: You were speaking too loudly

- Ask the following *Perspective Taking Questions*:

  - *"What was that like for (name of coach)?"*

    - Answers: Irritating; annoying; embarrassing

  - *"What do you think (name of coach) thought of me?"*

    - Answers: Weird; obnoxious; annoying

  - *"Is (name of coach) going to want to talk to me again?"*

    - Answers: Probably not; too weird

- Ask the behavioral coach the same *Perspective Taking Questions*:

  - *"What was that like for you?"*
  - *"What did you think of me?"*
  - *"Would you want to talk to me again?"*

- Explain, *"Remember, one of the rules for trading information and having a two-way conversation is to use good volume control."*

- Do not speak too loudly or the person may get annoyed or bothered by you
- If the person is annoyed or bothered, they may avoid speaking to you in future
- It can also be embarrassing when someone is speaking too loudly in public

- ***Have good body boundaries***

   [The instructor and behavioral coach should do an INAPPROPRIATE role-play with the instructor standing too close]

   o   Begin by saying, *"Watch this and tell me what I'm doing WRONG."*

   Example of an INAPPROPRIATE role-play:

   - Instructor: (Standing too close) *"Hi (insert name). How are you doing?"*
   - Coach: (Startled, moves back) *"Oh, I'm fine."*
   - Instructor: (Moves forward) *"What have you been up to?"*
   - Coach: (Looking annoyed, moving further back) *"Not much."*
   - Instructor: (Moves forward again) *"So how's school going?"*
   - Coach: (Looking around, trying to escape) *"Fine."*

   o   End by saying, *"Okay, time-out on that. So what did I do WRONG in that conversation?"*

   - Answer: You were standing too close

   o   Ask the following ***Perspective Taking Questions***:

   - *"What was that like for (name of coach)?"*
     - Answers: Uncomfortable; irritating; annoying; embarrassing
   - *"What do you think (name of coach) thought of me?"*
     - Answers: Weird; creepy; stalker
   - *"Is (name of coach) going to want to talk to me again?"*
     - Answers: Definitely not; too creepy

   o   Ask the behavioral coach the same ***Perspective Taking Questions***:

   - *"What was that like for you?"*
   - *"What did you think of me?"*
   - *"Would you want to talk to me again?"*

   o   Explain, *"One of the rules for trading information and having a two-way conversation is to have good body boundaries."*

   - Standing too close to someone is likely to make them feel uncomfortable
   - They may avoid you and not want to talk to you again
   - The general rule is to stand about an arm's length away (but do not measure first!)

[The instructor and behavioral coach should do an INAPPROPRIATE role-play with the instructor standing too far away]

- ○ Begin by saying, *"Watch this and tell me what I'm doing WRONG."*

    Example of an INAPPROPRIATE role-play:

    - ■ Instructor: (Standing across the room) *"Hi (insert name). How are you doing?"*
    - ■ Coach: (Straining to hear and looking confused) *"Oh, hi."*
    - ■ Instructor: (Still standing across the room) *"How are you doing?"*
    - ■ Coach: (Looking confused) *"Fine."*
    - ■ Instructor: (Still standing across the room) *"So what have you been up to?"*
    - ■ Coach: (Looking confused, looking around the room, trying to escape) *"Not much."*
    - ■ (Long awkward pause)

- ○ End by saying, *"Okay, time-out on that. So what did I do WRONG in that conversation?"*

    - ■ Answer: You were standing too far away

- ○ Ask the following ***Perspective Taking Questions***:

    - ■ *"What was that like for (name of coach)?"*

        - • Answers: Confusing; strange; embarrassing

    - ■ *"What do you think (name of coach) thought of me?"*

        - • Answers: Weird; odd; strange; oblivious

    - ■ *"Is (name of coach) going to want to talk to me again?"*

        - • Answers: Probably not; too embarrassing

- ○ Ask the behavioral coach the same ***Perspective Taking Questions***:

    - ■ *"What was that like for you?"*
    - ■ *"What did you think of me?"*
    - ■ *"Would you want to talk to me again?"*

- ○ Explain, *"Remember, one of the rules for trading information and having a two-way conversation is to have good body boundaries."*

    - ■ Standing too far away is awkward in a conversation and may make it feel like your conversation is too public
    - ■ The person may think you are strange for trying to have a conversation when you are standing so far away
    - ■ Saying hello across the hall in school is fine, but don't try to get into a lengthy conversation
    - ■ Again, the general rule is to stand about an arm's length away (but do not measure first!)

- *Make good eye contact*

  [The instructor and behavioral coach should do an INAPPROPRIATE role-play with the instructor making too little eye contact]

  ○ Begin by saying, *"Watch this and tell me what I'm doing WRONG."*

  Example of an INAPPROPRIATE role-play:

  - Coach: (Making eye contact) *"Hey (insert name)!"*
  - Instructor: (Looking away) *"Hi, how's it going?"*
  - Coach: (Confused) *"I'm good. How are you?"*
  - Instructor: (Looking away) *"I'm fine. What did you do this weekend?"*
  - Coach: (Trying to make eye contact) *"I went hiking."*
  - Instructor: (Looking around) *"Oh, that's cool, I like to hike."*
  - Coach: (Trying to make eye contact) *"Yeah, I like hiking too."*
  - Instructor: (Looking around) *"Who did you go with?"*
  - Coach: (Confused) *"I went with my sister."*
  - Instructor: (Looking away) *"Oh, that's nice."*
  - (Long awkward pause)

  ○ End by saying, *"Okay, time-out on that. So what did I do WRONG in that conversation?"*
    - Answer: You were not making eye contact

  ○ Ask the following *Perspective Taking Questions*:
    - *"What was that like for (name of coach)?"*
      • Answers: Confusing; awkward; weird
    - *"What do you think (name of coach) thought of me?"*
      • Answers: Disinterested; weird; strange; spacey
    - *"Is (name of coach) going to want to talk to me again?"*
      • Answers: Probably not; too weird; didn't seem interested

  ○ Ask the behavioral coach the same *Perspective Taking Questions*:
    - *"What was that like for you?"*
    - *"What did you think of me?"*
    - *"Would you want to talk to me again?"*

  ○ Explain, *"One of the rules for trading information and having a two-way conversation is to make good eye contact."*
    - When you **make good eye contact**, it shows them that you are interested in them
    - If you do not look at them, they will think you are not interested

[The instructor and behavioral coach should do an INAPPROPRIATE role-play with the instructor making too much eye contact]

○   Begin by saying, *"Watch this and tell me what I'm doing WRONG."*

Example of an INAPPROPRIATE role-play:

- Instructor: (Staring) *"Hey (insert name), how's it going?"*
- Coach: *"I'm good, how are you doing?"*
- Instructor: (Staring) *"I'm fine. What did you do this weekend?"*
- Coach: (Uncomfortable, looking away) *"I went hiking."*
- Instructor: (Still staring) *"That's cool! Who'd you go with?"*
- Coach: (Looking away) *"My sister."*
- Instructor: (Still staring) *"Nice, I like to go hiking too."*
- Coach: (Uncomfortable, looking away) *"Yeah?"*
- Instructor: (Still staring) *"There's this trail I like to go to by my house."*
- Coach: (Uncomfortable, looking away) *"Great."*
- (Long awkward pause)

○   End by saying, *"Okay, time-out on that. So what did I do WRONG in that conversation?"*
- Answer: You were making too much eye contact, you were staring at the person

○   Ask the following *Perspective Taking Questions*:
- *"What was that like for (name of coach)?"*
  • Answers: Uncomfortable; awkward; creepy; weird
- *"What do you think (name of coach) thought of me?"*
  • Answers: Stalker; predator; creepy; weird
- *"Is (name of coach) going to want to talk to me again?"*
  • Answers: No; too creepy; too awkward

○   Ask the behavioral coach the same *Perspective Taking Questions*:
- *"What was that like for you?"*
- *"What did you think of me?"*
- *"Would you want to talk to me again?"*

○   Explain, *"Remember, one of the rules for trading information and having a two-way conversation is to make good eye contact."*
- Staring at someone without looking away is creepy
- You will make the other person uncomfortable if you stare at them
- ***Make good eye contact***, but not too much eye contact
- Look away once in a while

Role-Play: Two-Way Conversations

[The instructor and a coach should demonstrate an APPROPRIATE role-play using all of the steps for having a *two-way conversation*]

- Begin by saying, *"Now that we know the rules for trading information and having a two-way conversation, watch this and tell us what we're doing RIGHT."*

    Example of an APPROPRIATE role-play:

    - Instructor: (Standing about an arm's length away, maintaining good eye contact, using appropriate volume) *"Hi (insert name). How's it going?"*
    - Coach: *"Oh, it's going well. How are you?"*
    - Instructor: *"I'm fine. So what have you been up to lately?"*
    - Coach: *"Oh, not much. Just studying a lot, but I'm going to the movies this weekend."*
    - Instructor: *"Oh, yeah. So what are you going to see?"*
    - Coach: *"I think I'm going to see that new sci-fi movie. What are you doing this weekend?"*
    - Instructor: *"I was thinking about going to the movies, too, but I already saw that one."*
    - Coach: *"Oh, yeah. Was it good?"*
    - Instructor: *"Yeah, it was really good. Do you like sci-fi?"*
    - Coach: *"Yeah. They're my favorite. What about you?"*
    - Instructor: *"They're my favorite, too!"*
    - Coach: *"Cool. What's your favorite movie?"*

- End by saying, *"Okay, time-out on that. So what did we do RIGHT in that conversation?"*

    - Answers: ***Asked open-ended questions, asked follow-up questions, not repetitive, listened, didn't police, didn't tease, were serious, used good volume control, used good body boundaries, made good eye contact***

- Ask, *"Did it seem like we wanted to talk to each other?"*

    - Answer: Yes

- Ask, *"How could you tell?"*

    - Answers: ***Talking to each other; looking at each other; facing each other***

- Ask the following *Perspective Taking Questions*:

    - *"What was that like for (name of coach)?"*

        - Answers: Nice; pleasant

    - *"What do you think (name of coach) thought of me?"*

        - Answers: Nice; interesting; pretty cool

    - *"Is (name of coach) going to want to talk to me again?"*

        - Answer: Yes

- Ask the behavioral coach the same *Perspective Taking Questions*:

  - *"What was that like for you?"*
  - *"What did you think of me?"*
  - *"Would you want to talk to me again?"*

Wrap Up

Say, *"So that's what it looks like to trade information and have a two-way conversation. Tomorrow we'll continue our discussion about good conversations. We'll be reviewing the rules for having a two-way conversation, practicing having good conversations, and finding common interests with our classmates."*

Calculate Points

Calculate the number of points earned by each teen (see Appendix E for the Daily Point Log):

- Do not publicly disclose the individual number of points

- Discourage attempts to compare number of points earned between teens

  - Remind them that they are working as a team to earn a bigger and better graduation party

Day Three: Lesson Review and Behavioral Rehearsal

Lesson Review: Two-Way Conversations

- Say, *"Yesterday we learned how to trade information and have a two-way conversation. Who can tell us what some of the rules are for having a two-way conversation?"*

[Have teens generate all of the rules. Be prepared to give prompts if necessary. Write the following buzzwords (**bold and italicized**) on the board and do not erase until the end of the lesson.]

- *Trade information (may include previous rules)*
- *Ask open-ended questions*
- *Ask follow-up questions*
- *Don't be repetitive*
- *Listen to your friend*
- *Don't police*
- *Don't tease*
- *Be a little more serious when you're first getting to know someone*
- *Use good volume control*
- *Have good body boundaries*
- *Make good eye contact*

Role-Play: Two-Way Conversations

[The instructor and a coach should demonstrate an APPROPRIATE role-play using all of the steps for having a *two-way conversation*]

- Say, *"Now we're going to show you an example of how to trade information and have a two-way conversation. Watch this conversation and tell us what we did RIGHT."*

  Example of an APPROPRIATE role-play:

  - Instructor: (Standing about an arm's length away, maintaining good eye contact, using appropriate volume) *"Hi (insert name). How's it going?"*
  - Coach: *"Oh, it's going well. How are you?"*
  - Instructor: *"I'm fine. So what are you doing this weekend?"*
  - Coach: *"I'm not sure. I was thinking about ordering a pizza and watching a movie at home or something. What about you?"*

- ■ Instructor: *"Oh, I have to study, but that sounds fun. So what movie are you going to watch?"*
- ■ Coach: *"I'm kind of in the mood for a good horror flick!"*
- ■ Instructor: *"Really? I love scary movies!"*
- ■ Coach: *"You do? That's cool. Not everyone's into them."*
- ■ Instructor: *"I know, right? So do you have any favorites?"*
- ■ Coach: *"I'm actually really into the classics right now. Old black and whites."*
- ■ Instructor: *"That sounds cool. I haven't seen too many of those."*
- ■ Coach: *"Well, you should come over some time and check them out."*
- ■ Instructor: *"That would be great!"*

- • End by saying, *"Okay, time-out on that. So what did we do RIGHT in that conversation?"*

  - ○ Answers: **Asked open-ended questions, asked follow-up questions, not repetitive, listened, didn't police, didn't tease, were serious, used good volume control, used good body boundaries, made good eye contact**

- • Ask, *"Did it seem like we wanted to talk to each other?"*

  - ○ Answer: Yes

- • Ask, *"How could you tell?"*

  - ○ Answers: **Talking to each other; looking at each other; facing each other**

- • Ask the following *Perspective Taking Questions*:

  - ○ *"What was that like for (name of coach)?"*

    - ■ Answers: Nice; pleasant

  - ○ *"What do you think (name of coach) thought of me?"*

    - ■ Answers: Nice; interesting; pretty cool

  - ○ *"Is (name of coach) going to want to talk to me again?"*

    - ■ Answer: Yes

- • Ask the behavioral coach the same *Perspective Taking Questions*:

  - ○ *"What was that like for you?"*
  - ○ *"What did you think of me?"*
  - ○ *"Would you want to talk to me again?"*

Behavioral Rehearsal: Two-Way Conversations

- • Say, *"Now that we know the rules for having a two-way conversation and we've seen what it looks like, we're going to have each of you practice with one of your classmates. Remember to trade information and find a common interest."*

- Assign teens to practice **trading information** and having a **two-way conversation** with someone else in the class

    ○ Assign pairs and move teens around to create appropriate dyads
    ○ If there is an uneven number of teens, create one triad

- Help facilitate the rehearsal when necessary by providing **prompting** and **feedback**, and **troubleshoot** when problems arise

    ○ Examples of **prompting**:

        ▪ *"You could ask each other about your interests or hobbies."*
        ▪ *"You could talk about your favorite books, movies, or television programs."*
        ▪ *"You could find out what the other person likes to do on the weekend."*

    ○ Examples of **feedback**:

        ▪ *"You may need to answer your own question."*
        ▪ *"Remember to ask follow-up questions."*
        ▪ *"Let's be careful not to ask too many closed-ended questions."*
        ▪ *"Remember, no policing."*
        ▪ *"We might want to be a little more serious at first."*

- Spend about five minutes on each dyad or triad

- If there is time, switch dyads/triads for an additional five minutes

- Then briefly have teens identify whether they were able to find a **common interest** by saying, *"It's time to wrap up your conversations. I heard lots of good trading information and two-way conversations. Let's go around the room and find out what common interests you found."*

    ○ Have teens identify **common interests**
    ○ Follow up **common interests** by asking, *"What could you do with that information if you were going to hang out?"*
    ○ Praise teens for their efforts

Homework Assignments

- [Assign the **in-class calls** for the week and write this on the In-Class Call Assignment Log (Appendix D) for future reference. If there is an uneven number of teens, assign someone **double duty**.]

- [Distribute the Parent Handout (found in the last section of this chapter) and inform teens that they should give this handout to their parents immediately. You may choose to email parents these handouts as an alternative, but you will need to notify them of the day and time of their teen's **in-class call**.]

- [Make sure all teens have a copy of the Phone Roster (Appendix C), and have them confirm that the information is correct. Be prepared to have the teens coordinate a day and time to make the **in-class call**, and then have each teen write the day and time of the call on the Phone Roster and Parent Handout.]

- Briefly explain the homework for the week by saying, *"We're going to continue to have you practice trading information and having two-way conversations this week."*

- Present the homework assignment for the coming week:

1. Teens should practice **trading information** and having a **two way conversation** with their parent this week

   a. Teens should go over the rules for **trading information** and having a **two-way conversation** from the Parent Handout with their parent before practicing

   b. Find one **common interest** to share with the class

2. **In-class call or video chat**

   a. Before the call:

      i. Before the class ends, teens should arrange to call another member of the class to practice **trading information** and having a **two-way conversation**

      ii. Set up a day and time to make the call

      iii. Write the day and time of the call on the Phone Roster and the Parent Handout

   b. During the call:

      i. Teens should **trade information** and have a **two-way conversation** on this call

      ii. Find a **common interest** to report back to the class

   c. After the call:

      i. Teens should discuss the call with their parent, identify **common interests**, and **troubleshoot** any problems

Wrap Up

Say, *"So those are your homework assignments for this week. Be sure to start working on these assignments right away. We'll be reviewing how they went at the beginning of next week. Tomorrow we'll continue our discussion about two-way conversations. We'll be reviewing the rules for having a two-way conversation, practicing having good conversations, and finding common interests with our classmates."*

Calculate Points

Calculate the number of points earned by each teen (see Appendix E for the Daily Point Log):

- Do not publicly disclose the individual number of points

- Discourage attempts to compare number of points earned between teens

  ○ Remind them that they are working as a team to earn a bigger and better graduation party

Days Four and Five: Teen Activity—Jeopardy

Lesson Review: Two-Way Conversations

- Say, *"This week we've been talking about how to trade information and have two-way conversations. Who can tell us what some of the rules are for having a two way conversation?"*

[Have teens generate all of the rules. Be prepared to give prompts if necessary. Write the following buzzwords (**bold and italicized**) on the board and do not erase until the end of the lesson.]

- ○ *Trade information (may include previous rules)*

- ○ *Ask open-ended questions*

- ○ *Ask follow-up questions*

- ○ *Don't be repetitive*

- ○ *Listen to your friend*

- ○ *Don't police*

- ○ *Don't tease*

- ○ *Be a little more serious when you're first getting to know someone*

- ○ *Use good volume control*

- ○ *Have good body boundaries*

- ○ *Make good eye contact*

Teen Activity: Jeopardy

Materials Needed

- Whiteboard and markers

- *Jeopardy Answer Sheets* for each teen

Rules

- Teens will compete in this game of **trading information**

- Like the television show **Jeopardy**, teens will be given answers and asked to respond in the form of a question

  - ○ Example:

    - ■ Instructor: *"The answer is Jimmy's favorite sport."*
    - ■ Teen: *"What is baseball?"*

  - ○ The teen does not have to answer in the form of a question (most do not)

- To promote interest and cooperation, points will be given for correct responses

- The purpose of *Jeopardy* is not to practice ***trading information*** or having a ***two-way conversation*** perfectly, since the teens will sound like they are ***interviewing*** when asking the questions

- The true purpose of *Jeopardy* is to improve:

  - ***Topic initiation***

    - Talking about a variety of topics, rather than only restricted interested

  - ***Listening skills***

    - Listening and remembering what people share about themselves

How to Play

- Write the ***Jeopardy Topics*** on the board where teens can see them

  - ***Favorite music***
  - ***Favorite weekend activity***
  - ***Favorite sport***
  - ***Favorite game***
  - ***Favorite movie***
  - ***Favorite television show***
  - ***Favorite book***
  - ***Eye color*** [Note: this is NOT to be asked, but noticed by using good eye contact]

- If the teens become bored with the current ***Jeopardy Topics***, encourage them to come up with their own topics and even name them

- Have teens practice ***trading information*** about the ***Jeopardy Topics*** in small groups for 2–3 minutes each

  - Change groups a few times (depending on time)
  - Prompt teens to ask relevant questions to the ***Jeopardy Topics*** when necessary

- While teens are ***trading information***, organize the ***Jeopardy Answer Sheets*** from the previous week according to category and mix the order of the answer sheets

- Write the Jeopardy categories on the board

- Once the teens have finished trading information, reconvene as a group and begin the ***Jeopardy Challenge***

  - Begin by having the teen with the most points that week pick the first category
  - Notify the class that if they raise their hand before the question has been asked fully, they are disqualified from answering that question
  - The person who raises their hand first gets to take the first guess
  - If they provide the wrong answer, the person who raised their hand second has a chance to answer, and so on
  - The teens get only one guess per question
  - Do not give teens clues

- You may need to enforce a time limit if teens take a long time to answer

- Do not correct the teens if they answer the questions in the incorrect format (i.e., instead of saying *"What is baseball?"* they say *"Baseball"*)

  o All that matters is that they remembered the information they obtained through **trading information** and having a **two-way conversation**

- The person who answers the question correctly gets a point and gets to choose the next category

- If no one answers correctly, the person about which the last question relates gets to pick the next category

- Encourage the teens to clap and cheer for each other during the game

- Give points for correct responses

- Keep track of the points on the board using a different colored marker than used during the lesson review (to differentiate from points earned during the didactic portion of the class)

- At the end of the game, the person with the most points is the **Jeopardy Challenge Winner**

- SAVE TEEN ANSWER SHEETS FOR NEXT WEEK

Homework Assignments

- [Be prepared to read off the **in-class call** assignments for the week as a reminder of the homework. This should be written on the In-Class Call Assignment Log (Appendix D). Make sure the teens have scheduled the **in-class call** and have the correct phone number.]

- Briefly remind teens of the homework for the week by saying, *"Remember, we're going to continue to have you practice trading information this week through simple and fun homework assignments."*

- Present the homework assignments for the coming week

  1. Teens should practice **trading information** and having a **two-way conversation** with their parent this week

     a. Teens should go over the rules for **trading information** and having a **two-way conversation** from the Parent Handout with their parent before practicing
     b. Find one **common interest** to share with the class

  2. **In-class call or video chat**

     a. Before the call:

        i.   Before the class ends, teens should arrange to call another member of the class to practice **trading information** and having a **two-way conversation**
        ii. Set up a day and time to make the call
        iii. Write the day and time of the call on the Phone Roster and the Parent Handout

   b. During the call:

      i. Teens should **trade information** and have a **two-way conversation** on this call

     ii. Find a **common interest** to report back to the class

   c. After the call:

      i. Teens should discuss the call with their parent, identify **common interests**, and **troubleshoot** any problems

Wrap Up

Say, *"So those are your homework assignments for this week. Be sure to start working on these assignments right away. We'll be reviewing how they went at the beginning of next week."*

Calculate Points

Calculate the number of points earned by each teen (see Appendix E for the Daily Point Log):

- Do not publicly disclose the individual number of points

- Discourage attempts to compare number of points earned between teens

   ○ Remind them that they are working as a team to earn a bigger and better graduation party

Parent Handout 2

PEERS® Program for the Education and Enrichment of Relational Skills

Two-Way Conversations

This week your teens will be learning how to have a **two-way conversation** with peers. There are very specific rules for having **two-way conversations**, which your teens will be practicing.

Didactic Lesson: Rules for Having a Two Way Conversation

* *Trade information* (review from last lesson)

* *Ask the other person about him or herself* (review from last lesson)

* *Answer your own questions* (review from last lesson)

* *Find a common interest* (review from last lesson)

* *Share the conversation* (review from last lesson)

* *Don't be a conversation hog* (review from last lesson)

* *Don't be an interviewer* (review from last lesson)

* *Don't get too personal at first* (review from last lesson)

* *Ask open-ended questions*

    ○ Questions should be *open-ended* so the person can give extended responses

        ▪ *Open-ended question*: *"What kind of movies do you like?"*

    ○ Repeated questions that are *closed-ended* only allow the person to give brief responses (e.g., *"yes/no"*) and end up sounding like an *interview*

        ▪ *Closed-ended question*: *"What is your favorite movie?"*

* *Ask follow-up questions*

    ○ *Follow-up questions* are those we ask on a specific topic to keep the conversation going

    ○ Example: A *follow-up question* to what kind of movies someone likes might be, *"Have you seen any good movies lately?"*

* *Don't be repetitive*

    ○ Don't talk about the same thing over and over even if it's a *common interest*

    ○ Try talking about different topics to keep it interesting

- *Listen to your friend*

  - This means that if you ask a question, listen to the answer
  - You're supposed to know the answer once you've asked the question
  - You should not ask the same question again
  - When you listen it shows that you're interested in your friend

- *Don't police*

  - Don't criticize people and point out their mistakes
  - People will be annoyed and they will think you're a know-it-all

- *Don't tease*

  - *Teasing* or *bantering* is risky behavior if you're trying to make and keep friends
  - Even if you think you're being funny, it may upset them or hurt their feelings
  - This is especially true when you are FIRST getting to know someone and they don't understand your sense of humor yet

- *Be a little more serious when you're first getting to know someone*

  - Don't act silly when you're FIRST getting to know someone
  - You might make the other person uncomfortable
  - They might not understand your sense of humor and they might think you're making fun of them

- *Use good volume control*

  - Don't speak too quietly or too loudly
  - [Parents may need to give feedback to teens on this]

- *Have good body boundaries*

  - Don't stand too close or too far away when talking to someone
  - Stand about an arm's length away
  - [Parents may need to give feedback to teens on this]

- *Make good eye contact*

  - Look the person in the eyes and smile when appropriate
  - Don't stare too much
  - Look away once in awhile

Homework Assignments

Every week your teen will have homework assignments to practice new and previously learned social skills. It is extremely helpful if parents assist teens in completing these assignments. The homework assignments for this week include the following:

1. Teens should practice *trading information* and having a *two way conversation* with their parent this week

    a. Teens should go over the rules for **trading information** and having a **two-way conversation** from the Parent Handout with their parent before practicing

    b. Find one **common interest** to share with the class

    c. After identifying **common interests**, parents should ask, *"What could we do with that information if we were going to hang out?"*

2. ***In-class call or video chat***

    a. Before the call:

        i. Teens should have arranged to call another member of the class to practice **trading information** (instructor has assigned the calls)

       ii. Teens should have set up a day and time to make the call (this information should be listed below and on your teen's Phone Roster)

    b. During the call:

        i. Teens should **trade information** and have a **two-way conversation** on this call

       ii. Find a **common interest** to report back to the class

    c. After the call:

        i. Teens should discuss the call with their parent, identify **common interests**, and **troubleshoot** any problems

       ii. After identifying **common interests**, parents should ask, *"What could you do with that information if you were going to hang out?"*

In-Class Call Assignment

Your teen has been assigned to be the **caller/receiver** (circle one) with:

Name:

Phone Number:

Day:

Time:

ELECTRONIC COMMUNICATION

Preparing for the Lesson

It seems that with every succeeding generation teens learn to use more sophisticated electronic communication at younger ages. Electronic communication is an integral part of teen culture, particularly text messaging, instant messaging (IM), and social networking sites like Facebook. The popularity of online games, like World of Warcraft, and video-sharing websites, like YouTube, are also dramatically increasing among teens. The focus of this lesson will be on how to effectively navigate these forms of electronic communication.

The purpose of this lesson is to help teens learn the appropriate uses of electronic forms of communication with peers. For some teens, the first portion of the didactic lesson on using the telephone will already be included in their repertoire. For others, using the telephone, apart from texting or video chatting, will be less familiar. Some teens will even claim that no one makes phone calls anymore. While it's true that fewer and fewer teens use the phone just to talk, it is still difficult to get through life and navigate social relationships without knowing how to make a phone call.

The challenge with this part of the lesson may be to keep your students' interest until you move into more sophisticated forms of electronic communication. The role-play demonstrations will be helpful in this respect. It can also be helpful to point out to the teens that although some of them may already know these skills, it is very easy to forget one or two of the steps. You might even have them think of a time when someone forgot one of the steps and how it affected their conversation. For example, you might say, *"I know it seems obvious that you should identify yourself when calling someone on the phone, but how many of you have had someone call you on the phone that didn't identify themselves and you had no idea who you were talking to? It seems obvious and yet people often forget!"*

During the online safety portion of the didactic lesson it is common for one or two teens to challenge the point that the Internet should not be used to make new friends for teens. With the rising popularity of social networking sites like Facebook, teens often use the Internet to communicate with strangers as well as friends. While the latter is perfectly appropriate, the former can be dangerous for teenagers. As described in previous lessons, the best way to handle objections from teens is to ask the class, *"What could be the problem with . . ."* In this case, you can ask the class, *"What could be the problem with teens making new friends on the Internet?"* The other teens will quickly offer that it can be dangerous, and may even launch into stories from the news about predators targeting children online. Once this point has been made sufficiently, remind teens that the Internet can actually be very helpful in strengthening current friendships and developing friendships with pre-existing acquaintances.

Day One: Homework Review

Homework Review

[Start with completed homework first. If you have time, you can inquire as to why others were unable to complete the assignment and try to **troubleshoot** how they might get it done for the coming week. When reviewing homework, be sure to use the buzzwords (**bold and italicized**) and **troubleshoot** issues that come up. Spend the majority of the homework review on the **in-class call**, as this is the most important assignment.]

[Note: Give multiple points for homework parts—not just one point per assignment.]

1. Practice **trading information** and having a **two-way conversation** with parents

   a. Say, *"One of your assignments this week was to practice trading information and having a two-way conversation with a parent. Raise your hand if you practiced trading information with one of your parents this week."*

      i. Ask the following questions:

         1. *"Who did you practice trading information with (mom, dad, etc.)?"*
         2. *"Did you find a common interest?"*

            a. When they identify **common interests** ask, *"What could you do with that information if you were going to hang out with your parent?"*

2. **In-class call or video chat**

   a. Say, *"The other assignment you had this week was to have a phone call or video chat with someone in the class in order to practice trading information and having a two-way conversation. Raise your hand if you did the in-class call."*

      i. Ask the following questions:

         1. *"Who did you talk to?"*
         2. *"Who called who?"*
         3. *"Did you trade information?"*
         4. *"Did you find a common interest?"*

            a. When they identify **common interests** ask, *"What could you do with that information if you were going to hang out?"*

         5. Avoid general questions like, *"How did it go?"*

      ii. Do not allow teens to talk about mistakes the other person made
      iii. Have the other person who participated in the call give their account immediately after, but not at the same time

Wrap Up

Say, *"Good work for those of you who completed your homework assignments. Tomorrow we will be talking about electronic forms of communication, like text messaging, instant messaging, voicemail, and the Internet."*

Calculate Points

Calculate the number of points earned by each teen (see Appendix E for the Daily Point Log):

- Do not publicly disclose the individual number of points

- Discourage attempts to compare number of points earned between teens

  - Remind them that they are working as a team to earn a bigger and better graduation party

Day Two: Didactic Lesson—Electronic Communication

Didactic Lesson: Electronic Communication

- Explain, *"Today we're going to be talking about electronic communication. This includes things like making phone calls, texting, instant messaging, sending emails, and using the Internet. Electronic communication is a very popular way for teens to talk to one another, so we need to know what the rules are."*

[Present the rules and steps for electronic communication by writing the buzzwords (**bold and italicized**) on the board. Do not erase the rules and steps until the end of the lesson.]

Phone Calls

- Say, *"One of the most popular ways for teens to communicate is through the phone, especially through texting and video chatting. We know fewer teens use the phone just to talk, but sometimes you just have to make a call. Because we don't use the phone as much in that way, it can be difficult to know how to begin and end phone calls. There are very specific steps for starting and ending phone calls."*

Starting Phone Calls

[The instructor and behavioral coach should do an INAPPROPRIATE role-play of starting a phone call]

- Begin by saying, *"Watch this and tell me what I'm doing WRONG."*

    Example of an INAPPROPRIATE role-play:

    - Instructor: (Hold a cell phone to your ear) *"Ring, ring."*
    - Coach: (Pick up a cell phone) *"Hello?"*
    - Instructor: *"Hey. What are you doing?"*
    - Coach: (Confused) *"Umm, watching TV."*
    - Instructor: *"Oh, what are you watching?"*
    - Coach: (Confused) *"Umm, some reality show."*
    - Instructor: *"Oh, I like reality shows."*
    - Coach: (Annoyed) *"Okay."*
    - Instructor: *"So what are you doing this weekend?"*
    - Coach: (Confused, annoyed) *"Umm . . . I don't know."*

- End by saying, *"Time-out on that. So what did I do WRONG in starting that phone call?"*

    - Answer: You did not ask for the person you were calling, give your name, ask how the person was doing, ask if the person could talk, or give a reason for calling

- Ask the following *Perspective Taking Questions*:

  ○ *"What was that like for (name of coach)?"*

    ▪ Answers: Strange; confusing; weird

  ○ *"What do you think (name of coach) thought of me?"*

    ▪ Answers: Weird; odd; creepy; stalker

  ○ *"Is (name of coach) going to want to talk to me again?"*

    ▪ Answers: Probably not; too weird

- Ask the behavioral coach the same *Perspective Taking Questions*:

  ○ *"What was that like for you?"*
  ○ *"What did you think of me?"*
  ○ *"Would you want to talk to me again?"*

- Present the *steps for starting a phone call*:

  1. *Ask for the person you are calling*

     a. Example: *"Hi. May I please speak to Jennifer?"*

  2. *Say who you are*

     a. Example: *"Hi Jennifer. This is Carrie."*

  3. *Ask how they are*

     a. Example: *"How's it going?"*

  4. *Ask if they can talk*

     a. Example: *"Can you talk right now?"*

  5. *Give a cover story for why you are calling*

     a. Example: *"I was just calling to see how you're doing."*
     b. *Cover stories* are reasons you do things (in this case, the reason you are calling)
     c. Have the teens come up with different examples of *cover stories* (see Table 4.1)

Table 4.1 Cover Story Examples

Reasons You Are Calling	Reasons You Have To Hang Up
"Just calling to see how you're doing."	*"I have to get going."*
"Just calling to hear what's up with you."	*"I better let you go."*
"I'm calling to get the homework."	*"I need to finish my homework."*
"I haven't talked to you in a while."	*"I have to eat dinner now."*
"I was wondering what you're up to."	*"My mom needs to use the phone."*

[The instructor and behavioral coach should do an APPROPRIATE role-play of starting a phone call]

- Begin by saying, *"Watch this and tell me what I'm doing RIGHT."*

  Example of an APPROPRIATE role-play:

  - Instructor: (Hold a cell phone to your ear) *"Ring, ring."*
  - Coach: (Pick up a cell phone) *"Hello?"*
  - Instructor: *"Hi. Can I speak to (insert name)?"*
  - Coach: *"This is (insert name)."*
  - Instructor: *"Hi. This is (insert name)."*
  - Coach: *"Oh, hey! How's it going?"*
  - Instructor: *"Pretty well. How are you?"*
  - Coach: *"I'm good."*
  - Instructor: *"So can you talk right now?"*
  - Coach: *"Sure."*
  - Instructor: *"So I was just calling to see how you've been doing."*
  - Coach: *"Oh, I'm good. Just busy with school."*
  - Instructor: *"Oh yeah? How's school going?"*
  - Coach: *"Fine. We have a school dance this weekend."*
  - Instructor: *"That sounds fun. Are you going?"*
  - Coach: *"I was thinking about it."*

- End by saying, *"Time-out on that. So what did I do RIGHT in starting that phone call?"*
  - Answer: Asked for the person you were calling, said who you were, asked how the person was doing, asked if the person could talk, and gave a *cover story* for calling

- Ask the following *Perspective Taking Questions*:
  - *"What was that like for (name of coach)?"*
    - Answers: Fine; comfortable; pleasant
  - *"What do you think (name of coach) thought of me?"*
    - Answers: Normal; cool; friendly
  - *"Is (name of coach) going to want to talk to me again?"*
    - Answer: Probably yes

- Ask the behavioral coach the same *Perspective Taking Questions*:
  - *"What was that like for you?"*
  - *"What did you think of me?"*
  - *"Would you want to talk to me again?"*

Ending Phone Calls

[The instructor and behavioral coach should do an INAPPROPRIATE role-play of ending a phone call]

- Begin by saying, *"So we're going to pick up where we left off in the phone call. Watch this and tell me what I'm doing WRONG in ending this call."*

   Example of an INAPPROPRIATE role-play:

   o Instructor and Coach: (Pick up where you left off, with cell phones to ears)
   o Instructor: *"So who's going to the dance?"*
   o Coach: *"I'm not sure. I haven't decided if I'm going to go. I don't really like to dance, but I like music."*
   o Instructor: *"Oh yeah, me too. What kind of music do you like?"*
   o Coach: *"I'm kind of into rap and R&B. What about you?"*
   o Instructor: (Uncomfortable, awkward) *"Oh, you like rap?"*
   o Coach: *"Yeah, don't you?"*
   o Instructor: (Looks panicked, not sure what to do, hangs up phone)
   o Coach: (Looks confused, stunned)

- End by saying, *"Time-out on that. So what did I do WRONG in ending that phone call?"*
   o Answer: You did not wait for a pause, give a reason for getting off the phone, say it was nice talking to the person, say you would talk to the person later, or say goodbye

- Ask the following *Perspective Taking Questions*:
   o *"What was that like for (name of coach)?"*
      ▪ Answers: Strange; confusing; weird
   o *"What do you think (name of coach) thought of me?"*
      ▪ Answers: Weird; odd; strange
   o *"Is (name of coach) going to want to talk to me again?"*
      ▪ Answers: Probably not; too weird

- Ask the behavioral coach the same *Perspective Taking Questions*:
   o *"What was that like for you?"*
   o *"What did you think of me?"*
   o *"Would you want to talk to me again?"*

- Present the *steps for ending a phone call*:

  1. *Wait for a bit of a pause*

     a. This is a transitional moment
     b. Do not interrupt

  2. *Give a cover story for why you have to go*

     a. Example: *"Well, I'd better get started on my homework."*
     b. *Cover stories* are reasons you do things (in this case, the reason you have to get off the phone)
     c. Have the teens come up with different examples of *cover stories* (see Table 4.1)

  3. *Tell the person it was nice talking*

     a. Example: *"It was nice talking to you."*

  4. *Tell the person you will talk to them later*

     a. Example: *"I'll talk to you later."*

  5. *Say goodbye*

     a. Example: *"Bye."*

[The instructor and behavioral coach should do an APPROPRIATE role-play of ending a phone call]

- Begin by saying, *"So we're going to pick up where we left off in the phone call. Watch this and tell me what I'm doing RIGHT in ending this call."*

  Example of an APPROPRIATE role-play:

  - Instructor and Coach: (Pick up where you left off, with cell phones to ears)
  - Instructor: *"So who's going to the dance?"*
  - Coach: *"I'm not sure. I haven't decided if I'm going to go. I don't really like to dance, but I like music."*
  - Instructor: *"Oh yeah, me too. What kind of music do you like?"*
  - Coach: *"I'm kind of into rap and R&B. What about you?"*
  - Instructor: *"I'm not really into rap, but R&B is pretty cool."* (Pause) *"Well my mom needs to use the phone, so I should probably get going . . ."*
  - Coach: *"Okay."*
  - Instructor: *". . . but it was good talking to you."*
  - Coach: *"You too. Thanks for calling."*
  - Instructor: *"I'll talk to you later."*
  - Coach: *"Sounds good."*
  - Instructor: *"Okay, bye!"*
  - Coach: *"Bye!"*
  - Instructor and Coach: (Hang up phones)

- End by saying, *"Time-out on that. So what did I do RIGHT in ending that phone call?"*

    ○ Answer: You waited for a pause, gave a *cover story* for getting off the phone, said it was nice talking, said you would talk to the person later, and said goodbye

- Ask the following *Perspective Taking Questions*:

    ○ *"What was that like for (name of coach)?"*

        ▪ Answers: Fine; normal

    ○ *"What do you think (name of coach) thought of me?"*

        ▪ Answers: Friendly; pleasant; normal

    ○ *"Is (name of coach) going to want to talk to me again?"*

        ▪ Answer: Probably yes

- Ask the behavioral coach the same *Perspective Taking Questions*:

    ○ *"What was that like for you?"*
    ○ *"What did you think of me?"*
    ○ *"Would you want to talk to me again?"*

Voicemail

- Explain, *"Sometimes we call someone on the phone and we get their voicemail. Lots of people feel uncomfortable leaving voicemail, but it doesn't have to be uncomfortable if we know the steps to follow."*

[The instructor and behavioral coach should do an INAPPROPRIATE role-play of leaving a voice-mail message]

- Begin by saying, *"Watch this and tell me what I'm doing WRONG."*

    Example of an INAPPROPRIATE role-play:
    ○ Instructor: (Hold a cell phone to your ear) *"Ring, ring."*
    ○ Coach: (Voicemail message) *"Hi. We can't get to the phone right now. Please leave a message. Beep."*
    ○ Instructor: *"Umm, it's me. Why aren't you home? I'm just sitting around doing nothing. Are you there? Are you screening? I thought you'd be home."* (Hang up cell phone)

- End by saying, *"Time-out on that. So what did I do WRONG in leaving that voicemail message?"*

    ○ Answer: You did not say your name, say who you were calling for, say when you were calling, give a *cover story* for calling, leave a phone number, or say goodbye

- Ask the following *Perspective Taking Questions*:

    ○ *"What is (name of coach) going to think of that message?"*

        ▪ Answers: Strange; weird

- ○ *"What do you think (name of coach) is going to think of me?"*

    - ■ Answers: Weird; odd; strange

- ○ *"Is (name of coach) going to want to talk to me after that?"*

    - ■ Answers: Probably not; won't know who to call anyway

- Ask the behavioral coach the same *Perspective Taking Questions*:

    - ○ *"What would you think of that message?"*
    - ○ *"What would you think of me?"*
    - ○ *"Would you want to talk to me after that?"*

- Present the *steps for leaving a voicemail message*

1. *Say who you are*

    a. Example: *"Hi, this is Carrie."*

2. *Say who you are calling for*

    a. Example: *"I'm calling for Jennifer."*

3. *Say when you are calling*

    a. Example: *"It's about 6 o'clock on Thursday night."*

4. *Give a cover story for calling*

    a. Example: *"I was just calling to see what you've been up to."*

5. *Leave your phone number*

    a. Example: *"Give me a call at 555–1212."*

6. *Say goodbye*

    a. Example: *"Talk to you soon. Bye."*

[The instructor and behavioral coach should do an APPROPRIATE role-play of leaving a voicemail message]

- Begin by saying, *"Watch this and tell me what I'm doing RIGHT."*

    Example of an APPROPRIATE role-play:

    - ○ Instructor: (Hold a cell phone to your ear) *"Ring, ring."*
    - ○ Coach: (Voicemail message) *"Hi. We can't get to the phone right now. Please leave a message. Beep."*
    - ○ Instructor: *"Hi, this is (insert name). I'm calling for (insert name). It's about 6 o'clock on Thursday evening. I was just calling to see what you've been up to. Give me a call at 555–1212. Talk to you soon. Bye."*

- End by saying, *"Time-out on that. So what did I do RIGHT in leaving that voicemail message?"*

  ○ Answer: Said who you were, said who you were calling for, left the time, gave a *cover story* for calling, left a phone number, and said goodbye

- Ask the following *Perspective Taking Questions*:

  ○ *"What is (name of coach) going to think of that message?"*

    ■ Answers: Fine; normal

  ○ *"What do you think (name of coach) is going to think of me?"*

    ■ Answers: Friendly; normal

  ○ *"Is (name of coach) going to want to talk to me after that?"*

    ■ Answer: Probably yes

- Ask the behavioral coach the same *Perspective Taking Questions*:

  ○ *"What would you think of that message?"*
  ○ *"What would you think of me?"*
  ○ *"Would you want to talk to me after that?"*

General Rules for Using Electronic Communication

Explain, *"Now that we have some rules around making phone calls, it's also important for us to understand the rules for things like texting, instant messaging, emailing, and using social networking sites. Some of the rules are similar, so they should be easy to remember."*

- *Use cover stories for contacting people you don't know well*

  ○ Say, *"Just like with phone calls, we need to use cover stories when we're texting, instant messaging, or emailing people we don't know well."*

  ○ Ask, *"What could be the problem with not using cover stories with people we don't know well?"*

    ■ Answer: They will wonder why you are contacting them, they may even ask, *"What do you want?"*

  ○ Ask, *"Do we always need to use cover stories for text messaging, instant messaging, and emailing our close friends?"*

    ■ Answer: No, but it does not hurt to use *cover stories* even with close friends

- ○ Have teens generate some examples of *cover stories*
    - ■ Examples:
        - • *"Thought I'd check out your Facebook page."*
        - • *"Wondering what you've been up to."*
        - • *"Just calling to see what you're doing this weekend."*
        - • *"Wanted to know if you're going to the game."*

- • ***Don't get too personal***
    - ○ Say, *"Another important rule for using electronic communication is don't get too personal. This is true even if you know the person well."*
    - ○ Ask, *"What could be the problem with getting too personal over texting, instant messaging, email, phone calls, or Facebook?"*
        - ■ Answer: Anyone could see or hear what you sent, you may embarrass the other person by getting too personal, you may embarrass yourself if other people see or hear what you sent
    - ○ Explain, *"Since you can't control who sees or hears what you send, a good rule is to only send what you are comfortable having anyone see or hear. Save the personal stuff for when you're actually with them in person."*

- • ***Use the two message rule***
    - ○ Say, *"Sometimes when we contact people electronically, we don't get ahold of them."*
    - ○ Ask, *"Roughly how many VOICEMAIL MESSAGES can we leave in a row without hearing back before we stop calling?"*
        - ■ Go around the room and have everyone cast a vote
    - ○ Explain, *"The answer is two times. It's called the two message rule and it means that we shouldn't leave more than two messages in a row without hearing back."*
    - ○ Ask, *"What could be the problem with leaving more than two messages in a row?"*
        - ■ Answer: The other person may be busy, they may not want to talk to you, you may seem creepy, they might think you are a stalker
    - ○ Ask, *"What if we don't leave a voicemail message? Is it okay to call and hang up more than two times in a row?"*
        - ■ Answer: No, they will see that you called; missed calls count in the ***two message rule***
    - ○ Ask, *"About how many TEXT MESSAGES can we send in a row without hearing back before we stop texting?"*
        - ■ Go around the room and have everyone cast a vote
    - ○ Explain, *"The answer is two times. It's called the two message rule!"*
    - ○ Ask, *"What could be the problem with sending more than two text messages in a row?"*
        - ■ Answer: The other person may be busy, they may not want to talk to you, you may seem creepy, they might think you are a stalker

- ○ Ask, *"About how many INSTANT MESSAGES can we send in a row without hearing back before we stop IMing?"*
    - Go around the room and have everyone cast a vote
- ○ Explain, *"The answer is two times. It's called the two message rule!"*
- ○ Ask, *"What could be the problem with sending more than two instant messages in a row?"*
    - Answer: The other person may be busy, they may not want to talk to you, you may seem creepy, they might think you are a stalker
- ○ Ask, *"About how many EMAILS can we send in a row without hearing back before we stop emailing?"*
    - Go around the room and have everyone cast a vote
- ○ Explain, *"The answer is two times. It's called the two message rule!"*
- ○ Ask, *"What could be the problem with sending more than two emails in a row?"*
    - Answer: The other person may be busy, they may not want to talk to you, you may seem creepy, they might think you are a stalker
- ○ Ask, *"Does the two message rule mean that we can leave TWO voicemails, TWO text messages, TWO instant messages, and TWO emails in a row without hearing back?"*
    - Answer: No, the **two message rule** crosses all forms of electronic communication
- ○ Explain, *"There's one exception to the two message rule. That's if we're trying to 'friend' someone on Facebook or some other social networking site. When we try to 'friend' someone, they have the option to accept or ignore our request."*
- ○ Ask, *"If someone ignores your 'friend' request, what should you do?"*
    - Answer: **Move on** and find someone else to "friend" that knows you and seems interested in you; do not try to "friend" the same person twice
- ○ Ask, *"What could be the problem with sending more than one 'friend' request?"*
    - Answer: They might think you are desperate, creepy, or a stalker

- • *Avoid cold calling*
    - ○ Say, *"Another rule for using electronic communication is that we need to avoid cold calling."*
    - ○ Ask, *"Does anyone know what cold calling is?"*
        - Answer: Cold calling is contacting someone who has not given you their phone number, IM, email, or screen name; it is what telemarketers do
    - ○ Explain the following:
        - Giving out a phone number, IM, email address, or screen name is giving someone permission to contact you
        - Just because you may have access to someone's contact information in a school directory or online directory does not give you permission to contact that person

- This includes inviting someone to be your "friend" on Facebook, or other social networking sites
  - You need to know the person if you try to "friend" them
- Ask, *"What could be the problem with cold calling someone without their permission?"*
  - Answer: They might think you are strange, weird, creepy, or a stalker; they may ask how you got their phone number
- Ask, *"What if you're Facebook friends with someone and they have their contact information on their profile page. Does that give you permission to contact them?"*
  - Answer: Not at all; that is still cold calling and they may think you are creepy and weird

Exchanging Contact Information

- Say, *"Instead of cold calling, we need to get permission to contact people. We do that by exchanging contact information, and there are very specific steps we need to follow."*

[The instructor and behavioral coach should do an INAPPROPRIATE role-play for exchanging contact information]

- Begin by saying, *"Watch this and tell me what I'm doing WRONG."*

  Example of an INAPPROPRIATE role-play:

  - Instructor: (Walks up to the coach) *"Hey, can I get your number?"*
  - Coach: (Startled, confused) *"What?"*
  - Instructor: *"Can I get your number? I thought I could call you sometime."*
  - Coach: (Confused, uncomfortable) *"Umm . . . no. I don't think so."*

- End by saying, "Time-out on that. So what did I do WRONG in asking for contact information?"
  - Answer: You randomly asked for the person's phone number, there was no context for asking for the person's number
- Ask the following *Perspective Taking Questions*:
  - *"What was that like for (name of coach)?"*
    - Answers: Strange; confusing; weird; creepy
  - *"What do you think (name of coach) thought of me?"*
    - Answers: Weird; odd; strange; creepy; stalker

- ○ *"Is (name of coach) going to want to talk to me again?"*

  - ■ Answers: No; too creepy

- Ask the behavioral coach the same *Perspective Taking Questions*:

  - ○ *"What was that like for you?"*
  - ○ *"What did you think of me?"*
  - ○ *"Would you want to talk to me again?"*

Present the *steps for exchanging contact information*:

1. *Trade information on several occasions*

2. *Find common interests*

3. *Use your common interests as a cover story for future contact*

4. *Assess interest*

5. *If not interested, change the subject*

6. *If interested, suggest exchanging contact information*

[The instructor and behavioral coach should do an APPROPRIATE role-play for exchanging contact information]

- Begin by saying, *"Watch this and tell me what I'm doing RIGHT."*

  Example of an APPROPRIATE role-play:

  - ○ Coach: (Looking at iPhone)
  - ○ Instructor: (Walks up to the coach) *"Hey (insert name). How's it going?"*
  - ○ Coach: *"Hi (insert name). It's going well. How are you?"*
  - ○ Instructor: *"I'm good. Hey, you know how we were talking about the new iPhone coming out soon?"*
  - ○ Coach: *"Yeah?"*
  - ○ Instructor: *"Did you hear they're releasing them this weekend?"*
  - ○ Coach: *"Yeah! I heard that! I'm all over that!"*
  - ○ Instructor: *"Oh yeah, me too! Forget the lines. I'm there!"*
  - ○ Coach: *"I know. Absolutely."*
  - ○ Instructor: *"Hey, we should go together."*
  - ○ Coach: *"That would be cool."*
  - ○ Instructor: *"Great. Let me get your number . . ."*
  - ○ Coach: *"Sure."*

- End by saying, *"Okay, time-out on that. So what did I do RIGHT in exchanging contact information?"*

- o Answer: Traded information on several occasions, found a common interest, used common interest as a cover story for future contact, assessed interest, suggested exchanging contact information

- Ask the following *Perspective Taking Questions*:

  - o *"What was that like for (name of coach)?"*

    - ▪ Answers: Fun; interesting; normal

  - o *"What do you think (name of coach) thought of me?"*

    - ▪ Answers: Friendly; cool; interesting

  - o *"Is (name of coach) going to want to talk to me again?"*

    - ▪ Answer: Yes; definitely

- Ask the behavioral coach the same *Perspective Taking Questions*:

  - o *"What was that like for you?"*
  - o *"What did you think of me?"*
  - o *"Would you want to talk to me again?"*

Staying Safe Online

- Say, *"We all know that the Internet is a very popular way for teens to socialize, and many of you are probably online and even use social networking sites like Facebook. But just like with any kind of communication, there are rules about how to be safe when you're online."*

- Explain, *"One of the rules for staying safe online is that teens should NOT use the Internet to make NEW friends."*

- Ask, *"What could be the problem with teens making new friends on the Internet?"*

  - o Answer: Because it is dangerous, you do not know who they are, the person could be a predator

- Ask, *"What's the difference between 'online friends' and 'real-life friends'?"*

  - o Answer: "Online friends" are people you may play games with online, but you do not know in real life; "real-life friends" are people you know in person

- Ask, *"What could be the problem with trying to turn 'online friends' into 'real-life friends'?"*

  - o Answer: You do not know who that person is, they could be dangerous, they could even be a predator

- Ask, *"Is it okay to use the Internet to develop stronger friendships with people we already know?"*

  - o Answer: Yes, absolutely

- Ask, *"Is it okay to use the Internet to reconnect with friends we haven't talked to in a while?"*

  - o Answer: Yes, absolutely

- Explain, *"The Internet is very useful for developing closer friendships with PRE-EXISTING friends, but we shouldn't use it to make new friends."*

  - Teenagers should not try to make NEW friends online
  - Use the Internet to develop closer friendships with PRE-EXISTING friends
  - Never give your personal information to a stranger online
  - Never agree to meet with a stranger from the Internet
  - Do not accept invitations to be "friends" with strangers on Facebook or other social networking sites
  - Use privacy settings on Facebook and other social networking sites so your account is not open for anyone to view

Wrap Up

Say, *"So those are the rules for using electronic communication. Tomorrow we'll be reviewing the rules for electronic communication, practicing our conversational skills, and finding common interests with our classmates."*

Calculate Points

Calculate the number of points earned by each teen (see Appendix E for the Daily Point Log):

- Do not publicly disclose the individual number of points
- Discourage attempts to compare number of points earned between teens

  - Remind them that they are working as a team to earn a bigger and better graduation party

Day Three: Lesson Review and Behavioral Rehearsal

Lesson Review: Electronic Communication

- Say, *"Yesterday we learned about the rules for using electronic communication, like how to start and end phone calls, leave voicemail messages, and how to be safe online."*

[Have teens generate all of the rules and steps for electronic communication. Be prepared to give prompts if necessary. Write the following buzzwords (**bold and italicized**) on the board and do not erase until the end of the lesson.]

- Ask, *"What are the steps for starting a phone conversation?"*

  1. ***Ask for the person you are calling***
  2. ***Say who you are***
  3. ***Ask how they are***
  4. ***Ask if they can talk***
  5. ***Give a cover story for why you are calling***

- Ask, *"What are the steps for ending a phone call?"*

  1. ***Wait for a bit of a pause***
  2. ***Give a cover story for why you have to go***
  3. ***Tell the person it was nice talking***
  4. ***Tell the person you will talk to them later***
  5. ***Say goodbye***

- Ask, *"What are the steps for leaving a voicemail?"*

  1. ***Say who you are***
  2. ***Say who you are calling for***
  3. ***Say when you are calling***
  4. ***Give a cover story for calling***
  5. ***Leave your phone number***
  6. ***Say goodbye***

- Ask, *"What are the general rules for electronic communication, like text messaging, instant messaging, emailing, and social networking sites?"*

  1. ***Use cover stories***

2. *Don't get too personal*

3. *Use the two message rule*

4. *Avoid cold calling*

- Ask, *"What are the steps for exchanging contact information?"*

    1. **Trade information on several occasions**

    2. **Find common interests**

    3. **Use your common interests as a cover story for future contact**

    4. **Assess interest**

    5. **If not interested, change the subject**

    6. **If interested, suggest exchanging contact information**

- Ask, *"Should teenagers ever use the Internet to make NEW friends?"*

    1. **Teenagers should not try to make NEW friends online**

    2. **Use the Internet to develop closer friendships with PRE-EXISTING friends**

Behavioral Rehearsal: Starting and Ending Phone Calls

- Have the teens practice **trading information** and having **two-way conversations** on the phone

- Be sure teens follow the **steps for starting and ending phone calls**

- Give teens approximately five minutes to practice in dyads

- Assign a "caller" and a "receiver"

    o Have the caller start the call
    o Have the receiver end the call (with a prompt from the instructor)
    o If there is an uneven number of teens, have one teen observe or practice with a behavioral coach

- Switch dyads and have teens practice with a new person

    o Switch the assignment of "caller" and "receiver" when possible

- Debrief at the end of the behavioral rehearsal

    o Have the "caller" identify how they **started the phone call**
    o Ask them if they **traded information**
    o Have teens identify any **common interests**
    o Have the "receiver" identify how they **ended the phone call**

- If there is time, have teens practice using the *steps for leaving voicemail messages*

Homework Assignments

- [Assign the *in-class calls* for the week and write this on the In-Class Call Assignment Log (Appendix D) for future reference. If there is an uneven number of teens, assign someone *double duty*.]

- [Distribute the Parent Handout (found in the last section of this chapter) and inform teens that they should give this handout to their parents immediately.]

- [Be prepared to have the teens coordinate a day and time to make the *in-class call* and then have each teen write the day and time of the call on the Phone Roster and Parent Handout.]

- Briefly explain the homework for the week by saying, *"We're going to continue to have you practice trading information, having two-way conversations, and using electronic communication this week."*

- Present the homework assignments for the coming week:

  1. Teens should practice *making phone calls* with their parent this week

     a. Teens should go over the rules for *starting and ending phone calls* from the Parent Handout with their parent before practicing
     b. Follow the steps for *starting and ending phone calls*, including using *cover stories*
     c. Find one *common interest* to share with the class

  2. *In-class call or video chat*

     a. Before the call:

        i. Before the class ends, teens should arrange to call another member of the class to practice *trading information* and having a *two-way conversation*
        ii. Set up a day and time to make the call
        iii. Write the day and time of the call on the Phone Roster and the Parent Handout

     b. During the call:

        i. Follow the steps for *starting and ending phone calls*, including using *cover stories*
        ii. Teens should *trade information* and have a *two-way conversation* on this call
        iii. Find a *common interest* to report back to the class

     c. After the call:

        i. Teens should discuss the call with their parent, identify *common interests*, and *troubleshoot* any problems

  3. *Bring a personal item*

     a. Bring a favorite item to share with the group on **Thursday and Friday of next week** (e.g., music, game, book, pictures)
     b. Be prepared to *trade information* about the item one-on-one with someone else in the class

Wrap Up

Say, *"So those are your homework assignments for this week. Be sure to start working on these assignments right away. We'll be reviewing how they went at the beginning of next week. Tomorrow we'll continue our discussion about electronic communication."*

Calculate Points

Calculate the number of points earned by each teen (see Appendix E for the Daily Point Log)

- Do not publicly disclose the individual number of points
- Discourage attempts to compare number of points earned between teens
  - Remind them that they are working as a team to earn a bigger and better graduation party

Days Four and Five: Teen Activity—Jeopardy

Lesson Review: Electronic Communication

- Say, *"This week we've been talking about the rules for using electronic communication. What are some of the rules and steps for electronic communication?"*

[Have teens generate all of the rules and steps for electronic communication. Be prepared to give prompts if necessary. Write the following buzzwords (**bold and italicized**) on the board and do not erase until the end of the lesson.]

- Ask, *"What are the steps for starting a phone conversation?"*

   1. ***Ask for the person you are calling***
   2. ***Say who you are***
   3. ***Ask how they are***
   4. ***Ask if they can talk***
   5. ***Give a cover story for why you are calling***

- Ask, *"What are the steps for ending a phone call?"*

   1. ***Wait for a bit of a pause***
   2. ***Give a cover story for why you have to go***
   3. ***Tell the person it was nice talking***
   4. ***Tell the person you will talk to them later***
   5. ***Say goodbye***

- Ask, *"What are the steps for leaving a voicemail?"*

   1. ***Say who you are***
   2. ***Say who you are calling for***
   3. ***Say when you are calling***
   4. ***Give a cover story for calling***
   5. ***Leave your phone number***
   6. ***Say goodbye***

- Ask, *"What are the general rules for electronic communication, like text messaging, instant messaging, emailing, and social networking sites?"*

  1. *Use cover stories*

  2. *Don't get too personal*

  3. *Use the two message rule*

  4. *Avoid cold calling*

- Ask, *"What are the steps for exchanging contact information?"*

  1. *Trade information on several occasions*

  2. *Find common interests*

  3. *Use your common interests as a cover story for future contact*

  4. *Assess interest*

  5. *If not interested, change the subject*

  6. *If interested, suggest exchanging contact information*

- Ask, *"Should teenagers ever used the Internet to make NEW friends?"*

  1. *Teenagers should not try to make NEW friends online*

  2. *Use the Internet to develop closer friendships with PRE-EXISTING friends*

Teen Activity: Jeopardy

Materials Needed

- Whiteboard and markers

- *Jeopardy Answer Sheets* for each teen

Rules

- Teens will compete in this game of *trading information*

- Like the television show *Jeopardy*, teens will be given answers and asked to respond in the form of a question

  o Example:

    - Instructor: *"The answer is Jimmy's favorite sport."*
    - Teen: *"What is baseball?"*

  o The teen does not have to answer in the form of a question (most do not)

- To promote interest and cooperation, points will be given for correct responses

- The purpose of *Jeopardy* is not to practice **trading information** or having a **two-way conversation** perfectly, since the teens will sound like they are **interviewing** when asking the questions

- The true purpose of *Jeopardy* is to improve:

    o *Topic initiation*

      ▪ Talking about a variety of topics, rather than only those of restricted interest

    o *Listening skills*

      ▪ Listening and remembering what people share about themselves

How to Play

- Write the *Jeopardy Topics* on the board where teens can see them

    o *Favorite music*
    o *Favorite weekend activity*
    o *Favorite sport*
    o *Favorite game*
    o *Favorite movie*
    o *Favorite television show*
    o *Favorite book*
    o *Eye color* [Note: this is NOT to be asked, but noticed by using good eye contact]

- If the teens become bored with the current *Jeopardy Topics*, encourage them to come up with their own topics and even name them

- Have teens practice **trading information** about the *Jeopardy Topics* in small groups for 2–3 minutes each

    o Change groups a few times (depending on time)
    o Prompt teens to ask relevant questions to the Jeopardy topics when necessary

- While teens are **trading information**, organize the *Jeopardy Answer Sheets* from the previous week according to category and mix the order of the answer sheets

- Write the Jeopardy categories on the board

- Once the teens have finished trading information, reconvene as a group and begin the *Jeopardy Challenge*

    o Begin by having the teen with the most points that week pick the first category
    o Notify the class that if they raise their hand before the question has been asked fully, they are disqualified from answering that question
    o The person who raises their hand first gets to take the first guess
    o If they provide the wrong answer, the person who raised their hand second has a chance to answer, and so on
    o The teens get only one guess per question
    o Do not give teens clues

- You may need to enforce a time limit if teens take a long time to answer

- Do not correct the teens if they answer the questions in the incorrect format (i.e., instead of saying *"What is baseball?"* they say *"Baseball"*)

  o All that matters is that they remembered the information they obtained through **trading information** and having a **two-way conversation**

- The person who answers the question correctly gets a point and gets to choose the next category

- If no one answers correctly, the person about which the last question relates gets to pick the next category

- Encourage the teens to clap and cheer for each other during the game

- Give points for correct responses

- Keep track of the points on the board using a different colored marker (to differentiate from points earned during the lesson review)

- At the end of the game, the person with the most points is the *Jeopardy Challenge Winner*

Homework Assignments

- [Be prepared to read off the **in-class call** assignments for the week as a reminder of the homework. This should be written on the In-Class Call Assignment Log (Appendix D). Make sure the teens have scheduled the **in-class call** and have the correct phone number.]

- Briefly explain the homework for the week by saying, *"We're going to continue to have you practice trading information, having two-way conversations, and using electronic communication this week."*

- Present the homework assignments for the coming week:

  1. Teens should practice **making phone calls** with their parent this week

     a. Teens should go over the rules for **starting and ending phone calls** from the Parent Handout with their parent before practicing
     b. Follow the steps for **starting and ending phone calls**, including using **cover stories**
     c. Find one **common interest** to share with the class

  2. **In-class call or video chat**

     a. Before the call:

        i. Before the class ends, teens should arrange to call another member of the class to practice **trading information** and having a **two-way conversation**
        ii. Set up a day and time to make the call
        iii. Write the day and time of the call on the Phone Roster and the Parent Handout

     b. During the call:

        i. Follow the steps for **starting and ending phone calls**, including using **cover stories**

        ii. Teens should **trade information** and have a **two-way conversation** on this call

        iii. Find a **common interest** to report back to the class

    c. After the call:

        i. Teens should discuss the call with their parent, identify **common interests**, and **troubleshoot** any problems

3. ***Bring a personal item***

    a. Bring a favorite item to share with the class on **Thursday and Friday of next week** (e.g., music, game, book, pictures)

    b. Be prepared to **trade information** about the item one-on-one with someone else in the class

Wrap Up

Say, *"So those are your homework assignments for this week. Be sure to start working on these assignments right away. We'll be reviewing how they went at the beginning of next week."*

Calculate Points

Calculate the number of points earned by each teen (see Appendix E for the Daily Point Log):

- Do not publicly disclose the individual number of points

- Discourage attempts to compare number of points earned between teens

    o Remind them that they are working as a team to earn a bigger and better graduation party

Parent Handout 3

PEERS® *Program for the Education and Enrichment of Relational Skills*

Electronic Communication

This week your teens will be learning how to use electronic forms of communication appropriately. There are very specific rules and steps for using electronic communication, which your teens will be practicing.

Steps for Starting and Ending Phone Calls

Starting phone calls:

1. *Ask for the person you are calling*

2. *Say who you are*

3. *Ask how they are*

4. *Ask if they can talk*

5. *Give a cover story for why you are calling*

Ending phone calls:

1. *Wait for a bit of a pause*

2. *Give a cover story for why you have to go*

3. *Tell the person it was nice talking*

4. *Tell the person you will talk to them later*

5. *Say goodbye*

Examples of Cover Stories

Reasons You Are Calling	Reasons You Have To Hang Up
"Just calling to see how you're doing."	"I have to get going."
"Just calling to hear what's up with you."	"I better let you go."
"I'm calling to get the homework."	"I need to finish my homework."
"I haven't talked to you in a while."	"I have to eat dinner now."
"I was wondering what you're up to."	"My mom needs to use the phone."

Steps for Leaving Voicemail Messages

1. *Say who you are*

2. *Say who you are calling for*

3. *Say when you are calling*

4. *Give a cover story for calling*

5. *Leave your phone number*

6. *Say goodbye*

General Rules for Electronic Communication

- *Use cover stories for contacting people you don't know well*

  o You do not need *cover stories* for contacting friends you are close to
  o If you are contacting someone you don't know well, it's best to have a *cover story*

    - *Cover stories* are reasons we do things

- *Don't get too personal*

  o Do not ask personal questions or share personal information over electronic communication
  o You do not know who may see or hear what you send
  o Only share what you are comfortable having anyone know

- Use the *two message rule*

  o Do not leave more than two messages in a row with no response

    - This is true for voicemail, texts, IMs, emails, and missed calls

  o Exception to the *two message rule*: If someone ignores your first "friend request" on Facebook or some other social networking site, do not make another attempt

- *Avoid cold calling*

  o Do not call someone that has not given you their contact information
  o Giving out a phone number, email address, or screen name is giving someone permission to contact you

Steps for Exchanging Contact Information

1. *Trade information on several occasions*

2. *Find common interests*

3. *Use your common interests as a cover story for future contact*

4. *Assess interest*

5. *If not interested, change the subject*

6. *If interested, suggest exchanging contact information*

Using the Internet Safely

- *Teens should NOT use the Internet to make NEW friends*

  o   Teens should never give personal information to a stranger online
  o   Teens should never agree to meet with a stranger from the Internet
  o   Teens should not accept invitations to be "friends" with strangers on Facebook or other social networking sites
  o   Parents should help teens set up privacy settings on social networking sites so that people who do not know them cannot access their account

- *The internet is best used to develop stronger friendships with PRE-EXISTING friends*

- Parents may want to monitor their teen's social networking pages discreetly to ensure that their teen is being safe and responsible

  o   This will also give parents a glimpse at which friends are appropriate

Homework Assignments

Every week your teen will have homework assignments to practice new and previously learned social skills. It is extremely helpful if parents assist teens in completing these assignments. The homework assignments for this week include the following:

1. Teens should practice ***making phone calls*** with their parent this week

   a. Teens should go over the rules for ***starting and ending phone calls*** from the Parent Handout with their parent before practicing
   b. Follow the steps for ***starting and ending phone calls***, including using ***cover stories***
   c. Find one ***common interest*** to share with the class

2. *In-class call or video chat*

   a. Before the call:

      i.   Teens should have arranged to call another member of the class to practice ***trading information*** (instructor has assigned the calls)
      ii. Teens should have set up a day and time to make the call (this information should be listed below and on your teen's Phone Roster)

   b. During the call:

      i.   Follow the steps for ***starting and ending phone calls***, including using ***cover stories***
      ii. Teens should ***trade information*** and have a ***two-way conversation*** on this call
      iii. Find a ***common interest*** to report back to the class

   c. After the call:

    i. Teens should discuss the call with their parent, identify **common interests**, and **trouble-shoot** any problems

3. **Bring a personal item**

    a. Bring a favorite item to share with the class on **Thursday and Friday of next week** (e.g., music, game, book, pictures)

    b. Be prepared to **trade information** about the item one-on-one with someone else in the class

---

In-Class Call Assignment

Your teen has been assigned to be the **caller/receiver** (circle one) with:

Name:

Phone Number:

Day:

Time:

CHOOSING APPROPRIATE FRIENDS

Preparing for the Lesson

Teens find themselves embedded in a multilevel system of peer affiliations. At the most intimate level of peer affiliation is the *clique*. This typically includes a few close friends, often identified as best friends. The next level of peer affiliation is the *social group*. This may include dozens of peers, all sharing some *common interest*. These *social groups* are often identified with a name or label, like the jocks or the gamers, which defines their *common interest*. Research shows that many socially accepted teens belong to more than one *social group*, floating naturally between different friendship networks, and often finding their best friends from among these *social groups*. The last level of peer affiliation is the *larger peer group*. This group typically includes teens around the same age, made up of individuals from different *cliques* or *social groups*, but who do not necessarily share *common interests* or socialize with one another. For most teens, the *larger peer group* may include the entire student body of a school.

Although several levels of peer affiliation are present throughout adolescence, the *social group*, which includes dozens of peers with *common interests*, is particularly crucial during middle school and high school. It is this level of peer affiliation that typically defines the social world of teens, often determining their reputation and defining who they will become friends with. Yet, for many teens with Autism Spectrum Disorder (ASD) and other social challenges, affiliation with a *social group* is not necessarily something they have given much thought. The problem with this oversight is that not identifying with a particular *social group* makes it difficult to find a *source of friends*. The purpose of this lesson is to help overcome this lapse.

Problems with group identification is a characteristic of many teens referred for social skills training. Typically, they have either failed to identify with a *social group* and are socially isolated (also known as *socially neglected teens*), or they have repeatedly attempted to make friends with teens from an inappropriate *social group* (common among *peer rejected teens*). *Socially neglected teens* often end up either completely withdrawn from peer social networks (i.e., the *loners*) or on the periphery of one or more inappropriate peer groups, (i.e., the *floaters*). *Peer rejected teens* tend to be the victims of teasing and bullying and often have bad reputations, making it difficult for them to make and keep friends.

By helping teens understand the function of *social groups*, you will assist them in identifying appropriate *sources of friends*. Your students will be looking to you as an expert in these matters, as most of the teens you will be working with will have heard of these *social groups*, but will not have given much thought to the function of them. Thus, it is important for you to have a good understanding of these *social groups* prior to the didactic lesson.

Some teens will incorrectly state that they would fit in with the popular kids or the jocks. One of the most important parts of the lesson is for you to gently dissuade teens from attempting to fit in with inappropriate *social groups*, while identifying more appropriate options based on the teen's interests. You will do this by asking, *"Have you ever tried to hang out with that group?"* If they say yes, you will ask, *"Did it seem like they accepted you?"* If they say yes, you will ask, *"How could you tell?"* Lesson content has teens identify behavioral signs of acceptance or rejection. If this discussion leads to the realization or admission of previous rejection, you will need to follow up by assisting the teen with finding a more appropriate *social group*. While these realizations can be painful, you will want to help normalize the experience by frequently using the buzzphrase, *"Friendship is a choice. We don't get to be friends with everyone, and everyone doesn't get to be friends with us."*

Some teens may come to your class with such a negative reputation that choosing a *social group* from within their school may not be a viable option. In these cases, finding an extracurricular activity outside of the school setting will be essential to identifying sources of potential friends. Parents are often an integral part of this process, which underscores the importance of distributing Parent Handouts and encouraging parent participation in the program.

For teens attending smaller schools where *social groups* are less relevant, this lesson will be helpful in identifying sources of new friends through extracurricular activities. Your support in identifying extracurricular activities will be essential to success in finding new *sources of friends* with *common interests* for the teens. If extracurricular activities are limited in your school, or are limited, simply identifying a few teens with *common interests* may be sufficient to get started.

Some teens may be enrolled in extracurricular activities without the benefit of generating closer friendships. For instance, a teen may enjoy attending a youth group, but would not consider asking any of the members for their phone number. Just because a teen enjoys a particular activity does not mean it fits the parameters of a *good source of friends*. Now may be a good time to find NEW extracurricular activities, since the teen will be more socially motivated. You may need to judge whether an extracurricular activity is socially productive or not, and if not, share this with the parent and encourage him or her to find better alternatives.

It will be critical to involve the teen in the process of joining an appropriate extracurricular activity where he or she has access to a *good potential source of friends* with *common interests*. It should be less a question of *DO* they want to join an extracurricular activity, and instead, *WHICH* one. Some teens may be reluctant to do this, but if the teen is socially motivated, with a little help from you and the parent, it will probably go more smoothly. If the teen has a functional extracurricular activity, with good friend options already, they do not need to look for new activities.

The *out-of-class call* is assigned for the first time this week, so this will also be a new experience for the now trained teen to try the new skills being taught. There may be some anxiety and/ or resistance by the teen to identify a person to call outside of the class. The parents may be helpful in identifying appropriate options for this phone call, while you can be helpful by encouraging getting the call done.

Day One: Homework Review

Homework Review

[Start with completed homework first. If you have time, you can inquire as to why others were unable to complete the assignment and try to **troubleshoot** how they might get it done for the coming week. When reviewing homework, be sure to use the buzzwords (**bold and italicized**) and **troubleshoot** issues that come up. Spend the majority of the homework review on the **in-class call**, as this is the most important assignment.]

[Note: Give multiple points for homework parts—not just one point per assignment.]

1. Practice **making phone calls** with a parent

   a. Say, *"One of your assignments this week was to practice following the steps for starting and ending a phone call with a parent. Raise your hand if you practiced making a phone call with one of your parents this week."*

      i. Ask, *"Who did you do the phone call with (mom, dad, etc.)?"*
      ii. Ask, *"How did you start the call?"*

         1. Have teens identify all the steps:

            a. **Ask for the person you are calling**
            b. **Say who you are**
            c. **Ask how they are**
            d. **Ask if they can talk**
            e. **Give a cover story for why you are calling**

      iii. Ask, *"Did you trade information?"*
      iv. Ask, *"Did you find a common interest?"*

         1. When they identify common interests ask, *"What could you do with that information if you were going to hang out?"*

      v. Ask, *"How did you end the call?"*

         1. Have teens identify all the steps:

            a. **Wait for a bit of a pause**
            b. **Give a cover story for why you have to go**
            c. **Tell the person it was nice talking**
            d. **Tell the person you will talk to them later**
            e. **Say goodbye**

2. **In-class call or video chat**

   a. Say, *"Another assignment this week was to practice trading information and having a two-way conversation with one of your classmates over the phone or video chat. Raise your hand if you did the in-class call."*

      i. Ask, *"Who did you talk to?"*

  ii. Ask, *"Who called who?"*

  iii. Ask, *"How did the conversation begin?"*

    1. Have teens identify all the relevant steps (if a phone call):

      a. *Ask for the person you are calling*

      b. *Say who you are*

      c. *Ask how they are*

      d. *Ask if they can talk*

      e. *Give a cover story for why you are calling*

  iv. Ask, *"Did you trade information?"*

  v. Ask, *"Did you find a common interest?"*

    1. When they identify common interests ask, *"What could you do with that information if you were going to hang out?"*

  vi. Ask, *"How did the conversation end?"*

    1. Have teens identify all the relevant steps (if a phone call):

      a. *Wait for a bit of a pause*

      b. *Give a cover story for why you have to go*

      c. *Tell the person it was nice talking*

      d. *Tell the person you will talk to them later*

      e. *Say goodbye*

  vii. Avoid general questions like, *"How did it go?"*

  viii. Do not allow teens to talk about mistakes the other person made

 b. Have the other person who participated in the call give their account immediately after, but not at the same time.

3. *Bring a personal item*

 a. Identify the favorite item the teen will bring to share with the class later this week (e.g., music, game, book, pictures)

Wrap Up

Say, *"Good work for those of you who completed your homework assignments. Tomorrow we will be talking about choosing appropriate friends."*

Calculate Points

Calculate the number of points earned by each teen (see Appendix E for the Daily Point Log):

- Do not publicly disclose the individual number of points

- Discourage attempts to compare number of points earned between teens

  ○ Remind them that they are working as a team to earn a bigger and better graduation party

Day Two: Didactic Lesson—Choosing Appropriate Friends

Didactic Lesson: Choosing Appropriate Friends

- Explain, *"Today we're talking about choosing appropriate friends. It's important to understand that friendship is a choice."*

- Ask, *"Do we get to be friends with everyone?"*

  o   Answer: No

- Ask, *"Does everyone get to be friends with us?"*

  o   Answer: No

- Explain, *"That's because having a friend is a CHOICE, and it's important that we CHOOSE our friends wisely. There are good choices and bad choices for choosing potential friends."*

- Present each of the GOOD suggestions below for choosing friends by saying, *"Do you want to choose someone who. . . ?"* (while nodding your head yes). Follow each point by saying, *"Why is it important to choose someone who . . .?"*

  o   *". . . is nice and friendly to you?"*
  o   *". . . is interested in you?"*
  o   *". . . likes the same things as you?"*
  o   *". . . is a similar age as you?"*

- Present each of the BAD suggestions below for choosing friends by saying, *"Do you want to choose someone who. . . ?"* (while shaking your head no). Follow each point by saying, *"What could be the problem with choosing someone who . . . ?"*

  o   *". . . is mean to you or makes fun of you?"*
  o   *". . . ignores you?"*
  o   *". . . is way more popular than you?"*
  o   *". . . has a bad reputation and could get you into trouble?"*

Social Groups

- Explain, *"Now that we understand that friendship is a CHOICE, and there are good choices and bad choices, we need to talk about WHERE you might find some of these good choices for friends. In most schools there are different groups of people that hang out, and they share some common interest. We call them 'social groups' and they usually have names, like the jocks, the cheerleaders, or the popular kids. What are some other social groups?"*

- Have teens brainstorm the different *social groups*

[Write the names of the *social groups* on the board and do not erase until the end of the lesson.]

Table 5.1 Different Social Groups Identified by Teens

Jocks	Nerds	Stoners/Burners/Druggies
Sports teams	Computer geeks/Techies	Gangs/Taggers
Cheerleaders	Gamers/Videogame geeks	Hip hop group
Popular kids	Science geeks	Metal heads/Rockers
Student council	Comic book geeks	Skaters
Drama club	Anime geeks/Manga geeks	Surfers
Choir/Chorus/Glee club	Cosplayers	Hipsters
Partiers	Larpers	Hippies/Granolas
Preppies	Math geeks/Mathletes	Artists
Brains/Smart kids	Movie buffs/Movie geeks	Musicians
Bookworms	Band geeks	Debate club/Debate team
Sports fans	Chess club/Chess team	Political groups
History buffs	Goths	ROTC/Military groups
Motor heads/Gear heads	Emos	Ethnic groups/Cultural groups
Bikers	Scene	Religious groups

- [When the teens begin to identify the different types of geeks, it will be important to present the following information and make a good pitch for being a geek. If you normalize and even promote the affiliation of being a geek, many if not most of the teens will identify themselves with one or more of these groups.]

- Explain, *"There are lots of different kinds of geeks, and it's actually kind of cool to be a geek. That's because a 'geek' is someone that's really interested in something and really good at it. You can't just be interested in something to be a geek, you have to know about it too."*

- Ask, *"For example, I might be really interested in computers, but if I don't know much about computers, do I get to be a computer geek?"*

  ○ Answer: No, absolutely not

- Explain, *"So computer geeks are really interested in computers and really good at using them. And are they proud to call themselves computer geeks?"*

  ○ Answer: Yes, absolutely

- Ask, *"What are some other kinds of geeks?"*

  ○ Answer: Videogame geeks or gamers, comic book geeks, anime geeks, science geeks, math geeks, band geeks, movie geeks

- Ask the following question about the different types of geeks listed below, *"What do the (insert name) geeks have in common?"* Follow each point by asking, *"And are they proud to call themselves (insert name) geeks?"*

  ○ Computer geeks or techies
  ○ Videogame geeks or gamers

- ○ Comic book geeks
- ○ Anime geeks
- ○ Science geeks
- ○ Math geeks
- ○ Band geeks
- ○ Movie geeks

Importance of Common Interests and Extracurricular Activities

- Explain, *"Something important to remember about these social groups is that they all share something in common with one another. For example, what do all the jocks have in common?"*
  - ○ Answer: Sports
- Ask, *"So if I'm interested in sports, but I don't actually play sports, do I get to be a jock?"*
  - ○ Answer: No, absolutely not, you're probably a sports fan
- Ask, *"Do I actually have to play on a team at school to be a jock?"*
  - ○ Answer: Usually
- Explain, *"A lot of these social groups hang out and even meet each other through extracurricular activities, sports, or clubs at school or in the community. So if our goal is to make and keep friends, and we know that friendships are based on common interests, then it's important for us to find an extracurricular activity where we might meet people that have the same interests as us."*
- Ask, *"So if I'm a computer geek or a techie, where can I meet other people that like computers?"*
  - ○ Answer: Computer clubs, computer classes, computer camp, computer expos
- Ask, *"If I'm a gamer, where can I meet other people that like videogames?"*
  - ○ Answer: Gaming clubs, arcades, gaming stores
- Ask, *"If I'm a comic book geek or an anime geek, where can I meet other people that like comic books or anime?"*
  - ○ Answer: Comic book clubs, anime clubs, comic book conventions, comic book stores
- Ask, *"If I'm a science geek, where can I meet other people that like science?"*
  - ○ Answer: Science clubs, science classes, robotics clubs, science camp

Finding Social Groups

- Ask, *"So now that we've identified all of these different social groups and talked about some of the places we might find teens who have common interests, let's talk about other ways we can identify and find these people. How can you tell which social group someone belongs to?*
  - ○ Answers:
    - Clothing, hair, appearance
    - Their interests, what they talk about
    - What they do during free time

- Who they hang out with
- Where they hang out
- Extracurricular activities they belong to

- Ask, *"If I'm a computer geek and I want to meet other people who like computers, how will I find them at school if there's not a computer club?"*

  - Answer: Computer geeks hang out in the computer lab, take computer classes, carry around laptops, talk about computers with their friends, and wear T-shirts with computer or technology logos

- Ask, *"If I'm a gamer and I want to meet other people who like videogames, how will I find them at school if there's not a gaming club?"*

  - Answer: Gamers carry around portable gaming devices, play videogames before and after school and at lunch, they talk about videogames with their friends, and often wear gaming T-shirts

- Ask, *"If I'm a comic book geek or an anime geek and I want to meet other people who like comics or anime, how will I find them at school if there's not a comic book or anime club?"*

  - Answer: Comic book geeks and anime geeks often carry around magazines of their favorite comics, they may draw characters on their notebooks, take art classes to improve their drawing, talk about comic books or anime with their friends, talk about attending comic book conventions, and wear T-shirts with comic book or anime characters

- Ask, *"If I'm a science geek and I want to meet other people who like science, how will I find them at school if there's not a science club?"*

  - Answer: Science geeks hang out in the science lab, take science classes, carry around science books or sci-fi books, talk about science with their friends, and wear T-shirts with science or sci-fi related logos

- Explain, *"So there are lots of ways to identify people with common interests even if we don't have extracurricular activities at school to make it simple."*

Assessing Peer Acceptance or Rejection

- Explain, *"Remember that friendship is a choice. We don't get to be friends with everyone and everyone doesn't get to be friends with us. There are good choices and bad choices. Sometimes people try to be friends with people that don't want to be friends with them. That would be a bad choice."*

- Ask, *"So how can you tell if you're ACCEPTED by a group?"*

  - Answer: See Table 5.2

- Ask, *"How can you tell if you're NOT ACCEPTED by a group?"*

  - Answer: See Table 5.2

- Explain, *"We know that it feels bad when people don't want to be our friend, but we have to remember that friendship is a choice. We don't get to be friends with everyone and everyone doesn't get to be friends with us. If someone doesn't want to be our friend, we need to move on and find other people that do."*

Table 5.2 Signs of Acceptance and Lack of Acceptance from Social Groups

Signs You Are Accepted	Signs You Are NOT Accepted
They seek you out to do things individually or in the group	They do not seek you out to do things
They talk to you and respond to your attempts to talk	They ignore you and/or do not respond to your attempts to talk
They give you their contact information	They do not give you their contact information
They ask for your contact information	They do not ask for your contact information
They text message, instant message, email, or call you just to talk	They do not text message, instant message, email, or call you
They respond to your text messages, instant messages, emails, or phone calls	They do not accept or return your calls or messages
They invite you to do things	They do not invite you to do things
They accept your invitations to do things	They do not accept your invitations or put off your invitations to do things
They add you to their social networking pages	They ignore your friend requests on social networking sites
They say nice things to you and give you compliments	They laugh or make fun of you

Importance of Having a Social Group

- Explain, *"One of the best ways to find friends is by identifying social groups and extracurricular activities with people with common interests. Having a social group to hang out with is particularly important for a lot of reasons."*

- Explain the following WITHOUT using a Socratic method:

  o Having a *social group* gives us a *source of friends* with *common interests*

     ▪ People usually develop close friendships with people in their *social group*
     ▪ Some people are in more than one *social group*
     ▪ Floating from one *social group* to the next makes it hard to develop close friendships
     ▪ Focusing on a FEW *social groups* (at most) is more likely to lead to close friendships

  o Having a *social group* protects teens from individual teasing

     ▪ Bullies like to pick on teens who are by themselves
     ▪ You are an easier target if you are alone and unprotected because no one is there to defend you
     ▪ Bullies are less likely to individually pick on teens who are in *social groups*
     ▪ Teens appear stronger and more protected when they are in a group

  o Between-group rivalry is common and normal among different *social groups*

     ▪ Teens bond over between-group rivalry

        • Example: Fans of sports teams often bond over rivalry with other teams

     ▪ They feel a sense of support and in-group solidarity with other group members
     ▪ They bond with the other group members over dislike of another *social group*

- Example: The jocks may dislike the nerds and the nerds may dislike the jocks

    ○ Each group may complain about the other, but group members bond over the rivalry and experience less loneliness and individual bullying

Wrap Up

Say, *"So those are some of the social groups common to teens and some of the reasons why they are important for making and keeping friends. It's important to think about where we might fit in within these social groups so that we can find a source of friends with common interests. Tomorrow we'll be reviewing the different social groups and thinking about extracurricular activities, and where we might meet people with common interests."*

Calculate Points

Calculate the number of points earned by each teen (see Appendix E for the Daily Point Log):

- Do not publicly disclose the individual number of points
- Discourage attempts to compare number of points earned between teens

    ○ Remind them that they are working as a team to earn a bigger and better graduation party

Day Three: Lesson Review and Behavioral Rehearsal

Lesson Review: Choosing Appropriate Friends

- Explain, *"Yesterday we talked about the different social groups common to teens. In order to develop close friendships with other people who have common interests, it can be helpful to find a group that you might fit in with. What were some of the social groups we identified?"*

- Have teens brainstorm the different **social groups**

- [Write the names of the **social groups** on the board and do not erase until the end of the lesson.]

Table 5.1 Different Social Groups Identified by Teens

Jocks	Nerds	Stoners/Burners/Druggies
Sports teams	Computer geeks/Techies	Gangs/Taggers
Cheerleaders	Gamers/Videogame geeks	Hip hop group
Popular kids	Science geeks	Metal heads/Rockers
Student council	Comic book geeks	Skaters
Drama club	Anime geeks/Manga geeks	Surfers
Choir/Chorus/Glee club	Cosplayers	Hipsters
Partiers	Larpers	Hippies/Granolas
Preppies	Math geeks/Mathletes	Artists
Brains/Smart kids	Movie buffs/Movie geeks	Musicians
Bookworms	Band geeks	Debate club/Debate team
Sports fans	Chess club/Chess team	Political groups
History buffs	Goths	ROTC/Military groups
Motor heads/Gear heads	Emos	Ethnic groups/Cultural groups
Bikers	Scene	Religious groups

Behavioral Rehearsal

- Ask, *"How can you find these social groups either at school or outside of school?"*

  - Answer: Join extracurricular activities, sports, or clubs related to the common interest, notice what people look like, what they carry around, where they hang out, who they hang out with, and what they talk about and do in their free time

- Explain, *"We've spent a lot of time during the last few weeks trading information about the things you like to do. Based on your interests, think about which social group you might fit in with. We're going to go around the room and I want everyone to think of 2–3 groups that they might fit in with based on your interests. Then I want you to think of a few extracurricular activities or clubs where you might find these kids."* [See Table 5.3 for assistance.]

- Ask each teen, *"So which groups do you think you might fit in with based on your interests?"*

  ○ Follow up with asking each teen the following questions:

    ▪ *"Have you ever tried to hang out with people from that group before?"*
    ▪ *"Did it seem like they wanted to hang out with you?"*
    ▪ *"How could you tell?"*

- Ask each teen, *"So where can you find other teens from these social groups?"*

  ○ Encourage identification and enrollment in extracurricular activities related to the **common interests**
  ○ If the teen has a bad reputation at school, the extracurricular activity should be outside of school for the time being

[You may need to assess whether teens are accepted or rejected by the identified **social group** and provide feedback to teens that appear to be rejected by reminding them, *"Friendship is a choice. We don't get to be friends with everyone and everyone doesn't get to be friends with us."* Then help them identify a new **social group** that might be more appropriate. Challenge teens that choose an antisocial group by **opening it up to the group** and asking, *"What could be the problem with choosing to hang out with (insert name of social group)?"* Do not allow teens to choose "floaters" (i.e., teens that float from one group to another) or "loners," as neither is a true **social group**. Be sure to write down the **social groups** and extracurricular activities the teens choose on the Homework Compliance Sheet (Appendix G) for future reference.]

Table 5.3 Possible Extracurricular Activities

Teen Interests	Related Activities
Computers	Join a computer club; attend computer camp; take computer classes; start a website with friends
Videogames; computer games	Join a gaming club; play videogames with friends; go to video arcades with friends
Chess	Join a chess club; play chess with friends; attend chess camp
Movies	Join a movie club; go to movies with friends; watch DVDs with friends; join an audio–visual (AV) club
Television	Watch favorite television shows with friends; join an audio–visual (AV) club
Comic books	Attend comic book conventions; share/trade/read comic books with friends; go to comic book stores with friends; take art classes
Sports	Try out for a team at school; play sports at a recreation center; join a junior league team; watch sporting events on TV with friends; go to sporting events with friends; attend a sports camp
Cars	Go to car shows with friends; take auto shop; look at car magazines with friends
Music	Go to concerts with friends; listen to music with friends; watch music videos with friends; read/share music magazines with friends; join the school band/orchestra; take music classes; start a band with friends
Science	Join a science club; attend science camp; go to science museum with friends; take science classes; join a robotics club
Photography	Join a photography club; volunteer for the yearbook; take photo journalism classes; take pictures with friends; start a photo website with friends; sign up on Instagram

Homework Assignments

- [Assign the *in-class calls* for the week and write this on the In-Class Call Assignment Log (Appendix D) for future reference. If there is an uneven number of teens, assign someone *double duty*.]

- [Distribute the Parent Handout (found in the last section of this chapter) and inform teens that they should give this handout to their parents immediately.]

- [Be prepared to have the teens coordinate a day and time to make the *in-class call* and then have each teen write the day and time of the call on the Phone Roster and Parent Handout.]

- Briefly explain the homework for the week by saying, *"We are going to continue to have you practice trading information and having two-way conversations this week. We also want you to begin to find extracurricular activities with your parents where you might meet new friends with common interests."*

- Present the homework assignments for the coming week:

1. ***Enroll in extracurricular activities***

   a. Teens and parents should DISCUSS and DECIDE on extracurricular activities based on the teen's interests and BEGIN TO ENROLL in these activities

      i. Criteria for a good extracurricular activity:

         1. Meets weekly or at least every other week
         2. Age range of other teens includes the social age of the teen
         3. Activity includes informal time so that the teen can interact with others
         4. Activity starts within the next couple of weeks

2. ***In-class call or video chat***

   a. Before the call:

      i. Before the class ends, teens should arrange to call another member of the class to practice *trading information* and having a *two-way conversation*
      ii. Set up a day and time to make the call
      iii. Write the day and time of the call on the Phone Roster and the Parent Handout

   b. During the call:

      i. Follow the steps for *starting and ending phone calls*, including using *cover stories*
      ii. Teens should *trade information* and have a *two-way conversation* on this call
      iii. Find a *common interest* to report back to the class

   c. After the call:

      i. Teens should discuss the call with their parent, identify *common interests*, and *trouble-shoot* any problems

3. ***Out-of-class call or video chat***

   a. Before the call:

      i. Choose someone the teen feels comfortable talking with around the same age

   b. During the call:

    i. Follow the steps for *starting and ending phone calls*, including using *cover stories*
    ii. Teens should *trade information* and have a *two-way conversation* on this phone call
    iii. Find a *common interest* to report back to the class

   c. After the call:

    i. Teens should discuss the call with their parent, identify *common interests*, and *trouble-shoot* any problems

4. ***Bring a personal item***

   a. Bring a favorite item to share with the class on **Thursday and Friday of next week** (e.g., music, game, book, pictures)
   b. Be prepared to *trade information* about the item one-on-one with someone else in the class

Wrap Up

Say, *"So those are your homework assignments for this week. Be sure to start working on these assignments right away. We'll be reviewing how they went at the beginning of next week. Tomorrow we'll continue our discussion about choosing appropriate friends."*

Calculate Points

Calculate the number of points earned by each teen (see Appendix E for the Daily Point Log):

• Do not publicly disclose the individual number of points

• Discourage attempts to compare number of points earned between teens

    ○ Remind them that they are working as a team to earn a bigger and better graduation party

Days Four and Five: Teen Activity—Trading Information about Personal Items

Lesson Review: Choosing Appropriate Friends

- Say, *"This week we've been talking about how to choose appropriate friends. Remember that the best sources of friends come from social groups and extracurricular activities and clubs where we share common interests with the other members. Yesterday we started talking about which social groups you might fit in with, based on your interests and where you might find these teens. Let's go around the room and have you identify the social groups and extracurricular activities you thought might work best for each of you."*

- Have teens identify:

  - The *social groups* they think they might fit in with
  - Some extracurricular activities or clubs where they might find teens with *common interests* (see Table 5.3 for assistance)

- Identify whether the teens are currently enrolled in these activities or if they need assistance with enrollment

  - If the teen is not enrolled in these activities, parent involvement may be necessary

Table 5.3 Possible Extracurricular Activities

Teen Interests	Related Activities
Computers	Join a computer club; attend computer camp; take computer classes; start a website with friends
Videogames; computer games	Join a gaming club; play videogames with friends; go to video arcades with friends
Chess	Join a chess club; play chess with friends; attend chess camp
Movies	Join a movie club; go to movies with friends; watch DVDs with friends; join an audio–visual (AV) club
Television	Watch favorite television shows with friends; join an audio–visual (AV) club
Comic books	Attend comic book conventions; share/trade/read comic books with friends; go to comic book stores with friends; take art classes
Sports	Try out for a team at school; play sports at a recreation center; join a junior league team; watch sporting events on TV with friends; go to sporting events with friends; attend a sports camp
Cars	Go to car shows with friends; take auto shop; look at car magazines with friends
Music	Go to concerts with friends; listen to music with friends; watch music videos with friends; read/share music magazines with friends; join the school band/orchestra; take music classes; start a band with friends
Science	Join a science club; attend science camp; go to science museum with friends; take science classes; join a robotics club
Photography	Join a photography club; volunteer for the yearbook; take photo journalism classes; take pictures with friends; start a photo website with friends; sign up on Instagram

Teen Activity: Trading Information about Personal Items

Materials Needed

- Teens bring personal items to **trade information** about

- If teens forget to bring personal items:

    ○ Cell phones with music and/or pictures may be used

    ○ T-shirts with logos of favorite pastimes are relevant

    ○ Teens can simply talk about their interests without personal items

Rules

- Break teens up into dyads

- Have teens practice **trading information** and having **two-way conversations** about their personal items

- Encourage teens to identify **common interests** through **trading information**

- Prompt teens to ask questions when appropriate

- Rotate teens approximately every five minutes

    ○ Match girls with girls and boys with boys whenever possible

    ○ It may be necessary to create triads if there is an uneven number of girls or boys

- Give points for **trading information** and **finding common interests**

- Debrief during the final five minutes of the class

    ○ Have teens recall what they learned about their peers through **trading information**

    ○ Have teens identify **common interests**

        ▪ Follow up by asking, *"What could you do with that information if you were going to hang out?"*

    ○ Give points for accurate recall of information

Homework Assignments

- [Be prepared to read off the **in-class call** assignments for the week as a reminder of the homework. This should be written on the In-Class Call Assignment Log (Appendix D). Make sure the teens have scheduled the **in-class call** and have the correct phone number.]

- Briefly remind teens of the homework for the week by saying, *"Remember, we're going to have you begin to enroll in extracurricular activities and continue to practice trading information and having two-way conversations this week."*

- Present the homework assignments for the coming week

1. *Enroll in extracurricular activities*

   a. Teens and parents should DISCUSS and DECIDE on extracurricular activities based on the teen's interests and BEGIN TO ENROLL in these activities

      i. Criteria for a good extracurricular activity:

         1. Meets weekly or at least every other week
         2. Age range of other teens includes the social age of the teen
         3. Activity includes informal time so that the teen can interact with others
         4. Activity starts within the next couple of weeks

2. *In-class call or video chat*

   a. Before the call:

      i. Before the class ends, teens should arrange to call another member of the class to practice *trading information* and having a *two-way conversation*
      ii. Set up a day and time to make the call
      iii. Write the day and time of the call on the Phone Roster and the Parent Handout

   b. During the call:

      i. Follow the steps for *starting and ending phone calls*, including using *cover stories*
      ii. Teens should *trade information* and have a *two-way conversation* on this call
      iii. Find a *common interest* to report back to the class

   c. After the call:

      i. Teens should discuss the call with their parent, identify *common interests*, and *troubleshoot* any problems

3. *Out-of-class call or video chat*

   a. Before the call:

      i. Choose someone the teen feels comfortable talking with around the same age

   b. During the call:

      i. Follow the steps for *starting and ending phone calls*, including using *cover stories*
      ii. Teens should *trade information* and have a *two-way conversation* on this phone call
      iii. Find a *common interest* to report back to the class

   c. After the call:

      i. Teens should discuss the call with their parent, identify *common interests*, and *troubleshoot* any problems

4. *Bring a personal item*

   a. Bring a favorite item to share with the class on **Thursday and Friday of next week** (e.g., music, game, book, pictures)
   b. Be prepared to *trade information* about the item one-on-one with someone else in the class

Wrap Up

Say, *"So those are your homework assignments for this week. Be sure to start working on these assignments right away. We'll be reviewing how they went at the beginning of next week."*

Calculate Points

Calculate the number of points earned by each teen (see Appendix E for the Daily Point Log):

- Do not publicly disclose the individual number of points
- Discourage attempts to compare number of points earned between teens
    - Remind them that they are working as a team to earn a bigger and better graduation party

Parent Handout 4

PEERS® *Program for the Education and Enrichment of Relational Skills*

Choosing Appropriate Friends

This week your teen will be learning how to choose appropriate friends through involvement in extracurricular activities and clubs. The best activities for finding friends are those where there are other teens with **common interests**. One of the most important jobs you have as your teen's social coach is to help him or her find a source of friends. This is often done through enrollment in extra-curricular activities and finding a *social group*. Extra-curricular activities and choice of *social group* should be based on your teen's interests. These will be the best methods for meeting other teens with **common interests**.

Social Groups

In most schools, there are *social groups* of teens that exist on campus. These *social groups* are generally formed through **common interests.** *Common interests are the foundation of friendship*, so it is important to think about which *social groups* your teen might fit in with based on his or her interests. Not all of the social groups listed below will be appropriate choices for friends (e.g., gang bangers, taggers, etc.), but these are the *social groups* that exist in many schools. You will have to help your teen identify which are the best *social groups* for him or her.

Different Social Groups Identified by Teens

Jocks	Nerds	Stoners/Burners/Druggies
Sports teams	Computer geeks/Techies	Gangs/aggers
Cheerleaders	Gamers/Videogame geeks	Hip hop group
Popular kids	Science geeks	Metal heads/Rockers
Student council	Comic book geeks	Skaters
Drama club	Anime geeks/Manga geeks	Surfers
Choir/Chorus/Glee club	Cosplayers	Hipsters
Partiers	Larpers	Hippies/Granolas
Preppies	Math geeks/Mathletes	Artists
Brains/Smart kids	Movie buffs/Movie geeks	Musicians
Bookworms	Band geeks	Debate club/Debate team
Sports fans	Chess club/Chess team	Political groups
History buffs	Goths	ROTC/Military groups
Motor heads/Gear heads	Emos	Ethnic groups/Cultural groups
Bikers	Scene	Religious groups

Finding Sources of Friends and Extracurricular Activities: Tips for Parents

- Encourage your teen to make friends with other teens at school:

  ○ Before or after school

- o Between classes
- o During lunch

- Help your teen develop hobbies or pursue special interests at school which could potentially include others (*get a list of clubs from the school by calling the school or going to the school's website*)

  - o Computer club
  - o Videogame club
  - o Science club
  - o Comic book or anime club
  - o Chess club

- Encourage your teen to participate in extracurricular activities at school

  - o Band/orchestra
  - o Choir/glee club
  - o Sports teams
  - o Yearbook
  - o School play (e.g., stage crew, set design, acting, etc.)
  - o Community service projects
  - o After-school programs

- Encourage your teen to pursue recreational activities in the community, particularly if your teen has a bad reputation at school

  - o Boy scouts or girl scouts
  - o YMCA/YWCA
  - o 4-H
  - o Community youth sports leagues
  - o Sports classes (e.g., swimming, tennis, golf, etc.)
  - o Teen activities through parks and recreation centers
  - o Drama clubs
  - o Dance classes
  - o Art classes
  - o Music classes
  - o Computer classes
  - o Martial arts classes
  - o Community clubs
  - o Hobby stores (e.g., Warhammer for making models)
  - o Teen book clubs (public library, book stores)
  - o Church/Temple/Mosque

    - ▪ Youth groups
    - ▪ Choir
    - ▪ Bible Study, Hebrew School, etc.

- Take your teen to places where he or she can be around other teens (be sure to check out these places in advance to make sure there is no gang activity)

  - o Recreational centers
  - o Local parks (e.g., basketball, etc.)
  - o Community pool

- Private gym
- Sports club/golf club
- Public library (during teen activities)

- Extracurricular activities should be based on your teen's interests

Teen Interests	Related Activities
Computers	Join a computer club; attend computer camp; take computer classes; start a website with friends
Videogames; computer games	Join a gaming club; play videogames with friends; go to video arcades with friends
Chess	Join a chess club; play chess with friends; attend chess camp
Movies	Join a movie club; go to movies with friends; watch DVDs with friends; join an audio-visual (AV) club
Television	Watch favorite television shows with friends; join an audio-visual (AV) club
Comic books	Attend comic book conventions; share/trade/read comic books with friends; go to comic book stores with friends; take art classes
Sports	Try out for a team at school; play sports at a recreation center; join a junior league team; watch sporting events on TV with friends; go to sporting events with friends; attend a sports camp
Cars	Go to car shows with friends; take auto shop; look at car magazines with friends
Music	Go to concerts with friends; listen to music with friends; watch music videos with friends; read/share music magazines with friends; join the school band/orchestra; take music classes; start a band with friends
Science	Join a science club; attend science camp; go to science museum with friends; take science classes; join a robotics club
Photography	Join a photography club; volunteer for the yearbook; take photo journalism classes; take pictures with friends; start a photo website with friends; sign up on Instagram

Assessing Peer Acceptance or Rejection

Signs of Acceptance and Lack of Acceptance from Social Groups

Signs You Are Accepted	Signs You Are NOT Accepted
They seek you out to do things individually or in the group	They do not seek you out to do things
They talk to you and respond to your attempts to talk	They ignore you and/or do not respond to your attempts to talk
They give you their contact information	They do not give you their contact information
They ask for your contact information	They do not ask for your contact information
They text message, instant message, email, or call you just to talk	They do not text message, instant message, email, or call you
They respond to your text messages, instant messages, emails, or phone calls	They do not accept or return your calls or messages
They invite you to do things	They do not invite you to do things
They accept your invitations to do things	They do not accept your invitations or put off your invitations to do things
They add you to their social networking pages	They ignore your friend requests on social networking sites
They say nice things to you and give you compliments	They laugh or make fun of you

Homework Assignments

Every week your teen will have homework assignments to practice new and previously learned social skills. It is extremely helpful if parents assist teens in completing these assignments. The homework assignments for this week include the following:

1. *Enroll in extracurricular activities*

   a. Teens and parents should DISCUSS and DECIDE on extracurricular activities based on the teen's interests and BEGIN TO ENROLL in these activities

      i. Criteria for a good extracurricular activity:

         1. Meets weekly or at least every other week
         2. Age range of other teens includes the social age of the teen
         3. Activity includes informal time so that the teen can interact with others
         4. Activity starts within the next couple of weeks

2. *In-class call or video chat*

   a. Before the call:

      i. Teens should have arranged to call another member of the class to practice *trading information* (instructor has assigned the calls)
      ii. Teens should have set up a day and time to make the call (this information should be listed below and on your teen's Phone Roster)

   b. During the call:

      i. Follow the steps for *starting and ending phone calls*, including using *cover stories*
      ii. Teens should *trade information* and have a *two-way conversation* on this call
      iii. Find a *common interest* to report back to the class

   c. After the call:

      i. Teens should discuss the call with their parent, identify *common interests*, and *trouble-shoot* any problems

3. *Out-of-class call or video chat*

   a. Before the call:

      i. Choose someone the teen feels comfortable talking with around the same age

   b. During the call:

      i. Follow the steps for *starting and ending phone calls*, including using *cover stories*
      ii. Teens should *trade information* and have a *two-way conversation* on this phone call
      iii. Find a *common interest* to report back to the class

   c. After the call:

      i. Teens should discuss the call with their parent, identify *common interests*, and *trouble-shoot* any problems

4. *Bring a personal item*

    a. Bring a favorite item to share with the class on **Thursday and Friday of next week** (e.g., music, game, book, pictures)

    b. Be prepared to *trade information* about the item one-on-one with someone else in the class

---

In-Class Call Assignment

Your teen has been assigned to be the **caller/receiver** (circle one) with:

Name:

Phone Number:

Day:

Time:

APPROPRIATE USE OF HUMOR

Preparing for the Lesson

While most of us will recognize that a good sense of humor can be socially magnetic and charming, *inappropriate use of humor is one of the fastest ways to push people away*. After only one inappropriate joke or off-color remark from an acquaintance and most people are done with that person. Unfortunately, humor is perhaps one of the more outstanding and obvious social deficits for many people with Autism Spectrum Disorder (ASD). Teens with ASD often have substantial deficits in understanding punch lines to jokes, particularly when sarcasm is involved. Even with these deficits, many teens with ASD like to tell jokes. Yet their humor tends to be inappropriate for their age: either too socially immature or excessively sophisticated for their audience. These deficits, coupled with insensitivity to feedback from others after joke telling, are the reasons for the inclusion of this lesson.

While some teens with ASD will relish in telling jokes, others are so confused by humor that they get upset, even angry, when people tell jokes. We call these teens *joke-refusers*. While they make up only a minority of teens with ASD, *joke-refusers* must come to understand that it is not their job to *police* others and insist that they not tell jokes. Instead, it will be important to remember that *friendship is a choice*. They don't have to be friends with *joke-tellers*, and *joke-tellers* don't have to be friends with them.

For some teens in your class, learning to use humor appropriately will be of paramount importance to developing friendships, particularly for those who engage in silly or immature humor or joke telling that no one else seems to understand. Many *peer-rejected* teens are oblivious to the negative *humor feedback* they receive. This causes them to be further rejected, and may even result in a bad reputation among peers. Teens who regularly engage in inappropriate use of humor are often seen as strange or weird by their peers, which may ultimately lead to teasing and bullying, if not simply *peer rejection*. Therefore, paying attention to one's *humor feedback* and learning to use humor appropriately will be critical for a select group of rejected teens that consider themselves *joke-tellers*. For some teens, failing to develop this one core skill may be the difference between success and failure in PEERS®. In other words, even if a teen was able to successfully master all of the other skills outlined in the PEERS® curriculum, if they continued to persist with inappropriate use of humor, it is likely that they would continue to experience rejection from peers.

One issue that may come up in this lesson relates to the misunderstanding about the role of *joke-receivers* and *joke-tellers*. To clarify, *joke-receivers* enjoy jokes. In fact, most *joke-receivers* also tell jokes. But unlike *joke-tellers* who consider themselves class clowns and full-time comedians, *joke-receivers* are not trying to be funny ALL of the time. It will be important for you to explain the difference and stress that very few people can be successful *joke-tellers*. Since **humor is one of the fastest ways to push people away**, if our goal is to make and keep friends, we should be careful with our humor and always **pay attention to our humor feedback**.

Another issue that may come up in this lesson will be teens who challenge the rules by claiming that most jokes are **insult jokes**, or that **dirty jokes** are very common among teenage boys. You should respond to these comments by acknowledging that these statements are true. Insult jokes are very common, and in certain circles, dirty jokes are too. The point that you will need to stress is that this behavior is very *risky* if you are trying to make and keep friends. You can present this idea by saying, *"Remember that humor is one of the fastest ways to push people away. If your goal is to make and keep friends, then telling these jokes is risky."* Like everything you teach in PEERS®, you are simply providing information about **ecologically valid skills** related to making and keeping friends. You are sharing what we know works through research. It is up to the teens to decide whether they will use that information.

Perhaps the greatest challenge in this lesson will involve addressing the re-emergence of symptoms of the "too cool for school syndrome." Some teens may hold onto their identity as a *joke-teller* despite repeated social failures. Teens may claim that he or she is a *joke-teller*, as this role may be seen as having a higher social standing; they may initially feel reluctant to identify themselves as *joke-receivers*, wrongly believing that this position may make them inferior.

This issue can be defused in two ways. First, the role of *joke-receiver* is presented and normalized as a helpful social role that most people fulfill. Very few people are successful *joke-tellers*. Most people are actually *joke-receivers* who enjoy jokes, but do not try to make jokes all of the time. It is helpful if the instructor and any behavioral coaches self-identify as *joke-receivers* during the lesson for the teens. Knowing this may help teens "save face" when they identify themselves as *joke-receivers.*

Second, part of the homework assignment involves **paying attention to humor feedback**, which will afford a good opportunity to challenge any wrongful notions about joke-telling. Your role, in discreetly pointing out **humor feedback** from peers during the lessons using subtle teachable moments, will be integral to this process. For example, if a teen makes an inappropriate joke during class and no one laughs, or worse, the class laughs at him or her, you might take the opportunity to gently ask, *"What was your humor feedback?"* Most students will be able to admit that their feedback was not good. This will give you the opportunity to remind the teen, *"Humor is one of the fastest ways to push people away, so if our goal is to make and keep friends, we need to be careful with our humor."*

Day One: Homework Review

Homework Review

[Start with completed homework first. If you have time, you can inquire as to why others were unable to complete the assignment and try to ***troubleshoot*** how they might get it done for the coming week. When reviewing homework, be sure to use the buzzwords (***bold and italicized***) and ***troubleshoot*** issues that come up. Spend the majority of the homework review on extracurricular activities and the ***out-of-class call*** as these were the most important assignments.]

[Note: Give multiple points for homework parts—not just one point per assignment.]

1. ***Enroll in extracurricular activities***

    a. Say, *"One of your assignments this week was for you and your parents to identify an extracurricular activity for you to join where you might meet other teens with common interests and then begin to enroll in those activities. Raise your hand if you found an extracurricular activity."*

        i. Ask, *"Which extracurricular activity did you choose?"*
        ii. Ask, *"Did you enroll in the activity?'*
        iii. Ask, *"Are there other teens your age in the group?'*
        iv. Ask, *"How often does it meet?"*
        v. Ask, *"Does this seem like a good place for you to make potential new friends?"*

2. ***Out-of-class call or video chat***

    a. Say, *"Another assignment this week was to trade information and have a two-way conversation with someone not in this class over the phone or video chat. Raise your hand if you did the out-of-class call."*

        i. Ask, *"Who did you talk to?"*
        ii. Ask, *"How did the conversation begin?"*

            a. Have teens identify all the relevant steps (if a phone call):

                1. ***Ask for the person you are calling***
                2. ***Say who you are***
                3. ***Ask how they are***
                4. ***Ask if they can talk***
                5. ***Give a cover story for why you are calling***

        iii. Ask, *"Did you trade information?"*
        iv. Ask, *"Did you find a common interest?"*

            a. When they identify common interests ask, *"What could you do with that information if you were going to hang out?"*

        v. Ask, *"How did the conversation end?"*

            a. Have teens identify all the relevant steps (if a phone call):

1. ***Wait for a bit of a pause***
2. ***Give a cover story for why you have to go***
3. ***Tell the person it was nice talking***
4. ***Tell the person you will talk to them later***
5. ***Say goodbye***

vi. Avoid general questions like, *"How did it go?"*

3. ***In-class call or video chat***

a. Say, *"Another assignment this week was to practice trading information and having a two-way conversation with one of your classmates over the phone or video chat. Raise your hand if you did the in-class call."*

i. Ask, *"Who did you talk to?"*
ii. Ask, *"Who called who?"*
iii. Ask, *"How did the conversation begin?"*

a. Have teens identify all the relevant steps (if a phone call):

1. ***Ask for the person you are calling***
2. ***Say who you are***
3. ***Ask how they are***
4. ***Ask if they can talk***
5. ***Give a cover story for why you are calling***

iv. Ask, *"Did you trade information?"*
v. Ask, *"Did you find a common interest?"*

a. When they identify common interests ask, *"What could you do with that information if you were going to hang out?"*

vi. Ask, *"How did the conversation end?"*

a. Have teens identify all the relevant steps (if a phone call):

1. ***Wait for a bit of a pause***
2. ***Give a cover story for why you have to go***
3. ***Tell the person it was nice talking***
4. ***Tell the person you will talk to them later***
5. ***Say goodbye***

vii. Avoid general questions like, *"How did it go?"*
viii. Do not allow teens to talk about mistakes the other person made

b. Have the other person who participated in the call give their account immediately after, but not at the same time.

4. ***Bring a personal item***

a. Identify the favorite item the teen will bring to share with the class later this week (e.g., music, game, book, pictures)

Wrap Up

Say, *"Good work for those of you who completed your homework assignments. Tomorrow we will be talking about appropriate use of humor."*

Calculate Points

Calculate the number of points earned by each teen (see Appendix E for the Daily Point Log):

- Do not publicly disclose the individual number of points
- Discourage attempts to compare number of points earned between teens
  - Remind them that they are working as a team to earn a bigger and better graduation party

Day Two: Didactic Lesson—Appropriate Use of Humor

Didactic Lesson: Appropriate Use of Humor

- Explain, *"Today we're going to be talking about appropriate use of humor. Humor is one way that people communicate and connect with each other. The problem is that when used inappropriately, humor is one of the fastest ways to push people away. So it's important that we understand the rules about using humor appropriately when trying to make and keep friends."*

[Present the rules for appropriate use of humor by writing the following buzzwords (**bold and italicized**) on the board. Do not erase the rules until the end of the lesson.]

- *Be serious when you're FIRST getting to know someone*

   ○ Explain, *"The first rule for appropriate use of humor is to be serious when you're FIRST getting to know someone."*
   ○ Ask, *"What could be the problem with acting silly and trying to be funny when we're FIRST getting to know someone?"*

      ▪ Answers:
         - They may not understand your sense of humor
         - They may think you're making fun of them
         - They may think you're weird

   ○ Ask, *"Is it okay to be less serious once you've gotten to know the person better?"*

      ▪ Answer: Yes

- *Don't repeat jokes*

   ○ Explain, *"Another rule for appropriate use of humor is don't repeat jokes to people that have already heard them."*
   ○ Ask, *"What could be the problem with repeating jokes to people that have already heard them?"*

      ▪ Answer: A joke usually isn't funny if you've already heard it, and it makes you look like you don't have any other material

   ○ Ask, *"What if I tell my friend Jessica a joke one day. Then the next day, our friend Ruth is there with Jessica and me. Ruth hasn't heard the joke, but Jessica has. Is it okay to repeat the joke then?"*

      ▪ No, never tell the same joke more than once in front of the same person

   ○ Ask, *"What if Jessica asks me to tell the joke to Ruth. Then is it okay to repeat the joke?"*

      ▪ Answer: Yes, then you can repeat the joke, but only when someone who has heard the joke asks you to repeat it

- *Humor should be age appropriate*

   ○ Explain, *"It's also important that humor be age appropriate. That means teenagers shouldn't be telling knock-knock jokes or really silly jokes that a five-year-old might tell."*

- ○ Ask, *"What could be the problem with telling jokes that aren't age appropriate?"*

  - ■ Answer: Because your friends won't think your jokes are funny if they are too immature

- ○ Ask, *"What about jokes that are overly mature, like jokes about politics or the stock market. If our friends don't know anything about those topics, what could be the problem with telling jokes like that?"*

  - ■ Answer: Because your friends won't think your jokes are funny if they're too sophisticated for your audience

- **Avoid insult jokes**

  - ○ Explain, *"Another rule for appropriate use of humor is to avoid insult jokes. These are jokes that make fun of another person."*
  - ○ Ask, *"What could be the problem with telling jokes that make fun of another person?"*

    - ■ Answer: You might hurt their feelings, they might not want to be friends with you, and you could get a bad reputation

  - ○ Explain, *"Insult jokes include jokes that make fun of someone's ethnicity, religion, or sexual orientation."*
  - ○ Ask, *"What could be the problem with telling jokes that make fun of someone's ethnicity, religion, or sexual orientation?"*

    - ■ Answer: You could insult someone, they might not want to be friends with you, and you could get a bad reputation

  - ○ Ask, *"What if the person isn't of that ethnicity, religion, or sexual orientation. Then is it okay to tell the joke?"*

    - ■ Answers:

      - • No, absolutely not
      - • Many people find these jokes offensive even if they are not from the targeted group
      - • The person might think you're racist or sexist, and may not want to be friends with you
      - • Even if the person you're telling the joke to is not offended, someone overhearing the joke may be upset
      - • Telling offensive jokes is a fast way to get a bad reputation and ensure that people won't want to be your friend

- **Avoid dirty jokes**

  - ○ Explain, *"Another important rule about humor is to avoid telling dirty jokes. Dirty jokes are usually about sex or body parts."*
  - ○ Ask, *"What could be the problem with telling dirty jokes?"*

    - ■ Answer: Dirty jokes often make other people uncomfortable and may give you a bad reputation

  - ○ Ask, *"What if everyone else was telling dirty jokes. Then is it okay to tell them?"*

■ Answer: No, you could still get a bad reputation if someone overhears, people might think you're weird or even call you perverted

- *Avoid inside jokes with people who won't get them*

  ○ Explain, *"Another rule for appropriate use of humor is to avoid inside jokes with people who won't get them. Inside jokes are those that only a few people would understand. They're usually specific to some context and are only shared by certain people."*

  ○ Ask, *"What could be the problem with telling inside jokes with people who won't get them?"*

    ■ Answer: The people not in on the joke will feel left out, you might hurt their feelings

  ○ Ask, *"What if I have an inside joke with my friends Jessica and Ruth. One day the three of us are with our friend Ashley and I want to tell the joke. Jessica and Ruth are in on the joke, but Ashley isn't. Is it okay for me to tell the inside joke then?"*

    ■ Answer: No, because Ashley won't get the joke and she might feel left out

  ○ Ask, *"What should I do if I accidentally tell the inside joke in front of Ashley who doesn't get it?"*

    ■ Answer: Explain the joke to Ashley

  ○ Ask, *"But is a joke ever funny if you have to explain it?"*

    ■ Answer: No, hardly ever

- *Think about whether it's the right time to tell jokes*

  ○ Explain, *"It's also important that we think about whether it's the RIGHT time or the WRONG time to tell jokes."*

  ○ Ask, *"When would be the RIGHT time to tell jokes?"*

    ■ Answer: Parties, get-togethers, free time, when other people are telling jokes

  ○ Ask, *"When would be the WRONG time to tell jokes?"*

    ■ Answer: During class, when the teacher is talking, during passing period when people are in a hurry, when people are sad

  ○ Say, *"Some people think it's a good time to tell jokes when someone is sad, like they might cheer the person up. What could be the problem with telling jokes when someone is sad?"*

    ■ Answer: It makes you look insensitive, like you don't care about your friend

- *Pay attention to your humor feedback*

  ○ Explain, *"One of the most important rules for using humor appropriately is that if you're going to tell a joke, you need to pay attention to your humor feedback. Humor feedback is the reaction people give you after you've told a joke."*

  ○ Ask, *"What could be the problem with not paying attention to your humor feedback?"*

    ■ Answer:

      • Because if people don't think you're funny, then maybe you shouldn't be trying to tell jokes

- • When you try to tell jokes and no one thinks you're funny, you may end up pushing people away
- • They may think you're weird or strange and not want to be your friend

○ Explain, *"When you're paying attention to your humor feedback, there are four types of reactions you should look for . . ."*

- ■ **Not laughing at all**
- ■ **Giving a courtesy laugh**
- ■ **Laughing at you**
- ■ **Laughing with you**

○ Ask, *"What does it mean if they DON'T LAUGH at all?*

- ■ Answer:
  - • They don't think what you said was funny
  - • **Bad humor feedback**

○ Ask, *"What does it mean if they give you a COURTESY LAUGH?"*

- ■ Answer:
  - • They're laughing to be polite, but don't think what you said was funny
  - • **Bad humor feedback**

○ Ask, *"What does it mean when they LAUGH AT YOU, and what does that look like?"*

- ■ Answer:
  - • See Table 6.1
  - • **Bad humor feedback**

○ Ask, *"What does it mean when they LAUGH WITH YOU, and what does that look like?"*

- ■ Answer:
  - • See Table 6.1
  - • **Good humor feedback**

○ Explain, *"One of the best ways to pay attention to humor feedback is to LOOK and LISTEN. That means you must WATCH the other person for their reaction. Simply listening to whether they laugh will not give you enough feedback."*

Table 6.1 Humor Feedback Signs

Laughing AT You	Laughing WITH You
Laugh and roll their eyes	Laugh and smile
Look at someone else and then laugh	Compliment your joke or sense of humor
Laugh before the joke is over	Laugh and shake their head yes
Long pause before they laugh	They say, *"That's a good one"* and smile
Laugh and make a face	They say, *"You're funny"* and smile
Laugh, point at you, and shake their head no	Ask you to tell another joke or start telling jokes themselves
Sarcastically say, *"You're funny"*	Say, *"I'll have to remember that one."*

Identifying Joke-Tellers

- Explain, *"Everyone has a different relationship with humor. Some people like to tell jokes, many people like to hear jokes, and some people don't like jokes at all. There are basically three types of people when it comes to humor."*

    ○ *Joke-tellers*

        ▪ Explain, *"Joke-tellers are people who like to tell jokes CONSTANTLY. They think they're the class clown, but a lot of the time people aren't laughing with them, they're laughing at them. Very few people are good joke-tellers."*

    ○ *Joke-receivers*

        ▪ Explain, *"Joke-receivers are people who enjoy humor, sometimes tell jokes, but aren't trying to be funny ALL the time. Joke-receivers like to laugh and occasionally tell jokes, but their identity isn't wrapped up in being the class clown. Most people are joke-receivers."*

    ○ *Joke-refusers*

        ▪ Explain, *"Joke-refusers are people who don't enjoy humor. They don't like telling jokes or hearing jokes. Humor may make them uncomfortable or feel confused."*

[It is useful for the instructor and any behavioral coaches to say they are *joke-receivers* to normalize this point. Point out that very few people are successful *joke-tellers*, and that most teens will be more successful *joke-receivers*. Point out that being a *joke-receiver* is equally fun, as the role still involves laughter and fun times with friends.]

- Go around the room and have each teen identify if they are more of a *joke-teller, joke-receiver,* or *joke-refuser*

    ○ Praise those who claim to be *joke-receivers*
    ○ Normalize anyone who claims to be a *joke-refuser* by saying, *"Friendship is a CHOICE and you don't have to be friends with people who are joke-tellers if that makes you uncomfortable."*
    ○ Remind any teen claiming to be a *joke-teller* that it is very difficult to be a *joke-teller*, and you expect them to **pay very close attention to their humor feedback**
    ○ Let teens know that we will be checking in with them next week to report on their **humor feedback**

Wrap Up

Say, *"So those are the rules for appropriate humor. We know that a lot of humor types, like insult jokes, are fairly common. But if your goal is to make and keep friends, you need to know that telling these kinds of jokes is risky. Remember, humor is one of the fastest ways to push people away. If we upset someone or insult someone with our humor, we may not get a second chance. We may even get a bad reputation. So we need to use humor appropriately, and if we're going to tell jokes, we need to pay attention to our humor feedback. Tomorrow we'll continue our discussion about appropriate use of humor."*

Calculate Points

Calculate the number of points earned by each teen (see Appendix E for the Daily Point Log)

- Do not publicly disclose the individual number of points
- Discourage attempts to compare number of points earned between teens
  - Remind them that they are working as a team to earn a bigger and better graduation party

Day Three: Lesson Review and Behavioral Rehearsal

Lesson Review: Appropriate Use of Humor

- Say, *"Yesterday we talked about appropriate use of humor. What are some of the rules for appropriate use of humor?"*

[Have teens generate all of the rules for appropriate use of humor. Be prepared to give prompts if necessary. Write the following bullet points and buzzwords (**bold and italicized**) on the board and do not erase until the end of the lesson.]

- ○ ***Be serious when you are FIRST getting to know someone***
- ○ ***Don't repeat jokes***
- ○ ***Humor should be age appropriate***
- ○ ***Avoid insult jokes***
- ○ ***Avoid dirty jokes***
- ○ ***Avoid inside jokes with people who won't get them***
- ○ ***Think about whether it's the right time to tell jokes***
- ○ ***Pay attention to your humor feedback***
  - ▪ ***Not laughing at all***
  - ▪ ***Giving a courtesy laugh***
  - ▪ ***Laughing AT you***
  - ▪ ***Laughing WITH you***

- Say, *"One of the best ways to pay attention to humor feedback is to LOOK and LISTEN to notice whether the person is laughing AT you or laughing WITH you. In order to do this, you must WATCH the other person for their reaction. Simply listening to whether they laugh will not give you enough feedback."*

- Ask, *"How you can tell if someone is laughing AT you or laughing WITH you?"* [See Table 6.1 for a list of possible humor feedback signs.]

Table 6.1 Humor Feedback Signs

Laughing AT You	Laughing WITH You
Laugh and roll their eyes	Laugh and smile
Look at someone else and then laugh	Compliment your joke or sense of humor
Laugh before the joke is over	Laugh and shake their head yes
Long pause before they laugh	They say, *"That's a good one"* and smile
Laugh and make a face	They say, *"You're funny"* and smile
Laugh, point at you, and shake their head no	Ask you to tell another joke or start telling jokes themselves
Sarcastically say, *"You're funny"*	Say, *"I'll have to remember that one."*

Behavioral Rehearsal: Paying Attention to Humor Feedback

- Have each teen practice *paying attention to their humor feedback*

  - Say, *"Now we're going to practice paying attention to our humor feedback. Remember that the most important way to pay attention to humor feedback is to LOOK and LISTEN. That means we need to WATCH the other person's reaction. Listening for whether they laughed or not is not enough, since they could be rolling their eyes or making a face."*

- Have each teen say the same joke to the instructor on two different occasions

  - Say, *"We're going to go around the room and each of you is going to say the same joke twice. This joke is not meant to be funny. In fact, it's a good example of humor that is not age appropriate for you. The reason we're using it is because it's simple and most people have heard the joke before."*

  - Teens will be telling this joke to the instructor while the rest of the class watches

    - Teen: *"Why did the chicken cross the road?"*
    - Instructor: *"I don't know."*
    - Teen: *"To get to the other side."*
    - Instructor: (Laughs at or laughs with)

  - Be sure that each teen uses the same joke or the group may get out of control
  - The instructor should randomly alternate between demonstrating *laughing AT* (e.g., laughing, rolling eyes, making a face, shaking head no) and *laughing WITH* (e.g., laughing, smiling, nodding head yes) throughout the exercise
  - On the FIRST OCCASION, the teen should have his or her EYES CLOSED when they tell the joke, and be *paying attention to their humor feedback*

    - When the joke is finished and the instructor has given a reaction, have the teen interpret the *humor feedback*

      - Say, *"Okay, now open your eyes. Tell us if you think that was laughing at you or laughing with you."*

    - Allow the teen to take a guess
    - Then have the rest of the teens (who had their eyes open) interpret the *humor feedback*
    - The instructor will tell them if they were correct or incorrect

  - On the SECOND OCCASION, the teen should have his or her EYES OPEN looking at the instructor when they tell the joke, and be *paying attention to their humor feedback*

    - When the joke is finished and the instructor has given a reaction, have the teen interpret the *humor feedback*

      - Say, *"Okay, so tell us if you think that was laughing at you or laughing with you."*

    - Allow the teen to take a guess
    - Then have the rest of the teens also interpret the *humor feedback*
    - The instructor will tell them if they were correct or incorrect

  - After each teen has finished *paying attention to their humor feedback*, ask which way was easier to interpret

- ■ Ask, *"Which way was easier to tell—eyes open or eyes closed?"*

    - • Answer: Eyes open

- The purpose of this demonstration is to show the teens that they need to WATCH the other person for their reaction by making eye contact

    - ○ When you do not WATCH the other person's reaction, you may miss out on the *humor feedback*

[During this exercise, it will be more difficult for the teens to interpret their *humor feedback* when their eyes are closed. Some teens may try to make a joke or be oppositional and say that it was easier with their eyes closed. Do not engage in a debate with the teen. Instead, *open it up to the group* and say, *"What do we think everyone? Is it generally easier to notice humor feedback with eyes open or eyes closed?"* The group will most likely say *"eyes open,"* and this will apply sufficient peer pressure so that the opposing teen will back down.]

Homework Assignments

- [Assign the *in-class calls* for the week and write this on the In-Class Call Assignment Log (Appendix D) for future reference. If there is an uneven number of teens, assign someone *double duty*.]

- [Distribute the Parent Handout (found in the last section of this chapter), and inform teens that they should give this handout to their parents immediately.]

- [Be prepared to have the teens coordinate a day and time to make the *in-class call*, and then have each teen write the day and time of the call on the Phone Roster and Parent Handout.]

- Briefly explain the homework for the week by saying, *"We are going to continue to have you practice paying attention to your humor feedback, trading information, and having two-way conversations this week."*

- Present the homework assignments for the coming week:

    1. *Pay attention to humor feedback*

        a. If the teen happens to tell a joke (this is NOT the assignment), notice whether people are *not laughing at all, giving a courtesy laugh, laughing AT you,* or *laughing WITH you*

        b. Discuss this *humor feedback* with your parent

            i. Teen and parent should decide if teen is more of a *joke-teller, joke-receiver,* or *joke-refuser*

    2. *Enroll in extracurricular activities*

        a. Teens and parents should DISCUSS and DECIDE on extracurricular activities based on the teen's interests and BEGIN TO ENROLL in these activities

i.   Criteria for a good extracurricular activity:

1.   Meets weekly or at least every other week
2.   Age range of other teens includes the social age of the teen
3.   Activity includes informal time so that the teen can interact with others
4.   Activity starts within the next couple of weeks

3.   ***In-class call or video chat***

a.   Before the call:

i.   Before the class ends, teens should arrange to call another member of the class to practice ***trading information*** and having a ***two-way conversation***
ii.   Set up a day and time to make the call
iii.   Write the day and time of the call on the Phone Roster and the Parent Handout

b.   During the call:

i.   Follow the steps for ***starting and ending phone calls***, including using ***cover stories***
ii.   Teens should ***trade information*** and have a ***two-way conversation*** on this call
iii.   Find a common ***interest*** to report back to the class

c.   After the call:

i.   Teens should discuss the call with their parent, identify ***common interests***, and ***troubleshoot*** any problems

4.   ***Out-of-class call or video chat***

a.   Before the call:

i.   Choose someone the teen feels comfortable talking with around the same age

b.   During the call:

i.   Follow the steps for ***starting and ending phone calls***, including using ***cover stories***
ii.   Teens should ***trade information*** and have a ***two-way conversation*** on this phone call
iii.   Find a ***common interest*** to report back to the class

c.   After the call:

i.   Teens should discuss the call with their parent, identify ***common interests***, and ***troubleshoot*** any problems

5.   ***Bring a personal item***

a.   Bring a favorite item to share with the class on **Wednesday, Thursday, and Friday of next week** (e.g., music, game, book, pictures)
b.   Be prepared to ***trade information*** about the item

Wrap Up

Say, *"So those are your homework assignments for this week. Be sure to start working on these assignments right away. We'll be reviewing how they went at the beginning of next week. Tomorrow we'll continue our discussion about humor and practice our conversational skills."*

Calculate Points

Calculate the number of points earned by each teen (see Appendix E for the Daily Point Log):

- Do not publicly disclose the individual number of points
- Discourage attempts to compare number of points earned between teens
  - Remind them that they are working as a team to earn a bigger and better graduation party

Days Four and Five: Teen Activity—Trading Information about Personal Items

Lesson Review: Appropriate Use of Humor

- Say, *"This week we've been talking about appropriate use of humor. What are some of the rules for appropriate use of humor?"*

[Have teens generate all of the rules for appropriate use of humor. Be prepared to give prompts if necessary. Write the following bullet points and buzzwords (**bold and italicized**) on the board and do not erase until the end of the lesson.]

- *Be serious when you are FIRST getting to know someone*
- *Don't repeat jokes*
- *Humor should be age appropriate*
- *Avoid insult jokes*
- *Avoid dirty jokes*
- *Avoid inside jokes with people who won't get them*
- *Think about whether it's the right time to tell jokes*
- *Pay attention to your humor feedback*

  - *Not laughing at all*
  - *Giving a courtesy laugh*
  - *Laughing AT you*
  - *Laughing WITH you*

Teen Activity: Trading Information about Personal Items

Materials Needed

- Teens bring personal items to *trade information* about

- If teens forget to bring personal items:

  - Cell phones with music and/or pictures may be used
  - T-shirts with logos of favorite pastimes are relevant
  - Teens can simply talk about their interests without personal items

Rules

- Break teens up into dyads

- Have teens practice *trading information* and having *two-way conversations* about their personal items

- Encourage teens to identify *common interests* through *trading information*

- Prompt teens to ask questions when appropriate

- Rotate teens approximately every five minutes

  ○ Match girls with girls and boys with boys whenever possible
  ○ It may be necessary to create triads if there are an uneven numbers of girls or boys

- Give points for **trading information** and **finding common interests**

- Debrief during the final five minutes of the class

  ○ Have teens recall what they learned about their peers through **trading information**
  ○ Have teens identify **common interests**

    ▪ Follow up by asking, "*What could you do with that information if you were going to hang out?*"

  ○ Give points for accurate recall of information

Homework Assignments

- [Be prepared to read off the **in-class call** assignments for the week as a reminder of the homework. This should be written on the In-Class Call Assignment Log (Appendix D). Make sure the teens have scheduled the **in-class call** and have the correct phone number.]

- Briefly remind teens of the homework for the week by saying, "*Remember, we are going to have you continue to pay attention to your humor feedback, trade information, and practice having two-way conversations this week.*"

- Present the homework assignments for the coming week:

  1. *Pay attention to humor feedback*

     a. If the teen happens to tell a joke (this is NOT the assignment), notice whether people are **not laughing at all, giving a courtesy laugh, laughing AT you,** or **laughing WITH you**

     b. Discuss this **humor feedback** with your parent

        i. Teen and parent should decide if teen is more of a **joke-teller, joke-receiver,** or **joke-refuser**

  2. *Enroll in extracurricular activities*

     a. Teens and parents should DISCUSS and DECIDE on extracurricular activities based on the teen's interests and BEGIN TO ENROLL in these activities

        i. Criteria for a good extracurricular activity:

           1. Meets weekly or at least every other week
           2. Age range of other teens includes the social age of the teen
           3. Activity includes informal time so that the teen can interact with others
           4. Activity starts within the next couple of weeks

3. ***In-class call or video chat***

   a. Before the call:

      i. Before the class ends, teens should arrange to call another member of the class to practice ***trading information*** and having a ***two-way conversation***
      ii. Set up a day and time to make the call
      iii. Write the day and time of the call on the Phone Roster and the Parent Handout

   b. During the call:

      i. Follow the steps for ***starting and ending phone calls***, including using ***cover stories***
      ii. Teens should ***trade information*** and have a ***two-way conversation*** on this call
      iii. Find a ***common interest*** to report back to the class

   c. After the call:

      i. Teens should discuss the call with their parent, identify ***common interests***, and ***troubleshoot*** any problems

4. ***Out-of-class call or video chat***

   a. Before the call:

      i. Choose someone the teen feels comfortable talking with around the same age

   b. During the call:

      i. Follow the steps for ***starting and ending phone calls***, including using ***cover stories***
      ii. Teens should ***trade information*** and have a ***two-way conversation*** on this phone call
      iii. Find a ***common interest*** to report back to the class

   c. After the call:

      i. Teens should discuss the call with their parent, identify ***common interests***, and ***troubleshoot*** any problems

5. ***Bring a personal item***

   a. Bring a favorite item to share with the class on **Wednesday, Thursday, and Friday of next week** (e.g., music, game, book, pictures)
   b. Be prepared to ***trade information*** about the item

Wrap Up

Say, *"So those are your homework assignments for this week. Be sure to start working on these assignments right away. We'll be reviewing how they went at the beginning of next week."*

Calculate Points

Calculate the number of points earned by each teen (see Appendix E for the Daily Point Log):

- Do not publicly disclose the individual number of points
- Discourage attempts to compare number of points earned between teens
  - Remind them that they are working as a team to earn a bigger and better graduation party

Parent Handout 5

PEERS® *Program for the Education and Enrichment of Relational Skills*

Appropriate Use of Humor

This week your teen will be learning about the rules for appropriate use of humor. When used inappropriately, *humor is one of the fastest ways to push people away*, and can make it difficult to form friendships. Parents can be extremely helpful in providing **humor feedback** to teens.

Rules about Appropriate Use of Humor

- *Be serious when you are FIRST getting to know someone*

  - They may not understand your sense of humor
  - They may think you're making fun of them
  - They may think you're weird

- *Don't repeat jokes*

  - Never tell the same joke more than once in front of the same person
  - A joke is rarely funny if you've already heard it

- *Humor should be age appropriate*

  - Teens should avoid immature joke telling
  - Overly mature or sophisticated joke telling can be confusing with the wrong audience

- *Avoid insult jokes*

  - Don't tell jokes at other people's expense
  - Don't tell racial, ethnic, religious, or sexist jokes
  - People may get upset or feel insulted and the teen could get a bad reputation

- *Avoid dirty jokes*

  - Dirty jokes are usually sexual in nature or focus on certain body parts
  - Dirty jokes often make other people uncomfortable and may give the teen a bad reputation

- *Avoid inside jokes with people who won't get them*

  - Inside jokes are those that only a few people would understand, are specific to a context, and only shared by certain people
  - Don't tell inside jokes to people who won't get them, unless you are willing to explain it to them

    - If you have to explain a joke, it usually isn't funny

- *Think about whether it's the right time to tell jokes*

  - Jokes aren't funny if they're told at the wrong time

    - Right times: Parties, get-togethers, free time, when other people are telling jokes
    - Wrong times: During class, when the teacher is talking, during passing period when people are in a hurry, when people are sad

- *Pay attention to your humor feedback*

  - Notice the reaction you get from others by LOOKING and LISTENING

    - *Not laughing at all*
    - *Giving a courtesy laugh*
    - *Laughing at you*
    - *Laughing with you*

  - You must WATCH the person for their reaction
  - If you only listen, you will miss valuable information
  - *Paying attention to your humor feedback* will give you valuable information about whether you should be a:

    - *Joke-teller*

      - Someone who tries to be funny ALL the time

    - *Joke-receiver*

      - Someone who likes to tell jokes sometimes but isn't committed to being funny ALL the time

    - *Joke-refuser*

      - Someone who does not enjoy humor

Homework Assignments

Every week your teen will have homework assignments to practice new and previously learned social skills. It is extremely helpful if parents assist teens in completing these assignments. The homework assignments for this week include the following:

1. *Pay attention to humor feedback*

   a. If the teen happens to tell a joke (this is NOT the assignment), notice whether people are *not laughing at all, giving a courtesy laugh, laughing AT you,* or *laughing WITH you*
   b. Discuss this *humor feedback* with your parent

      i. Teen and parent should decide if teen is more of a *joke-teller, joke-receiver,* or *joke-refuser*

2. *Enroll in extracurricular activities*

   a. Teens and parents should DISCUSS and DECIDE on extracurricular activities based on the teen's interests and BEGIN TO ENROLL in these activities

     i.   Criteria for a good extracurricular activity:

        1.   Meets weekly or at least every other week
        2.   Age range of other teens includes the social age of the teen
        3.   Activity includes informal time so that the teen can interact with others
        4.   Activity starts within the next couple of weeks

3. ***In-class call or video chat***

   a. Before the call:

     i.   Teens should have arranged to call another member of the class to practice ***trading information*** (instructor has assigned the calls)
     ii. Teens should have set up a day and time to make the call (this information should be listed below and on your teen's Phone Roster)

   b. During the call:

     i.   Follow the steps for ***starting and ending phone calls***, including using ***cover stories***
     ii. Teens should ***trade information*** and have a ***two-way conversation*** on this call
     iii. Find a ***common interest*** to report back to the class

   c. After the call:

     i.   Teens should discuss the call with their parent, identify ***common interests***, and ***trouble-shoot*** any problems

4. ***Out-of-class call or video chat***

   a. Before the call:

     i.   Choose someone the teen feels comfortable talking with around the same age

   b. During the call:

     i.   Follow the steps for ***starting and ending phone calls***, including using ***cover stories***
     ii. Teens should ***trade information*** and have a ***two-way conversation*** on this phone call
     iii. Find a ***common interest*** to report back to the class

   c. After the call:

     i.   Teens should discuss the call with their parent, identify ***common interests***, and ***trouble-shoot*** any problems

5. ***Bring a personal item***

   a. Bring a favorite item to share with the class on **Wednesday, Thursday, and Friday of next week** (e.g., music, game, book, pictures)
   b. Be prepared to ***trade information*** about the item

In-Class Call Assignment

Your teen has been assigned to be the **caller/receiver** (circle one) with:

Name:

Phone Number:

Day:

Time:

STARTING AND JOINING CONVERSATIONS

Preparing for the Lesson

Knowing how to start and join conversations with others is a critical ingredient for making and keeping friends. This is the process by which we meet people. If you were to ask teens what advice they are often given by adults to meet new people, they will probably tell you that they are told to *"go up and introduce yourself"* or *"go up and say hi."* Sadly, these are not *ecologically valid social skills* used by socially successful teens. In fact, those strategies are likely to result in some form of rejection. Research suggests that successful entries into a group of teens in conversation begin with low-risk tactics such as waiting and listening until positive feedback from the conversing peers permits entry. Unsuccessful entry attempts might include disrupting an ongoing conversation by asking for information or disagreeing.

For many teens, this week marks a pivotal lesson in that they are now being taught skills to help them approach new potential friends. Up until this point, teens have been working on improving their communication skills and identifying appropriate friends. They should now have the prerequisite skills for developing new friendships.

Teens will be taught the basic steps of *peer entry* (i.e., how to start individual conversations and how to join group conversations with peers). When teaching *peer entry*, it is helpful to break down these complex social behaviors into discrete steps. Teens with Autism Spectrum Disorder (ASD) often think in concrete and literal ways. Breaking down complex social skills into easily digestible parts through the presentation of steps of behavior will make the skills far more palatable.

A critical aspect of success with *peer entry* skills will be identifying the appropriate *social group* or members of a *social group* with which to *start and join conversations*. This point cannot be understated. If teens choose to *start individual conversations* or *join group conversations* with peers who are likely to reject them, perhaps because of poor choices in *social groups*, this may only make them feel defeated and increase their social anxiety and avoidant behavior. You will need to be very specific with teens in having them identify which *social group* they plan to enter conversation with and where. If there are serious questions about whether the teen will be accepted by this group, for the time being it may be advisable to have the teen choose a different *social group* that is less likely to reject them.

One of the more common difficulties with this lesson for socially anxious teens is having trouble initiating all of the steps for *joining a group conversation* during the behavioral rehearsal exercise and teen activity. One way to overcome this anxiety is to walk through the steps with the teen, side-by-side, essentially *joining the group conversation* together. This may ease some nervousness so that the teen may be able to independently *join group conversations* during future rehearsals. For teens that are particularly socially anxious and reluctant to complete this rehearsal or assignment, it may be helpful to have them practice just the first few steps of ***peer entry***, which involve ***listening, watching, identifying the topic***, and ***finding common interests***, while establishing proximity and interest in the group. In subsequent sessions, the teen may be encouraged to add additional steps as he or she feels more comfortable.

Another common issue that comes up in the behavioral rehearsal for ***joining group conversations*** is that teens will often ***wait for the perfect pause***. Perhaps it is due to their tendency to follow rules and be exacting in their utilization of rules that compels them to wait for the ***perfect pause*** during ***peer entry***. You will notice this immediately when you observe a teen ***listening*** and ***watching from a distance*** with no effort to move toward the group. You can coach the teen in the moment by asking questions like, *"Do you know what they're talking about?" "Do you know anything about that topic?" "What are you waiting for?" "Is there ever a PERFECT pause?" "There's never a PERFECT pause, so go ahead and join, just try not to interrupt too much."* You might even point out moments when it would be appropriate to join, like when the conversation is going from one person to the next.

Another issue that may come up during the behavioral rehearsal is that teens choose not to ***join group conversations*** because they don't know about the topic that is being discussed. Since this is a very appropriate response, you will want to praise them for having good judgment. Then, in order to facilitate practice, you should ask the other students to change the topic so the teen can join appropriately. This will be artificial, but the teens won't mind since this is just for practice. Be sure that the new topic is something that the teen attempting to join knows something about it.

Finally, for some teens with intellectual or executive functioning challenges, the number of steps presented in this lesson may be overwhelming. In that case, it is recommended that you simplify the lesson to include the following abbreviated steps. Tables 7.1 and 7.2 present suggestions for how you might abbreviate the lessons for certain students.

Table 7.1 Abbreviated Steps for Starting Individual Conversations

Traditional Steps	*Abbreviated Steps*
Casually look over	*Find a common interest*
Use a prop	*Mention the common interest*
Find a common interest	*Trade information*
Mention the common interest	
Trade information	
Assess interest	
Introduce yourself	

Table 7.2 Abbreviated Steps for Joining Group Conversations

Traditional Steps	*Abbreviated Steps*
Listen to the conversation	*Watch and listen*
Watch from a distance	*Wait for a pause*
Use a prop	*Mention the topic*
Identify the topic	
Find a common interest	
Move closer	
Wait for a pause	
Mention the topic	
Assess interest	
Introduce yourself	

Day One: Homework Review

Homework Review

[Start with completed homework first. If you have time, you can inquire as to why others were unable to complete the assignment and try to **troubleshoot** how they might get it done for the coming week. When reviewing homework, be sure to use the buzzwords (**bold and italicized**) and **troubleshoot** issues that come up. Spend the majority of the homework review on extracurricular activities and the **out-of-class call**, as these were the most important assignments.]

[Note: Give multiple points for homework parts—not just one point per assignment.]

1. *Pay attention to humor feedback*

   a. Say, *"Last week we talked about appropriate use of humor. One of your assignments this week was to pay attention to your humor feedback if you happened to tell a joke. The assignment was NOT to tell a joke. If you happened to tell a joke this week, raise your hand if you paid attention to your humor feedback."*

      i. Say, *"I don't want to know what joke you told, I just want to know what your humor feedback was. Were they laughing AT you, laughing WITH you, giving a courtesy laugh, or NOT laughing at all?"*

      ii. Ask, *"How could you tell?"*

      iii. Ask, *"So are you done paying attention to your humor feedback?"*

         1. Answer: No

      iv. Ask, *"When will you pay attention to your humor feedback?"*

         1. Answer: Every time they tell a joke

      v. Ask, *"How will you pay attention to your humor feedback?"*

         1. Answer: By LOOKING and LISTENING

2. *Enroll in extracurricular activities*

   a. Say, *"Another assignment was that you and your parents were supposed to identify an extracurricular activity for you to join where you might meet other teens with common interests, and then begin to enroll in those activities. Raise your hand if you found an extracurricular activity."*

      i. Ask, *"Which extracurricular activity did you choose?"*

      ii. Ask, *"Did you enroll in the activity?'*

      iii. Ask, *"Are there other teens your age in the group?'*

      iv. Ask, *"How often does it meet?"*

      v. Ask, *"Does this seem like a good place for you to make potential new friends?"*

3. *Out-of-class call or video chat*

   a. Say, *"Another assignment this week was to trade information and have a two-way conversation with someone not in this class over the phone or video chat. Raise your hand if you did the out-of-class call."*

    i.   Ask, *"Who did you talk to?"*

    ii. Ask, *"How did the conversation begin?"*

        1.   Have teens identify all the relevant steps (if a phone call):

           a. ***Ask for the person you are calling***
           b. ***Say who you are***
           c. ***Ask how they are***
           d. ***Ask if they can talk***
           e. ***Give a cover story for why you are calling***

    iii. Ask, *"Did you trade information?"*

    iv. Ask, *"Did you find a common interest?"*

        1.   When they identify common interests ask, *"What could you do with that information if you were going to hang out?"*

    v.   Ask, *"How did the conversation end?"*

        1.   Have teens identify all the relevant steps (if a phone call):

           a. ***Wait for a bit of a pause***
           b. ***Give a cover story for why you have to go***
           c. ***Tell the person it was nice talking***
           d. ***Tell the person you will talk to them later***
           e. ***Say goodbye***

    vi. Avoid general questions like, *"How did it go?"*

4. ***In-class call or video chat***

    a. Say, *"Another assignment this week was to practice trading information and having a two-way conversation with one of your classmates over the phone or video chat. Raise your hand if you did the in-class call."*

        i.   Ask, *"Who did you talk to?"*

        ii. Ask, *"Who called who?"*

        iii. Ask, *"How did the conversation begin?"*

           1.   Have teens identify all the relevant steps (if a phone call):

              a. ***Ask for the person you are calling***
              b. ***Say who you are***
              c. ***Ask how they are***
              d. ***Ask if they can talk***
              e. ***Give a cover story for why you are calling***

        iv. Ask, *"Did you trade information?"*

        v.   Ask, *"Did you find a common interest?"*

           1.   When they identify common interests ask, *"What could you do with that information if you were going to hang out?"*

vi.   Ask, *"How did the conversation end?"*

1.   Have teens identify all the relevant steps (if a phone call):

   a.   ***Wait for a bit of a pause***
   b.   ***Give a cover story for why you have to go***
   c.   ***Tell the person it was nice talking***
   d.   ***Tell the person you will talk to them later***
   e.   ***Say goodbye***

vii.   Avoid general questions like, *"How did it go?"*
viii.   Do not allow teens to talk about mistakes the other person made

b.   Have the other person who participated in the call give their account immediately after, but not at the same time

4.   ***Bring a personal item***

a.   Identify the favorite item the teen will bring to share with the class later this week (e.g., music, game, book, pictures)

Wrap Up

Say, *"Good work for those of you who completed your homework assignments. Tomorrow we will be talking about the rules for starting and joining conversations."*

Calculate Points

Calculate the number of points earned by each teen (see Appendix E for the Daily Point Log):

- Do not publicly disclose the individual number of points

- Discourage attempts to compare number of points earned between teens

   o   Remind them that they are working as a team to earn a bigger and better graduation party

Day Two: Didactic Lesson—Starting and Joining Conversations

Didactic Lesson: Starting and Joining Conversations

- Explain, *"Knowing how to meet new groups of people can be difficult. Sometimes adults give the wrong advice about what to do. What do most adults tell teens to do to meet new people?"*

  ○ Answer: Go up and say *"Hi"* or go up and introduce yourself

- Explain, *"That's NOT actually how it's done. Imagine what would happen if you went up and randomly said, 'Hi,' or walked over and said, 'Hi, I'm (insert name).' What do you think the other teens would think of you?"*

  ○ Answer: That you're weird; odd; strange

- Explain, *"Instead of doing something that might be seen as strange, we're going to talk about the specific steps you can follow for starting individual conversations and joining group conversations."*

Starting Individual Conversations

[The instructor and behavioral coach should do an INAPPROPRIATE role-play with the instructor starting a random conversation.]

- Begin by saying, *"We're going to do a role-play. Watch this and tell me what I'm doing WRONG in starting this conversation."*

  Example of an INAPPROPRIATE role-play:

  - Coach: (Looking at iPhone)
  - Instructor: (Walks up abruptly) *"Hey, did you go to the comic book convention last night?"*
  - Coach: (Confused) *"What?"*
  - Instructor: *"The comic book convention. Were you there?"*
  - Coach: (Confused) *"The comic book convention?"*
  - Instructor: *"Yeah, did you go last night?"*
  - Coach: (Confused) *"Umm . . . no."*
  - Instructor: *"Oh, I was there. It was awesome. You should have gone. Do you like comic books?"*
  - Coach: (Annoyed, looking at phone) *"Umm . . . yeah I do."*
  - Instructor: (interrupts) *"Why didn't you go then? You should have gone. Everyone was there."*
  - Coach: (Sarcastic, annoyed, looking at phone) *"That's great."*
  - Instructor: *"So are you going next week?"*
  - Coach: (Annoyed) *"What?"*
  - Instructor: *"You should go. It's going to be really good."*
  - Coach: (Annoyed, looking at phone, ignoring) *"Okay."*
  - (Long awkward pause)

- End by saying, *"Time out on that. So what did I do WRONG in trying to start that conversation?"*

  o Answer: You walked up and talked about something completely random

- Ask, *"Did it seem like (insert name) wanted to talk to me?"*

  o Answer: No

- Ask, *"How could you tell?"*

  o Answer: Gave short answers, didn't look at you, turned away from you

- Ask the following *Perspective Taking Questions*:

  o *"What was that like for (name of coach)?"*

    ▪ Answers: Confusing; weird; odd

  o *"What do you think (name of coach) thought of me?"*

    ▪ Answers: Weird; odd; strange

  o *"Is (name of coach) going to want to talk to me again?"*

    ▪ Answers: No; too weird

- Ask the behavioral coach the same *Perspective Taking Questions*:

  o *"What was that like for you?"*
  o *"What did you think of me?"*
  o *"Would you want to talk to me again?"*

Steps for Starting Individual Conversations

[Present the steps for *starting an individual conversation* by writing the following buzzwords (**bold and italicized**) on the board. Do not erase the steps until the end of the lesson.]

1. *Casually look over*

   a. Explain, *"When you're considering starting a conversation with someone, it's helpful to first show interest in the person by casually looking at them for a second or two, but not staring at them."*

      i. Ask, *"Why would it be a good idea to casually look over?"*

         1. Answer: It shows you are interested in them

2. *Use a prop*

   a. Explain, *"As you're casually looking over, it's helpful to use a prop like a mobile phone, gaming device, or a book to give the appearance that you're focused on some other activity."*

      i. Ask, *"Why would it be a good idea to use a prop?"*

         1. Answer: Then you don't look like you're staring at them, you look distracted by something else

3. *Find a common interest*

   a. Explain, *"While you're casually and covertly watching the person, you need to find some kind of common interest that you both appear to share."*

   b. Ask, *"Why is it important to have a common interest?"*

      i.   Answer: It gives you something to talk about, an excuse for starting a conversation

4. *Mention the common interest*

   a. Explain, *"Once you've identified a common interest, you'll want to make a comment, ask a question, or give a compliment about the common interest."*

   b. Ask, *"Why is it important to mention the common interest?"*

      i.   Answer: This is your excuse for talking to them

5. *Trade information*

   a. Explain, *"Next, you need to trade information about the common interest by asking follow-up questions, answering your own questions, and sharing relevant information about yourself."*

   b. Ask, *"Why is it important to trade information?"*

      i.   Answer: This is how you will get to know each other

6. *Assess interest*

   a. Explain, *"Then you need to assess the interest of the person you're trying to talk to. If they don't seem interested in talking to you, you should move on. You can tell if someone wants to talk to you by asking yourself the following questions . . ."*

      i.   *Are they talking to me?*
      ii. *Are they looking at me?*
      iii. *Are they facing me (or giving me the cold shoulder)?*

7. *Introduce yourself*

   a. Explain, *"If they seem interested in talking to you, the final step for starting an individual conversation is to introduce yourself if you've never met. If they don't seem interested, you should move on without introducing yourself."*

Role-Play: Starting an Individual Conversation

[The instructor and behavioral coach should do an APPROPRIATE role-play with the instructor following the steps for *starting an individual conversation*.]

- Begin by saying, *"We're going to do another role-play. Watch this and tell me what I'm doing RIGHT in starting this conversation."*

Example of an APPROPRIATE role-play:

- Instructor and Coach: (Standing a few feet away from each other)
- Coach: (Looking at iPhone)
- Instructor: (Holding iPhone, looks over at coach) *"Hey, is that the new iPhone?"*
- Coach: (Looks over and smiles) *"Yeah, it is."*
- Instructor: (Smiles) *"Oh, that's cool. I've been wanting to get one."*
- Coach: *"You should. It's great."*
- Instructor: *"I know. I have the old one. Is the new one a lot better?"*
- Coach: *"Oh yeah, it's awesome. It's lightweight too."*
- Instructor: *"Yeah, I definitely need to get one. I thought they were sold out."*
- Coach: *"They might be. I ordered mine early."*
- Instructor: *"That was smart."*
- Coach: (Smiles casually)
- Instructor: *"I'm (insert name) by the way."*
- Coach: *"Oh, hi. I'm (insert name)."*
- Instructor and Coach: (Smile, don't shake hands)

- End by saying, *"Time out on that. So what did I do RIGHT in starting that conversation?"*

  o Answer: ***Casually looked over, used a prop, found a common interest, mentioned the common interest, traded information, assessed interest,*** and ***introduced self***

- Ask, *"Did it seem like (insert name) wanted to talk to me?"*

  o Answer: Yes

- Ask, *"How could you tell?"*

  o Answer: ***Talked to you, looked at you, faced you***

- Ask the following *Perspective Taking Questions*:

  o *"What was that like for (name of coach)?"*

    ■ Answers: Nice; normal; pleasant

  o *"What do you think (name of coach) thought of me?"*

    ■ Answers: Friendly; cool; interesting

  o *"Is (name of coach) going to want to talk to me again?"*

    ■ Answers: Yes, probably

- Ask the behavioral coach the same *Perspective Taking Questions*:

  o *"What was that like for you?"*
  o *"What did you think of me?"*
  o *"Would you want to talk to me again?"*

Joining Group Conversations

- Explain, *"Another way to make new friends is by joining the conversations of teens that you're trying to get to know better. These are not the steps for joining conversations of people we know well. With good friends we can just walk up and say hello. These are the steps we use for joining group conversations with people we either don't know or only know slightly."*

[The instructor and behavioral coach should do an INAPPROPRIATE role-play, with the instructor barging into a conversation. If there is only one behavioral coach, you can select the highest-functioning teen in the class and ask them to assist with the role-play. Be sure to give them an overview of what you plan to do before the role-play demonstration. This is best done before the class begins. The teen will often feel flattered to be included in the exercise. When using teens, it is best to let them naturally trade information with the coach, rather than trying to provide them with a script.]

- Begin by saying, *"We're going to do another role-play where I'll try to join a group conversation with people I don't know well. Watch this and tell me what I'm doing WRONG."*

Example of an INAPPROPRIATE role-play:

- Instructor: (Standing several feet from the two coaches)
- Coach 1: *"Hi (insert name). How was your weekend?"*
- Coach 2: *"It was good. How was yours?"*
- Coach 1: *"It was pretty good. What did you do?"*
- Coach 2: *"I did a little homework and watched some movies."*
- Coach 1: *"Oh yeah? What movies did you watch?"*
- Coach 2: *"I watched a couple of sci-fi movies."*
- Coach 1: *"Really? I love sci-fi movies . . ."*
- Instructor: (Walks over abruptly, interrupts) *"Hey guys. Have you been to the new water park?"*
- Coach 1: (Startled, confused) *"Umm . . . no."* (Turning away from the instructor) *"So anyway, you were saying that you watched some sci-fi movies . . ."*
- Instructor: (Interrupts) *"So I'm going to that new water park next week. Have you guys been there?"*
- Coach 2: (Looking annoyed, rolling eyes) *"Umm . . . no."* (Turning away from the instructor) *"So, anyway. Yeah, I watched some sci-fi movies."*
- Coach 1: *"That's cool. I'm into sci-fi too . . ."*
- Instructor: (Interrupts) *"So you guys should go to this new water park. It's supposed to be really cool!"*
- Coach 1 and 2: (Looking annoyed, ignoring comments, rolling eyes)

- End by saying, "Time out on that. So what did I do WRONG in trying to join that conversation?"
  - Answer: You barged in and were off topic

- Ask, *"Did it seem like they wanted to talk to me?"*

  o   Answer: No

- Ask, *"How could you tell?"*

  o   Answer: They weren't **talking to you**, weren't **looking at you**, and weren't **facing you**

- Ask the following *Perspective Taking Questions*:

  o   *"What was that like for (names of coaches)?"*

  ▪   Answers: Irritating; annoying; frustrating

  o   *"What do you think (names of coaches) thought of me?"*

  ▪   Answers: Rude; obnoxious; annoying; weird

  o   *"Are (names of coaches) going to want to talk to me again?"*

  ▪   Answers: No; too annoying

- Ask the behavioral coaches the same *Perspective Taking Questions*:

  o   *"What was that like for you?"*
  o   *"What did you think of me?"*
  o   *"Would you want to talk to me again?"*

Steps for Joining Group Conversations

[Present the steps for *joining a group conversation* by writing the following buzzwords (**bold and italicized**) on the board. Do not erase the steps until the end of the lesson.]

1. *Listen to the conversation*

   a. Explain, *"Before you try to enter a group conversation between people you either don't know or only know slightly, you first need to discreetly listen to the conversation and try to figure out what they're talking about."*
   b. Ask, *"Why is it important to listen to the conversation?"*

      i.   Answer: You need to know what the topic is before you join

2. *Watch from a distance*

   a. Explain, *"While you're listening, you should also be inconspicuously watching from a distance. This means you should occasionally look over toward the group for a second or two at a time, without staring at them."*
   b. Ask, *"Why would it be important to watch from a distance?"*

      i.   Answer: It shows you're interested in the group

3. *Use a prop*

   a. Explain, *"While you're listening and watching the conversation, it's helpful to use a prop like a mobile phone, a gaming device, or a book to make it look like you're focused on something else."*

   b. Ask, *"Why would it be a good idea to use a prop?"*

      i. Answer: It makes it seem like you're occupied with something else, doesn't look like you're eavesdropping

4. *Identify the topic*

   a. Explain, *"The most important goal of listening to the conversation will be to identify the topic being discussed."*

   b. Ask, *"Why is it important to identify the topic?"*

      i. Answer: Because you need to be able to talk about that topic if you are going to join the conversation

5. *Find a common interest*

   a. Explain, *"Before you attempt to join a conversation, you need to make sure you share a common interest in the topic."*

   b. Ask, *"Why is it important to find a common interest?"*

      i. Answer: Your **common interest** will be your excuse for joining

6. *Move closer*

   a. Explain, *"Around the time you start to make a bit more eye contact and you've decided to join the conversation, you should move a bit closer to the group. Usually about an arm or two lengths away is good."*

   b. Ask, *"Why is it important to move closer?"*

      i. Answer: It shows interest, alerts the group you are joining, and to stand far away and try to talk to the group would seem weird

7. *Wait for a pause*

   a. Explain, *"The next step is to wait for a brief pause in the conversation just before joining."*

   b. Ask, *"Why is it important to wait for a pause in the conversation?"*

      i. Answer: If you don't wait for a brief pause, you may be interrupting the conversation

   c. Ask, *"Is there ever a PERFECT PAUSE?"*

      i. Answer: **There's never a perfect pause**, so just try not to interrupt too much, the best time to join is when one person stops talking and another is just beginning to talk

8. *Mention the topic*

   a. Explain, *"You should join the conversation by making a comment or asking a question about the topic."*

   b. Ask, *"Why is it important to mention the topic?"*

      i. Answer: This is your reason for joining the conversation

9. *Assess interest*

   a. Explain, *"You also need to make sure the group wants to talk to you by asking yourself the following questions . . ."*

      i. *Are they talking to me?*
      ii. *Are they looking at me?*
      iii. *Are they facing me (or did they close the circle)?*

         1. When people talk in groups, they talk in circles
         2. When they want to talk to you, they **open the circle**
         3. When they don't want to talk to you, they **close the circle**

10. *Introduce yourself*

    a. Explain, *"If you've been accepted, the final step for entering a group conversation is to introduce yourself to anyone you don't know. You only do this after you've been talking for several minutes and you're sure you've been accepted into the conversation."*

Role-Play: Joining Group Conversations

[The instructor and two behavioral coaches should do an APPROPRIATE role-play with the instructor *joining a group conversation*.]

- Begin by saying, *"We're going to do another role-play. Watch this and tell me what I'm doing RIGHT in joining this conversation."*

   Example of an APPROPRIATE role-play:

   - Instructor: (Standing several feet from the two coaches, looking at a cell phone)
   - Coach 1: *"Hi (insert name). How was your weekend?"*
   - Coach 2: *"It was good. How was yours?"*
   - Coach 1: *"It was pretty good. What did you do?"*
   - Coach 2: *"Oh, I did a little homework and watched some movies."*
   - Instructor: (Looking over at the coaches periodically)
   - Coach 1: *"Oh yeah? What movies did you watch?"*
   - Coach 2: *"I watched a couple of sci-fi movies."*
   - Instructor: (Looking over, showing interest)
   - Coach 1: *"How fun. I love sci-fi movies!"*
   - Coach 2: *"Really? That's cool."*
   - Coach 1: *"So which ones did you watch?"*
   - Coach 2: *"I did a little Star Wars marathon."*
   - Instructor: (Looking over, showing interest)
   - Coach 1: *"That's awesome. Those are classic."*
   - Coach 2: *"I know, right? Phantom Menace is my favorite. How about you?"*
   - Coach 1: *"Definitely Episode 1! Hard to beat that one."*
   - Instructor: (Walks a little closer, making more eye contact)

- Coach 1 and 2: (Look over at the instructor)
- Instructor: (Waits for a brief pause) *"So you guys are into Star Wars?"*
- Coach 1 and 2: (Looking over at the instructor) *"Yeah. Are you?"*
- Instructor: *"Oh definitely. Actually, I'm not sure if you heard, but they're showing Episodes 1–3 next week at this old theater downtown."*
- Coach 2: (Open the circle)*"No way!"*
- Coach 1: (Opens the circle) *"Really? I hadn't heard about that."*
- Coach 2: *"That's so cool."*
- Instructor: *"I know. It's been a long time since I've seen them on the big screen."*
- Coach 1: *"Me too. I'm going to have to check that out."*
- Instructor: *"You should."* (Brief pause) *"I'm (insert name) by the way."*
- Coach 2: *"Oh cool. I'm (insert name)."*
- Coach 1: *"Hey, I'm (insert name)."*
- (Smile, nod heads, don't shake hands)

- End by saying, *"Time out on that. So what did I do RIGHT in joining that conversation?"*
  - Answer: ***Listened and watched, used a prop, identified the topic, found a common interest, moved closer, waited for a pause, mentioned the topic, assessed interest***, and ***introduced yourself***

- Ask, *"Did it seem like they wanted to talk to me?"*
  - Answer: Yes

- Ask, *"How could you tell?"*
  - Answer: They were ***talking to you, looking at you***, and ***facing you*** (they ***opened the circle***)

- Ask the following ***Perspective Taking Questions***:
  - *"What was that like for (names of coaches)?"*
    - Answers: Nice; pleasant
  - *"What do you think (names of coaches) thought of me?"*
    - Answers: Nice; interesting; pretty cool
  - *"Are (names of coaches) going to want to talk to me again?"*
    - Answer: Yes, probably

- Ask the behavioral coaches the same ***Perspective Taking Questions***:
  - *"What was that like for you?"*
  - *"What did you think of me?"*
  - *"Would you want to talk to me again?"*

Wrap Up

Say, *"So those are the steps for starting and joining conversations. Tomorrow we'll continue our discussion about starting and joining conversations, and we'll begin to practice joining conversations with our classmates."*

Calculate Points

Calculate the number of points earned by each teen (see Appendix E for the Daily Point Log):

- Do not publicly disclose the individual number of points

- Discourage attempts to compare number of points earned between teens

    o   Remind them that they are working as a team to earn a bigger and better graduation party

Day Three: Lesson Review and Behavioral Rehearsal

Lesson Review: Starting and Joining Conversations

Steps for Starting Individual Conversations

- Say, *"Yesterday we worked on starting and joining conversations. Who can tell us what the steps are for starting individual conversations?"*

[Have teens generate all of the steps for starting and joining conversations. Be prepared to give prompts if necessary. Write the following bullet points and buzzwords (**bold and italicized**) on the board and do not erase until the end of the lesson.]

1. *Casually look over*

2. *Use a prop*

3. *Find a common interest*

4. *Mention the common interest*

5. *Trade information*

6. *Assess interest*

   a. *Are they talking to me?*
   b. *Are they looking at me?*
   c. *Are they facing me (or giving me the cold shoulder)?*

7. *Introduce yourself (if they are interested)*

Steps for Joining Group Conversations

- Say, *"Those were the steps for starting an individual conversation. Who can tell us what the steps are for joining group conversations?"*

1. *Listen to the conversation*

2. *Watch from a distance*

3. *Use a prop*

4. *Identify the topic*

5. *Find a common interest*

6. *Move closer*

7. *Wait for a pause*

8. *Mention the topic*

9. *Assess interest*

> i. *Are they talking to me?*
> ii. *Are they looking at me?*
> iii. *Are they facing me?*
>
> > 1. *Did they open the circle or close the circle?*

10. *Introduce yourself (if they are interested)*

Role-Play: Joining Group Conversations

[The instructor and two behavioral coaches should do an APPROPRIATE role-play with the instructor joining a group conversation.]

- Begin by saying, *"We're going to do a role-play. Watch this and tell me what I'm doing RIGHT in joining this conversation."*

Example of an APPROPRIATE role-play:

- Instructor: (Standing several feet from the two coaches, looking at cell phone)
- Coach 1: *"Hi (insert name). How was your weekend?"*
- Coach 2: *"It was good. How was yours?"*
- Coach 1: *"It was pretty good. What did you do?"*
- Coach 2: *"Oh, I played tennis."*
- Instructor: (Looking over at the coaches periodically)
- Coach 1: *"Oh yeah? I didn't know you played tennis."*
- Coach 2: *"Yeah, I've been playing for years. Do you play?"*
- Instructor: (Looking over, showing interest)
- Coach 1: *"I do actually!"*
- Coach 2: *"So where do you play?"*
- Coach 1: *"Usually at the courts on campus."*
- Coach 2: *"No way! That's where I play too."*
- Instructor: (Looking over, showing interest)
- Coach 1: *"You're kidding? I can't believe we've never run into each other."*
- Coach 2: *"I know, right?"*
- Instructor: (Walks a little closer, making more eye contact)
- Coach 1 and 2: (Look over at the instructor)
- Instructor: (Waits for a brief pause) *"So you guys play tennis?"*
- Coach 1 and 2: (Looking over at the instructor) *"Yeah. Do you?"*
- Instructor: *"Yeah. I play at the campus courts too."*
- Coach 2: (Opening the circle) *"Oh that's funny."*
- Coach 1: (Opening the circle) *"I know, right? We all play there, but never run into each other."*
- Coach 2: (Slight laugh) *"So what do you play? Singles or doubles?"*
- Coach 1: *"I play both, but mostly singles."*
- Instructor: *"I play both too. What about you?"*

- Coach 2: *"Singles if I want a workout. Doubles if I'm feeling lazy."*
- [Laughs]
- Instructor: *"I'm (insert name) by the way."*
- Coach 2: *"Oh cool. I'm (insert name)."*
- Coach 1: *"Hey, I'm (insert name)."*
- (Smile, nod heads, don't shake hands)

- End by saying, *"Time out on that. So what did I do RIGHT in joining that conversation?"*
  - Answer: **Listened and watched, used a prop, identified the topic, found a common interest, moved closer, waited for a pause, mentioned the topic, assessed interest**, and **introduced yourself**

- Ask, *"Did it seem like they wanted to talk to me?"*
  - Answer: Yes

- Ask, *"How could you tell?"*
  - Answer: They were **talking to you, looking at you**, and **facing you** (they **opened the circle**)

- Ask the following *Perspective Taking Questions*:
  - *"What was that like for (names of coaches)?"*
    - Answers: Nice; pleasant
  - *"What do you think (names of coaches) thought of me?"*
    - Answers: Nice; interesting; pretty cool
  - *"Are (names of coaches) going to want to talk to me again?"*
    - Answer: Yes, probably

- Ask the behavioral coaches the same *Perspective Taking Questions*:
  - *"What was that like for you?"*
  - *"What did you think of me?"*
  - *"Would you want to talk to me again?"*

Behavioral Rehearsal: Joining Group Conversations

- Break teens up into small groups (no less than three teens per group)
  - Match girls with girls and boys with boys, whenever possible
- Have each teen practice *joining a group conversation*
  - Separate the teen from the group and have him or her identify the steps for *joining group conversations* (they may need to look at the board at first)

- ○ Then have the teen practice using these steps by *joining a group conversation* with their peers who will already be *trading information* about their personal items
- ○ Remind the other teens that they should accept everyone into these conversations
- ○ Teens may need you to provide prompting for specific steps, such as:

  - ■ *"Do you know what they're talking about?"*
  - ■ *"Do you know anything about that subject?"*
  - ■ *"Do you want to use anything while you're listening?"*
  - ■ *"What are you waiting for before you join?"*
  - ■ *"Is there ever a PERFECT PAUSE?"*
  - ■ *"Do you want to move closer before you join?"*
  - ■ *"When you join, do you want to be on topic?"*

- In the event that a teen incorrectly attempts to join, call a *"time-out"* and use this teachable moment to gently point out the error, while providing feedback on how to more appropriately attempt to join

  - ○ Have the teen try again until he or she is successful

- Once the teen has successfully joined, call a *"time-out"* and have the other teens applaud

  - ○ Instructor should briefly point out the steps that the teen followed for *joining the group conversation*

- Rotate teens after each has successfully joined

- Each teen should practice at least once

- Give points for following the steps for *joining a group conversation*

Homework Assignments

- [Assign the *in-class calls* for the week and write this on the In-Class Call Assignment Log (Appendix D) for future reference. If there is an uneven number of teens, assign someone *double duty*.]

- [Distribute the Parent Handout (found in the last section of this chapter) and inform teens that they should give this handout to their parents immediately.]

- [Be prepared to have the teens coordinate a day and time to make the *in-class call* and then have each teen write the day and time of the call on the Phone Roster and Parent Handout.]

- Briefly explain the homework for the week by saying, *"We're going to continue to have you practice joining group conversations this week."*

- Present the homework assignments for the coming week:

1. Practice *joining a group conversation* between at least two teens you feel comfortable with

   a. Before *joining*:

      i.   Think of a place where you are likely to be accepted and you don't have a bad reputation

  b. During the conversation:

      i.   Follow the steps for *joining a group conversation*

  c. After *joining*:

      i.   Parents and teen should discuss how the teen *joined the group conversation*

      ii. Parents should help teen *troubleshoot* any problems that may have arisen

2. ***Pay attention to humor feedback***

  a. If the teen happens to tell a joke (this is NOT the assignment), notice whether people are ***not laughing at all, giving a courtesy laugh, laughing AT you***, or ***laughing WITH you***

  b. Discuss this ***humor feedback*** with your parent

      i.   Teen and parent should decide if teen is more of a ***joke-teller, joke-receiver***, or ***joke-refuser***

3. ***Enroll in extracurricular activities***

  a. Teens and parents should DISCUSS and DECIDE on extracurricular activities based on the teen's interests and BEGIN TO ENROLL in these activities

      i.   Criteria for a good extracurricular activity:

           1. Meets weekly or at least every other week
           2. Age range of other teens includes the social age of the teen
           3. Activity includes informal time so that the teen can interact with others
           4. Activity starts within the next couple of weeks

  b. Teen should ***start an individual conversation*** with someone at this extracurricular activity

      i.   ***Trade information*** and ***find common interests*** while having a ***two-way conversation***

4. ***In-class call or video chat***

  a. Before the call:

      i.   Before the class ends, teens should arrange to call another member of the class to practice ***trading information*** and having a ***two-way conversation***
      ii. Set up a day and time to make the call
      iii. Write the day and time of the call on the Phone Roster and the Parent Handout

  b. During the call:

      i.   Follow the steps for ***starting and ending phone calls***, including using ***cover stories***
      ii. Teens should ***trade information*** and have a ***two-way conversation*** on this call
      iii. Find a ***common interest*** to report back to the class

c. After the call:

    i. Teens should discuss the call with their parent, identify *common interests*, and *troubleshoot* any problems

5. *Out-of-class call or video chat*

    a. Before the call:

        i. Choose someone the teen feels comfortable talking with around the same age

    b. During the call:

        i. Follow the steps for *starting and ending phone calls*, including using *cover stories*
        ii. Teens should *trade information* and have a *two-way conversation* on this phone call
        iii. Find a *common interest* to report back to the class

    c. After the call:

        i. Teens should discuss the call with their parent, identify *common interests*, and *troubleshoot* any problems

6. *Bring a personal item*

    a. Bring a favorite item to share with the class on **Wednesday, Thursday and Friday of next week** (e.g., music, game, book, pictures)
    b. Be prepared to *trade information* about the item

Wrap Up

Say, *"So those are your homework assignments for this week. Be sure to start working on these assignments right away. We'll be reviewing how they went at the beginning of next week. Tomorrow we will continue our discussion about starting and joining conversations."*

Calculate Points

Calculate the number of points earned by each teen (see Appendix E for the Daily Point Log):

- Do not publicly disclose the individual number of points

- Discourage attempts to compare number of points earned between teens

    ○ Remind them that they are working as a team to earn a bigger and better graduation party

Days Four and Five: Teen Activity—Joining Group Conversations

Lesson Review: Starting and Joining Conversations

Steps for Starting Individual Conversations

- Say, *"Yesterday we worked on starting and joining conversations. Who can tell us what the steps are for starting individual conversations?"*

[Have teens generate all of the steps for starting and joining conversations. Be prepared to give prompts if necessary. Write the following bullet points and buzzwords (**bold and italicized**) on the board and do not erase until the end of the lesson.]

1. *Casually look over*

2. *Use a prop*

3. *Find a common interest*

4. *Mention the common interest*

5. *Trade information*

6. *Assess interest*

    a. *Are they talking to me?*
    b. *Are they looking at me?*
    c. *Are they facing me (or giving me the cold shoulder)?*

7. *Introduce yourself (if they're interested)*

Steps for Joining Group Conversations

- Say, *"Those were the steps for starting an individual conversation. Who can tell us what the steps are for joining group conversations?"*

1. *Listen to the conversation*

2. *Watch from a distance*

3. *Use a prop*

4. *Identify the topic*

5. *Find a common interest*

6. *Move closer*

7. *Wait for a pause*

8. *Mention the topic*

9. *Assess interest*

   a. *Are they talking to me?*
   b. *Are they looking at me?*
   c. *Are they facing me?*

      i. *Did they open the circle or close the circle?*

10. *Introduce yourself (if they're interested)*

Teen Activity: Joining Group Conversations

Materials Needed

- Teens bring personal items to *trade information* about

- If teens forget to bring personal items:

  ○ Cell phones with music and/or pictures may be used
  ○ T-shirts with logos of favorite pastimes are relevant
  ○ Teens can simply talk about their interests without personal items

Rules

- Break teens up into small groups (no less than three teens per group)

  ○ Match girls with girls and boys with boys, whenever possible

- Have teens practice *trading information* about their personal items while taking turns *joining a group conversation*

- For teens practicing *trading information about personal items*:

  ○ Encourage teens to identify *common interests* through *trading information*
  ○ Prompt teens to ask questions when appropriate

- For teens practicing *joining a group conversation*:

  ○ Separate the teen from the group and have him or her identify the *steps for joining group conversations* (they may need to look at the board at first)
  ○ Then have the teen practice using these steps by *joining a group conversation* with their peers in which the others will be *trading information* about their personal items
  ○ Remind the other teens that they should accept everyone into these conversations
  ○ Teens may need you to provide prompting for specific steps, such as:

    ■ *"Do you know what they're talking about?"*
    ■ *"Do you know anything about that topic?"*
    ■ *"Do you want to use anything while you're listening?"*
    ■ *"What are you waiting for before you join?"*

- "*Is there ever a PERFECT PAUSE?*"
- "*Do you want to move closer before you join?*"
- "*When you join, do you want to be on topic?*"

- In the event that a teen incorrectly ***joins the group conversation***, call a "*time-out*" and use this teachable moment to gently point out the error, while providing feedback on how to more appropriately attempt to join

  ○ Have the teen try again until he or she is successful

- Once the teen has successfully joined, call a "*time-out*" and have the other teens applaud

  ○ Briefly point out the ***steps for joining a group conversation*** that the teen followed

- Each teen should practice ***joining a group conversation*** at least once

- Give points for following the ***steps for joining a group conversation***

Homework Assignments

- [Be prepared to read off the ***in-class call*** assignments for the week as a reminder of the homework. This should be written on the In-Class Call Assignment Log (Appendix D). Make sure the teens have scheduled the ***in-class call*** and have the correct phone number.]

- Briefly remind teens of the homework for the week by saying, "*Remember, we're going to continue to have you practice joining group conversations this week.*"

- Present the homework assignments for the coming week:

  1. Practice ***joining a group conversation*** between at least two teens you feel comfortable with

     a. Before ***joining***:

        i. Think of a place where you are likely to be accepted and you don't have a bad reputation

     b. During the conversation:

        i. Follow the steps for ***joining a group conversation***

     c. After ***joining***:

        i. Parents and teen should discuss how the teen ***joined the group conversation***
        ii. Parents should help teen ***troubleshoot*** any problems that may have arisen

  2. ***Pay attention to humor feedback***

     a. If the teen happens to tell a joke (this is NOT the assignment), notice whether people are ***not laughing at all, giving a courtesy laugh, laughing AT you***, or ***laughing WITH you***

b. Discuss this *humor feedback* with your parent

  i. Teen and parent should decide if teen is more of a *joke-teller, joke-receiver*, or *joke-refuser*

3. *Enroll in extracurricular activities*

  a. Teens and parents should DISCUSS and DECIDE on extracurricular activities based on the teen's interests and BEGIN TO ENROLL in these activities

  i. Criteria for a good extracurricular activity:

  1. Meets weekly or at least every other week
  2. Age range of other teens includes the social age of the teen
  3. Activity includes informal time so that the teen can interact with others
  4. Activity starts within the next couple of weeks

  b. Teen should *start an individual conversation* with someone at this extracurricular activity

  i. *Trade information* and *find common interests* while having a *two-way conversation*

4. *In-class call or video chat*

  a. Before the call:

  i. Before the class ends, teens should arrange to call another member of the class to practice *trading information* and having a *two-way conversation*
  ii. Set up a day and time to make the call
  iii. Write the day and time of the call on the Phone Roster and the Parent Handout

  b. During the call:

  i. Follow the steps for *starting and ending phone calls*, including using *cover stories*
  ii. Teens should *trade information* and have a *two-way conversation* on this call
  iii. Find a *common interest* to report back to the class

  c. After the call:

  i. Teens should discuss the call with their parent, identify *common interests*, and *troubleshoot* any problems

5. *Out-of-class call or video chat*

  a. Before the call:

  i. Choose someone the teen feels comfortable talking with around the same age

  b. During the call:

  i. Follow the steps for *starting and ending phone calls*, including using *cover stories*
  ii. Teens should *trade information* and have a *two-way conversation* on this phone call
  iii. Find a *common interest* to report back to the class

    c. After the call:

        i. Teens should discuss the call with their parent, identify **common interests**, and **troubleshoot** any problems

6. **Bring a personal item**

    a. Bring a favorite item to share with the class on **Wednesday, Thursday and Friday of next week** (e.g., music, game, book, pictures)

    b. Be prepared to **trade information** about the item

Wrap Up

Say, *"So those are your homework assignments for this week. Be sure to start working on these assignments right away. We'll be reviewing how they went at the beginning of next week."*

Calculate Points

Calculate the number of points earned by each teen (see Appendix E for the Daily Point Log):

- Do not publicly disclose the individual number of points

- Discourage attempts to compare number of points earned between teens

    ○ Remind them that they are working as a team to earn a bigger and better graduation party

Parent Handout 6

PEERS® *Program for the Education and Enrichment of Relational Skills*

Starting and Joining Conversations

This week your teens will be learning how to start and join conversations with people they want to know better. The rules for starting and joining conversations with casual acquaintances are very specific and are presented below.

Didactic Lesson: Starting and Joining Conversations

Steps for Starting Individual Conversations

1. *Casually look over*
2. *Use a prop*
3. *Find a common interest*
4. *Mention the common interest*
5. *Trade information*
6. *Assess interest*
   a. *Are they talking to me?*
   b. *Are they looking at me?*
   c. *Are they facing me (or giving me the cold shoulder)?*
7. *Introduce yourself (if they're interested)*

Steps for Joining Groups Conversations

1. *Listen to the conversation*
2. *Watch from a distance*
3. *Use a prop*
4. *Identify the topic*
5. *Find a common interest*
6. *Move closer*
7. *Wait for a pause*
8. *Mention the topic*
9. *Assess interest*

   a. *Are they talking to me?*

   b. *Are they looking at me?*

   c. *Are they facing me?*

      i. When people talk in groups, they talk in circles

      ii. When they accept you in the conversation, they *open the circle*

      iii. When they don't accept you in the conversation, they *close the circle*

10. *Introduce yourself (if they're interested)*

Homework Assignments

Every week your teen will have homework assignments to practice new and previously learned social skills. It is extremely helpful if parents assist teens in completing these assignments. The homework assignments for this week include the following:

1. Practice *joining a group conversation* between at least two teens you feel comfortable with

   a. Before *joining*:

      i. Teen should think of a place where he or she is likely to be accepted and doesn't have a bad reputation

   b. During the conversation:

      i. Follow the steps for *joining a group conversation*

   c. After *joining*:

      i. Parents and teens should discuss how the teen *joined the group conversation*

      ii. Parents should help teen *troubleshoot* any problems that may have arisen

2. *Pay attention to humor feedback*

   a. If the teen happens to tell a joke (this is NOT the assignment), notice whether people are *not laughing at all, giving a courtesy laugh, laughing AT you,* or *laughing WITH you*

   b. Discuss this *humor feedback* with your parent

      i. Teen and parent should decide if teen is more of a *joke-teller, joke-receiver,* or *joke-refuser*

3. *Enroll in extracurricular activities*

   a. Teens and parents should DISCUSS and DECIDE on extracurricular activities based on the teen's interests and BEGIN TO ENROLL in these activities

      i. Criteria for a good extracurricular activity:

         1. Meets weekly or at least every other week

         2. Age range of other teens includes the social age of the teen

         3. Activity includes informal time so that the teen can interact with others

         4. Activity starts within the next couple of weeks

   b. Teen should *start an individual conversation* with someone at this extracurricular activity

      i. *Trade information* and *find common interests* while having a *two-way conversation*

4. *In-class call or video chat*

   a. Before the call:

      i. Teens should have arranged to call another member of the class to practice *trading information* (instructor has assigned the calls)

      ii. Teens should have set up a day and time to make the call (this information should be listed below and on your teen's Phone Roster)

   b. During the call:

      i. Follow the steps for *starting and ending phone calls*, including using *cover stories*

      ii. Teens should *trade information* and have a *two-way conversation* on this call

      iii. Find a *common interest* to report back to the class

   c. After the call:

      i. Teens should discuss the call with their parent, identify *common interests*, and *trouble-shoot* any problems

5. ***Out-of-class call or video chat***

   a. Before the call:

      i. Choose someone the teen feels comfortable talking with around the same age

   b. During the call:

      i. Follow the steps for *starting and ending phone calls*, including using *cover stories*

      ii. Teens should *trade information* and have a *two-way conversation* on this phone call

      iii. Find a *common interest* to report back to the class

   c. After the call:

      i. Teens should discuss the call with their parent, identify *common interests*, and *trouble-shoot* any problems

6. ***Bring a personal item***

   a. Bring a favorite item to share with the class on **Wednesday, Thursday and Friday of next week** (e.g., music, game, book, pictures)

   b. Be prepared to *trade information* about the item

In-Class Call Assignment

Your teen has been assigned to be the **caller/receiver** (circle one) with:

Name:

Phone Number:

Day:

Time:

WEEK 7

EXITING CONVERSATIONS

Preparing for the Lesson

The primary purpose of this lesson is to help teens recover from unsuccessful attempts at entering group conversations. Some teens with Autism Spectrum Disorder (ASD) are puzzled when they try to join conversations and their entry attempts do not go as planned. Although this could happen to anyone, for a socially awkward teen, this can add to their confusion when peers do not respond as expected.

One of the common social errors committed by teens with ASD is that they fail to notice when they are not being accepted into conversations. They may persist in forcing conversations, often resulting in frustration and annoyance from their conversational partners, and possibly even resulting in a bad reputation among the larger peer group when this pattern persists. Bridging on the last lesson, the current lesson reviews the important social cues to which teens should attend in order to determine if they are accepted into a conversation (i.e., verbal cues, eye contact, body language). The role-play demonstrations, along with the *Perspective Taking Questions* in this lesson, will be helpful in improving teens' social awareness and understanding of social cognition during *peer entry*. Conducting inappropriate role-play demonstrations of *peer entry* attempts, followed by questions like, *"Did it seem like they wanted to talk to me?," "How could you tell?," "What do you think that was like for them?," "What do you think they thought of me?,"* and *"Are they going to want to talk to me again?,"* will assist teens in better understanding the social cues related to acceptance and rejection in conversational entry.

This lesson primarily focuses on teaching teens how to extricate themselves when they are not accepted in conversations in a way that minimizes the negative social impact. Unfortunately, *peer exiting* strategies can only be taught after the teens are taught how to join conversations. If teens have only confined their entry attempt to just watching and listening to the conversation, it's relatively easy for them to extricate themselves when the group is not receptive to their entry. It's only after they have begun to contribute to the conversation and have been turned down that knowing how to exit is more complicated.

Hopefully, most or all of the teens have attempted to join a conversation as part of the previous homework assignment. If they followed the instructions from this assignment, they would have attempted to enter a group that is likely to be receptive and accepting of their *peer entry* attempt, making it less likely that they will need to utilize *peer exiting* strategies.

The most common reason for teen *peer entry* attempts to be turned down is that the teen has a bad reputation among his or her peers, and/or the teen chose the wrong group of peers to join in conversation. In the event that the teen has a bad reputation, it will be important to identify other **sources of potential friends** through involvement in extracurricular activities in which the teen is unknown. These activities are usually found in the community, rather than the school, and will most likely require parental support for enrollment. Meanwhile, you will need to work with the teen on identifying a more accepting **social group** to practice **peer entry** skills within the following week.

Whatever the cause of the entry attempts being turned down, teens will need to be reassured that this is common (even for adults), and that they do not need to take it too personally. It can be very helpful if you normalize this experience by telling the teens that even you (and perhaps the coaches) get turned down from joining conversations from time to time. If these efforts are successful in normalizing the experience for the teens, they will be more willing to attempt to join conversations in the future.

Although the bulk of this lesson focuses on how to **exit conversations** when either **never accepted** or when **initially accepted and then excluded**, the lesson also provides strategies for how to **exit conversations when fully accepted**. In this case, the common social error made by teens with ASD is to simply walk away when done speaking, with no acknowledgment of their departure or where they are going. Since this behavior is hardly likely to lead to social success, the portion of the lesson on **exiting conversations when fully accepted** will be quite useful.

Because this lesson is fairly straightforward, you should not expect much push back from the teens. One issue that may come up relates to the number of personnel needed to conduct the role-play demonstrations in this lesson. To adequately demonstrate peer entry and exiting strategies in weeks 6 and 7, you will need three "actors" for your role-play demonstrations. If you only have one instructor and one coach in your class, you may want to "borrow" another member of the teaching staff for a few moments during the role-play demonstrations. Alternatively, as previously described in the week 6 lesson guide, selecting the highest-functioning teen in the class and asking him or her to assist with the role-play is another option. Be sure to give the student an overview of what you plan to do before the role-play demonstration. This is best done before the class begins. The teen will often feel flattered to be included in the exercise. When using teens in role-play demonstrations, it is best to let them naturally **trade information** with the coach, rather than trying to provide them with a script.

As explained in the Preparing for the Lesson section for week 1, although this manual provides scripts of how to demonstrate inappropriate and appropriate social behavior, *role-play scripts are not intended to be read verbatim*. They are simply intended to provide a guide for how you might conduct role-plays. Hopefully, you have taken this advice to heart and have not been reading the script aloud to your class. In this case, you have been creating your own dialogue and hopefully having fun with the process. One thing to keep in mind with the role-play demonstrations this week is that when demonstrating inappropriate behavior, make sure that everything you are demonstrating is WRONG. In other words, if you are exiting the conversation inappropriately, you should also be joining the conversation inappropriately. To do one aspect of a role-play appropriately and the other inappropriately would be confusing for your students.

Day One: Homework Review

Homework Review

[Start with completed homework first. If you have time, you can inquire as to why others were unable to complete the assignment and try to **troubleshoot** how they might get it done for the coming week. When reviewing homework, be sure to use the buzzwords (**bold and italicized**) and **troubleshoot** issues that come up. Spend the majority of the homework review on **joining a group conversation**, extracurricular activities, and the **out-of-class call**, as these were the most important assignments.]

[Note: Give multiple points for homework parts—not just one point per assignment.]

1. *Joining a group conversation*

   a. Say, *"Last week we went over the steps for joining conversations with people we know only slightly. One of your assignments this week was to practice joining a conversation with a group that you were likely to be accepted by. Raise your hand if you practiced joining a group conversation this week."*

      i. Ask, *"Where did you join?"*
      ii. Ask, *"How did you join?"*

         1. Be sure they followed the ***steps for joining a group conversation***:

            a. ***Listen to the conversation***
            b. ***Watch from a distance***
            c. ***Use a prop***
            d. ***Identify the topic***
            e. ***Find a common interest***
            f. ***Move closer***
            g. ***Wait for a pause***
            h. ***Mention the topic***
            i. ***Assess interest***
            j. ***Introduce yourself*** (if appropriate)

      iii. Ask, *"Did it seem like they wanted to talk to you?"*

         1. Ask, *"How could you tell?"*

            a. ***Talking to you***
            b. ***Looking at you***
            c. ***Facing you (opened the circle)***

2. *Enroll in extracurricular activities*

   a. Say, *"Another assignment was that you and your parents were supposed to identify an extracurricular activity for you to join where you might meet other teens with common interests, and then begin to enroll in those activities. Raise your hand if you found an extracurricular activity."*

      i. Ask, *"Which extracurricular activity did you choose?"*
      ii. Ask, *"Did you enroll in the activity?'*
      iii. Ask, *"Are there other teens your age in the group?'*

iv. Ask, *"How often does it meet?"*

v. Ask, *"Does this seem like a good place for you to make potential new friends?"*

b. Say, *"You were also supposed to follow the steps for starting a conversation with someone from this extracurricular activity. Raise your hand if you started a conversation with someone from your extracurricular activity."*

i. Ask, *"Who did you start the conversation with?"*

ii. Ask, *"How did you start the conversation?"*

1. Be sure they followed the ***steps for starting an individual conversation***:

a. ***Casually look over***

b. ***Use a prop***

c. ***Find a common interest***

d. ***Mention the common interest***

e. ***Trade information***

f. ***Assess interest***

g. ***Introduce yourself*** (if appropriate)

iii. Ask, *"Did it seem like they wanted to talk to you?"*

1. Ask, *"How could you tell?"*

a. ***Talking to you***

b. ***Looking at you***

c. ***Facing you***

3. ***Out-of-class call or video chat***

a. Say, *"Another assignment this week was to trade information and have a two-way conversation with someone not in this class over the phone or video chat. Raise your hand if you did the out-of-class call."*

i. Ask, *"Who did you talk to?"*

ii. Ask, *"How did the conversation begin?"*

a. Have teens identify all the relevant steps (if a phone call):

1. ***Ask for the person you are calling***

2. ***Say who you are***

3. ***Ask how they are***

4. ***Ask if they can talk***

5. ***Give a cover story for why you are calling***

iii. Ask, *"Did you trade information?"*

iv. Ask, *"Did you find a common interest?"*

a. When they identify common interests ask, *"What could you do with that information if you were going to hang out?"*

v. Ask, *"How did the conversation end?"*

a. Have teens identify all the relevant steps (if a phone call):

1. *Wait for a bit of a pause*
2. *Give a cover story for why you have to go*
3. *Tell the person it was nice talking*
4. *Tell the person you will talk to them later*
5. *Say goodbye*

   vi. Avoid general questions like, *"How did it go?"*

4. *In-class call or video chat*

  a. Say, *"Another assignment this week was to practice trading information and having a two-way conversation with one of your classmates over the phone or video chat. Raise your hand if you did the in-class call."*

     i. Ask, *"Who did you talk to?"*
    ii. Ask, *"Who called who?"*
   iii. Ask, *"How did the conversation begin?"*

      a. Have teens identify all the relevant steps (if a phone call):

1. *Ask for the person you are calling*
2. *Say who you are*
3. *Ask how they are*
4. *Ask if they can talk*
5. *Give a cover story for why you are calling*

    iv. Ask, *"Did you trade information?"*
     v. Ask, *"Did you find a common interest?"*

      a. When they identify common interests ask, *"What could you do with that information if you were going to hang out?"*

    vi. Ask, *"How did the conversation end?"*

      a. Have teens identify all the relevant steps (if a phone call):

1. *Wait for a bit of a pause*
2. *Give a cover story for why you have to go*
3. *Tell the person it was nice talking*
4. *Tell the person you will talk to them later*
5. *Say goodbye*

    vii. Avoid general questions like, *"How did it go?"*
   viii. Do not allow teens to talk about mistakes the other person made

  b. Have the other person who participated in the call give their account immediately after, but not at the same time

5. *Pay attention to humor feedback*

  a. Say, *"Another one of your assignments this week was to pay attention to your humor feedback if you happened to tell a joke. The assignment was NOT to tell a joke. If you happened to tell a joke this week, raise your hand if you paid attention to your humor feedback."*

     i. Say, *"I don't want to know what joke you told, I just want to know what your humor feedback was. Were they laughing AT you, laughing WITH you, giving a courtesy laugh, or NOT laughing at all?"*

    ii. Ask, *"How could you tell?"*

    iii. Ask, *"So are you done paying attention to your humor feedback?"*

       1. Answer: No

    iv. Ask, *"When will you pay attention to your humor feedback?"*

       1. Answer: Every time they tell a joke

    v. Ask, *"How will you pay attention to your humor feedback?"*

       1. Answer: By LOOKING and LISTENING

6. ***Bring a personal item***

    a. Identify the favorite item the teen will bring to share with the class later this week (e.g., music, game, book, pictures)

Wrap Up

Say, *"Good work for those of you who completed your homework assignments. Tomorrow we'll be talking about how to exit conversations."*

Calculate Points

Calculate the number of points earned by each teen (see Appendix E for the Daily Point Log):

- Do not publicly disclose the individual number of points

- Discourage attempts to compare number of points earned between teens

  - Remind them that they are working as a team to earn a bigger and better graduation party

Day Two: Didactic Lesson—Exiting Conversations

Didactic Lesson: Exiting Conversations

- Explain, *"Last week we talked about the steps for starting and joining conversations. This week we're going to talk about exiting conversations. Sometimes, even when we follow all of the steps for joining conversations, some people will still not want to talk to us. It happens to everyone and it's not a big deal."*

- Ask, *"For example, if someone tried to join ten different conversations, on average how many times out of ten do you think they will get turned down?"*

    o   Go around the room and have everyone take a guess
    o   Write the answers on the board

- Say, *"The answer is FIVE OUT OF TEN TIMES! That means half the time we try to join conversations we're not going to be accepted, and it's not a big deal. It happens to everyone."*

- Ask, *"Do you think we should give up trying?"*

    o   Answer: No, don't let this stop you from trying in the future

Reasons for Being Turned Down in Conversations

- Explain, *"There are many reasons for being turned down when we're trying to start or join conversations. Even though we won't be invited to join half of the time, it's important to think about why we might have been turned down and what we can do differently next time."*

- Using the Socratic method, have teens come up with reasons for being turned down and what they can do differently next time (see Table 8.1 for examples)

    o   Ask the question, *"What are some reasons why you might be turned down?"*
    o   Follow up each answer with, *"What could you do differently next time?"*

Table 8.1 Reasons for Being Turned Down in Conversations

Reasons for Being Turned Down	What to Do Differently Next Time
They want to talk privately	Try again later and listen before you join
They are stuck up or mean	Try a different group
You broke one of the rules for joining	Try again later, following the steps
You got too personal	Try a different group, don't get too personal
They are in a clique and don't want to make new friends	Try a different group
They are talking about something you do not know about	Try a different group that is talking about something you know about
You have a bad reputation with them	Try a different group that does not know or care about your reputation
They did not understand that you were trying to join	Try again later, following the steps

Steps for Exiting Conversations

- Explain, *"Since we know that it's common for people to not let us join their conversations and that it's not a big deal, we need to know what to do in these situations. Just like with joining conversations, there are very specific steps we need to follow for exiting conversations."*

[The instructor and two behavioral coaches should do an INAPPROPRIATE role-play with the instructor **joining a group conversation** inappropriately and **exiting the conversation** inappropriately. If there is only one behavioral coach, you can select the highest-functioning teen in the class and ask him or her to assist with the role-play. Be sure to give the teen an overview of what you plan to do before the role-play demonstration. This is best done before the class begins. The teen will often feel flattered to be included in the exercise. When using teens, it is best to let them naturally **trade information** with the coach, rather than trying to provide them with a script.]

- Begin by saying, *"We're going to do a role-play where I'll try to join a group conversation, but I'm not going to be accepted. Watch this and tell me what I'm doing WRONG."*

    Example of an INAPPROPRIATE role-play:

    - Instructor: (Standing several feet away)
    - Coach 1: *"Hi (insert name). How've you been doing?"*
    - Coach 2: *"I've been pretty good. How about you?"*
    - Coach 1: *"I'm good. Hey, didn't you tell me you like comic books? Did you go to that big comic book convention last weekend?"*
    - Coach 2: *"Yeah, I went on Saturday! It was great! Did you go?"*
    - Instructor: (Walks over abruptly, interrupts) *"Hey guys. What are you talking about?"*
    - Coach 2: (Startled, confused) *"What?"*
    - Coach 1: (Annoyed): *"We were just talking. So anyway, you went to the . . ."*
    - Coach 1 and 2: (Turning away from the instructor, closing the circle)
    - Instructor: (Interrupts) *"So what are you guys doing this weekend?"*
    - Coach 1: (Annoyed, ignoring, rolling eyes) *"So you went to the comic book convention? How was it?"*
    - Coach 2: (Ignoring) *"It was great! So why didn't you go?"*
    - Coach 1: (Ignoring) *"I had other plans, but I was thinking about going to the next one . . ."*
    - Instructor: (Interrupts) *"Hey, have you guys been to that new indoor water park?"*
    - Coach 1 and 2: (Annoyed, rolling eyes, ignoring)
    - Coach 2: *"Well, if you do go, let me know because I want to go again . . ."*
    - Instructor: (Interrupts) *"So have you been before? I'm supposed to go this weekend. I guess they have these really cool slides . . ."*
    - Coaches 1 and 2: (Looking annoyed, ignoring comments)
    - Coach 2: (Under breath, rolling eyes): *"How annoying?"*
    - Coach 1: (Making a face, rolling eyes) *"I know, right?"*
    - Instructor: (Angry) *"What's your problem? I was just trying to talk to you guys. You don't have to be so rude!"* (Storms off)
    - Coaches 1 and 2: (Look at each other and laugh)

- End by saying, *"Time out on that. So what did I do WRONG in trying to join that conversation?"*

  - Answer: You barged in and were off topic

- Ask, *"Did it seem like they wanted to talk to me?"*

  - Answer: No

- Ask, *"How could you tell?"*

  - Answer: They **didn't talk to you**, they **didn't look at you** (except to roll their eyes and make faces), and **they weren't facing you** (they **closed the circle**)

- Ask, *"What should I have done when I realized they didn't want to talk to me?"*

  - Answer: You shouldn't have tried to force them to talk, you shouldn't have gotten upset, you should have moved on

- Ask the following *Perspective Taking Questions*:

  - *"What was that like for (names of coaches)?"*

    - Answers: Irritating; annoying; frustrating

  - *"What do you think (names of coaches) thought of me?"*

    - Answers: Rude; obnoxious; annoying; weird

  - *"Are (names of coaches) going to want to talk to me again?"*

    - Answers: No; too annoying

- Ask the behavioral coaches the same *Perspective Taking Questions*:

  - *"What was that like for you?"*
  - *"What did you think of me?"*
  - *"Would you want to talk to me again?"*

Steps for Exiting Conversations when Never Accepted

- Say, *"Instead of getting upset and not taking no for an answer, we need to know how to exit conversations appropriately. In this case, I was NEVER ACCEPTED into that conversation. So these are the steps I should have followed . . ."*

[Present the steps for *exiting a conversation when never accepted* by writing the following bullet points and buzzwords (**bold and italicized**) on the board. Do not erase the steps until the end of the lesson.]

1. *Keep your cool*

   a. Explain, *"The first step for exiting a conversation we've never been accepted into is to keep your cool. This means don't get upset or try to force them to talk to you."*
   b. Ask, *"What could be the problem with getting upset and losing your cool?"*

  i.   Answer: They are going to think you're weird, they will be less likely to want to talk to you in the future, they may tell other teens about your reaction which could give you a bad reputation

2. *Look away*

  a.   Explain, *"The next step for exiting a conversation we've never been accepted into is to look away. This means you shouldn't stare. Instead, you should casually stop eye contact and look in a different direction."*

  b.   Ask, *"What does it tell the group when you start to look away?"*

  i.   Answer: Your attention is now somewhere else, you're not interested in what they're talking about anymore

  c.   Explain, *"We want to be careful not to draw too much attention to ourselves when we look away. That means choosing something to look at that doesn't involve looking over your shoulder or turning you whole head and body around."*

  d.   Ask, *"What could be the problem with turning your whole head and body around to look away?"* (Demonstrate turning in the opposite direction)

  i.   Answer: This would look strange and would draw attention to your behavior, the group might think the behavior was weird and might laugh or make fun of you

  e.   Explain, *"So just try looking to one side or the other. You could even pull out your cell phone or some other prop as a way of looking away."*

3. *Turn away*

  a.   Explain, *"After we've kept our cool and looked away, the next step for exiting a conversation is to turn away. This means that you casually and slowly turn your body away from the group."*

  b.   Ask, *"What does it tell the group when you turn away?"*

  i.   Answer: That you are about to walk away, that you've lost interest in what they're saying, that you're preparing to leave

  c.   Say, *"It's also important to turn your body away in the direction that you're already looking. What could be the problem with turning your body in a different direction from where you were looking?"* (Demonstrate looking in one direction and turning your body in another)

  i.   Answer: This would also look strange and would draw attention to your behavior, the group would think this was odd behavior, they would probably think you were weird

4. *Walk away*

  a.   Explain, *"The last step for exiting a conversation when you're never accepted is to walk away. This doesn't mean storming off or walking away quickly. Instead, you will want to SLOWLY and calmly walk away."*

  b.   Ask, *"What could be the problem with walking off quickly?"*

  i.   Answer: Walking off quickly will draw attention to you, instead you want to walk away so casually they don't even notice you've left

c.   Say, *"It's also important that we walk away in the direction that we're looking and facing. What could be the problem with walking in a different direction from where you were looking and facing?"* (Demonstrate looking in one direction, turning in another direction, and walking in a separate direction)

   i.   Answer: This would look very odd and would draw attention to you, this strange behavior could give you a bad reputation

Role-Play: Exiting a Conversation when Never Accepted

[The instructor and two behavioral coaches should do an APPROPRIATE role-play with the instructor *joining a group conversation* appropriately and *exiting the conversation* appropriately.]

- Begin by saying, *"We're going to do another role-play. Watch this and tell me what I'm doing RIGHT."*

   Example of an APPROPRIATE role-play:

   - Instructor: (Standing several feet away, looking at a cell phone)
   - Coach 1: *"Hi (insert name). How've you been doing?"*
   - Coach 2: *"I've been pretty good. How about you?"*
   - Coach 1: *"I'm good. Hey, didn't you tell me you like comic books? Did you go to that big comic book convention last weekend?"*
   - Instructor: (Looks over briefly, slightly smiles)
   - Coach 2: *"Yeah, I went on Saturday! It was great! Did you go?"*
   - Coach 1: *"I had other plans, but I was thinking about going to the next one."*
   - Instructor: (Looks over again)
   - Coach 2: *"Well, if you do go, let me know because I want to go again."*
   - Coach 1: *"Definitely. I'll let you know. That would be fun!"*
   - Instructor: (Move closer, waits for a pause, looks at Coach 2): *"So you went to the comic book convention?"*
   - Coach 1 and 2: (Ignoring, close the circle)
   - Coach 1: *"So did you meet all the famous authors?"*
   - Instructor: (Casually looks away)
   - Coach 2: *"Yeah, I did! It was so crazy."*
   - Instructor: (Casually turns away)
   - Coach 1: *"Was everyone dressed up?"*
   - Instructor: (Slowly walks away in the direction looking and facing)
   - Coach 2: *"So many people were dressed up! It was so much fun!"*
   - Coaches 1 and 2: (Don't appear to notice that the instructor has left)

- End by saying, *"Time out on that. So what did I do RIGHT in JOINING that conversation?"*

   ○   Answer: **Listened and watched, used a prop, identified the topic, found a common interest, moved closer, waited for a pause, mentioned the topic**

- Ask, *"Did it seem like they wanted to talk to me?"*

  ○   Answer: No

- Ask, *"How could you tell?"*

  ○   Answer: **Didn't talk to you, didn't look at you, didn't face you (closed the circle)**

- Ask, *"What did I do RIGHT in exiting that conversation?"*

  ○   Answer: **Kept your cool, looked away, turned away, walked away**

- Ask the following *Perspective Taking Questions*:

  ○   *"What was that like for (names of coaches)?"*

  ■   Answers: Fine; normal

  ○   *"What do you think (names of coaches) thought of me?"*

  ■   Answers: Not much; didn't notice you

  ○   *"Are (names of coaches) going to want to talk to me again?"*

  ■   Answer: Not sure; maybe

- Ask the behavioral coaches the same *Perspective Taking Questions*:

  ○   *"What was that like for you?"*
  ○   *"What did you think of me?"*
  ○   *"Would you want to talk to me again?"*

Steps for Exiting Conversations when Initially Accepted and then Excluded

- Explain, *"In some cases, we may have been initially accepted into a conversation, but then something happens to shut us out of the conversation, like we've been excluded. For example, you may have joined a conversation and initially the group spoke to you, but then you notice that they've closed the circle, are ignoring your comments, and are no longer talking to you or looking at you. In this case, leaving without saying anything would seem awkward, so we have different steps for exiting these kinds of conversations."*

[Present the steps for *exiting a conversation when initially accepted and then excluded* by writing the following buzzwords (**bold and italicized**) on the board. Do not erase the steps until the end of the lesson.]

1. *Keep your cool*

   a.   Explain, *"The first step for exiting a conversation when you are initially accepted and then excluded is to keep your cool. Just like before, you need to stay calm and not get upset."*
   b.   Ask, *"What could be the problem with getting upset?"*

   i.   Answer: They may think you are weird, they will be less likely to want to talk to you in the future, they may tell other teens about your reaction which could give you a bad reputation

2. *Look away*

   a. Explain, *"The next step is to slowly look away as if you're distracted by something. Just like before, you could look to one side or the other, or look at a personal item like a mobile phone."*

   b. Ask, *"What does it tell the group when you start to look away?"*

      i. Answer: Your attention is now somewhere else, you're not interested in what they're talking about anymore

3. *Wait for a brief pause*

   a. Explain, *"The next step is to wait for a pause in the conversation before you say anything. Just like with entering a conversation, there's never a perfect pause, so just try not to interrupt too much."*

   b. Ask, *"Why would you need to wait for a pause before saying anything?"*

      i. Answer: They might be annoyed if you interrupted them

4. *Give a brief cover story for leaving*

   a. Explain, *"The next step is to give a brief cover story for leaving the conversation. Remember, cover stories are reasons you have to do something. Some examples in this case are . . ."*

      i. *"Well, gotta go."*
      ii. *"I'd better go."*
      iii. *"Take care."*
      iv. *"See you later."*

   b. Explain, *"In this case, cover stories need to be VERY BRIEF. The reality is that they're done talking to you, so they're not really that concerned with where you're going."*

   c. Ask, *"Why do we need to give a cover story before leaving?"*

      i. Answer: Even though they're done talking to you, if you don't give some acknowledgement that you're leaving, it will seem weird

5. *Walk away*

   a. Explain, *"The last step for exiting a conversation when initially accepted and then excluded is to walk away."*

   b. Ask, *"Should we wait for them to make some kind of reply to our cover story before we walk away?"*

      i. Answer: No, after you've **given a brief cover story**, don't wait for the group to respond, just casually and calmly walk away

Role-Play: Exiting a Conversation when Initially Accepted and then Excluded

[The instructor and two behavioral coaches should do an APPROPRIATE role-play with the instructor **joining a group conversation** appropriately and **exiting the conversation** appropriately.]

- Begin by saying, *"We're going to do another role-play. Watch this and tell me what I'm doing RIGHT."*

Example of an APPROPRIATE role-play:

- Instructor: (Standing several feet away, looking at a cell phone)
- Coach 1: *"Hi (insert name). How've you been doing?"*
- Coach 2: *"I've been pretty good. How about you?"*
- Coach 1: *"I'm good. Hey, didn't you tell me you like comic books? Did you go to that big comic book convention last weekend?"*
- Instructor: (Looks over briefly, smiles slightly)
- Coach 2: *"Yeah, I went on Saturday! It was great! Did you go?"*
- Coach 1: *"I had other plans, but I was thinking about going to the next one."*
- Instructor: (Looks over again)
- Coach 2: *"Well, if you do go, let me know because I want to go again."*
- Coach 1: *"Definitely. I'll let you know. That would be fun!"*
- Instructor: (Moves closer, waits for a pause, looks at Coach 2): *"So you went to the comic book convention?"*
- Coach 2: (Looks over, turns toward instructor) *"Yeah."*
- Instructor: *"I love comic books. I really wanted to go to that convention."*
- Coach 2: *"Oh, you should have. It was cool."*
- Instructor: *"So where was it?"*
- Coach 2: *"It was downtown."* (Looks away, turns away, starts to close the circle)
- Coach 1: (Turned away from instructor) *"So anyway, when is the next one?"*
- Instructor: (Begins to look away)
- Coach 2: *"I'm not sure, but I think it's next month."*
- Coach 1: *"We should figure out when it is and get tickets."*
- Instructor: (Waits for a brief pause) *"Well, see you later."* (Starts to walk away)
- Coaches 1 and 2: (Casually look over) *"Yeah. See ya."*

- End by saying, *"Time out on that. So what did I do RIGHT in JOINING that conversation?"*
  - Answer: **Listened and watched, used a prop, identified the topic, found a common interest, moved closer, waited for a pause, mentioned the topic**

- Ask, *"Did it seem like they wanted to talk to me?"*
  - Answer: At first, but then they pushed you out of the conversation

- Ask, *"How could you tell?"*
  - Answer: **Stopped talking to you, stopped looking at you, closed the circle**

- Ask, *"What did I do RIGHT in exiting that conversation?"*
  - Answer: **Kept your cool, looked away, waited for a pause, gave a brief cover story, walked away**

- Ask the following *Perspective Taking Questions*:

- ○ *"What was that like for (names of coaches)?"*
  - ■ Answers: Fine; normal
- ○ *"What do you think (names of coaches) thought of me?"*
  - ■ Answers: Not much; normal
- ○ *"Are (names of coaches) going to want to talk to me again?"*
  - ■ Answer: Maybe
- Ask the behavioral coaches the same *Perspective Taking Questions*:
  - ○ *"What was that like for you?"*
  - ○ *"What did you think of me?"*
  - ○ *"Would you want to talk to me again?"*

Exiting Conversations when Fully Accepted

- Say, *"Sometimes we have to exit conversations even when we've been fully accepted. Just like when we're not accepted, there are specific steps we need to follow."*

[The instructor and two behavioral coaches should do an INAPPROPRIATE role-play with the instructor *exiting a conversation* inappropriately.]

- Begin by saying, *"Watch this role-play and tell me what I'm doing WRONG."*

    Example of an INAPPROPRIATE role-play:

    - ■ Coach 1 and 2, and Instructor: (Standing around and talking)
    - ■ Instructor: *"So what did you guys do this weekend?"*
    - ■ Coach 1: *"I actually went and saw that new sci-fi movie. I forget what it's called."*
    - ■ Coach 2: *"That fantasy sci-fi one that's in the theatres right now and just came out on Friday?"*
    - ■ Coach 1: *"Yeah. That's the one."*
    - ■ Coach 2: *"Oh, I want to see that."*
    - ■ Instructor: *"I know what you guys are talking about."*
    - ■ Coach 1: *"Did you see that one?"*
    - ■ Instructor: *"Yeah, I saw it last weekend too."*
    - ■ Coach 2: *"Oh, really. How was it?"*
    - ■ Coach 1: *"It was good. I liked it."* (Turns to Instructor) *"Did you like it?"*
    - ■ Instructor: *"Yeah, I thought it was really good actually."*
    - ■ Coach 2: *"I'm going to try to see it this weekend I think."*
    - ■ Coach 1: *"You really should. It's cool."*
    - ■ Instructor: *"It's really good. You should see it."*
    - ■ Coach 2: *"Awesome. I definitely will."*
    - ■ (Long pause)
    - ■ Instructor: (Looks awkward, abruptly walks away)
    - ■ Coach 1 and 2: (Shocked, confused, look at each other)

- Coach 2: (Confused) *"What was that all about?"*
- Coach 1: (Confused) *"I have no idea."*
- Coach 1 and 2: (Shake head in disbelief)

- End by saying, *"Time out on that. So what did I do WRONG in exiting that conversation?"*

  ○ Answer: You barged off for no reason

- Ask the following *Perspective Taking Questions*:

  ○ *"What was that like for (names of coaches)?"*

    - Answers: Confusing; surprising; shocking

  ○ *"What do you think (names of coaches) thought of me?"*

    - Answers: Rude; weird; odd

  ○ *"Are (names of coaches) going to want to talk to me again?"*

    - Answer: Not sure; maybe too weird

- Ask the behavioral coaches the same *Perspective Taking Questions*:

  ○ *"What was that like for you?"*
  ○ *"What did you think of me?"*
  ○ *"Would you want to talk to me again?"*

Steps for Exiting Conversations when Fully Accepted

- Explain, *"Instead of just walking away or barging off when we have to leave, we should follow the steps for exiting conversations when we've been fully accepted."*

[Present the steps for **exiting a conversation when fully accepted** by writing the following buzzwords (**bold and italicized**) on the board. Do not erase the steps until the end of the lesson.]

1. ***Wait for a brief pause***

   a. Explain, *"The first step for exiting a conversation when you've been fully accepted is to wait for a brief pause in the conversation before saying anything about leaving."*
   b. Ask, *"Why is it important to wait for a brief pause in the conversation before saying anything?"*

      i. Answer: It would be rude to interrupt someone unless it was urgent

2. ***Give a specific cover story for leaving***

   a. Explain, *"The next step is to give a SPECIFIC cover story for why you're leaving. In this case, because you've been fully accepted, your cover story will be specific and a little longer."*
   b. Ask, *"If you just said, 'Gotta go,' what do you think your friends are going to think?"*

    i.   Answer: Your friends may think you don't want to talk to them, or they may wonder where you're going, they may even ask *"Where are you going?"*

    c.   Explain, *"Instead, be more specific by saying something like, 'Well, I better get to class,' or 'I have to head home,' or 'My ride is here.' In this case, you need to give some SPECIFIC reason for why you have to leave so your friends won't be confused or offended."*

3. ***Say you'll see them later***

    a.   Explain, *"If you're planning on seeing your friends again, the next step usually involves saying something like, 'Talk to you later' or 'See you later'."*

    b.   Ask, *"Why would it be a good idea to say, 'Talk to you later' or 'See you later'?"*

        i.   Answer: It lets your friends know that you want to hang out again and that you're just leaving because you have to go, not because you want to go

4. ***Say goodbye***

    a.   Explain, *"As you're leaving, the next step is to say goodbye. Some people will also wave, give a hug or kiss, or give a fist bump or a pound."*

    b.   Ask, *"Why is it important to say goodbye before you leave?"*

        i.   Answer: It's polite and doesn't feel as abrupt as simply walking away without saying goodbye

5. ***Walk away***

    a.   Explain, *"The last step for exiting a conversation when you've been fully accepted is to walk away. In this case, if you've followed all the steps, walking away won't seem rude or abrupt to your friends."*

Role-Play: Exiting a Conversation when Fully Accepted

[The instructor and two behavioral coaches should do an APPROPRIATE role-play with the instructor ***exiting a conversation*** appropriately.]

- Begin by saying, *"Watch this role-play and tell me what I'm doing RIGHT."*

    Example of an APPROPRIATE role-play:

    ■ Coach 1 and 2, and Instructor: (Standing around and talking)
    ■ Instructor: *"So what did you guys do this weekend?"*
    ■ Coach 1: *"I actually went and saw that new sci-fi movie. I forget what it's called."*
    ■ Coach 2: *"That fantasy sci-fi one that's in the theatres right now and just came out on Friday?"*
    ■ Coach 1: *"Yeah. That's the one."*
    ■ Coach 2: *"Oh, I want to see that."*
    ■ Instructor: *"I know what you guys are talking about."*
    ■ Coach 1: *"Did you see that one?"*

- Instructor: *"Yeah, I saw it last weekend too."*
- Coach 2: *"Oh, really. How was it?"*
- Coach 1: *"It was good. I liked it."* (Turns to Instructor) *"Did you like it?"*
- Instructor: *"Yeah, I thought it was really good actually."*
- Coach 2: *"I'm going to try to see it this weekend I think."*
- Coach 1: *"You really should. It's cool."*
- Instructor: *"It's really good. You should see it."*
- Coach 2: *"Awesome. I definitely will."*
- Instructor: (Look away, waits for a pause) *"Hey guys, my ride's here, so I've got to get going."*
- Coach 2: *"Okay."*
- Coach 1: *"Alright."*
- Instructor: *"It was good talking to you guys."*
- Coach 1 and 2: *"You too."*
- Instructor: *"See you tomorrow."* (Waves, smiles, casually walks away)
- Coach 2: (Waves, smiles) *"Bye, see you."*
- Coach 1: (Waves, smiles) *"Bye."*

- End by saying, *"Time out on that. So what did I do RIGHT in exiting that conversation?"*
  - Answer: **Waited for a pause, gave a specific cover story, said see you later, said goodbye, walked away**

- Ask the following **Perspective Taking Questions**:
  - *"What was that like for (names of coaches)?"*
    - Answers: Fine; pleasant; normal; interesting
  - *"What do you think (names of coaches) thought of me?"*
    - Answers: Friendly; interesting; cool
  - *"Are (names of coaches) going to want to talk to me again?"*
    - Answers: Yes; definitely

- Ask the behavioral coaches the same **Perspective Taking Questions**:
  - *"What was that like for you?"*
  - *"What did you think of me?"*
  - *"Would you want to talk to me again?"*

Wrap Up

Say, *"So those are the steps for exiting conversations. Tomorrow we'll continue our discussion about exiting conversations, and we'll be practicing the steps for exiting conversations with our classmates."*

Calculate Points

Calculate the number of points earned by each teen (see Appendix E for the Daily Point Log):

- Do not publicly disclose the individual number of points

- Discourage attempts to compare number of points earned between teens

    o Remind them that they are working as a team to earn a bigger and better graduation party

Day Three: Lesson Review and Behavioral Rehearsal

Lesson Review: Exiting Conversations

Steps for Exiting Conversations when Never Accepted

- Say, *"Yesterday we talked about exiting conversations. Who can tell us the steps for exiting conversations when we're NEVER accepted?"*

[Have teens generate all of the steps for *exiting conversations*. Be prepared to give prompts if necessary. Write the following buzzwords (**bold and italicized**) on the board and do not erase until the end of the lesson.]

1. ***Keep your cool***
2. ***Look away***
3. ***Turn away***
4. ***Walk away***

Steps for Exiting Conversations when Initially Accepted and then Excluded

- Say, *"Who can tell us the steps for exiting conversations when we're INITIALLY ACCEPTED AND THEN EXCLUDED?"*

1. ***Keep your cool***
2. ***Look away***
3. ***Wait for a brief pause***
4. ***Give a brief cover story for leaving***
5. ***Walk away***

Steps for Exiting Conversations when Fully Accepted

- Say, *"Who can tell us the steps for exiting conversations when we're FULLY ACCEPTED?"*

1. ***Wait for a brief pause***
2. ***Give a specific cover story for leaving***
3. ***Say you'll see them later***
4. ***Say goodbye***
5. ***Walk away***

Role-Play: Exiting a Conversation when Never Accepted

[The instructor and two behavioral coaches should do an APPROPRIATE role-play with the instructor *joining a group conversation* appropriately and *exiting the conversation* appropriately.]

- Begin by saying, *"We're going to do a role-play of exiting a conversation when NEVER ACCEPTED. Watch this and tell me what I'm doing RIGHT."*

  Example of an APPROPRIATE role-play:

  - Instructor: (Standing several feet away, looking at a cell phone)
  - Coach 1: *"Hi (insert name). How've you been doing?"*
  - Coach 2: *"I've been pretty good. How about you?"*
  - Coach 1: *"I'm good. Hey, are you going to that music festival this weekend?"*
  - Instructor: (Looks over briefly, smiles slightly)
  - Coach 2: *"Yeah, I am! Are you going?"*
  - Coach 1: *"I was thinking about it."*
  - Instructor: (Looks over again)
  - Coach 2: *"You totally should. It's going to be so much fun!"*
  - Coach 1: *"I really want to. Do you think I can still get tickets?"*
  - Coach 2: *"I think so."*
  - Instructor: (Moves closer, waits for a pause) *"So are you guys going to the music festival?"*
  - Coach 1 and 2: (Ignoring, close the circle)
  - Coach 1: *"So it's not sold out?"*
  - Instructor: (Casually looks away)
  - Coach 2: *"No, I don't think so. I just got my tickets this morning."*
  - Instructor: (Casually turns away)
  - Coach 1: *"Oh really? I should definitely check that out."*
  - Instructor: (Slowly walks away in the direction looking and facing)
  - Coach 2: *"Well if you get tickets, definitely let me know. We can hang out."*
  - Coach 1: *"Of course. That would be so much fun!"*
  - Coaches 1 and 2: (Don't appear to notice that the instructor has left)

- End by saying, *"Time out on that. So what did I do RIGHT in JOINING that conversation?"*
  - Answer: **Listened and watched, used a prop, identified the topic, found a common interest, moved closer, waited for a pause, mentioned the topic**

- Ask, *"Did it seem like they wanted to talk to me?"*
  - Answer: No

- Ask, *"How could you tell?"*
  - Answer: **Didn't talk to you, didn't look at you, didn't face you (closed the circle)**

- Ask, *"What did I do RIGHT in exiting that conversation?"*

    o Answer: ***Kept your cool, looked away, turned away, walked away***

- Ask the following *Perspective Taking Questions*:

    o *"What was that like for (names of coaches)?"*

        ▪ Answers: Fine; normal

    o *"What do you think (names of coaches) thought of me?"*

        ▪ Answers: Not much; didn't notice you

    o *"Are (names of coaches) going to want to talk to me again?"*

        ▪ Answer: Not sure; maybe

- Ask the behavioral coaches the same *Perspective Taking Questions*:

    o *"What was that like for you?"*
    o *"What did you think of me?"*
    o *"Would you want to talk to me again?"*

Behavioral Rehearsal: Exiting Conversations when Never Accepted

- Break teens up into small groups (no less than three teens per group)

    o Match girls with girls and boys with boys, whenever possible

- Have each teen practice *joining and exiting a group conversation*

    o Begin by separating the teen from the group and have him or her identify the steps for *joining group conversations*
    o Then have the teen practice using these steps by *joining a group conversation* with their peers who will already be *trading information* about their personal items
    o Remind the other teens that they should accept everyone into these conversations
    o Teens may need you to provide prompting for specific steps, such as:

        ▪ *"Do you know what they're talking about?"*
        ▪ *"Do you know anything about that subject?"*
        ▪ *"Do you want to use anything while you're listening?"*
        ▪ *"What are you waiting for before you join?"*
        ▪ *"Is there ever a PERFECT PAUSE?"*
        ▪ *"Do you want to move closer before you join?"*
        ▪ *"When you join, do you want to be on topic?"*

- In the event that a teen incorrectly attempts to join, call a *"time-out"* and use this teachable moment to gently point out the error, while providing feedback on how to attempt to join more appropriately

    o Have the teen try again until he or she is successful

- Once the teen has successfully *joined the conversation*, pull them out and say, *"That was great! Now imagine they NEVER ACCEPTED you into the conversation. What are the steps for exiting a conversation when you're NEVER ACCEPTED?"*

  ○ Have the teen verbally go over the steps for *exiting a conversation when never accepted* before they make the attempt to *exit the conversation* (they may need to look at the board at first)

- Then have the teen demonstrate how they would *exit the conversation if never accepted*

- In the event that a teen incorrectly exits, call a *"time-out"* and use this teachable moment to gently point out the error, while providing feedback on how to exit more appropriately

  ○ Have the teen try again until he or she is successful

- Once the teen has successfully *exited the conversation*, call a *"time-out"* and have the other teens applaud

  ○ Briefly point out the steps that the teen followed for *joining and exiting the group conversation*

- Each teen should practice at least once

- Give points for following the steps for *joining and exiting a group conversation*

Homework Assignments

- [Distribute the Parent Handout (found in the last section of this chapter) and inform teens that they should give this handout to their parents immediately.]

- Briefly explain the homework for the week by saying, *"We're going to continue to have you practice joining and exiting conversations this week."*

- Present the homework assignments for the coming week:

1. Practice *joining a group conversation* between at least two teens you feel comfortable with

   a. Before *joining*:

      i. Think of a place where you are likely to be accepted and you don't have a bad reputation

   b. During the conversation:

      i. Follow the steps for *joining a group conversation*
      ii. *Assess interest* and follow the steps for *exiting a conversation* if needed

   c. After *joining*:

      i. Parents and teen should discuss how the teen *joined and exited the group conversation* (if relevant)
      ii. Parents should help teen *troubleshoot* any problems that may have arisen

2. ***Enroll in extracurricular activities***

   a. Teens and parents should DISCUSS and DECIDE on extracurricular activities based on the teen's interests and BEGIN TO ENROLL in these activities

      i. Criteria for a good extracurricular activity:

         1. Meets weekly or at least every other week
         2. Age range of other teens includes the social age of the teen
         3. Activity includes informal time so that the teen can interact with others
         4. Activity starts within the next couple of weeks

   b. Teen should ***start an individual conversation*** with someone at this extracurricular activity

      a. ***Trade information*** and ***find common interests*** while having a ***two-way conversation***

3. ***Out-of-class call or video chat***

   a. Before the call:

      i. Choose someone the teen feels comfortable talking with around the same age

   b. During the call:

      i. Follow the steps for ***starting and ending phone calls***, including using ***cover stories***
      ii. Teens should ***trade information*** and have a ***two-way conversation*** on this phone call
      iii. Find a ***common interest*** to report back to the class

   c. After the call:

      i. Teens should discuss the call with their parent, identify ***common interests***, and ***troubleshoot*** any problems

4. Bring an inside game

   a. Bring an inside game to share with the class on **Wednesday, Thursday, and Friday of next week** (e.g., age appropriate board game, card game, etc.)
   b. Do not bring a solitary game (like a portable gaming device) or something that you are unwilling to share or are worried about breaking or losing

Wrap Up

Say, *"So those are your homework assignments for this week. Be sure to start working on these assignments right away. We'll be reviewing how they went at the beginning of next week. Tomorrow we'll continue our discussion about exiting conversations, and we'll be practicing exiting conversations with our classmates."*

Calculate Points

Calculate the number of points earned by each teen (see Appendix E for the Daily Point Log):

- Do not publicly disclose the individual number of points
- Discourage attempts to compare number of points earned between teens
  - Remind them that they are working as a team to earn a bigger and better graduation party

Day Four: Teen Activity—Joining and Exiting Conversations

Lesson Review: Exiting Conversations

Steps for Exiting Conversations when Never Accepted

- Say, *"This week we've been talking about exiting conversations. Who can tell us the steps for exiting conversations when we're NEVER accepted?"*

[Have teens generate all of the steps for *exiting conversations*. Be prepared to give prompts if necessary. Write the following buzzwords (**bold and italicized**) on the board and do not erase until the end of the lesson.]

1. *Keep your cool*
2. *Look away*
3. *Turn away*
4. *Walk away*

Steps for Exiting Conversations when Initially Accepted and then Excluded

- Say, *"Who can tell us the steps for exiting conversations when we're INITIALLY ACCEPTED AND THEN EXCLUDED?"*

1. *Keep your cool*
2. *Look away*
3. *Wait for a brief pause*
4. *Give a brief cover story for leaving*
5. *Walk away*

Steps for Exiting Conversations when Fully Accepted

- Say, *"Who can tell us the steps for exiting conversations when we're FULLY ACCEPTED?"*

1. *Wait for a brief pause*
2. *Give a specific cover story for leaving*
3. *Say you'll see them later*
4. *Say goodbye*
5. *Walk away*

Teen Activity: Exiting a Conversation when Initially Accepted and then Excluded

Materials Needed

- Teens bring personal items to *trade information* about

- If teens forget to bring personal items:

    ○ Cell phones with music and/or pictures may be used
    ○ T-shirts with logos of favorite pastimes are relevant
    ○ Teens can simply talk about their interests without personal items

Rules

- Break teens up into small groups (no less than three teens per group)

    ○ Match girls with girls and boys with boys, whenever possible

- Have teens practice *trading information* about their personal items while taking turns *joining and exiting a group conversation*

- For teens practicing *trading information about personal items:*

    ○ Encourage teens to identify *common interests* through *trading information*
    ○ Prompt teens to ask questions when appropriate

- For teens practicing *joining a group conversation*:

    ○ Separate the teen from the group and have him or her identify the *steps for joining group conversations*
    ○ Then have the teen practice using these steps by *joining a group conversation* with their peers in which the others will be *trading information* about their personal items
    ○ Remind the other teens that they should accept everyone into these conversations
    ○ Teens may need you to provide prompting for specific steps, such as:

        ▪ *"Do you know what they're talking about?"*
        ▪ *"Do you know anything about that topic?"*
        ▪ *"Do you want to use anything while you're listening?"*
        ▪ *"What are you waiting for before you join?"*
        ▪ *"Is there ever a PERFECT PAUSE?"*
        ▪ *"Do you want to move closer before you join?"*
        ▪ *"When you join, do you want to be on topic?"*

- In the event that a teen incorrectly *joins the group conversation*, call a *"time-out"* and use this teachable moment to gently point out the error, while providing feedback on how to attempt to join more appropriately

    ○ Have the teen try again until he or she is successful

- Once the teen has successfully *joined the conversation*, pull them out and say, *"That was great! Now imagine they INITIALLY ACCEPTED you into the conversation and then EXCLUDED you. What are the steps for exiting a conversation when you're INITIALLY ACCEPTED AND THEN EXCLUDED?"*

  - Have the teen verbally go over the steps for *exiting a conversation when initially accepted and then excluded* before they make the attempt to *exit the conversation* (they may need to look at the board at first)

- Then have the teen demonstrate how they would *exit a conversation when initially accepted and then excluded*

- In the event that a teen incorrectly exits, call a *"time-out"* and use this teachable moment to gently point out the error, while providing feedback on how to exit more appropriately

  - Have the teen try again until he or she is successful

- Once the teen has successfully *exited the conversation*, call a *"time-out"* and have the other teens applaud

  - Briefly point out the steps that the teen followed for *joining and exiting the group conversation*

- Each teen should practice at least once

- Give points for following the steps for *joining and exiting a group conversation*

Homework Assignments

- Briefly explain the homework for the week by saying, *"We're going to continue to have you practice joining and exiting conversations this week."*

- Present the homework assignments for the coming week:

1. Practice *joining a group conversation* between at least two teens you feel comfortable with

   a. Before *joining*:

      i. Think of a place where you are likely to be accepted and you don't have a bad reputation

   b. During the conversation:

      i. Follow the steps for *joining a group conversation*
      ii. *Assess interest* and follow the steps for *exiting a conversation* if needed

   c. After *joining*:

      i. Parents and teen should discuss how the teen *joined and exited the group conversation* (if relevant)
      ii. Parents should help teen *troubleshoot* any problems that may have arisen

2. *Enroll in extracurricular activities*

   a. Teens and parents should DISCUSS and DECIDE on extracurricular activities based on the teen's interests and BEGIN TO ENROLL in these activities

      i. Criteria for a good extracurricular activity:

         1. Meets weekly or at least every other week
         2. Age range of other teens includes the social age of the teen
         3. Activity includes informal time so that the teen can interact with others
         4. Activity starts within the next couple of weeks

   b. Teen should **start an individual conversation** with someone at this extracurricular activity

      i. **Trade information** and **find common interests** while having a **two-way conversation**

3. *Out-of-class call or video chat*

   a. Before the call:

      i. Choose someone the teen feels comfortable talking with around the same age

   b. During the call:

      i. Follow the steps for **starting and ending phone calls**, including using **cover stories**
      ii. Teens should **trade information** and have a **two-way conversation** on this phone call
      iii. Find a **common interest** to report back to the class

   c. After the call:

      i. Teens should discuss the call with their parent, identify **common interests**, and **troubleshoot** any problems

4. *Bring an inside game*

   a. Bring an inside game to share with the class on **Wednesday, Thursday, and Friday of next week** (e.g., age appropriate board game, card game, etc.)
   b. Do not bring a solitary game (like a portable gaming device) or something that you are unwilling to share or are worried about breaking or losing

Wrap Up

Say, *"So those are your homework assignments for this week. Be sure to start working on these assignments right away. We'll be reviewing how they went at the beginning of next week."*

Calculate Points

Calculate the number of points earned by each teen (see Appendix E for the Daily Point Log):

- Do not publicly disclose the individual number of points

- Discourage attempts to compare number of points earned between teens

  - Remind them that they are working as a team to earn a bigger and better graduation party

Day Five: Teen Activity—Joining and Exiting Conversations

Lesson Review: Exiting Conversations

Steps for Exiting Conversations When Never Accepted

- Say, *"This week we've been talking about exiting conversations. Who can tell us the steps for exiting conversations when we're NEVER accepted?"*

[Have teens generate all of the steps for *exiting conversations*. Be prepared to give prompts if necessary. Write the following buzzwords (**bold and italicized**) on the board and do not erase until the end of the lesson.]

1. *Keep your cool*

2. *Look away*

3. *Turn away*

4. *Walk away*

Steps for Exiting Conversations When Initially Accepted and Then Excluded

- Say, *"Who can tell us the steps for exiting conversations when we're INITIALLY ACCEPTED AND THEN EXCLUDED?"*

1. *Keep your cool*

2. *Look away*

3. *Wait for a brief pause*

4. *Give a brief cover story for leaving*

5. *Walk away*

Steps for Exiting Conversations When Fully Accepted

- Say, *"Who can tell us the steps for exiting conversations when we're FULLY ACCEPTED?"*

1. *Wait for a brief pause*

2. *Give a specific cover story for leaving*

3. *Say you'll see them later*

4. *Say goodbye*

5. *Walk away*

Teen Activity: Exiting a Conversation When Fully Accepted

Materials Needed

- Teens bring personal items to *trade information* about

- If teens forget to bring personal items:

  - Cell phones with music and/or pictures may be used
  - T-shirts with logos of favorite pastimes are relevant
  - Teens can simply talk about their interests without personal items

Rules

- Break teens up into small groups (no less than three teens per group)

  - Match girls with girls and boys with boys, whenever possible

- Have teens practice *trading information* about their personal items while taking turns *joining and exiting a group conversation*

- For teens practicing *trading information about personal items*:

  - Encourage teens to identify *common interests* through *trading information*
  - Prompt teens to ask questions when appropriate

- For teens practicing *joining a group conversation*:

  - Separate the teen from the group and have him or her identify the *steps for joining group conversations*
  - Then have the teen practice using these steps by *joining a group conversation* with their peers in which the others will be *trading information* about their personal items
  - Remind the other teens that they should accept everyone into these conversations
  - Teens may need you to provide prompting for specific steps, such as:

    - *"Do you know what they're talking about?"*
    - *"Do you know anything about that topic?"*
    - *"Do you want to use anything while you're listening?"*
    - *"What are you waiting for before you join?"*
    - *"Is there ever a PERFECT PAUSE?"*
    - *"Do you want to move closer before you join?"*
    - *"When you join, do you want to be on topic?"*

- In the event that a teen incorrectly *joins the group conversation*, call a *"time-out"* and use this teachable moment to gently point out the error, while providing feedback on how to attempt to join more appropriately

  - Have the teen try again until he or she is successful

- Once the teen has successfully *joined the conversation*, pull them out and say, *"That was great! Now imagine that you've been FULLY ACCEPTED into the conversation, but you have to leave. What are the steps for exiting a conversation when you're FULLY ACCEPTED?"*

  o Have the teen verbally go over the steps for *exiting a conversation when fully accepted* before they make the attempt to *exit the conversation* (they may need to look at the board at first)

- Then have the teen demonstrate how they would *exit a conversation when fully accepted*

- In the event that a teen incorrectly exits, call a *"time-out"* and use this teachable moment to gently point out the error, while providing feedback on how to exit more appropriately

  o Have the teen try again until he or she is successful

- Once the teen has successfully *exited the conversation*, call a *"time-out"* and have the other teens applaud

  o Briefly point out the steps that the teen followed for *joining and exiting the group conversation*

- Each teen should practice at least once

- Give points for following the steps for *joining and exiting a group conversation*

Homework Assignments

- Briefly explain the homework for the week by saying, *"We're going to continue to have you practice joining and exiting conversations this week."*

- Present the homework assignments for the coming week:

  1. Practice *joining a group conversation* between at least two teens you feel comfortable with

     a. Before *joining*:

        i. Think of a place where you are likely to be accepted and you don't have a bad reputation

     b. During the conversation:

        i. Follow the steps for *joining a group conversation*
        ii. *Assess interest* and follow the steps for *exiting a conversation* if needed

     c. After *joining*:

        i. Parents and teen should discuss how the teen *joined and exited the group conversation* (if relevant)
        ii. Parents should help teen *troubleshoot* any problems that may have arisen

  2. *Enroll in extracurricular activities*

     a. Teens and parents should DISCUSS and DECIDE on extracurricular activities based on the teen's interests and BEGIN TO ENROLL in these activities

    i.   Criteria for a good extracurricular activity:

        1.   Meets weekly or at least every other week
        2.   Age range of other teens includes the social age of the teen
        3.   Activity includes informal time so that the teen can interact with others
        4.   Activity starts within the next couple of weeks

  b. Teen should **start an individual conversation** with someone at this extracurricular activity

    i.   **Trade information** and **find common interests** while having a **two-way conversation**

3. ***Out-of-class call or video chat***

  a. Before the call:

    i.   Choose someone the teen feels comfortable talking with around the same age

  b. During the call:

    i.   Follow the steps for **starting and ending phone calls**, including using **cover stories**
    ii. Teens should **trade information** and have a **two-way conversation** on this phone call
    iii. Find a **common interest** to report back to the class

  c. After the call:

    i.   Teens should discuss the call with their parent, identify **common interests**, and **troubleshoot** any problems

4. ***Bring an inside game***

  a. Bring an inside game to share with the class on **Wednesday, Thursday, and Friday of next week** (e.g., age appropriate board game, card game, etc.)
  b. Do not bring a solitary game (like a portable gaming device) or something that you are unwilling to share or are worried about breaking or losing

Wrap Up

Say, *"So those are your homework assignments for this week. Be sure to start working on these assignments right away. We'll be reviewing how they went at the beginning of next week."*

Calculate Points

Calculate the number of points earned by each teen (see Appendix E for the Daily Point Log):

- Do not publicly disclose the individual number of points

- Discourage attempts to compare number of points earned between teens

  - Remind them that they are working as a team to earn a bigger and better graduation party

Parent Handout 7

PEERS® *Program for the Education and Enrichment of Relational Skills*

Exiting Conversations

This week your teens will be learning how to *exit conversations* in which they are not accepted. Approximately 50 percent of attempts to *join conversations* are unsuccessful. It will be helpful for you to normalize this for your teen, to help him or her understand that it is not a big deal, does not have to be taken personally, and that he or she should not give up trying in the future.

Questions to Ask when Assessing Interest

Review from last week:

1. *Are they talking to me?*

2. *Are they looking at me?*

3. *Are they facing me?*

    a. When people talk in groups, they talk in circles
    b. When they accept you in the conversation, they *open the circle*
    c. When they don't accept you in the conversation, they *close the circle*

Reasons for Being Turned Down in Conversations

Reasons for Being Turned Down	*What to Do Differently Next Time*
They want to talk privately	Try again later and listen before you join
They are stuck up or mean	Try a different group
You broke one of the rules for joining	Try again later, following the steps
You got too personal	Try a different group, don't get too personal
They are in a clique and don't want to make new friends	Try a different group
They are talking about something you do not know about	Try a different group that is talking about something you know
You have a bad reputation with them	Try a different group that does not know or care about your reputation
They did not understand that you were trying to join	Try again later, following the steps

Steps for Exiting Conversations when Never Accepted

1. *Keep your cool*

2. *Look away*

3. *Turn away*

4. *Walk away*

Steps for Exiting Conversation when Initially Accepted and then Excluded

1. *Keep your cool*

2. *Look away*

3. *Wait for a brief pause*

4. *Give a brief cover story for leaving*

   a. Examples:

      i.   *"Well, gotta go."*
      ii. *"I'd better go."*
      iii. *"Take care."*
      iv. *"See you later."*

5. *Walk away*

Steps for Exiting Conversations when Fully Accepted

1. *Wait for a brief pause*

2. *Give a specific cover story for leaving*

   a. Examples:

      i.   *"Well, I better get to class."*
      ii. *"I have to head home."*
      iii. *"My ride is here."*

3. *Say you'll see them later*

4. *Say goodbye*

5. *Walk away*

Homework Assignments

Every week your teen will have homework assignments to practice new and previously learned social skills. It is extremely helpful if parents assist teens in completing these assignments. The homework assignments for this week include the following:

1. Practice *joining a group conversation* between at least two teens you feel comfortable with

   a. Before *joining*:

  i. Teen should think of a place where he or she is likely to be accepted and doesn't have a bad reputation

 b. During the conversation:

  i. Follow the steps for *joining a group conversation*

  ii. *Assess interest* and follow the steps for *exiting a conversation* if needed

 c. After *joining*:

  i. Parents and teen should discuss how the teen *joined and exited the group conversation* (if relevant)

  ii. Parents should help teen *troubleshoot* any problems that may have arisen

2. *Enroll in extracurricular activities*

 a. Teens and parents should DISCUSS and DECIDE on extracurricular activities based on the teen's interests and BEGIN TO ENROLL in these activities

  i. Criteria for a good extracurricular activity:

   1. Meets weekly or at least every other week
   2. Age range of other teens includes the social age of the teen
   3. Activity includes informal time so that the teen can interact with others
   4. Activity starts within the next couple of weeks

 b. Teen should *start an individual conversation* with someone at this extracurricular activity

  i. *Trade information* and *find common interests* while having a *two-way conversation*

3. *Out-of-class call or video chat*

 a. Before the call:

  i. Choose someone the teen feels comfortable talking with around the same age

 b. During the call:

  i. Follow the steps for *starting and ending phone calls*, including using *cover stories*
  ii. Teens should *trade information* and have a *two-way conversation* on this phone call
  iii. Find a *common interest* to report back to the class

 c. After the call:

  i. Teens should discuss the call with their parent, identify *common interests*, and *troubleshoot* any problems

4. *Bring an inside game*

 a. Bring an inside game to share with the class on **Wednesday, Thursday, and Friday of next week** (e.g., age appropriate board game, card game, etc.)

 b. Do not bring a solitary game (like a portable gaming device) or something that you are unwilling to share or are worried about breaking or losing

WEEK 8

GOOD SPORTSMANSHIP

Preparing for the Lesson

The content of this lesson is concerned with rules for *good sportsmanship*. Since common activities for teens during get-togethers and other peer social interactions include the playing of games, videogames, and sports (particularly for boys), it is essential that teens know how to interact harmoniously during these activities.

Individuals with social difficulties have been shown to have different priorities in their social goals when compared to individuals without social problems, particularly when it comes to playing games and sports. Research has found that children and teens with social difficulties tend to focus more on obtaining tangible rewards and less on relationship enhancing. Many teens will be accustomed to thinking of winning being the ultimate goal in game playing and sports. Although they may also want to be liked by others, they frequently set *good sportsmanship* at a low priority. It will be your responsibility to challenge these priorities by pointing out that *if our goal is to make and keep friends, then our goal during games and sports should be to make sure everyone is having a good time.*

The rules for *good sportsmanship* are based heavily upon *ecologically valid social skills* used by socially successful teens, as well as rules addressing common social errors often committed by teens with Autism Spectrum Disorder (ASD). One of the more common social errors committed by teens with ASD is the tendency to enforce rules and *police* others during play. Week 2 of PEERS® introduced the *no policing* rule to teens in the context of having *two-way conversations*. This same tendency to point out mistakes, which appears to be a product of excessive rule-following, may also make an appearance in game playing. Within the context of games and sports, we refer to this tendency as either *refereeing* or *coaching*. Both involve the act of pointing out mistakes, but are slightly different with regard to *intent*. Consider the roles of both *referees* and *coaches* in games and sports. The job of a *referee* is to enforce rules, point out rule violations, and make sure everyone is playing fairly. The job of a *coach* is to help the players play better by offering suggestions and guidance. Although these two roles are similar, the intent is somewhat different. Referees intend to enforce rules, while coaches intend to help others. While both of these roles are important in organized sports, *refereeing* or *coaching* other players during recreational activities (when the goal is to simply have fun) is not a good way to make and keep friends.

Just presenting the rules for *good sportsmanship* to teens has no evidential basis for promoting generalization of these skills. Instead, reinforcing *good sportsmanship* by teens during in-class games and outdoor sports activities will promote the use of this important social skill. Behavioral coaching with a points system (or "token economy") is the optimal intervention in this case. This involves: (1) intervening during teachable moments to point out *good sportsmanship* rule violations, and (2) reinforcing the use of *good sportsmanship* during game playing using a token economy.

When intervening during teachable moments, you will want to pull teens aside when you see *good sport* violations and remind teens about appropriate good sportsmanship behavior. You will do this by asking questions like, *"What could be the problem with hogging the ball?," "What could be the problem with refereeing others?,"* or *"What could be the problem with coaching others?"* Gently pointing out these social errors during teachable moments will help teens to apply these skills in more natural settings.

Reinforcing the use of good sportsmanship by teens will involve rewarding them with points when you see instances of good sportsmanship during game playing with classmates. This will occur in the context of the behavioral rehearsal exercise on Day Three and the teen activity on Days Four and Five. To prepare for these exercises, you will need to ensure that you and each of your coaches has a Good Sportsmanship Point Log (Appendix F) to track the distribution of points. Teens will be receiving points for good sportsmanship (equivalent to what they have been earning for participation and completing homework assignments) while playing games and sports. Just like the points they are earning in class, these points should be earned toward graduation prizes and the graduation party in week 16. You will provide points on a *continuous reinforcement schedule* for the first few weeks of good sportsmanship practice (i.e., give a point during every instance of good sportsmanship), and eventually fade into providing points on an *intermittent reinforcement schedule* in the last few weeks of the program (i.e., give points intermittently for good sportsmanship, while providing verbal praise in the absence of points).

Teens should receive points for behaviors such as: *praising, following the rules, not refereeing, not coaching, sharing and taking turns, not being competitive, suggesting a change if bored, helping and showing concern when someone is injured, not being a bad winner, not being a sore loser,* and *saying "good game" at the end of the game.* The manner in which you provide points will be critical to the success of the reinforcement. This involves stating why the teen is receiving a point in a very specific way. You will do this by saying something like, *"Jimmy gets a point for being a good sport!"* Notice that the order includes: (1) saying the teen's name first to get his or her attention, (2) stating what the reward is (i.e., getting a point), and (3) stating the reason for the reward (i.e., being a *good sport*). Examples include: *"Jimmy gets a point for saying 'good job'!," "Jenny gets a point for taking turns!," "Johnny gets a point for giving a high five!," "Julie gets a point for saying 'good game'!,"* or *"Joey gets a point for praising!"*

When giving out points, make sure that you speak loudly enough so that the other teens can hear. The social comparison will encourage and prompt other teens to *praise* and be *good sports*. Be sure to keep track of points on the Good Sportsmanship Point Log (Appendix F) throughout every behavioral rehearsal exercise and teen activity. Also be aware that in order to practice good sportsmanship during these exercises, you are asking teens to bring inside games to play three days this week, on Wednesday, Thursday, and Friday (Days Three, Four, and Five).

Day One: Homework Review

Homework Review

[Start with completed homework first. If you have time, you can inquire as to why others were unable to complete the assignment and try to *troubleshoot* how they might get it done for the coming week. When reviewing homework, be sure to use the buzzwords (***bold and italicized***) and *troubleshoot* issues that come up. Spend the majority of the homework review on ***joining a group conversation***, extracurricular activities, and the ***out-of-class call***, as these were the most important assignments.]

[Note: Give multiple points for homework parts—not just one point per assignment.]

1. *Joining a group conversation*

    a. Say, *"Last week we went over the steps for joining and exiting conversations. One of your assignments this week was to practice joining a conversation with a group that you were likely to be accepted by. Raise your hand if you practiced joining a group conversation this week."*

        i. Ask, *"Where did you join?"*
        ii. Ask, *"How did you join?"*

            1. Be sure they followed the ***steps for joining a group conversation***:

                a. ***Listen to the conversation***
                b. ***Watch from a distance***
                c. ***Use a prop***
                d. ***Identify the topic***
                e. ***Find a common interest***
                f. ***Move closer***
                g. ***Wait for a pause***
                h. ***Mention the topic***
                i. ***Assess interest***
                j. ***Introduce yourself*** (if appropriate)

        iii. Ask, *"Did it seem like they wanted to talk to you?"*

            1. Ask, *"How could you tell?"*

                a. ***Talking to you***
                b. ***Looking at you***
                c. ***Facing you (opened the circle)***

        iv. Ask, *"Did you need to exit the conversation?"*

            1. If they ***exited the conversation***, be sure they followed the steps based on whether they were ***never accepted, initially accepted and then excluded***, or ***fully accepted***

2. *Enroll in extracurricular activities*

   a. Say, *"Another assignment was that you and your parents were supposed to identify an extracurricular activity for you to join where you might meet other teens with common interests and then begin to enroll in those activities. Raise your hand if you found an extracurricular activity."*

      i. Ask, *"Which extracurricular activity did you choose?"*
      ii. Ask, *"Did you enroll in the activity?"*
      iii. Ask, *"Are there other teens your age in the group?'*
      iv. Ask, *"How often does it meet?"*
      v. Ask, *"Does this seem like a good place for you to make potential new friends?"*

   b. Say, *"You were also supposed to follow the steps for starting a conversation with someone from this extracurricular activity. Raise your hand if you started a conversation with someone from your extracurricular activity?"*

      i. Ask, *"Who did you start the conversation with?"*
      ii. Ask, *"How did you start the conversation?"*

         1. Be sure they followed the *steps for starting an individual conversation*:

            a. *Casually look over*
            b. *Use a prop*
            c. *Find a common interest*
            d. *Mention the common interest*
            e. *Trade information*
            f. *Assess interest*
            g. *Introduce yourself* (if appropriate)

      iii. Ask, *"Did it seem like they wanted to talk to you?"*

         1. Ask, *"How could you tell?"*

            a. *Talking to you*
            b. *Looking at you*
            c. *Facing you*

3. *Out-of-class call or video chat*

   a. Say, *"Another assignment this week was to trade information and have a two-way conversation with someone not in this class over the phone or video chat. Raise your hand if you did the out-of-class call."*

      i. Ask, *"Who did you talk to?"*
      ii. Ask, *"How did the conversation begin?"*

         a. Have teens identify all the relevant steps (if a phone call):

            1. *Ask for the person you are calling*
            2. *Say who you are*
            3. *Ask how they are*
            4. *Ask if they can talk*
            5. *Give a cover story for why you are calling*

iii. Ask, *"Did you trade information?"*

iv. Ask, *"Did you find a common interest?"*

    a. When they identify common interests ask, *"What could you do with that information if you were going to hang out?"*

v. Ask, *"How did the conversation end?"*

    a. Have teens identify all the relevant steps (if a phone call):

        1. **Wait for a bit of a pause**
        2. **Give a cover story for why you have to go**
        3. **Tell the person it was nice talking**
        4. **Tell the person you will talk to them later**
        5. **Say goodbye**

vi. Avoid general questions like, *"How did it go?"*

4. **Bring an inside game**

    a. Identify the inside game the teen will bring to share with the class later in the week (e.g., age appropriate board game, card game, etc.)

Wrap Up

Say, *"Good work for those of you who completed your homework assignments. Tomorrow we'll be talking about good sportsmanship."*

Calculate Points

Calculate the number of points earned by each teen (see Appendix E for the Daily Point Log):

- Do not publicly disclose the individual number of points

- Discourage attempts to compare number of points earned between teens

    ○ Remind them that they are working as a team to earn a bigger and better graduation party

Day Two: Didactic Lesson—Good Sportsmanship

Didactic Lesson: Good Sportsmanship

- Explain, *"Today we're going to talk about good sportsmanship. Good sportsmanship is an important part of making and keeping friends because a lot of teens socialize around playing games and sports."*

- Ask, *"What is the most important goal when you're playing games and sports with friends?"*

  - Answer: That everyone has a good time

- Explain, *"So if our goal is to make and keep friends, then when we play sports, videogames, or other games, we need to be good sports."*

- Ask, *"Why is it important to be a good sport?"*

  - Answer: It is more fun for everyone

- Ask, *"What could be the problem with being a poor sport when playing games or sports?"*

  - Answer: Our friends won't want to play with us, we may get a bad reputation

[Present the ***rules of good sportsmanship*** by writing the following buzzwords (***bold and italicized***) on the board. Do not erase the rules until the end of the lesson.]

- ***Praise* your friend**

  - Say, *"One of the most important parts of being a good sport is to give praise. Who can tell us what praise is?"*

    - Answer: Praise is a kind of compliment

  - Ask, *"Why is it important to praise your friend when you're playing games or sports?"*

    - Answer: It makes them feel good, shows that you are a ***good sport***

  - Ask, *"What are some examples of praise you could give during a game?"*

    - Answers:

      - *"Nice move!"*
      - *"Nice try."*
      - *"Great shot!"*
      - *"Good job!"*
      - High five
      - Thumbs up
      - Pound or fist bump (bump closed fists)
      - Clapping

  - Explain, *"Praising a friend by saying 'good job' or 'nice shot' is a simple way to ensure that your friend has a nice time and that the game remains fun."*

- *Play by the rules*

    - Explain, *"Another important rule of good sportsmanship is to play by the rules. This means you shouldn't cheat or try to make up different rules in the middle of a game, which could be seen as cheating."*
    - Ask, *"What could be the problem with cheating or not playing by the rules?"*

        - Answer: If you do this enough times, you could get a bad reputation and fewer people will want to play games and sports with you

- *Don't be a referee*

    - Say, *"Another rule for being a good sport is don't be a referee. What is a referee?"*

        - Answer: Someone who calls plays during a game, points out rule violations, enforces the rules of a game

    - Ask, *"What could be the problem with acting like a referee during a game?"*

        - Answer: Teens don't like to hang out with people who boss them around

    - Ask, *"So what do you do if your friends don't play by the rules and it really bothers you?"*

        - Answer: It's not your business to **referee** them, just **go with the flow in the moment**, remember that **friendship is a choice, you don't have to be friends with everyone and everyone doesn't have to be friends with you**, and if it bothers you that much, you don't have to hang out with them

- *Don't be a coach*

    - Explain, *"It's also important that when we're trying to be a good sport that we don't coach other players. Some kids try to be helpful and give advice during a game, the way that a coach might."*
    - Ask, *"What could be the problem with coaching your friends?"*

        - Answer: Teens don't like to hang out with other teens who tell them what to do, you will seem bossy and controlling, they may think you're a know-it-all

    - Explain, *"Even though you may only be trying to help, it may seem like you're being bossy. So unless your friend asks, don't try to help by giving advice."*
    - Say, *"For example, if you see your friend struggling with a videogame that you're really good at, what could you offer to do instead of coaching?"*

        - Answer: You can offer to help by saying something like, *"Would you like me to show you how to get to the next level?"*

    - Ask, *"If your friend doesn't want your help, what should you do?"*

        - Answer: **Don't be a coach**, stop giving advice, they may find it obnoxious and annoying, you may seem bossy and controlling

- *Share and take turns*

    - Say, *"Another rule for being a good sport is to share and take turns. This is the opposite of being a ball hog or someone who doesn't share the controller."*

- Ask, *"What is a 'ball hog'?"*
    - Answer: Someone who doesn't share the ball or take turns
- Ask, *"What could be the problem with being a 'ball hog' or not taking turns during a game?"*
    - Answer: No one will want to play with you, it's not fun for other people
- Ask, *"What could be the problem with hogging the controller when you're playing a videogame?"*
    - Answer: No one will want to play with you; it's not fun for other people
- Ask, *"What should you do instead of hogging the ball or not sharing the controller?"*
    - Answer: **Share and take turns**
- Ask, *"Why is it important to share and take turns?"*
    - Answer: Then it will be fun for everyone

- **Don't be competitive**
    - Explain, *"Another rule for being a good sport is don't be competitive. That means don't try to win at all costs."*
    - Ask, *"What could be the problem with being competitive when playing games and sports with friends?"*
        - Answer: It's not fun for the other people, you seem selfish and rude
    - Ask, *"What about organized sports? Is it okay to be competitive if you're playing in an organized team or league?"*
        - Answer: Yes, but you can still be a **good sport**
    - Ask, *"What is the purpose of games and sports with friends?"*
        - Answer: To have fun
    - Explain, *"Focusing on winning at all costs is not a good idea for developing friends. So if your goal is to make and keep friends, don't be competitive."*

- **Help and show concern if someone is injured** (outdoor sports)
    - Explain, *"Sometimes when we play physical sports, people can get hurt or injured. When that happens, it's important to help and show concern. That means if your friend falls down during a game, ask if they're okay and offer to help."*
    - Ask, *"What could be the problem with just walking by, not saying anything, not offering help, and not showing concern?"*
        - Answer: You'll look like you don't care, your friends may get upset with you, and you could get a bad reputation for being cold and uncaring

- **Suggest a change if bored**
    - Say, *"Sometimes people get bored with games and sports. What could you do if you get bored in the middle of a game?"*
        - Answer: Suggest playing something else, **suggest a change** in activity, ask if they want to do something else

- ○ Ask, *"What could be the problem with just walking away or saying 'I'm bored' in the middle of a game?"*

  - ■ Answer: It's rude, you might hurt the other person's feelings, you might look like a ***poor sport***, you could get a bad reputation for being rude

- ○ Ask, *"What could you say instead of saying 'I'm bored'?"*

  - ■ Answer: You could say:

    - • *"When we're done do you want to play something else?"*
    - • *"How about after this game we get something to eat?"*
    - • *"Do you want to do something else?"*

- ○ Ask, *"What if your friend doesn't want to do something else?"*

  - ■ Answer: Don't make a big deal out of it, just ***go with the flow in the moment***, remember that ***friendship is a choice***, if your friend never wants to do what you suggest you don't have to hang out with him or her

- • ***Don't be a bad winner***

  - ○ Say, *"Sometimes when people win games, they get really excited and they gloat. They might jump up and down, cheer for themselves, and do the 'end zone dance.' That's being a bad winner."*
  - ○ Ask, *"What could be the problem with gloating and being a bad winner?"*

    - ■ Answer: It makes the other person feel bad, it embarrasses the person who lost, they may not want to play with you again

  - ○ Ask, *"What should you do instead of being a bad winner?"*

    - ■ Answer: ***Act like winning wasn't a big deal***

- • ***Don't be a sore loser***

  - ○ Say, *"Another rule for being a good sport is to avoid sulking or getting angry if you lose. That's being a sore loser."*
  - ○ Ask, *"What could be the problem with sulking, getting angry, and being a sore loser?"*

    - ■ Answer: It makes you look like a ***poor sport***, it takes away the enjoyment of winning for the other person, they may not want to play with you again

  - ○ Ask, *"What should you do instead of being a sore loser?"*

    - ■ Answer: ***Act like losing wasn't a big deal***

- • ***At the end of a game say "good game"***

  - ○ Say, *"The final rule for being a good sport relates to what we should do at the end of the game. What should you say and do at the end of a game?"*

    - ■ Answer: ***Say "good game,"*** give a high five, give a pound or fist bump

  - ○ Ask, *"Why is it important to say 'good game' at the end of a game?"*

    - ■ It shows that you're a ***good sport***, it makes the other person feel good

Wrap Up

Say, *"So those are the rules for being a good sport. Tomorrow we'll continue our discussion about good sportsmanship and practice being good sports with our classmates."*

Calculate Points

Calculate the number of points earned by each teen (see Appendix E for the Daily Point Log):

- Do not publicly disclose the individual number of points
- Discourage attempts to compare number of points earned between teens
  - Remind them that they are working as a team to earn a bigger and better graduation party

Day Three: Lesson Review and Behavioral Rehearsal

Lesson Review: Good Sportsmanship

• Say, *"Yesterday we went over the rules for being a good sport. Who can tell me some of the rules for being a good sport?"*

[Have teens generate all of the rules for **good sportsmanship**. Be prepared to give prompts if necessary. Write the following buzzwords (**bold and italicized**) on the board and do not erase until the end of the lesson.]

- ○ *Praise*
  - ▪ Examples:
    - • *"Nice move!"*
    - • *"Nice try."*
    - • *"Great shot!"*
    - • *"Good job!"*
    - • High five
    - • Thumbs up
    - • Pound or fist bump (bump closed fists)
    - • Clapping

- ○ *Play by the rules*

- ○ *Don't be a referee*

- ○ *Don't be a coach*

- ○ *Share and take turns*
  - ▪ *Don't be a ball hog*
  - ▪ *Share the controller*

- ○ *Don't be competitive*

- ○ *Help and show concern if someone is injured* (outdoor sports)

- ○ *Suggest a change if bored*

- ○ *Don't be a bad winner*

- ○ *Don't be a sore loser*

- ○ *At the end of a game say "good game"*

Behavioral Rehearsal: Good Sportsmanship

Materials Needed

- Indoor games brought by teens

- In the event that teens forget to bring indoor games, have board games and card games available to use if possible

Rules

- Notify teens they will be practicing *good sportsmanship*

- Break teens up into dyads

  - If there is an uneven number of teens, create one triad

- When possible, girls should be paired with girls and boys should be paired with boys

- Teens will then play indoor games while practicing *good sportsmanship*

- Games are chosen from appropriate *inside games* brought by teens and other available games provided by the instructor

  - Have teens negotiate what they will play

    - They may need to compromise by playing one game for half the time and then switching games midway

  - You may need to assist teens in understanding the rules for specific games

    - Try to avoid acting as a referee if disagreements occur
    - Encourage teens to work out their differences by being *good sports*

  - You may need to prompt teens to be *good sports* and *praise* their partners, saying things like:

    - *"Johnny just made a nice move, what could you say?"*
    - *"Jenny got a lucky hand, what could you say?"*
    - *"What do we say at the end of the game?"*

- Teens receive points while playing games for practicing:

  - *Praising*
  - *Playing by the rules*
  - *Not refereeing*
  - *Not coaching*
  - *Sharing and taking turns*
  - *Not being competitive*
  - *Helping and showing concern if someone is injured* (outdoor sports)
  - *Suggesting a change if bored*
  - *Not being a bad winner*
  - *Not being a sore loser*
  - *Saying "good game" at the end of the game*

- When giving points:
  - ○ Say the teen's name first to get his or her attention
  - ○ State what the reward is (i.e., getting a point)
  - ○ Give the reason for the reward (i.e., being a **good sport**)
    - ■ Examples:
      - • *"Jimmy gets a point for saying 'good job'!"*
      - • *"Jenny gets a point for taking turns!"*
      - • *"Johnny gets a point for giving a high five!"*
      - • *"Julie gets a point for saying 'good game'!"*
      - • *"Joey gets a point for praising!"*
  - ○ Speak loudly when giving out points so other teens can hear
    - ■ The social comparison will encourage other teens to **praise** and be **good sports**
- Be sure to keep track of points on the Good Sportsmanship Point Log (see Appendix F)

Homework Assignments

- [Distribute the Parent Handout (found in the last section of this chapter) and inform teens that they should give this handout to their parents immediately.]

- Briefly explain the homework for the week by saying, *"We're going to continue to have you practice being good sports this week."*

- Present the homework assignments for the coming week:

1. Practice **being a good sport**

   a. This can be done anytime during the week when the teen plays games (videogames, computer games, board games, card games) or sports

2. Practice **joining a group conversation** between at least two teens you feel comfortable with

   a. Before **joining**:

      i. Think of a place where you are likely to be accepted and you don't have a bad reputation

   b. During the conversation:

      i. Follow the steps for **joining a group conversation**
      ii. **Assess interest** and follow the steps for **exiting a conversation** if needed

   c. After **joining**:

      i. Parents and teen should discuss how the teen **joined and exited the group conversation** (if relevant)
      ii. Parents should help teen **troubleshoot** any problems that may have arisen

3. *Enroll in extracurricular activities*

   a. Teens and parents should DISCUSS and DECIDE on extracurricular activities based on the teen's interests and BEGIN TO ENROLL in these activities

      i. Criteria for a good extracurricular activity:

         1. Meets weekly or at least every other week
         2. Age range of other teens includes the social age of the teen
         3. Activity includes informal time so that the teen can interact with others
         4. Activity starts within the next couple of weeks

   b. Teen should *start an individual conversation* with someone at this extracurricular activity

      i. *Trade information* and *find common interests* while having a *two-way conversation*

4. *Out-of-class call or video chat*

   a. Before the call:

      i. Choose someone the teen feels comfortable talking with around the same age

   b. During the call:

      i. Follow the steps for *starting and ending phone calls*, including using *cover stories*
      ii. Teens should *trade information* and have a *two-way conversation* on this phone call
      iii. Find a *common interest* to report back to the class

   c. After the call:

      i. Teens should discuss the call with their parent, identify *common interests*, and *troubleshoot* any problems

5. *Bring an inside game*

   a. Bring an inside game to share with the class on **Thursday and Friday of next week** (e.g., age appropriate board game, card game, etc.)
   b. Do not bring a solitary game (like a portable gaming device) or something that you are unwilling to share or are worried about breaking or losing

Wrap Up

Say, *"So those are your homework assignments for this week. Be sure to start working on these assignments right away. We'll be reviewing how they went at the beginning of next week. Tomorrow we'll continue our discussion about good sportsmanship and we'll practice being good sports with our classmates."*

Calculate Points

Calculate the number of points earned by each teen (see Appendix E for the Daily Point Log):

- Do not publicly disclose the individual number of points
- Discourage attempts to compare number of points earned between teens
    - Remind them that they are working as a team to earn a bigger and better graduation party

Days Four and Five: Teen Activity—Good Sportsmanship

Lesson Review: Good Sportsmanship

- Say, *"This week we've been working on the rules for being a good sport. Who can tell me some of the rules for being a good sport?"*

[Have teens generate all of the rules for **good sportsmanship**. Be prepared to give prompts if necessary. Write the following buzzwords (**bold and italicized**) on the board and do not erase until the end of the lesson.]

- ○ *Praise*
    - ■ Examples:
        - • *"Nice move!"*
        - • *"Nice try."*
        - • *"Great shot!"*
        - • *"Good job!"*
        - • High five
        - • Thumbs up
        - • Pound or fist bump (bump closed fists)
        - • Clapping

- ○ *Play by the rules*

- ○ *Don't be a referee*

- ○ *Don't be a coach*

- ○ *Share and take turns*
    - ■ *Don't be a ball hog*
    - ■ *Share the controller*

- ○ *Don't be competitive*

- ○ *Help and show concern if someone is injured* (outdoor sports)

- ○ *Suggest a change if bored*

- ○ *Don't be a bad winner*

- ○ *Don't be a sore loser*

- ○ *At the end of a game say "good game"*

Teen Activity: Good Sportsmanship

Materials Needed

- Indoor games brought by teens

- In the event that teens forget to bring indoor games, have board games and card games available to use if possible

Rules

- Notify teens they will be practicing *good sportsmanship*

- Break teens up into dyads

  ○ If there is an uneven number of teens, create one triad

- When possible, girls should be paired with girls and boys should be paired with boys

- Teens will then play indoor games while practicing *good sportsmanship*

- Games are chosen from appropriate *inside games* brought by teens and other available games provided by the instructor

  ○ Have teens negotiate what they will play

    ▪ They may need to compromise by playing one game for half the time and then switching games midway

  ○ You may need to assist teens in understanding the rules for specific games

    ▪ Try to avoid acting as a referee if disagreements occur
    ▪ Encourage teens to work out their differences by being *good sports*

  ○ You may need to prompt teens to be *good sports* and *praise* their partners, saying things like:

    ▪ *"Johnny just made a nice move, what could you say?"*
    ▪ *"Jenny got a lucky hand, what could you say?"*
    ▪ *"What do we say at the end of the game?"*

- Teens receive points while playing games for practicing:

  ○ *Praising*
  ○ *Playing by the rules*
  ○ *Not refereeing*
  ○ *Not coaching*
  ○ *Sharing and taking turns*
  ○ *Not being competitive*
  ○ *Helping and showing concern if someone is injured* (outdoor sports)
  ○ *Suggesting a change if bored*
  ○ *Not being a bad winner*

- ○ *Not being a sore loser*
- ○ *Saying "good game" at the end of the game*
- When giving points:
  - ○ Say the teen's name first to get his or her attention
  - ○ State what the reward is (i.e., getting a point)
  - ○ Give the reason for the reward (i.e., being a *good sport*)
    - ■ Examples:
      - • *"Jimmy gets a point for saying 'good job'!"*
      - • *"Jenny gets a point for taking turns!"*
      - • *"Johnny gets a point for giving a high five!"*
      - • *"Julie gets a point for saying 'good game'!"*
      - • *"Joey gets a point for praising!"*
  - ○ Speak loudly when giving out points so other teens can hear
    - ■ The social comparison will encourage other teens to *praise* and be *good sports*
- Be sure to keep track of points on the Good Sportsmanship Point Log (see Appendix F)

Homework Assignments

- Briefly explain the homework for the week by saying, *"We're going to continue to have you practice being good sports this week."*

- Present the homework assignments for the coming week:

  1. Practice *being a good sport*

     a. This can be done anytime during the week when the teen plays games (videogames, computer games, board games, card games) or sports

  2. Practice *joining a group conversation* between at least two teens you feel comfortable with

     a. Before *joining*:

        i. Think of a place where you are likely to be accepted and you don't have a bad reputation

     b. During the conversation:

        i. Follow the steps for *joining a group conversation*
        ii. *Assess interest* and follow the steps for *exiting a conversation* if needed

     c. After *joining*:

        i. Parents and teen should discuss how the teen *joined and exited the group conversation* (if relevant)
        ii. Parents should help teen *troubleshoot* any problems that may have arisen

3. *Enroll in extracurricular activities*

   a. Teens and parents should DISCUSS and DECIDE on extracurricular activities based on the teen's interests and BEGIN TO ENROLL in these activities

      i. Criteria for a good extracurricular activity:

         1. Meets weekly or at least every other week
         2. Age range of other teens includes the social age of the teen
         3. Activity includes informal time so that the teen can interact with others
         4. Activity starts within the next couple of weeks

   b. Teen should **start an individual conversation** with someone at this extracurricular activity

      i. **Trade information** and **find common interests** while having a **two-way conversation**

4. *Out-of-class call or video chat*

   a. Before the call:

      i. Choose someone the teen feels comfortable talking with around the same age

   b. During the call:

      i. Follow the steps for **starting and ending phone calls**, including using **cover stories**
      ii. Teens should **trade information** and have a **two-way conversation** on this phone call
      iii. Find a **common interest** to report back to the class

   c. After the call:

      i. Teens should discuss the call with their parent, identify **common interests**, and **troubleshoot** any problems

5. *Bring an inside game*

   a. Bring an inside game to share with the class on **Thursday and Friday of next week** (e.g., age appropriate board game, card game, etc.)
   b. Do not bring a solitary game (like a portable gaming device) or something that you are unwilling to share or are worried about breaking or losing

Wrap Up

Say, *"So those are your homework assignments for this week. Be sure to start working on these assignments right away. We'll be reviewing how they went at the beginning of next week."*

Calculate Points

Calculate the number of points earned by each teen (see Appendix E for the Daily Point Log)

- Do not publicly disclose the individual number of points
- Discourage attempts to compare number of points earned between teens
    - Remind them that they are working as a team to earn a bigger and better graduation party

Parent Handout 8

PEERS® *Program for the Education and Enrichment of Relational Skills*

Good Sportsmanship

This week your teens will be learning how to be a *good sport* during games and sports activities. There are very specific rules for being a *good sport*.

Rules for Good Sportsmanship

- *Praise* your friends

  - Examples of praise during games:

    - *"Nice move!"*
    - *"Nice try."*
    - *"Nice shot!"*
    - *"Good job!"*
    - High five
    - Thumbs up
    - Pound or fist bump (bumping closed fists)
    - Clapping

- *Play by the rules*

  - *Don't cheat*
  - Don't make up rules in the middle of a game

- *Don't be a referee*

  - Don't try to call plays or boss the other players around
  - Teens don't like to hang out with people who boss them around

- *Don't be a coach*

  - Unless your friend asks, don't try to "help" by giving advice
  - Even though you may only be trying to help, it may seem like you're being bossy
  - Teens don't like to hang out with other teens who tell them what to do

- *Share and take turns*

  - *Don't be a ball hog* during a sporting game
  - *Share the controller* if you're playing a videogame

- *Don't be competitive*

  - The goal when playing with friends is not to win, but to have fun
  - Being competitive makes you look like a *poor sport*
  - They may not want to play with you again

- *Help and show concern if someone is injured* (outdoor sports)

    ○ Offer help if someone is injured

    ○ Show concern if someone gets hurt

- *Suggest a change if bored*

    ○ Don't walk away or say *"I'm bored"* in the middle of a game

        ▪ It might hurt the other person's feelings

        ▪ You might look like a *poor sport*

    ○ If you're bored say, *"How about when we're done with this we play something else?"*

- *Don't be a bad winner*

    ○ Don't gloat if you win

    ○ This makes the other person feel bad and they may not want to play with you again

    ○ *Act like winning wasn't a big deal*

- *Don't be a sore loser*

    ○ Don't sulk or get angry if you lose

    ○ This makes you look like a *poor sport* and they may not want to play with you again

    ○ *Act like losing wasn't a big deal*

- *At the end of a game say "good game"*

    ○ This shows that you're a *good sport*

    ○ It makes the other person feel good

Homework Assignments

Every week your teen will have homework assignments to practice new and previously learned social skills. It is extremely helpful if parents assist teens in completing these assignments. The homework assignments for this week include the following:

1. Practice *being a good sport*

    a. This can be done anytime during the week when the teen plays games (videogames, computer games, board games, card games) or sports

2. Practice *joining a group conversation* between at least two teens you feel comfortable with

    a. Before *joining*:

        i. Teen should think of a place where he or she is likely to be accepted and doesn't have a bad reputation

    b. During the conversation:

        i. Follow the steps for *joining a group conversation*

        ii. *Assess interest* and follow the steps for *exiting a conversation* if needed

   c. After *joining*:

      i. Parents and teen should discuss how the teen *joined and exited the group conversation* (if relevant)

      ii. Parents should help teen *troubleshoot* any problems that may have arisen

3. ***Enroll in extracurricular activities***

   a. Teens and parents should DISCUSS and DECIDE on extracurricular activities based on the teen's interests and BEGIN TO ENROLL in these activities

      i. Criteria for a good extracurricular activity:

         1. Meets weekly or at least every other week
         2. Age range of other teens includes the social age of the teen
         3. Activity includes informal time so that the teen can interact with others
         4. Activity starts within the next couple of weeks

   b. Teen should *start an individual conversation* with someone at this extracurricular activity

      i. *Trade information* and *find common interests* while having a *two-way conversation*

4. ***Out-of-class call or video chat***

   a. Before the call:

      i. Choose someone the teen feels comfortable talking with around the same age

   b. During the call:

      i. Follow the steps for *starting and ending phone calls*, including using *cover stories*
      ii. Teens should *trade information* and have a *two-way conversation* on this phone call
      iii. Find a *common interest* to report back to the class

   c. After the call:

      i. Teens should discuss the call with their parent, identify *common interests*, and *troubleshoot* any problems

5. ***Bring an inside game***

   a. Bring an inside game to share with the class on **Thursday and Friday of next week** (e.g., age appropriate board game, card game, etc.)

   b. Do not bring a solitary game (like a portable gaming device) or something that you are unwilling to share or are worried about breaking or losing

GET-TOGETHERS

Preparing for the Lesson

The focus of this lesson is on teaching teens how to organize and have successful *get-togethers* with potential friends. Socially accepted teens have frequent *get-togethers* with friends, both in their homes and in the community. They turn school acquaintances into close friends by spending time with friends outside of the school setting. Therefore, learning the skills necessary to be successful at having *get-togethers* is particularly important in helping teens make and keep friends. Research indicates that the best way to form close friendships is through organizing and frequently having social contact outside of structured interactions like school and extracurricular activities. In fact, studies show that getting together with friends after school is correlated with more social contacts at school. Since most teens with Autism Spectrum Disorder (ASD) tend to have fewer social interactions with peers outside of school, learning how to organize and have successful *get-togethers* will be a pivotal skill toward the development of closer friendships for these socially challenged teens.

The ideal circumstance would be to help teens organize *get-togethers* in their homes, where parents can unobtrusively observe the interactions and provide social coaching. This allows parents to monitor and intervene appropriately when necessary. However, given the variability of parent involvement in school-based programs like this, having *get-togethers* in the community may be a more viable option for some, since many teens may prefer socializing with friends outside of their homes. Community-based *get-togethers* may actually be more appropriate if family members tend to be intrusive, if living accommodations are uncomfortable in some way for the teen, or if teens simply live too far away from one another, making travel inconvenient.

Wherever the *get-togethers* take place, it is highly recommended that they be *activity-based*. In other words, *get-togethers* should be organized around some pre-determined activity in which all of the attendees share a *common interest*. Having *activity-based get-togethers* lessens the pressure of maintaining conversation throughout the time spent together. Research suggests that most teenagers (particularly boys) play videogames during *get-togethers*, so this will be a common activity. Other common activities include going to the movies and sharing meals. Table 10.1 highlights other common *activity-based get-togethers* identified by teens.

While the rules and steps of this lesson are rarely intuitive for teens with ASD and other social challenges, the lesson is fairly straightforward, so your students will probably not have too much difficulty understanding the principles of the lesson. The most common challenge about this lesson is the lack of choices for potential guests for *get-togethers*. The "gold standard" is someone with whom the teen wishes to get to know better and who appears to be interested in becoming closer friends. Options from successful *out-of-class call* assignments are usually helpful in this

Table 10.1 Common Activity-Based Get-Togethers Identified by Teens

Public Activities	*Indoor Activities*	*Amusement Parks*
Movie theaters	Computer/Videogames	Gaming centers
Malls	Surf the Internet	Video arcades
Comic book conventions	Social networking sites	Laser tag
Comic book stores	Listen to music	Circus
Gaming stores	Rent movies	Miniature golf parks
Science expos	Watch TV	Water parks
Science museums	Card games	Go-carting
Warhammer	Board games	Batting cages
Concerts	Ping pong	Golf ranges
Bowling	Pool	Zoos
Dog parks	Air hockey	Aquariums
Beach/Lake/River	Darts	State and county fairs
Mealtime Activities	*Pair Sports*	*Group Sports*
Restaurants	Swimming	Basketball
Ice cream shops	Skateboarding	Baseball
Frozen yogurt shops	Shooting baskets	Soccer
Order pizza	Bike riding	Touch football
Barbeque	Roller skating	Airsoft
Sushi	Tennis	Volleyball
Cook a meal	Skiing	Badminton
Picnic	Surfing	Water polo
Bake	Hiking	Bocce ball

regard. In the absence of having someone to fill the gold standard, a close friend or a distant family member around the same age would be acceptable options until someone more appropriate can be identified. The most important part of this assignment is that a *get-together* actually takes place so that the teen can practice the skills just learned. If such practice does not occur soon after learning, the skills are unlikely to be used at a later time.

In some cases, even when teens are given the option of choosing close friends or relatives, they may still have difficulty identifying someone to have a *get-together* with. In these cases, the problem may be related to one or two different issues: a *bad reputation* and/or no *source of potential friends*. Some teens referred to social skills training will be suffering from a *bad reputation* among the larger peer group, making it difficult to make friends with other teens. If a teen has a *bad reputation*, it is unlikely that others will want to socialize with him or her because teens get their reputations based on whom they hang out with. For teens struggling with a *bad reputation*, it will be critical that the teen find a *source of potential friends* outside of the place where the reputation exists. For most teens this will be in the community, far away from the school setting.

If you find that one of your students is struggling to identify people to have *get-togethers* with, the simplest and most likely explanation is that he or she does not have a *source of friends*. Whether this is due to a *bad reputation* will require further investigation on your part. Either way, you will need to help this student find a *source of potential friends* with *common interests* if he or she is to be successful in utilizing the skills in PEERS®. This point highlights the importance of including parents in the class whenever possible, as parents often play an important role in identifying and enrolling teens in extracurricular activities outside of the school setting.

Day One: Homework Review

Homework Review

[Start with completed homework first. If you have time, you can inquire as to why others were unable to complete the assignment and try to *troubleshoot* how they might get it done for the coming week. When reviewing homework, be sure to use the buzzwords (***bold and italicized***) and *troubleshoot* issues that come up. Spend the majority of the homework review on *joining a group conversation*, extracurricular activities, and the *out-of-class call*, as these were the most important assignments.]

[Note: Give multiple points for homework parts—not just one point per assignment.]

1. *Being a good sport*

   a. Say, *"Last week we learned the rules for being a good sport. One of your assignments this week was to practice being a good sport. This may have happened at school during gym class, during your extracurricular activities, or when you were hanging out with friends. Raise your hand if you practiced being a good sport this week."*

      i.   Ask, *"Where did you practice being a good sport?"*
      ii. Ask, *"What did you do or say to show that you were a good sport?"*

2. *Joining a group conversation*

   a. Say, *"Another one of your assignments this week was to practice joining a conversation with a group that you were likely to be accepted by. Raise your hand if you practiced joining a group conversation this week."*

      i.   Ask, *"Where did you join?"*
      ii. Ask, *"How did you join?"*

         1. Be sure they followed the *steps for joining a group conversation*:

            a. *Listen to the conversation*
            b. *Watch from a distance*
            c. *Use a prop*
            d. *Identify the topic*
            e. *Find a common interest*
            f. *Move closer*
            g. *Wait for a pause*
            h. *Mention the topic*
            i. *Assess interest*
            j. *Introduce yourself* (if appropriate)

      iii. Ask, *"Did it seem like they wanted to talk to you?"*

         1. Ask, *"How could you tell?"*

            a. *Talking to you*
            b. *Looking at you*
            c. *Facing you (opened the circle)*

    iv. Ask, *"Did you need to exit the conversation?"*

        1. If they **exited the conversation**, be sure they followed the steps based on whether they were **never accepted**, **initially accepted and then excluded**, or **fully accepted**

3. **Enroll in extracurricular activities**

    a. Say, *"Another assignment was that you and your parents were supposed to identify an extracurricular activity for you to join where you might meet other teens with common interests, and then begin to enroll in those activities. Raise your hand if you found an extra-curricular activity."*

      i. Ask, *"Which extracurricular activity did you choose?"*

      ii. Ask, *"Did you enroll in the activity?'*

      iii. Ask, *"Are there other teens your age in the group?'*

      iv. Ask, *"How often does it meet?"*

      v. Ask, *"Does this seem like a good place for you to make potential new friends?"*

    b. Say, *"You were also supposed to follow the steps for starting a conversation with someone from this extracurricular activity. Raise your hand if you started a conversation with someone from your extracurricular activity?"*

      i. Ask, *"Who did you start the conversation with?"*

      ii. Ask, *"How did you start the conversation?"*

        1. Be sure they followed the **steps for starting an individual conversation**:

          a. **Casually look over**

          b. **Use a prop**

          c. **Find a common interest**

          d. **Mention the common interest**

          e. **Trade information**

          f. **Assess interest**

          g. **Introduce yourself** (if appropriate)

      iii. Ask, *"Did it seem like they wanted to talk to you?"*

        1. Ask, *"How could you tell?"*

          a. **Talking to you**

          b. **Looking at you**

          c. **Facing you**

4. **Out-of-class call or video chat**

    a. Say, *"Another assignment this week was to trade information and have a two-way conversation with someone not in this class over the phone or video chat. Raise your hand if you did the out-of-class call."*

      i. Ask, *"Who did you talk to?"*

      ii. Ask, *"How did the conversation begin?"*

1. Have teens identify all the relevant steps (if a phone call):

    a. *Ask for the person you are calling*
    b. *Say who you are*
    c. *Ask how they are*
    d. *Ask if they can talk*
    e. *Give a cover story for why you are calling*

iii. Ask, *"Did you trade information?"*
iv. Ask, *"Did you find a common interest?"*

   a. When they identify common interests ask, *"What could you do with that information if you were going to hang out?"*

v. Ask, *"How did the conversation end?"*

   a. Have teens identify all the relevant steps (if a phone call):

      1. *Wait for a bit of a pause*
      2. *Give a cover story for why you have to go*
      3. *Tell the person it was nice talking*
      4. *Tell the person you will talk to them later*
      5. *Say goodbye*

vi. Avoid general questions like, *"How did it go?"*

5. *Bring an inside game*

   a. Identify the inside game the teen will bring to share later this week (e.g., age appropriate board game, card game, etc.)

Wrap Up

Say, *"Good work for those of you who completed your homework assignments. Tomorrow we'll be talking about having successful get-togethers."*

Calculate Points

Calculate the number of points earned by each teen (see Appendix E for the Daily Point Log)

*   Do not publicly disclose the individual number of points

*   Discourage attempts to compare number of points earned between teens

    o   Remind them that they are working as a team to earn a bigger and better graduation party

Day Two: Didactic Lesson—Get-Togethers

Didactic Lesson: Get-Togethers

- Explain, *"Today we're going to be talking about how to have successful get-togethers with friends. Having get-togethers is a way to hang out with friends and get to know each other better. This is how close friendships develop. Sadly, if we're not having get-togethers with our friends outside of school or extracurricular activities, we're probably not close friends."*

- Say, *"A good way to start a close friendship is to invite someone over to your home for a get-together. This means you're the host of the get-together. What's the difference between a host and a guest?"*

  - Answer: The host organizes the get-together, the guest attends the get-together, it is the job of the host to make sure the guest has a good time

- Explain, *"In order to make sure that your get-togethers are successful, we need to be familiar with the rules and steps for having get-togethers."*

[Present the rules and steps for **get-togethers** by writing the following buzzwords (**bold and italicized**) on the board. Do not erase the rules and steps until the end of the lesson.]

Preparing for Get-Togethers

- ***Make plans using the four W's***

  - Explain, *"The first part of having a successful get-together involves planning the get-together. This means you will need to decide beforehand, with your friend, what you're going to do and who is going to be there. We call these the four W's."*

  - ***WHO is going to be there***

    - Say, *"One part of planning involves deciding WHO is going to be there. Why is it important that everyone invited to a get-together knows in advance who is going to be there?"*

      - Answer: Because you don't want your friends to be surprised if there are other people at the ***get-together***, certain people may not get along and wouldn't want to be around each other

  - ***WHAT you're going to do***

    - Say, *"Another part of planning the get-together involves figuring out WHAT you're going to do beforehand. Why is it important to figure out what you're going to do?"*

      - Answer: Because ***get-togethers*** are easier and more fun if you plan activities, you don't want your friends to get bored if there is nothing to do

    - Ask, *"Should your activities be based on your common interests?"*

      - Answer: Yes

- ■ Ask, *"What are some activities that teens enjoy doing during get-togethers?"*

  - • Have teens brainstorm ideas (see Table 10.1 for suggestions)

- ○ *WHERE you're going to get-together*

  - ■ Say, *"It's also important to figure out WHERE the get-together is going to take place before-hand. Why is it important to figure out where the get-together is going to be?"*

    - • Answer: Because the *get-together* may never happen if no one knows where to go

- ○ *WHEN you're going to get-together*

  - ■ Say, *"We also need to figure out WHEN the get-together is going to take place beforehand. Why is it important to figure out when the get-together is going to happen?"*

    - • Answer: Because if you do not decide in advance when you're going to get together, your schedules may become full and the *get-together* might never take place

- ○ *HOW the get-together is going to happen*

  - ■ Say, *"Depending on what we're doing, we may also need to figure out HOW the get-together is going to happen, like who is going to drive or if we need to get tickets. Why is it important to figure out how the get-together is going to happen?"*

    - • Answer: If you don't work out the details in advance, the *get-together* may never happen

- • *Have other activities ready*

  - ○ Say, *"Even though you should have decided beforehand what you're going to do, if your friend is coming over to your home you'll need to have some other activities ready. Why would it be important to have other things to do?"*

    - ■ Answer: Because teens get bored easily, so you need to have other options ready, having a variety of activities ready will be helpful

  - ○ Ask, *"Should these other activities be based on your common interests?"*

    - ■ Answer: Yes

  - ○ Ask, *"What are some activities that you can have ready for your friends in case you get bored?"*

    - ■ Answer: DVDs, videogames, computer games, board games, card games, sports equipment

- • *Put away personal items you don't want others to share or see*

  - ○ Say, *"Another important part of preparing for a get-together involves putting away any personal items you don't want to share or let other people see. Why would it be important to put away these things beforehand?"*

    - ■ Answer: Because you don't want to be rude and tell your friends they can't see or touch your things, it's easier to put personal items away in advance so your friends don't even know they're there, this includes food you're unwilling to share

- *Make sure your space is presentable*

  - Explain, *"Another important part of preparing for a get-together is to make sure your room or personal space is cleaned up and presentable. That means that if the get-together is in your home, make sure your room is picked up. If you're driving, make sure your car isn't messy."*

  - Ask, *"What could be the problem with having a messy room or car?"*

    - Answer: If your room or car is a mess, your friends may think you are a slob, cleaning up before having company over is a sign of respect for your guests, not cleaning up is seen as rude

Steps for Beginning Get-Togethers

Explain, *"Now that we know the rules for planning and preparing for get-togethers, we need to talk about the steps for beginning get-togethers at your home."*

1. *Greet your guest*

   a. Say, *"When having a get-together in your home, the first step when your guests arrive is to greet them at the door. How do we greet our guests?"*

      i. Answer: Say hello and ask them how they're doing, some people will hug or give a casual acknowledgement like a head nod or a pound (bump fists)

2. *Invite them in*

   a. Say, *"Next, we need to invite them in. This involves saying something like, 'Come in' and moving out of the doorway so they can come inside. What happens if we forget to invite them in?"*

      i. Answer: They end up standing at the door waiting to come in, this can be awkward

3. *Introduce them to anyone they don't know*

   a. Say, *"Once we've invited our guest in, we need to introduce them to anyone they don't know. Why is it important to introduce them to anyone they don't know?"*

      i. Answer: If they don't know everyone, they might feel awkward and left out

4. *Give them a tour*

   a. Say, *"If this is the first time your friends have been to your home, you should show them around a little. Why is it important to give your friends a little tour?"*

      i. Answer: It's your job to make your guests feel welcome, they should know where the bathroom is located and be familiar with the surroundings in order to feel welcome, friends usually want to see your room too

5. *Offer them refreshments*

   a. Say, *"Next, you'll want to offer your friends something to eat or drink. Why is it important to offer your guests refreshments?"*

      i. Answer: They may be hungry or thirsty, it's polite to offer guests in your home food and beverages

6. *Ask them what they want to do*

    a. Say, *"Even though you should have planned with them what you're going to do, you should still ask your guest what they want to do when they're settled. Why is it a good idea to ask them what they want to do?"*

        i. Answer: It's your job as the host to make sure your guest has a good time, at least check in to make sure they still want to do what you planned, they might want to do something different in the end

Role-Play: Beginning a Get-Together

[The instructor and the behavioral coach should do an APPROPRIATE role-play with the instructor *beginning a get-together* following the steps.]

- Begin by saying, *"We're going to do a role-play. Watch this and tell me what I'm doing RIGHT in beginning this get-together."*

    Example of an APPROPRIATE role-play:

- Coach: (Knocks on door)
- Instructor: (Opens door) *"Hi (insert name)! How are you?"*
- Coach: *"Hi! I'm fine. How are you?"*
- Instructor: *"Fine, thanks. Come on in."* (Moves aside so the coach can enter)
- Coach: (Enters) *"Thanks."*
- Instructor: *"I don't think you've met my other friend before. This is (insert name of another coach or teen). This is (insert name of coach just arriving)."*
- Coach: *"Nice to meet you."*
- Instructor: *"So I guess you've never been here before. I should show you around real quick. (Give an imaginary tour.) This is the living room. The kitchen is through there. The bathroom is just around the corner. And my bedroom is upstairs."*
- Coach: *"Cool. Thanks."*
- Instructor: *"Can I get you something to eat or drink?"*
- Coach: *"I'm okay. Thanks anyway."*
- Instructor: (Looking at the two coaches) *"So what do you guys want to do?"*
- Coach: *"Maybe we could play some videogames?"*

- End by saying, *"Time out on that. So what did I do RIGHT in beginning that get-together?"*

    ○ Answer: **Greeted your guest, invited your guest in, introduced your guests, gave a tour, offered refreshments, asked your guests what they wanted to do**

- Ask the following *Perspective Taking Questions*:

    ○ *"What was that like for (name of coach)?"*

        ■ Answers: Fine; normal

- ○ *"What do you think (name of coach) thought of me?"*

  - ▪ Answers: Friendly; normal; a good host

- ○ *"Is (name of coach) going to want to hang out with me again?"*

  - ▪ Answer: Maybe; so far so good

- Ask the behavioral coach the same ***Perspective Taking Questions***:

  - ○ *"What was that like for you?"*
  - ○ *"What did you think of me?"*
  - ○ *"Would you want to hang out with me again?"*

Rules for During Get-Togethers

Explain, *"So now that we know how to begin the get-together, we need to know what to do during the get-together. There are some important rules for making sure your get-together is a success."*

- ***The guest gets to pick the activities at your home***

  - ○ Say, *"The first rule for having a get-together in your home is that the guests get to pick the activities. Why is it important to let the guests pick the activities?"*

    - ▪ Answer: Because it's the host's job to make sure the guests have a good time

  - ○ Say, *"There's one exception to this rule. What do you think you should do if your guest wants to do something dangerous or inappropriate?"*

    - ▪ Answer: Don't go along with it, consider whether this is a good choice for a friend

  - ○ Say, *"Not everyone knows the rule that the guest is supposed to pick the activities. So what do you do if you're at a friend's house and they want to choose all the activities?"*

    - ▪ Answer: **Go with the flow in the moment, don't police** him or her, remember that **friendship is a choice**, if your friend never wants to do what you want to do you don't have to hang out with him or her anymore

- ***Be a good sport***

  - ○ Say, *"When we're having a get-together and we're playing games or sports, it's important to be a good sport. Why is it important to be a good sport?"*

    - ▪ Answer: Because they will be less likely to want to hang out with you if you're a **poor sport**, if you're a **good sport** they're more likely to have fun and want to hang out again

- ***Give compliments***

  - ○ Explain, *"Another way to have successful get-togethers is to give compliments. That means if you notice things about your friends that you like, you should let them know. Like telling someone you like their outfit or that you think they're good at something."*

  - ○ Ask, *"Why is it is important to compliment your friend?"*

- Answer: Because it makes them feel good and shows that you're a nice person

- **Be loyal to your friends**

  - Explain, *"Another rule for having a successful get-together is to be loyal to your friends. This means you shouldn't argue with, criticize, or make fun of your friends."*

  - Ask, *"What could be the problem with arguing, criticizing, or making fun of your friends?"*

    - Answer: You don't seem like a good friend, they may not want to hang out with you again

- **Stick up for your friends**

  - Ask, *"If your job is to be loyal to your friends, what should you do if you're having a group get-together and someone else argues, criticizes, or makes fun of your friend?*

    - Answer: You should stick up for your friends and try to keep the peace, this is especially true if you're the host because your job is to make sure everyone is having a nice time

- **Don't ignore your friends**

  - Say, *"Another important rule for having get-togethers is don't ignore your friends. Is it okay to ignore one friend to talk to another friend during a get-together?"*

    - Answer: No, because it's your job to make sure all your friends are having fun, your friends should feel like they have your attention

  - Ask, *"What if someone unexpectedly calls, texts, or stops by during your get-together. Should you take their call, text them back, or invite them over?"*

    - Answer: No, you should wait to call or text them back, or tell them you're busy and that you'll get back to them later

  - Ask, *"Should you mention that you're having a get-together to the friend who is trying to reach you?"*

    - Answer: No, because it might make them feel excluded, it might hurt their feelings, they might ask to join the **get-together**

  - Ask, *"What could be the problem with inviting your other friend into your get-together unexpectedly?"*

    - Answer: It's rude and might make your other guest feel like they weren't good enough, when you decide **WHO** is going to be at the **get-together**, it's like a contract where you don't make changes

  - Ask, *"Is it okay to ask your guests if someone else can come over unexpectedly?"*

    - Answer: No, because your guests may feel obligated to say yes even though they may not want to

  - Ask, *"What if your friend wants to call, text, or invite other people into your get-together?"*

    - Answer: ***Go with the flow in the moment***, remember that ***friendship is a choice***, if your friend always wants to talk to or invite other people into your ***get-togethers***, you don't have to hang out with them

- *Suggest a change if you get bored*

  - Ask, *"Do people sometimes get bored during get-togethers?"*

    - Answer: Yes

  - Ask, *"What could be the problem with saying 'I'm bored' or walking away from your friends during a get-together?"*

    - Answer: You would seem rude, they might not want to hang out with you again

  - Explain, *"Instead of saying you're bored or walking away, you should suggest a change. You can do this by saying, 'How about when we're done with this we do something else?' just like during games and sports."*

  - Ask, *"What should you do if your friend doesn't want to do what you suggest for a change?"*

    - Answer: **Go with the flow in the moment**, let them pick the activity instead, remember that **friendship is a choice**, if your friend never wants to do what you suggest, you don't have to hang out with him or her again

- *Trade information at least 50 percent of the time*

  - Say, *"Another important rule for having a get-together is that you should be talking and trading information at least 50 percent of the time. Why is it important to trade information at least half of the time?"*

    - Answer: Because this is how you get to know one another and **find common interests**, if you don't talk and **trade information**, you won't get to know one another and become closer friends

Steps for Ending Get-Togethers

Explain, *"Now that we know the rules for what to do during a get-together, we need to talk about how to end a get-together."*

1. *Wait for a pause in activities*

   a. Say, *"The first step in ending a get-together is to wait for a pause in the activities. That means don't interrupt what you're doing unless you have to. What could be the problem with interrupting an activity to end a get-together?"*

      i. Answer: It may seem abrupt, your friends may think you just don't want to hang out with them anymore

2. *Give a cover story for leaving or ending the get-together*

   a. Say, *"The next step is to give a cover story for leaving or ending the get-together. Remember, cover stories are reasons we do things. What are some examples of reasons you might have to leave or end a get-together?"*

      i. Examples:

1. *"I have to go soon."*
2. *"I have to start my homework now."*
3. *"My mom said it's time for dinner."*
4. *"I have to go to bed soon."*

b. Ask, *"What could be the problem with not giving a cover story for ending a get-together?"*

   i. Answer: Your friends may think you don't want to hang out with them anymore

3. ***Start walking your friend to the door***

   a. Say, *"If the get-together is in your home, the next step is to stand up and start walking your friend to the door. Why is it important to walk your friend to the door?"*

      i. Answer: Because it's rude to make them find their way out, if you don't stand up and start walking them to the door, they may not leave, they are waiting for your cue about what to do

4. ***Thank your friend for getting together***

   a. Say, *"The next step for ending a get-together is to thank your friend for getting together. Why is it important to thank your friend?"*

      i. Answer: Because it makes them feel nice, it shows that you appreciate them

5. ***Tell your friend you had a good time***

   a. Say, *"If you had a good time, you should tell your friend as you're walking him or her to the door. Why is it important to tell your friend you had a good time?"*

      i. Answer: It shows them that you enjoy being around them, it makes them feel good

6. ***Say goodbye and you'll see them later***

   a. Explain, *"Finally, as you're walking your friend out, it's important to say goodbye. You might even say 'I'll see you later' or 'I'll see you at school' as you're saying goodbye. This is also a nice time to try to make future plans to get-together."*
   b. Ask, *"Why is it important to say goodbye and that you'll see them later?"*

      i. Answer: It shows that you enjoyed their company and want to see them again

Role-Play: Ending a Get-Together

[The instructor and the behavioral coach should do an APPROPRIATE role-play with the instructor ***ending a get-together*** following the steps.]

- Begin by saying, *"We're going to do another role-play. Watch this and tell me what I'm doing RIGHT in ending this get-together."*

Example of an APPROPRIATE role-play:

- Instructor and Coach: (Sitting down)
- Instructor: *"That was fun playing videogames. You're really good."*
- Coach: *"Thanks, so are you."*
- Instructor: (Little pause) *"Well, my mom said we're having dinner now."*
- Coach: *"Oh, okay."*
- Instructor: (Stands up and starts walking to the door) *"Thanks for coming over!"*
- Coach: (Follows instructor to the door) *"Thanks for having me over!"*
- Instructor: *"It was really fun!"*
- Coach: *"Yeah, I had a good time, too."*
- Instructor: *"We should hang out again soon."*
- Coach *"That would be cool."*
- Instructor: (Opens the door) *"So I guess I'll see you at school tomorrow."*
- Coach: *"Okay. Sounds good."* (Walks through the door)
- Instructor: *"Take care. Bye!"* (Waves)
- Coach: (Waves) *"Bye!"*

- End by saying, *"Time out on that. So what did I do RIGHT in ending that get-together?"*
  - Answer: **Waited for a pause in the activity, gave a cover story, started walking your friend to the door, thanked your friend for coming over, said you had a good time, said you would see your friend later, said goodbye**

- Ask the following *Perspective Taking Questions*:
  - *"What was that like for (name of coach)?"*
    - Answers: Fine; normal
  - *"What do you think (name of coach) thought of me?"*
    - Answers: Friendly; normal; a good host
  - *"Is (name of coach) going to want to hang out with me again?"*
    - Answer: Yes; probably

- Ask the behavioral coach the same *Perspective Taking Questions*:
  - *"What was that like for you?"*
  - *"What did you think of me?"*
  - *"Would you want to hang out with me again?"*

Wrap Up

Say, *"So those are the rules and steps for having successful get-togethers. Tomorrow we'll continue our discussion about get-togethers and practice the rules and steps we've learned today."*

Calculate Points

Calculate the number of points earned by each teen (see Appendix E for the Daily Point Log):

- Do not publicly disclose the individual number of points
- Discourage attempts to compare number of points earned between teens
    - Remind them that they are working as a team to earn a bigger and better graduation party

Day Three: Lesson Review and Behavioral Rehearsal

Lesson Review: Get-Togethers

- Say, *"Yesterday we talked about the rules and steps for having get-togethers. What are some of the rules and steps for having successful get-togethers?"*

[Have teens generate all of the rules and steps for ***get-togethers***. Be prepared to give prompts if necessary. Write the following buzzwords (***bold and italicized***) on the board and do not erase until the end of the lesson.]

Preparing for Get-Togethers

- ○ *Make plans using the four W's*
  - ■ *WHO is going to be there*
  - ■ *WHAT you're going to do*
  - ■ *WHERE you're going to get together*
  - ■ *WHEN you're going to get together*
  - ■ *HOW the get-together is going to happen*

- ○ *Have other activities ready*

- ○ *Put away personal items you don't want others to share or see*

- ○ *Make sure your space is presentable*

Steps for Beginning Get-Togethers

1. *Greet your guest*

2. *Invite them in*

3. *Introduce them to anyone they don't know*

4. *Give them a tour*

5. *Offer them refreshments*

6. *Ask them what they want to do*

Rules for During Get-Togethers

- ○ *The guest gets to pick the activities at your home*

- ○ *Be a good sport*

- ○ *Give compliments*

- ○ *Be loyal to your friends*

- ○ *Stick up for your friends*

- ○ *Don't ignore your friends*

- ○ *Suggest a change if you get bored*

- ○ *Trade information at least 50 percent of the time*

Steps for Ending Get-Togethers

1. *Wait for a pause in activities*

2. *Give a cover story for leaving or ending the get-together*

   a. *"I have to go soon."*
   b. *"I have to start my homework now."*
   c. *"My mom said it's time for dinner."*
   d. *"I have to go to bed soon."*

3. *Start walking your friend to the door*

4. *Thank your friend for getting together*

5. *Tell your friend you had a good time*

6. *Say goodbye and you'll see them later*

Role-Plays: Beginning and Ending a Get-Together

[The instructor and the behavioral coach should do an APPROPRIATE role-play with the instructor *beginning a get-together* following the steps.]

- Begin by saying, *"We're going to do a role-play. Watch this and tell me what I'm doing RIGHT in beginning this get-together."*

   Example of an APPROPRIATE role-play:

   - Coach: (Knocks on door)
   - Instructor: (Opens door) *"Hi (insert name)! How are you?"*
   - Coach: *"Hi! I'm fine. How are you?"*
   - Instructor: *"Fine, thanks. Come on in."* (Moves aside so the coach can enter)
   - Coach: (Enters) *"Thanks."*
   - Instructor: *"I don't think you've met my friend before. This is (insert name of another coach or teen). This is (insert name of coach just arriving)."*

- Coach: *"Nice to meet you."*
- Instructor: *"So I guess you've never been here before. I should show you around real quick. (Give an imaginary tour.) This is the living room. The kitchen is through there. The bathroom is just around the corner. And my bedroom is upstairs."*
- Coach: *"Cool. Thanks."*
- Instructor: *"Can I get you something to eat or drink?"*
- Coach: *"Thanks anyway. I'm okay."*
- Instructor: (Looking at the two coaches) *"So what do you guys want to do?"*
- Coach: *"Maybe we could play some videogames?"*

- End by saying, *"Time out on that. So what did I do RIGHT in beginning that get-together?"*

  - Answer: **Greeted your guest, invited your guest in, introduced your guests, gave a tour, offered refreshments, asked your guests what they wanted to do**

- Ask the following **Perspective Taking Questions**:

  - *"What was that like for (name of coach)?"*

    - Answers: Fine; normal

  - *"What do you think (name of coach) thought of me?"*

    - Answers: Friendly; normal; a good host

  - *"Is (name of coach) going to want to hang out with me again?"*

    - Answer: Maybe; so far so good

- Ask the behavioral coach the same **Perspective Taking Questions**:

  - *"What was that like for you?"*
  - *"What did you think of me?"*
  - *"Would you want to hang out with me again?"*

[The instructor and the behavioral coach should do an APPROPRIATE role-play with the instructor **ending a get-together** following the steps.]

- Begin by saying, *"We're going to do another role-play. Watch this and tell me what I'm doing RIGHT in ending this get-together."*

  Example of an APPROPRIATE role-play:

  - Instructor and Coach: (sitting down)
  - Instructor: *"That was fun playing videogames. You're really good."*
  - Coach: *"Thanks, so are you."*
  - Instructor: (Little pause) *"Well, my mom said we're having dinner now."*
  - Coach: *"Oh, okay."*

-     ■ Instructor: (Stands up and starts walking to the door) *"Thanks for coming over!"*
-     ■ Coach: (Follows instructor to the door) *"Thanks for having me over!"*
-     ■ Instructor: *"It was really fun!"*
-     ■ Coach: *"Yeah, I had a good time, too."*
-     ■ Instructor: *"We should hang out again soon."*
-     ■ Coach: *"That would be cool."*
-     ■ Instructor: (Opens the door) *"So I guess I'll see you at school tomorrow."*
-     ■ Coach: *"Okay. Sounds good."* (Walks through the door)
-     ■ Instructor: *"Take care. Bye!"* (Waves)
-     ■ Coach: (Waves) *"Bye!"*

- End by saying, *"Time out on that. So what did I do RIGHT in ending that get-together?"*
  - ○ Answer: **Waited for a pause in the activity, gave a cover story, started walking your friend to the door, thanked your friend for coming over, said you had a good time, said you would see your friend later, said goodbye**

- Ask the following **Perspective Taking Questions**:
  - ○ *"What was that like for (name of coach)?"*
    - ■ Answers: Fine; normal
  - ○ *"What do you think (name of coach) thought of me?"*
    - ■ Answers: Friendly; normal; a good host
  - ○ *"Is (name of coach) going to want to hang out with me again?"*
    - ■ Answer: Yes; probably

- Ask the behavioral coach the same **Perspective Taking Questions**:
  - ○ *"What was that like for you?"*
  - ○ *"What did you think of me?"*
  - ○ *"Would you want to hang out with me again?"*

Behavioral Rehearsal: Beginning and Ending Get-Togethers

- Notify teens they will be practicing *beginning and ending get-togethers*

- Break teens up into small groups (no less than three teens)
  - ○ When possible, girls should be paired with girls and boys should be paired with boys

- Have teens practice *beginning a get-together*

  - ○ Assign *"hosts"* and *"guests"*

    - ■ One teen will be the *"host"*
    - ■ One teen will be the *"arriving guest"*
    - ■ The other teens will be the *"guests that have already arrived"*

- Begin by having the *"host"* verbally go over the steps for **beginning a get-together** (they may need to look at the board at first)
- The *"arriving guest"* should step outside and knock on the door
- The *"guests that have already arrived"* should be seated somewhere near
- Have the *"host"* follow the steps for **beginning the get-together**
- Each teen should have an opportunity to be a *"host,"* an *"arriving guest,"* and a *"guest that has already arrived"*

- Have teens practice **ending a get-together**

  - Assign *"hosts"* and *"guests"*

    - One teen will be the *"host"*
    - The other teens will be the *"guests"*

  - Have the *"host"* verbally go over the steps for **ending a get-together** (they may need to look at the board at first)
  - The *"hosts"* and *"guests"* should be seated before they begin so that the *"host"* has to stand up and start walking the *"guests"* to the door
  - Have the *"host"* follow the steps for **ending the get-together**

    - *"Guests"* should actually leave and then come back at the end of the role-play

  - Each teen should have an opportunity to be a *"host"* and a *"guest"*

Homework Assignments

- Briefly explain the homework for the week by saying, *"We're going to continue to have you practice having get-togethers this week."*

- Present the homework assignments for the coming week:

  1. Teens are to have a **get-together** with a friend

     a. Follow the steps for **preparing for the get-together**
     b. **Get-togethers** should be **activity-based**
     c. **Trade information** and **find common interests** at least 50 percent of the time
     d. Initial **get-togethers** with new friends should be limited to approximately two hours (depending on the activity)

  2. Practice **being a good sport**

     a. This can be done within the context of the **get-together** or anytime during the week when the teen plays games or sports

  3. Practice **joining a group conversation** between at least two teens you feel comfortable with

     a. Before **joining**:

        i. Think of a place where you are likely to be accepted and you don't have a bad reputation

    b. During the conversation:

        i.   Follow the steps for *joining a group conversation*

        ii. *Assess interest* and follow the steps for *exiting a conversation* if needed

    c. After *joining*:

        i.   Parents and teen should discuss how the teen *joined and exited the group conversation* (if relevant)

        ii. Parents should help teen *troubleshoot* any problems that may have arisen

4. *Bring an inside game*

    a. Bring an inside game to share with the class on **Thursday and Friday of next week** (e.g., age appropriate board game, card game, etc.)

    b. Do not bring a solitary game (like a portable gaming device) or something that you are unwilling to share or are worried about breaking or losing

Wrap Up

Say, *"So those are your homework assignments for this week. Be sure to start working on these assignments right away. We'll be reviewing how they went at the beginning of next week. Tomorrow we'll continue our discussion about get-togethers."*

Calculate Points

Calculate the number of points earned by each teen (see Appendix E for the Daily Point Log):

- Do not publicly disclose the individual number of points

- Discourage attempts to compare number of points earned between teens

    ■ Remind them that they are working as a team to earn a bigger and better graduation party

Days Four and Five: Teen Activity—Get-Togethers and Good Sportsmanship

Lesson Review: Get-Togethers

- Say, *"This week we've been talking about the rules and steps for having get-togethers. What are some of the rules and steps for having successful get-togethers?"*

[Have teens generate all of the rules and steps for **get-togethers**. Be prepared to give prompts if necessary. Write the following buzzwords (**bold and italicized**) on the board and do not erase until the end of the lesson.]

Preparing for Get-Togethers

- *Make plans using the four W's*

  - *WHO is going to be there*
  - *WHAT you're going to do*
  - *WHERE you're going to get together*
  - *WHEN you're going to get together*
  - *HOW the get-together is going to happen*

- *Have other activities ready*

- *Put away personal items you don't want others to share or see*

- *Make sure your space is presentable*

Steps for Beginning Get-Togethers

1. *Greet your guest*

2. *Invite them in*

3. *Introduce them to anyone they don't know*

4. *Give them a tour*

5. *Offer them refreshments*

6. *Ask them what they want to do*

Rules for During Get-Togethers

- *The guest gets to pick the activities at your home*

- *Be a good sport*

- *Give compliments*

- ○ *Be loyal to your friends*

- ○ *Stick up for your friends*

- ○ *Don't ignore your friends*

- ○ *Suggest a change if you get bored*

- ○ *Trade information at least 50 percent of the time*

Steps for Ending Get-Togethers

1. *Wait for a pause in activities*

2. *Give a cover story for leaving or ending the get-together*

   a. *"I have to go soon."*
   b. *"I have to start my homework now."*
   c. *"My mom said it's time for dinner."*
   d. *"I have to go to bed soon."*

3. *Start walking your friend to the door*

4. *Thank your friend for getting together*

5. *Tell your friend you had a good time*

6. *Say goodbye and you'll see them later*

Teen Activity: Get-Togethers and Good Sportsmanship

Materials Needed

- Indoor games brought by teens

- In the event that teens forget to bring indoor games, have board games and card games available to use if possible

Rules

- Notify teens they will be practicing *beginning and ending get-togethers* and *good sportsmanship*

- Break teens up into small groups (no less than three teens)

  - ○ When possible, girls should be paired with girls and boys should be paired with boys

- Have teens practice *beginning a get-together*

  - ○ Assign *"hosts"* and *"guests"*

    - One teen will be the *"host"*

- One teen will be the *"arriving guest"*
- The other teens will be the *"guests that have already arrived"*

  ○ Begin by having the *"host"* verbally go over the steps for **beginning a get-together** (they may need to look at the board at first)
  ○ The *"arriving guest"* should step outside and knock on the door
  ○ The *"guests that have already arrived"* should be seated somewhere near
  ○ Have the *"host"* follow the steps for **beginning the get-together**
  ○ Each teen should have an opportunity to be a *"host,"* an *"arriving guest,"* and a *"guest that has already arrived"*

- Have teens practice **good sportsmanship** during **get-togethers**

  ○ Teens will play indoor games while practicing **good sportsmanship**
  ○ Games are chosen from appropriate **inside games** brought by teens and other available games provided by the instructor

    - Have teens negotiate what they will play

      • The last *"host"* should ask his or her *"guests"* what they want to play
      • They may need to compromise by playing one game for half the time and then switching games midway

  ○ You may need to assist teens in understanding the rules for specific games

    - Try to avoid acting as a referee if disagreements occur
    - Encourage teens to work out their differences by being **good sports**

  ○ You may need to prompt teens to be **good sports** and **praise** their partners, saying things like:

    - *"Johnny just made a nice move, what could you say?"*
    - *"Jenny got a lucky hand, what could you say?"*
    - *"What do we say at the end of the game?"*

  ○ Teens receive points while playing games for practicing:

    - *Praising*
    - *Playing by the rules*
    - *Not refereeing*
    - *Not coaching*
    - *Sharing and taking turns*
    - *Not being competitive*
    - *Helping and showing concern if someone is injured* (outdoor sports)
    - *Suggesting a change if bored*
    - *Not being a bad winner*
    - *Not being a sore loser*
    - *Saying "good game" at the end of the game*

  ○ When giving points:

    - Say the teen's name first to get his or her attention
    - State what the reward is (i.e., getting a point)

- Give the reason for the reward (i.e., being a *good sport*)

  - Examples:

    - *"Jimmy gets a point for saying 'good job'!"*
    - *"Jenny gets a point for taking turns!"*
    - *"Johnny gets a point for giving a high five!"*
    - *"Julie gets a point for saying 'good game'!"*
    - *"Joey gets a point for praising!"*

- Speak loudly when giving out points so other teens can hear

  - The social comparison will encourage other teens to *praise* and be *good sports*

  - Be sure to keep track of points on the Good Sportsmanship Point Log (see Appendix F)

- Have teens practice *ending a get-together*

  - Assign *"hosts"* and *"guests"*

    - One teen will be the *"host"*
    - The other teens will be the *"guests"*

  - Have the *"host"* verbally go over the steps for *ending a get-together* (they may need to look at the board at first)
  - The *"hosts"* and *"guests"* should be seated before they begin so that the *"host"* has to stand up and start walking the *"guests"* to the door
  - Have the *"host"* follow the steps for *ending the get-together*

    - *"Guests"* should actually leave and then come back at the end of the role-play

  - Each teen should have an opportunity to be a *"host"* and a *"guest"*

Homework Assignments

- Briefly explain the homework for the week by saying, *"We're going to continue to have you practice having get-togethers this week."*

- Present the homework assignment for the coming week:

  1. Teens are to have a *get-together* with a friend

     a. Follow the steps for *preparing for the get-together*
     b. *Get-togethers* should be *activity-based*
     c. *Trade information* and *find common interests* at least 50 percent of the time
     d. Initial *get-togethers* with new friends should be limited to approximately two hours (depending on the activity)

  2. Practice *being a good sport*

     a. This can be done within the context of the *get-together* or anytime during the week when the teen plays games or sports

3. Practice *joining a group conversation* between at least two teens you feel comfortable with

    a. Before *joining*:

        i. Think of a place where you are likely to be accepted and you don't have a bad reputation

    b. During the conversation:

        i. Follow the steps for *joining a group conversation*
        ii. *Assess interest* and follow the steps for *exiting a conversation* if needed

    c. After *joining*:

        i. Parents and teen should discuss how the teen *joined and exited the group conversation* (if relevant)
        ii. Parents should help teen *troubleshoot* any problems that may have arisen

4. *Bring an inside game*

    a. Bring an inside game to share with the class on **Thursday and Friday of next week** (e.g., age appropriate board game, card game, etc.)
    b. Do not bring a solitary game (like a portable gaming device) or something that you are unwilling to share or are worried about breaking or losing

Wrap Up

Say, *"So those are your homework assignments for this week. Be sure to start working on these assignments right away. We'll be reviewing how they went at the beginning of next week."*

Calculate Points

Calculate the number of points earned by each teen (see Appendix E for the Daily Point Log):

- Do not publicly disclose the individual number of points

- Discourage attempts to compare number of points earned between teens

    - Remind them that they are working as a team to earn a bigger and better graduation party

Parent Handout 9

PEERS® *Program for the Education and Enrichment of Relational Skills*

Get-Togethers

This week your teens will be learning how to have successful get-togethers with peers. Having get-togethers is an important part of developing friendships in adolescence. Parents play a critical role in supporting teens to organize get-togethers and make sure they go smoothly. Specific suggestions about how to help your teen have a successful get-together are provided below.

Get-togethers should be *activity-based* whenever possible to avoid boredom and to take the pressure off having to converse the whole time. Activities should be based on the *common interests* of everyone.

Common Activity-Based Get-Togethers Identified by Teens

Public Activities	Indoor Activities	Amusement Parks
Movie theaters	Computer/Videogames	Gaming centers
Malls	Surf the Internet	Video arcades
Comic book conventions	Social networking sites	Laser tag
Comic book stores	Listen to music	Circus
Gaming stores	Rent movies	Miniature golf parks
Science expos	Watch TV	Water parks
Science museums	Card games	Go-carting
Warhammer	Board games	Batting cages
Concerts	Ping pong	Golf ranges
Bowling	Pool	Zoos
Dog parks	Air hockey	Aquariums
Beach/Lake/River	Darts	State and county fairs

Mealtime Activities	Pair Sports	Group Sports
Restaurants	Swimming	Basketball
Ice-cream shops	Skateboarding	Baseball
Frozen-yogurt shops	Shooting baskets	Soccer
Order pizza	Bike riding	Touch football
Barbeque	Roller skating	Airsoft
Sushi	Tennis	Volleyball
Cook a meal	Skiing	Badminton
Picnic	Surfing	Water polo
Bake	Hiking	Bocce ball

Preparing for Get-Togethers

- *Make plans using the four W's*

  - *WHO is going to be there*
  - *WHAT you're going to do*

- *WHERE you're going to get together*
- *WHEN you're going to get together*
- *HOW the get-together is going to happen*

- *Have other activities ready*

  - DVDs, videos
  - Videogames, computer games
  - Board games, card games
  - Sports equipment

- *Put away personal items you don't want others to share or see*

- *Make sure your space is presentable*

  - Clean your room or car when relevant

Steps for Beginning Get-Togethers

1. *Greet your guest*

2. *Invite them in*

3. *Introduce them to anyone they don't know*

4. *Give them a tour*

5. *Offer them refreshments*

6. *Ask them what they want to do*

Rules for During Get-Togethers

- *The guest gets to pick the activities at your home*

  - This is because it's your job to make sure the guest has a good time
  - The only exception is if your guest wants to do something dangerous or inappropriate

- *Be a good sport*

  - Following the rules for being a *good sport* when playing games and sports

- *Give compliments*

  - This shows that you're nice and a good friend

- *Be loyal to your friends*

  - Don't argue, criticize, or make fun of your friends

- *Stick up for your friends*

  - If one friend is picking on another friend, you need to stick up for them and keep the peace (especially if you're the host)

- *Don't ignore your friends*

  - No text messaging, emailing, or instant messaging (unless it's your friend's idea)
  - If someone unexpectedly calls, texts, or stops by during your *get-together*:

    - Don't invite them over
    - Don't ignore your friend to talk with them
    - Tell them you're busy and that you'll get back to them later

- *Suggest a change if you get bored*

  - If you're bored say, *"How about when we're done with this we play something else?"*
  - If your friend doesn't want to do what you suggest, have them suggest the next activity

- *Trade information at least 50 percent of the time*

  - This is how you get to know each other and develop a closer friendship

Steps for Ending Get-Togethers

1. *Wait for a pause in activities*

2. *Give a cover story for leaving or ending the get-together*

   a. *"I have to go soon."*
   b. *"I have to start my homework now."*
   c. *"My mom said it's time for dinner."*
   d. *"I have to go to bed soon."*

3. *Start walking your friend to the door*

4. *Thank your friend for getting together*

5. *Tell your friend you had a good time*

6. *Say goodbye and you'll see them later*

Parent Tips to Help Teens Have Good Get-Togethers

- Provide a safe and comfortable environment in your home

  - Allow your teen's friends to hang out at your home with some privacy
  - Check on conversations by offering snacks

    - Unobtrusively observe
    - Do not intrude on conversations unless it is to offer snacks
      - Hint: Make several trips with the food at various times in order to monitor the *get-together*

  - Do not allow siblings to join the *get-together*

- ○ Help your teen organize an activity that would be of ***common interest*** to your teen and his or her friends

- Remind your teen prior to the ***get-together*** that at least 50 percent of the time should be spent ***trading information***

- Try to limit first-time ***get-togethers*** to no more than two hours (depending on the activity) to lessen the pressure on your teen

  - ○ It's better to have your teen's friend leave wanting more than to have them tire of one another

- Help your teen by providing a ***cover story*** at the end of the ***get-together*** (e.g., *"It's time to say goodbye to your friend. We need to eat dinner."*)

Homework Assignments

Every week your teen will have homework assignments to practice new and previously learned social skills. It is extremely helpful if parents assist teens in completing these assignments. The homework assignments for this week include the following:

1. Teens are to have a ***get-together*** with a friend

   a. Follow the steps for ***preparing for the get-together***
   b. ***Get-togethers*** should be ***activity-based***
   c. ***Trade information*** and ***find common interests*** at least 50 percent of the time
   d. Initial ***get-togethers*** with new friends should be limited to approximately two hours (depending on the activity)

2. Practice ***being a good sport***

   a. This can be done within the context of the ***get-together*** or anytime during the week when the teen plays games or sports

3. Practice ***joining a group conversation*** between at least two teens you feel comfortable with

   a. Before ***joining***:

      i. Think of a place where you are likely to be accepted and you don't have a bad reputation

   b. During the conversation:

      i. Follow the steps for ***joining a group conversation***
      ii. ***Assess interest*** and follow the steps for ***exiting a conversation*** if needed

   c. After ***joining***:

      i. Parents and teen should discuss how the teen ***joined and exited the group conversation*** (if relevant)
      ii. Parents should help teen ***troubleshoot*** any problems that may have arisen

4. *Bring an inside game*

    a. Bring an inside game to share with the class on **Thursday and Friday of next week** (e.g., age appropriate board game, card game, etc.)

    b. Do not bring a solitary game (like a portable gaming device) or something that you are unwilling to share or are worried about breaking or losing

HANDLING ARGUMENTS

Preparing for the Lesson

The purpose of the lesson this week is to teach teens basic skills to resolve arguments and disagreements with peers. Misunderstandings and disagreements are common among teenagers, and when infrequent and not too explosive, they do not need to result in the termination of friendships. Yet, some teens that lack skills for resolving arguments may be unable to see a way out of disagreements and may choose to end friendships.

Difficulty with problem resolution is somewhat characteristic of teens with Autism Spectrum Disorder (ASD), as they have a tendency to think concretely with little flexibility. For many teens with ASD, interpreting friendship status may be very black and white. For example, they might imagine that when they are getting along with others, they are friends, but when they are not getting along with others, they are not friends. An important goal of this lesson is to help teens understand that occasional arguments with friends do not need to result in the dissolution of friendship. Rather, through appropriate conflict resolution, friendships should be able to be maintained despite periodic disagreements. Yet, some teens that find themselves engaged in frequent and/or explosive conflicts with specific friends may need to reexamine the appropriateness of their friendship choices.

Research suggests that teens are more attentive to emotional reaction and resolution of conflict than the frequency of conflicts with peers. Successful negotiation of conflict may even result in closer friendships for some. Perhaps the ability to work through problems without terminating the relationship ultimately strengthens the commitment to these friendships.

A number of studies have investigated the effective strategies used by adolescents and adults to resolve conflict. This lesson incorporates these findings into teaching teens how to deal with conflict with peers following simple and concrete steps. The greatest challenge in this lesson involves helping teens understand that they must complete EACH STEP in this series of steps in order to successfully resolve arguments with others. Many teens will pick and choose which steps to use, rather than using each of the steps as a whole. Some teens may disagree with the lesson, making statements like, *"It never works to just say you're sorry"* or *"It doesn't work to just explain your side."* The reality is that statements like that are actually true. It rarely does work to ONLY say you are sorry, or ONLY explain your side. It is the combination of ALL of the steps that lead to effective conflict resolution.

The role-play demonstration in day two will assist you in driving home the point that all of the steps must be followed. In this role-play, you and a behavioral coach will demonstrate **handling an argument** by presenting each step individually and in succession, adding a new step in each phase of the role-play, while timing out in between the steps to have teens identify whether it feels like the argument is over. Conducting the role-play by showing all of the steps together in one unified whole will not convince teens that they must follow ALL of the steps. Don't make that mistake when conducting the first role-play demonstration on day two. Your second role-play demonstration of **handling an argument** on day three can involve all the steps in a unified sequence, as the point will already have been made.

Another challenge in this lesson relates to the step in which teens are told to **repeat what the other person said**. Essentially, this step is intended to involve *active and empathic listening*. The challenge with this step is that many teens with ASD and other social challenges struggle to understand emotions and communicate empathy. They may have difficulty understanding and labeling emotions in themselves and others, which impedes their ability to listen actively and express empathy during arguments. Consequently, you will present a simpler alternative to *active and empathic listening* through the rule to **repeat what the other person said**. In this case, you will give teens a sentence stem to help them through the process. Teens will be instructed that they can demonstrate that they are listening and showing empathy by saying, *"It sounds like . . ."* Examples might include, *"It sounds like you're upset," "It sounds like I made you mad,"* or *"It sounds like I hurt your feelings."* Although this sentence stem will help teens to demonstrate *active and empathic listening*, these statements may sound a bit artificial. If teens are socially savvy enough to discern the artificiality of these statements, then they may be well-equipped enough to provide more empathic responses. Feel free to encourage teens to use more empathic responses when appropriate. For those who struggle to communicate empathy, sticking to simple sentences that begin with *"It sounds like . . ."* should be sufficient to communicate that they are listening actively.

One question that may come up in this lesson relates to what to do if the situation is reversed and the teen is upset with someone else. In this situation the steps involved are the same, with just the order changed. To begin with, the person who is upset will want to **explain his or her side** while **keeping their cool**. The other person should also have a chance to **explain his or her side**, which will involve **listening** and **repeating what they said. Trying to solve the problem** will be equally important, and may involve the teen **suggesting what they want the other person to do** if a resolution is not automatically offered. Finally, all arguments should end with some type of **apology** from both sides, even if it's simply to say, *"I'm sorry that this happened."*

While this lesson may have limited immediate applicability for some teens, as with all other skills, the maximum effectiveness of the lesson comes with practice between classes. If there are no peer interactions with conflict, then the teen may not get to try out the skills being taught. Consequently, it is recommended that you encourage teens to practice following the steps for **handling arguments** at home with their parents during behavioral rehearsal exercises, utilize opportunities for practice during real sibling conflict, and have parents hold on to the Parent Handout for a time when conflict is present in one of their teen's friendships.

Day One: Homework Review

Homework Review

[Start with completed homework first. If you have time, you can inquire as to why others were unable to complete the assignment and try to **troubleshoot** how they might get it done for the coming week. When reviewing homework, be sure to use the buzzwords (**bold and italicized**) and **troubleshoot** issues that come up. Spend the majority of the homework review on **get-togethers** and **joining a group conversation**, as these were the most important assignments.]

[Note: Give multiple points for homework parts—not just one point per assignment.]

1. **Get-together**

    a. Say, *"Your main homework assignment this week was to have a get-together with a friend. Raise your hand if you had a get-together this week."*

    i. Ask, *"Who did you have a get-together with?"*
    ii. Ask, *"Did you talk beforehand to figure out what you were going to do?"*
    iii. Ask, *"What did you end up doing?"*
    iv. Ask, *"Who got to pick the activities?"* (Answer: Should be the guest)
    v. Ask, *"Did you trade information?"*

    1. If yes, follow up by asking, *"What percentage of the time did you trade information?"* (Answer: Should be at least 50 percent)

    vi. Ask, *"Did you have a good time?"*
    vii. Ask, *"Did your friend have a good time?"*
    viii. Ask, *"Is this someone you might want to have a get-together with again?"*

2. **Being a good sport**

    a. Say, *"Another assignment this week was to practice being a good sport. This may have happened during your get-together, at school during gym class, or during your extracurricular activities. Raise your hand if you practiced being a good sport this week."*

    i. Ask, *"Where did you practice being a good sport?"*
    ii. Ask, *"What did you do or say to show that you were a good sport?"*

3. **Joining a group conversation**

    a. Say, *"Another one of your assignments this week was to practice joining a conversation with a group that you were likely to be accepted by. Raise your hand if you practiced joining a group conversation this week."*

    i. Ask, *"Where did you join?"*
    ii. Ask, *"How did you join?"*

    1. Be sure they followed the **steps for joining a group conversation**:

      a. *Listen to the conversation*

      b. *Watch from a distance*

      c. *Use a prop*

      d. *Identify the topic*

      e. *Find a common interest*

      f. *Move closer*

      g. *Wait for a pause*

      h. *Mention the topic*

      i. *Assess interest*

      j. *Introduce yourself* (if appropriate)

iii. Ask, *"Did it seem like they wanted to talk to you?"*

    1. Ask, *"How could you tell?"*

        a. *Talking to you*

        b. *Looking at you*

        c. *Facing you (opened the circle)*

iv. Ask, *"Did you need to exit the conversation?"*

    1. If they *exited the conversation*, be sure they followed the steps based on whether they were *never accepted*, *initially accepted and then excluded*, or *fully accepted*

4. *Bring an inside game*

    a. Identify the inside game the teen will bring to share later this week (e.g., age appropriate board game, card game, etc.)

Wrap Up

Say, *"Good work for those of you who completed your homework assignments. Tomorrow we will be talking about how to manage arguments with friends."*

Calculate Points

Calculate the number of points earned by each teen (see Appendix E for the Daily Point Log):

- Do not publicly disclose the individual number of points

- Discourage attempts to compare number of points earned between teens

  - Remind them that they are working as a team to earn a bigger and better graduation party

Day Two: Didactic Lesson—Handling Arguments

Didactic Lesson: Handling Arguments

Explain, *"Today we're going to be talking about how to manage arguments and disagreements. Arguments with friends are common, and OCCASIONAL arguments that aren't too explosive shouldn't have to end your friendship. If you're having frequent and explosive arguments with a friend, you may need to consider whether this friendship is a good choice. Because we know that OCCASIONAL arguments are common, it's important to know how to manage them so they don't hurt our friendships."*

[Present the steps for **handling arguments** by writing the following buzzwords (**bold and italicized**) on the board. Do not erase the steps until the end of the lesson.]

1. ***Keep your cool***

   a. Say, *"The first step for handling a disagreement with a friend is to keep your cool. This means you need to stay calm and don't get upset. What are some ways people keep their cool?"*

      i. Answer: Take deep breaths, count to ten silently, take some time to cool down before you talk

   b. Ask, *"What could be the problem with losing your cool during an argument?"*

      i. Answer: Because if you lose your cool you may end up saying something you regret or ruining your friendship

2. ***Listen to the other person***

   a. Explain, *"The next step for handling an argument with a friend is to listen. That means if your friend is upset, you need to listen before you share your side."*

   b. Ask, *"Why is it important to listen to the other person's side?"*

      i. Answer: Listening is an important part of communication and helps us to understand the other person's perspective

3. ***Repeat what they said***

   a. Explain, *"The next step is to repeat back what they said to let them know you're listening to them."*

   b. Ask, *"Why would it be important to repeat back what the other person said?"*

      i. Answer: It shows them that you're listening, makes them feel like you care, makes them feel heard, shows that you have empathy

   c. Explain, *"Repeating statements usually start with, 'It sounds like . . .'"*

      i. Examples:

         1. *"It sounds like you're upset."*
         2. *"It sounds like you're angry."*
         3. *"It sounds like your feelings are hurt."*

d. Have each of the teens give an example of how to **repeat what the other person said** by presenting the following complaints and then having teens generate corresponding **repeating statements**

   i. Say, *"I feel bad when you tell jokes about me."*

      1. Example: *"It sounds like I upset you."*

   ii. Say, *"I feel bad when you make fun of me."*

      1. Example: *"It sounds like what I said made you feel bad."*

   iii. Say, *"I feel frustrated when you tell jokes about me."*

      1. Example: *"It sounds like I made you upset."*

   iv. Say, *"I feel embarrassed when you laugh at me in front of everybody."*

      1. Example: *"It sounds like I made you feel bad."*

   v. Say, *"It hurts my feelings when you don't call me back."*

      1. Example: *"It sounds like I hurt your feelings."*

   vi. Say, *"I feel upset when you say those things."*

      1. Example: *"It sounds like I upset you."*

   vii. Say, *"I don't like it when you tell other people my secrets."*

      1. Example: *"It sounds like I hurt your feelings."*

   viii. Say, *"I don't like it when you talk to me like that."*

      1. Example: *"It sounds like you're upset with me."*

   ix. Say, *"I feel hurt when you blow me off."*

      1. Example: *"It sounds like I hurt your feelings."*

   x. Say, *"It makes me mad when you treat me that way."*

      1. Example: *"It sounds like you're mad at me."*

4. **Explain your side**

   a. Explain, *"The next step is to explain your side. Many people will jump to do this step first, but you need to WAIT until you've kept your cool, listened, and repeated what they've said. When you're explaining your side, you should avoid telling the other person that they're wrong. Instead, calmly explain your side of the story."*

   b. Ask, *"What could be the problem with telling the other person that they're wrong?"*

      i. Answer: This will only upset them and escalate the argument, they are not likely to agree, they will most likely get more upset with you

5. *Say you're sorry*

   a. Explain, *"The next step for handling an argument with a friend is to say you're sorry. Even if you don't think you've done anything wrong, it's important to say you're sorry."*

   b. Ask, *"Why is it important to say you're sorry when someone is upset?"*

      i. Answer: Because the person is feeling bad and wants you to acknowledge that you're sorry they're feeling that way, arguments are rarely over until you've said you're sorry in some way

   c. Explain, *"Saying that you're sorry doesn't mean that you have to admit you did anything wrong. You can simply say you're sorry they feel that way."*

      i. Examples:

         1. *"I'm sorry you're upset."*
         2. *"I'm sorry this happened."*
         3. *"I'm sorry your feelings got hurt."*

6. **Try to solve the problem**:

   a. Explain, *"The last step in handling an argument with a friend is to try to solve the problem. This can be done is several ways."*

      i. **Tell them what you'll do differently**

         1. Examples:

            a. *"I'll try not to upset you again."*
            b. *"I'll try not to do that again."*
            c. *"I'll try to be more careful next time."*

      ii. **Ask them what they want you to do**

         1. Examples:

            a. *"What can I do to make it up to you?"*
            b. *"What would you like me to do?"*
            c. *"What can I do to fix this?"*

      iii. **Suggest what you want them to do** (if you're upset with them)

         1. Examples:

            a. *"I'd like it if you didn't do that again."*
            b. *"I wish you'd be more careful next time."*
            c. *"I'd appreciate it if you didn't say that again."*

   b. **Keep your cool if you can't solve the problem**

      i. Explain, *"If you can't solve the problem, then you at least need to keep your cool. Don't expect the other person to admit they're wrong. Your goal isn't to get them to apologize or admit they're wrong. Your goal is to try to end the argument."*

Role-Play: Handling an Argument

[The instructor and the behavioral coach should do an APPROPRIATE role-play with the instructor *handling an argument* following the steps. Each step should be presented individually and in succession, adding a new step in each phase of the role-play. Explain that you are going to act out a typical teen dispute several times, each time adding a new step. This will illustrate the importance of following EACH STEP.]

- Say, *"The first two steps of handling an argument are to keep your cool and to listen to the other person. Watch this role-play and tell me which steps I'm following."*

- [Demonstrate keeping your cool and listening to the other person]

  Example of an INCOMPLETE role-play:

  - Coach: *"I'm so mad at you (insert name)! I heard that you were talking behind my back and you told everyone that I got grounded for getting a bad grade on my math test."*
  - Instructor: (Keeping cool, not getting upset, listening)
  - Coach: *"I can't believe you told everyone that! That was supposed to be a secret. And now everyone knows. That's so uncool."*
  - Instructor: (Keeping cool, not getting upset, listening)

- Say, *"Time out on that. So which of the steps did I follow?"*

  - Answer: **Kept your cool, listened to the other person**

- Ask, *"Does it feel like the argument is over?"*

  - Answer: No

- Explain, *"The next step is to repeat what the person said. Watch this and tell me which steps I'm following."*

- [Demonstrate **keeping your cool**, **listening to the other person**, and **repeating what the person** said by saying, **"It sounds like . . ."**]

  Example of an INCOMPLETE role-play:

  - Coach: *"I'm so mad at you (insert name)! I heard that you were talking behind my back and you told everyone that I got grounded for getting a bad grade on my math test."*
  - Instructor: (Keeping cool, not getting upset, listening)
  - Coach: *"I can't believe you told everyone that! That was supposed to be a secret. And now everyone knows. That's so uncool."*
  - Instructor: *"It sounds like you're really upset with me."*
  - Coach: *"Yeah, I'm upset! I told you that in secret. You weren't supposed to say anything. Now everyone knows my business and is making fun of me."*
  - Instructor: (Looks apologetic)

- Say, *"Time out on that. So which of the steps did I follow?"*

  ○ Answer: **Kept your cool, listened to the other person, repeated what they said**

- Ask, *"Does it feel like the argument is over?"*

  ○ Answer: No

- Explain, *"The next step is to explain your side. Watch this and tell me which steps I'm following."*

- [Demonstrate **keeping your cool, listening to the other person, repeating what the person said** by saying, **"It sounds like . . ."** and **explaining your side**]

  Example of an INCOMPLETE role-play:

  - Coach: *"I'm so mad at you (insert name)! I heard that you were talking behind my back and you told everyone that I got grounded for getting a bad grade on my math test."*
  - Instructor: (Keeping cool, not getting upset, listening)
  - Coach: *"I can't believe you told everyone that! That was supposed to be a secret. And now everyone knows. That's so uncool."*
  - Instructor: *"It sounds like you're really upset with me."*
  - Coach: *"Yeah, I'm upset! I told you that in secret. You weren't supposed to say anything. Now everyone knows my business and is making fun of me."*
  - Instructor: (Looks apologetic) *"I didn't realize that was a secret. I didn't think I was talking behind your back because I thought people already knew. I didn't realize people were going to make fun of you."*
  - Coach: *"Well they are and it's your fault! If you hadn't said anything then none of this would have happened."*
  - Instructor: (Looks apologetic)

- Say, *"Time out on that. So which of the steps did I follow?"*

  ○ Answer: **Kept your cool, listened to the other person, repeated what they said, explained your side**

- Ask, *"Does it feel like the argument is over?"*

  ○ Answer: No

- Explain, *"The next step is to say you're sorry. Watch this and tell me which steps I'm following."*

- [Demonstrate **keeping your cool, listening to the other person, repeating what the person said** by saying, **"It sounds like . . . ,"** **explaining your side**, and **saying you're sorry**]

  Example of an INCOMPLETE role-play:

  - Coach: *"I'm so mad at you (insert name)! I heard that you were talking behind my back and you told everyone that I got grounded for getting a bad grade on my math test."*

- Instructor: (Keeping cool, not getting upset, listening)
- Coach: *"I can't believe you told everyone that! That was supposed to be a secret. And now everyone knows. That's so uncool."*
- Instructor: *"It sounds like you're really upset with me."*
- Coach: *"Yeah, I'm upset! I told you that in secret. You weren't supposed to say anything. Now everyone knows my business and is making fun of me."*
- Instructor: (Looks apologetic) *"I didn't realize that was a secret. I didn't think I was talking behind your back because I thought people already knew. I didn't realize people were going to make fun of you."*
- Coach: *"Well they are and it's your fault! If you hadn't said anything then none of this would have happened."*
- Instructor: (Looks apologetic) *"I'm sorry I upset you. I didn't mean to share your secrets."*
- Coach: *"Well you did, and it's too late to do anything about it now."*

- Say, *"Time out on that. So which of the steps did I follow?"*
  - Answer: **Kept your cool, listened to the other person, repeated what they said, explained your side, said you were sorry**

- Ask, *"Does it feel like the argument is over?"*
  - Answer: No

- Explain, *"The next step is to **try to solve the problem**. Watch this and tell me which steps I'm following."*

- Demonstrate all of the steps by **keeping your cool, listening to the other person, repeating what the person said** by saying, *"It sounds like . . . ,"* **explaining yourself, saying you're sorry**, and **trying to solve the problem**

Example of a COMPLETE role-play:

- Coach: *"I'm so mad at you (insert name)! I heard that you were talking behind my back and you told everyone that I got grounded for getting a bad grade on my math test."*
- Instructor: (Keeping cool, not getting upset, listening)
- Coach: *"I can't believe you told everyone that! That was supposed to be a secret. And now everyone knows. That's so uncool."*
- Instructor: *"It sounds like you're really upset with me."*
- Coach: *"Yeah, I'm upset! I told you that in secret. You weren't supposed to say anything. Now everyone knows my business and is making fun of me."*
- Instructor: (Looks apologetic) *"I didn't realize that was a secret. I didn't think I was talking behind your back because I thought people already knew. I didn't realize people were going to make fun of you."*
- Coach: *"Well they are and it's your fault! If you hadn't said anything then none of this would have happened."*
- Instructor: (Looks apologetic) *"I'm sorry I upset you. I didn't mean to share your secrets."*

- Coach: *"Well you did, and it's too late to do anything about it now."*
- Instructor: *"You're right. But I didn't mean for that to happen. From now on I'll be more careful about not telling people your business and I promise not to talk behind your back."*
- Coach: (Long pause) *"Okay, fine."* (Said reluctantly, still a little annoyed)

- Say, *"Time out on that. So which of the steps did I follow?"*

  - Answer: **Kept your cool, listened to the other person, repeated what they said, explained your side, said you were sorry, tried to solve the problem**

- Ask, *"Does it feel like the argument is over?"*

  - Answer: Yes, as much as it can be for now

- Ask the following **Perspective Taking Questions**:

  - *"What was that like for (name of coach) in the end?"*

    - Answers: Controlled; civilized; polite

  - *"What do you think (name of coach) thought of me in the end?"*

    - Answers: Good listener; empathic; apologetic

  - *"Is (name of coach) going to want to hang out with me again?"*

    - Answer: Yes, the friendship may even be stronger moving forward

- Ask the behavioral coach the same **Perspective Taking Questions**:

  - *"What was that like for you in the end?"*
  - *"What did you think of me in the end?"*
  - *"Would you want to hang out with me again?"*

- Explain, *"So remember, each of the steps doesn't work alone. The steps only work when they're done together. If you leave out a step, the argument may not be over, so be sure to follow ALL of the steps in this order."*

Wrap Up

Say, *"So those are the steps for handling arguments with friends. Tomorrow we'll continue our discussion about handling arguments and each of you will practice using these steps."*

Calculate Points

Calculate the number of points earned by each teen (see Appendix E for the Daily Point Log)

- Do not publicly disclose the individual number of points

- Discourage attempts to compare number of points earned between teens

  - Remind them that they are working as a team to earn a bigger and better graduation party

Day Three: Lesson Review and Behavioral Rehearsal

Lesson Review: Handling Arguments

- Say, *"Yesterday we worked on handling arguments. Who can tell us the steps for handling an argument or disagreement?"*

[Have teens generate all of the steps for **handling arguments**. Be prepared to give prompts if necessary. Write the following bullet points and buzzwords (**bold and italicized**) on the board and do not erase until the end of the lesson.]

1. *Keep your cool*

2. *Listen to the other person*

3. *Repeat what they said*

4. *Explain your side*

5. *Say you're sorry*

6. *Try to solve the problem*

   a. *Keep your cool if you can't solve the problem*

Role-Play: Handling an Argument

[The instructor and the behavioral coach should do an APPROPRIATE role-play with the instructor **handling an argument** following all of the steps in sequence without stopping.]

- Begin by saying, *"We're going to do a role-play. Watch this and tell me what I'm doing RIGHT in handling this argument."*

Example of an APPROPRIATE role-play:

- Coach: *"(insert name), what happened Friday night? You completely stood me up!"*
- Instructor: (Keeping cool, not getting upset, listening)
- Coach: *"We had plans to go to the movies. I called you, I texted you, but I didn't hear anything. What happened?"*
- Instructor: (Looks apologetic) *"It sounds like you're really upset."*
- Coach: *"Yeah, I'm really upset! You completely stood me up. I could have done something else, but instead I was waiting around for you all night. I don't understand. What happened?"*
- Instructor: (Looks apologetic) *"Well, here's the thing . . . you know how I have all my numbers and all my plans in my phone? Well I left my phone in my locker on Friday, so I didn't get your messages. I still don't have my phone actually. Plus, I thought we were hanging out this weekend, not last weekend. So I completely misunderstood."*

- ■ Coach: *"No, we had plans for last Friday. We talked about it and I was looking forward to it. I don't need my phone to remember when we're hanging out! It's just really uncool because I wanted to see this movie and I ended up sitting around waiting for you on a Friday night!"*
- ■ Instructor: (Looks apologetic) *"No, you're right. I'm really sorry this happened."*
- ■ Coach: *"You should be sorry. I was sitting around all night. There were so many things I could have done. It wasn't cool."*
- ■ Instructor: (Looks apologetic) *"I know, it wasn't cool. I'll really try not to depend on my phone so much. I was really looking forward to going to the movie with you too. Maybe you could let me try to make it up to you and we could go to the movie this weekend?"*
- ■ Coach: (Still a little annoyed) *"I don't know, I'll think about it."*

- Say, *"Time out on that. So which of the steps did I follow?"*

  - ○ Answer: **Kept your cool, listened to the other person, repeated what they said, explained your side, said you were sorry, tried to solve the problem**

- Ask, *"Does it feel like the argument is over?"*

  - ○ Answer: Yes, as much as it can be for now

- Ask the following *Perspective Taking Questions*:

  - ○ *"What was that like for (name of coach) in the end?"*

    - ■ Answers: Controlled; civilized; polite

  - ○ *"What do you think (name of coach) thought of me in the end?"*

    - ■ Answers: Good listener; empathic; apologetic

  - ○ *"Is (name of coach) going to want to hang out with me again?"*

    - ■ Answer: Yes; the friendship may even be stronger moving forward

- Ask the behavioral coach the same *Perspective Taking Questions*:

  - ○ *"What was that like for you in the end?"*
  - ○ *"What did you think of me in the end?"*
  - ○ *"Would you want to hang out with me again?"*

Behavioral Rehearsal: Handling an Argument

- Go around the room and have each teen practice following each of these steps in a behavioral rehearsal with the instructor

  - ○ The instructor should accuse each teen of something different
  - ○ The teens should feel free to look at the board in order to follow the steps for handling the disagreement

- ■ The instructor may need to point to a certain step on the board if the teen gets stuck as a reminder of what to do next

  - • Try not to interrupt the behavioral rehearsal to offer verbal prompts

- ■ If the teen does something inappropriate, call a time-out and gently point out the error, then have the teen start again from the beginning until he or she is successful in following all of the steps sequentially

- ○ Use different examples of typical teen disputes for each teen behavioral rehearsal

  - ■ Examples:

    - • You're hurt because the teen made fun of you
    - • You're upset because the teen told your secret
    - • You're hurt because you felt ignored by the teen in the hallway
    - • You're annoyed because the teen didn't call when they said they would
    - • You feel betrayed because the teen didn't pick you for his or her team
    - • You're mad because the teen was hanging out with your "enemy"
    - • You're hurt because the teen didn't invite you to his or her get-together
    - • You're angry because the teen laughed when people were teasing you
    - • You're upset because the teen didn't save you a seat at lunch
    - • You feel betrayed because the teen didn't come to your defense when someone accused you of something

Homework Assignments

- • Briefly explain the homework for the week by saying, *"We're going to have you practice handling arguments and continue having get-togethers this week."*

- • Present the homework assignments for the coming week:

  1. Practice **handling an argument**

     a. Parents and teen should practice **handling an argument** following the steps

     b. If it comes up this week, teens should practice **handling an argument** with a friend or a sibling following the steps

        i. Parents and teen should discuss how the teen **handled the argument**

  2. Teens are to have a **get-together** with a friend

     a. Follow the steps for **preparing for the get-together**

     b. **Get-togethers** should be **activity-based**

     c. **Trade information** and **find common interests** at least 50 percent of the time

     d. Initial **get-togethers** with new friends should be limited to approximately two hours (depending on the activity)

  3. Practice **being a good sport**

     a. This can be done within the context of the **get-together** or anytime during the week when the teen plays games or sports

4. ***Bring an inside game***

    a. Bring an inside game to share with the class on **Thursday and Friday of next week** (e.g., age appropriate board game, card game, etc.)

    b. Do not bring a solitary game (like a portable gaming device) or something that you are unwilling to share or are worried about breaking or losing

Wrap Up

Say, *"So those are your homework assignments for this week. Be sure to start working on these assignments right away. We'll be reviewing how they went at the beginning of next week. Tomorrow we'll continue our discussion about handling arguments and we'll practice having get-togethers and good sportsmanship."*

Calculate Points

Calculate the number of points earned by each teen (see Appendix E for the Daily Point Log)

- Do not publicly disclose the individual number of points

- Discourage attempts to compare number of points earned between teens

    ○ Remind them that they are working as a team to earn a bigger and better graduation party

Days Four and Five: Teen Activity—Get-Togethers and Good Sportsmanship

Lesson Review: Handling Arguments

- Say, *"This week we've been talking about how to handle arguments. Who can tell us the steps for handling arguments and disagreements?"*

[Have teens generate all of the steps for **handling arguments**. Be prepared to give prompts if necessary. Write the following bullet points and buzzwords (**bold and italicized**) on the board and do not erase until the end of the lesson.]

1. *Keep your cool*

2. *Listen to the other person first*

3. *Repeat what they said*

4. *Explain your side*

5. *Say you're sorry*

6. *Try to solve the problem*

    a. *Keep your cool if you can't solve the problem*

Teen Activity: Get-Togethers and Good Sportsmanship

Materials Needed

- Indoor games brought by teens

- In the event that teens forget to bring indoor games, have board games and card games available to use if possible

Rules

- Notify teens they will be practicing *beginning and ending get-togethers* and *good sportsmanship*

- Break teens up into small groups (no less than three teens)

    ○ When possible, girls should be paired with girls and boys should be paired with boys

- Have teens practice *beginning a get-together*

    ○ Assign *"hosts"* and *"guests"*

        ■ One teen will be the *"host"*

- One teen will be the *"arriving guest"*
- The other teens will be the *"guests that have already arrived"*

○ Begin by having the *"host"* verbally go over the steps for **beginning a get-together**

1. *Greet your guest*
2. *Invite them in*
3. *Introduce them to anyone they don't know*
4. *Give them a tour*
5. *Offer them refreshments*
6. *Ask them what they want to do*

○ The *"arriving guest"* should step outside and knock on the door
○ The *"guests that have already arrived"* should be seated somewhere near
○ Have the *"host"* follow the steps for **beginning the get-together**
○ Each teen should have an opportunity to be a *"host,"* an *"arriving guest,"* and a *"guest that has already arrived"*

- Have teens practice **good sportsmanship** during **get-togethers**

○ Teens will play indoor games while practicing **good sportsmanship**
○ Games are chosen from appropriate **inside games** brought by teens and other available games provided by the instructor

- Have teens negotiate what they will play

  - The last *"host"* should ask his or her *"guests"* what they want to play
  - They may need to compromise by playing one game for half the time and then switching games midway

○ You may need to assist teens in understanding the rules for specific games

- Try to avoid acting as a referee if disagreements occur
- Encourage teens to work out their differences by being **good sports**

○ You may need to prompt teens to be **good sports** and **praise** their partners, saying things like:

- *"Johnny just made a nice move, what could you say?"*
- *"Jenny got a lucky hand, what could you say?"*
- *"What do we say at the end of the game?"*

○ Teens receive points while playing games for practicing:

- *Praising*
- *Playing by the rules*
- *Not refereeing*
- *Not coaching*
- *Sharing and taking turns*
- *Not being competitive*
- *Helping and showing concern if someone is injured* (outdoor sports)
- *Suggesting a change if bored*
- *Not being a bad winner*

- *Not being a sore loser*
- *Saying "good game" at the end of the game*

o When giving points:

- Say the teen's name first to get his or her attention
- State what the reward is (i.e., getting a point)
- Give the reason for the reward (i.e., being a *good sport*)

• Examples:

o *"Jimmy gets a point for saying 'good job'!"*
o *"Jenny gets a point for taking turns!"*
o *"Johnny gets a point for giving a high five!"*
o *"Julie gets a point for saying 'good game'!"*
o *"Joey gets a point for praising!"*

- Speak loudly when giving out points so other teens can hear

• The social comparison will encourage other teens to *praise* and be *good sports*

o Be sure to keep track of points on the Good Sportsmanship Point Log (see Appendix F)

• Have teens practice *ending a get-together*

o Assign *"hosts"* and *"guests"*

- One teen will be the *"host"*
- The other teens will be the *"guests"*

o Have the *"host"* verbally go over the steps for *ending a get-together*

1. *Wait for a pause in activities*
2. *Give a cover story for leaving or ending the get-together*
3. *Start walking your friend to the door*
4. *Thank your friend for getting together*
5. *Tell your friend you had a good time*
6. *Say goodbye and you'll see them later*

o The *"hosts"* and *"guests"* should be seated before they begin so that the *"host"* has to stand up and start walking the *"guests"* to the door
o Have the *"host"* follow the steps for *ending the get-together*

- *"Guests"* should actually leave and then come back at the end of the role-play

o Each teen should have an opportunity to be a *"host"* and a *"guest"*

Homework Assignments

- Briefly explain the homework for the week by saying, *"We're going have you practice handling arguments and continue practicing having get-togethers this week."*

- Present the homework assignments for the coming week:

1. Practice *handling an argument*

   a. Parents and teen should practice *handling an argument* following the steps
   b. If it comes up this week, teens should practice *handling an argument* with a friend or a sibling following the steps

      i. Parents and teen should discuss how the teen *handled the argument*

2. Teens are to have a *get-together* with a friend

   a. Follow the steps for *preparing for the get-together*
   b. *Get-togethers* should be *activity-based*
   c. *Trade information* and *find common interests* at least 50 percent of the time
   d. Initial *get-togethers* with new friends should be limited to approximately two hours (depending on the activity)

3. Practice *being a good sport*

   a. This can be done within the context of the *get-together* or anytime during the week when the teen plays games or sports

4. *Bring an inside game*

   a. Bring an inside game to share with the class on **Thursday and Friday of next week** (e.g., age appropriate board game, card game, etc.)
   b. Do not bring a solitary game (like a portable gaming device) or something that you are unwilling to share or are worried about breaking or losing

Wrap Up

Say, *"So those are your homework assignments for this week. Be sure to start working on these assignments right away. We'll be reviewing how they went at the beginning of next week."*

Calculate Points

Calculate the number of points earned by each teen (see Appendix E for the Daily Point Log):

- Do not publicly disclose the individual number of points

- Discourage attempts to compare number of points earned between teens

  ○ Remind them that they are working as a team to earn a bigger and better graduation party

Parent Handout 10

PEERS® *Program for the Education and Enrichment of Relational Skills*

Handling Arguments

This week your teens will be learning how to handle arguments and disagreements. There are very specific steps for handling arguments, which are presented below. These steps should be followed in the order presented WITHOUT MISSING ANY STEPS. If your teen misses a step, their argument may not get resolved.

Steps for Handling Arguments

1. *Keep your cool*

   a. Stay calm
   b. Don't get upset

2. *Listen to the other person*

   a. Listen to the other person's side first
   b. This will help you to understand what the argument is about
   c. Listening is an important part of communication and helps us to understand the other person's perspective

3. *Repeat what they said*

   a. Try to repeat back what they said to you to let them know you're listening
   b. Repeating statements usually start with, *"It sounds like . . ."*

      i. Examples:

         1. *"It sounds like you're upset."*
         2. *"It sounds like you're angry."*
         3. *"It sounds like your feelings are hurt."*

4. *Explain your side*

   a. Calmly *explain your side* of the story
   b. Avoid telling the other person that they're wrong

      i. This will only upset them and escalate the argument

5. *Say you're sorry*

   a. It is helpful to *say you're sorry* in an argument
   b. *Saying you're sorry* doesn't mean that you admit you did anything wrong
   c. You can simply say you're sorry they feel that way

    i. Examples:

      1. *"I'm sorry you're upset."*

      2. *"I'm sorry this happened."*

      3. *"I'm sorry your feelings got hurt."*

6. ***Try to solve the problem***:

    a. ***Tell them what you'll do differently***

      i. Examples:

        1. *"I'll try not to upset you again."*

        2. *"I'll try not to do that again."*

        3. *"I'll try to be more careful next time."*

    b. ***Ask them what they want you to do***

      i. Examples:

        1. *"What can I do to make it up to you?"*

        2. *"What would you like me to do?"*

        3. *"What can I do to fix this?"*

    c. ***Suggest what you want them to do*** (if you're upset with them)

      i. Examples:

        1. *"I'd like it if you didn't do that again."*

        2. *"I wish you'd be more careful next time."*

        3. *"I'd appreciate it if you didn't say that again."*

    d. ***Keep your cool if you can't solve the problem***

      i. Don't expect them to admit they were wrong

        1. Your goal is not to get them to apologize or admit they were wrong

        2. Your goal is to try to end the disagreement

Homework Assignments

Every week your teen will have homework assignments to practice new and previously learned social skills. It is extremely helpful if parents assist teens in completing these assignments. The homework assignments for this week include the following:

1. Practice ***handling an argument***

    a. Parents and teen should practice ***handling an argument*** following the steps

    b. If it comes up this week, teens should practice ***handling an argument*** with a friend or a sibling following the steps

      i. Parents and teen should discuss how the teen ***handled the argument***

2. Teens are to have a *get-together* with a friend

    a. Follow the steps for *preparing for the get-together*
    b. *Get-togethers* should be *activity-based*
    c. *Trade information* and *find common interests* at least 50 percent of the time
    d. Initial *get-togethers* with new friends should be limited to approximately two hours (depending on the activity)

3. Practice *being a good sport*

    a. This can be done within the context of the *get-together* or anytime during the week when the teen plays games or sports

4. *Bring an inside game*

    a. Bring an inside game to share with the class on **Thursday and Friday of next week** (e.g., age appropriate board game, card game, etc.)
    b. Do not bring a solitary game (like a portable gaming device) or something that you are unwilling to share or are worried about breaking or losing

CHANGING REPUTATIONS

Preparing for the Lesson

The didactic lesson for this week focuses on *changing reputations*. Research suggests that bad reputations among peers are stable over time and negatively impact a teen's ability to interact appropriately with peers, due to the expectations and attributions of the larger peer group. Studies have found that even when children and adolescents with bad reputations attempt to engage peers through appropriate interactions, they are less likely to receive positive feedback than if a more well-liked child made the same attempt. The reason for these findings might simply be explained by the fact that *teens get their reputations based on who they hang out with*. Sadly, if a teen has a bad reputation, very few people will want to be friends with that teen for fear of "catching" their bad reputation by association.

The content of this lesson will provide teens with helpful steps about how to jump-start *changing a reputation*. The first step of this process involves *laying low*, which refers to "keeping a low profile" and avoiding attention for a period of time. The idea here is that the teen should actually "drop off the radar" for a bit, often by discontinuing whatever behaviors were giving him or her a bad reputation, and instead try to *follow the crowd*. The process of *laying low* is long and sometimes arduous for teens, and will probably need to continue well after your class ends. This is because it typically takes several months for a reputation to "die down." The length of time needed is often determined by how bad the reputation is and will need to be judged on a case-by-case basis. Summer break is often a good time for teens to *lay low*, as many teens often return after summer vacation seemingly transformed. When summer break is not an option, teens may need to *lay low* for more than a few months during the school year.

During the *laying low* period, you should encourage teens to find a *source of friends* outside of the place where he or she has a bad reputation, which is usually not the school setting. Finding extracurricular activities in the community, away from classmates, is often the best *source of friends* for teens struggling with bad reputations at school. The main point is that you do not want teens to be socially isolated during the *laying low* period. Instead, they should be finding friends who either do not know about their reputation or do not care about it.

Because finding an alternative *source of friends* can be a complicated business, it is helpful to have parents involved in the process. Moreover, since the next step for *changing a reputation* is to do something dramatic to get the attention back on you, like *changing your look*, parental involvement will also be useful, if not critical. This is because *changing your look*, which is intended to be a physical manifestation of some kind of internal change, often involves changing hairstyles or wardrobes. Consequently, having parents involved in this process improves the likelihood that the teen will be successful in *changing his or her reputation*.

For teens that are unable to *change their look*, it is possible to use the other steps described in this lesson, such as allowing their reputation to "die down" by avoiding attempts to make friends from within the peer group with which they have a negative reputation, by *laying low* for a while, and by *owning up to their previous reputation* when confronted about it. The latter step can be done by simply saying something like, *"I know people thought that about me, but I'm different now"* in response to negative comments about his or her reputation.

One of the most common issues that may arise with this lesson is resistance to the steps *following the crowd* or *changing your look*. Interestingly, in our experience through the UCLA PEERS® Clinic, this resistance is usually not from teens, but from parents. Many parents will reject the notion that their child should conform to the social norms of the dominant peer group, often stating that he or she should be allowed to be an "individual" and not a "lemming." Of course, choosing to *follow the crowd* is a personal choice and should not be forced upon anyone, and of course, everyone is entitled to their own individuality. Do not make the mistake of thinking that it is your job to convince teens or their parents that they must change in order to fit in. Instead, your job is simply to provide information about how teens that have been successful at *changing their reputations* have done it. The decision to change is a deeply personal choice, and it is ultimately up to each teen whether they choose to use this information.

Rather than rejecting these steps, many students take this strategy to heart and immediately come back to school with new haircuts and new clothes. Yet, *changing your look* is not enough to *change a reputation*. Instead, it is the combination of ALL of the steps that leads to success. *Laying low* is critical to letting your reputation die down. If done correctly, the larger peer group should forget all about the teen with the bad reputation. *Following the crowd* is essential to showing others that you are not so different after all. Likewise, *owning up to your previous reputation* is equally important to showing that you have changed. If a teen gets defensive and denies his or her previous reputation when confronted by peers, no one will believe he or she has changed. The notion that the teen has changed in some meaningful way (manifested by a change in his or her physical appearance) is essential to *changing a reputation*. Those teens in PEERS® who were able to successfully *change their reputations* typically report using ALL of the steps presented in this lesson (not just a few). So you should encourage your students to use ALL of the steps in this lesson in the order presented to promote success.

Choosing an appropriate *social group* will also be a critical step to success. Just because a teen may follow all of the steps outlined in this lesson does not mean he or she can now be friends with the most popular kids in school, for example. *Friendship is a choice—there are good choices and bad choices*. A good choice in friends would be finding an accepting group of people around the same age with common interests. Consequently, you may need to revisit the lesson on *Choosing Appropriate Friends* in Chapter 5 (Week 4) to help your students identify appropriate *sources of friends* when they get to this step.

Finally, because the steps involved in *changing a reputation* often take at least a few months to complete, you may need to come up with a plan of action following the end of your class or check back with students periodically to make sure they are on the right track.

Day One: Homework Review

Homework Review

[Start with completed homework first. If you have time, you can inquire as to why others were unable to complete the assignment and try to **troubleshoot** how they might get it done for the coming week. When reviewing homework, be sure to use the buzzwords (**bold and italicized**) and **troubleshoot** issues that come up. Spend the majority of the homework review on **handling arguments** and having **get-togethers**, as these were the most important assignments.]

[Note: Give multiple points for homework parts—not just one point per assignment.]

1. *Handling arguments*

   a. Say, *"One of your assignments was to practice handling an argument with a friend or a sibling if it came up this week. You may also have practiced with your parent during a role-play exercise. Raise your hand if you had a chance to practice handling an argument this week."*

      i. Ask, *"Who did you practice handling an argument with?"*
      ii. Ask, *"Which steps did you follow to resolve the argument?"*
      iii. If teens did not practice, have them go over the steps for handling arguments:

         1. *Keep your cool*
         2. *Listen to the other person*
         3. *Repeat what they said*
         4. *Explain your side*
         5. *Say you're sorry*
         6. *Try to solve the problem*

2. *Get-together*

   a. Say, *"Your main homework assignment this week was to have a get-together with a friend. Raise your hand if you had a get-together this week."*

      i. Ask, *"Who did you have a get-together with?"*
      ii. Ask, *"Did you talk beforehand to figure out what you were going to do?"*
      iii. Ask, *"What did you end up doing?"*
      iv. Ask, *"Who got to pick the activities?"* (Answer: Should be the guest)
      v. Ask, *"Did you trade information?"*

         1. If yes, follow up by asking, *"What percentage of the time did you trade information?"* (Answer: Should be at least 50 percent)

      vi. Ask, *"Did you have a good time?"*
      vii. Ask, *"Did your friend have a good time?"*
      viii. Ask, *"Is this someone you might want to have a get-together with again?"*

3. *Being a good sport*

   a. Say, *"Another assignment this week was to practice being a good sport. This may have happened during your get-together, at school during gym class, or during your extracurricular activities. Raise your hand if you practiced being a good sport this week."*

   i. Ask, *"Where did you practice being a good sport?"*

   ii. Ask, *"What did you do or say to show that you were a good sport?"*

4. ***Bring an inside game***

  a. Identify the inside game the teen will bring to share later this week (e.g., age appropriate board game, card game, etc.)

Wrap Up

Say, *"Good work for those of you who completed your homework assignments. Tomorrow we'll be talking about strategies for changing a reputation."*

Calculate Points

Calculate the number of points earned by each teen (see Appendix E for the Daily Point Log):

- Do not publicly disclose the individual number of points

- Discourage attempts to compare number of points earned between teens

  ○ Remind them that they are working as a team to earn a bigger and better graduation party

Day Two: Didactic Lesson—Changing Reputations

Didactic Lesson: Changing Reputations

- Explain, *"This week we're going to be talking about how to change a reputation. Some people have bad reputations, which makes it difficult to make and keep friends. This is because we get our reputations based on who we hang out with, so if we have a bad reputation, very few people will want to be friends with us."*

- Ask the following questions and let teens come up with different explanations:

  - *"What is a bad reputation?"*

    - Answer: A low opinion held by the larger peer group about a particular teen

  - *"Are bullies the only ones with bad reputations?"*

    - Answer: No, teens who are teased and bullied often have bad reputations too, teens who stand out in an unusual way may also have a bad reputation

- *"How do you get a bad reputation?"*

  - Answers:

    - Getting into physical fights or being aggressive toward others
    - Hanging out with teens who get in trouble
    - Talking back to teachers or adults
    - Teasing or bullying other teens
    - Skipping school
    - Getting bad grades, not doing homework, not listening to teachers
    - Doing drugs, drinking alcohol, smoking
    - Stealing, damaging property, breaking the law
    - Telling on peers, getting peers into trouble with adults, *policing* others
    - Wearing unusual clothes, wearing the same clothes all the time
    - Having a strange appearance from others
    - Having unusual interests, engaging in unusual behaviors
    - Excessively talking, being a *conversation hog*
    - Trying to be a *joke-teller* all the time
    - Engaging in self-injurious behavior
    - Having bad hygiene or poor grooming
    - Having emotional outbursts, crying spells
    - Having behavioral outbursts, tantrums, yelling, cursing, going into rages

- Ask, *"Is it ever easy to change a reputation?"*

  - Answer: No, it's difficult and time consuming to *change a reputation*

- Ask, *"What do most parents do to help their kids escape a bad reputation?"*

  - Answer: Change schools

- Ask, *"Does that always work?"*

  ○ Answer: No, reputations often follow people

- Explain, *"Reputations often follow people either because other people hear about their reputation through the grapevine or because the person keeps doing whatever gave them a bad reputation to begin with."*

Steps for Changing a Reputation

- Explain, *"Changing a reputation is difficult to do and usually takes time, but it can be done. People who've been successful at changing their reputation usually follow very specific steps. None of these steps alone will change a reputation. Instead, ALL of these steps need to be followed together."*

[Present the steps for **changing reputations** by writing the following buzzwords (**bold and italicized**) on the board. Do not erase the steps until the end of the lesson.]

1. *Lay low*

   a. Say, *"The first step for changing a reputation is to lay low. This means you need to keep a low profile for a while and not draw attention to yourself. This will give your reputation a chance to die down before you try to make friends. What could be the problem with trying to make new friends when you have a bad reputation?"*

      i. Answer: People may not want to associate with you because of your reputation, they would be afraid they would "catch" your reputation by association

   b. Ask, *"Do you lay low for just a few days or few weeks?"*

      i. Answer: No, you should lay low for several months to let your reputation die down

   c. Explain, *"It takes several months to lay low and let your reputation die down. If you do this right, people will forget all about you. Summer break is a great time to lay low. If it's not the summer, you many need to lay low for several months during the school year."*

   d. Ask, *"Does that mean you shouldn't be trying to make friends anywhere?"*

      i. Answer: No, you can make friends somewhere people don't know or care about your reputation

   e. Explain, *"When you're laying low, you may want to join extracurricular activities or clubs where people don't know or care about your reputation. Sometimes this is in the community away from school."*

2. *Follow the crowd*

   a. Say, *"The next step for changing a reputation is to follow the crowd. This means that you should try to fit in with the crowd and not stand out in any unusual way. What do people sometimes do to stand out from the crowd in a bad way?"*

      i. Answer: They might **police** people, be a **conversation hog**, try to be a **joke-teller**, dress strangely, have poor hygiene, behave in unusual ways, etc.

b. Explain, *"So if you're going to follow the crowd, you need to avoid doing things that make you stand out in some unusual way. That might include being overly emotional or aggressive, or telling on peers for minor offences. It could also include dressing differently, having bad hygiene, or talking about unusual interests. All of these things could give someone a bad reputation."*

3. ***Change your look to change your rep***

   a. Explain, *"After you've laid low for a while and tried to follow the crowd, the next step is to do something dramatic to get the attention back on you. We call this changing your look to change your rep. This might include wearing different clothes, getting a new hairstyle, wearing new glasses, getting in shape, or even wearing make-up for girls. You want to change your look because when you look different, people naturally think there's something different about you. Changing your look is the physical representation that you've changed."*

   b. Ask, *"What do teens do when they notice something different about you?"*

      i. Answer: They approach you and start asking questions, they notice something is different about you and usually comment on it

   c. Explain, *"By changing your look, you're drawing positive attention to yourself. You're letting people know that there's something new and improved about you. But this should only be done after a period of laying low for a while, and a 'make-over' alone won't change your reputation."*

4. ***Own up to your previous reputation***

   a. Say, *"Once people start to notice that you're different you'll have to prove it. This involves owning up to your previous reputation. That means you have to acknowledge what people used to think of you. Once people notice there's something different about you, they may ask about it. Let them know you've changed and you're different now."*

   b. Ask, *"Why is it important to own up to your previous reputation?"*

      i. Answer: Because if you don't **own up to your previous reputation** and change certain things about yourself that people didn't like, no one is going to believe that you're different

   c. Explain, *"You should expect people to call you out on your previous reputation. When they do, you don't have to agree with them. You just have to own up to the fact that people thought that about you."*

   d. Ask, *"What would people think if you said, 'I was never like that! You just didn't know me!'?"*

      i. Answer: They would think you haven't changed, it's the same old you with a new haircut and new clothes, you wouldn't get to **change your reputation**

   e. Explain, *"If you try to disprove your previous reputation by saying 'You just didn't know me' or 'I was never like that', they're less likely to believe that you're different and your reputation will stay the same."*

   f. Say, *"Instead, when people call you out on your old reputation you could say, 'I know people used to think that about me, but I'm different now.' Why would it be important to own up to your previous reputation instead of trying to disprove it?"*

      i. Answer: When you own up to your previous reputation you don't seem defensive, it seems like you may have changed, they're more likely to believe you're different if you don't try to deny what they thought of you

5. ***Find a new social group***

   a. Explain, *"The last step for changing a reputation is to find a new social group. Remember, you get your reputation based on whom you hang out with. Once your reputation has died down a bit, you'll want to find friends that don't know or care about your previous reputation that you have common interests with."*

   b. Ask, *"Does that mean you get to be friends with the most popular people at school?"*

      i. Answer: No, probably not

   c. Explain, *"You need to think about which group you might fit in with and try to make friends in that group. You may need to go somewhere new to find potential friends, like new clubs, teams, or youth groups."*

- Explain, *"Remember that in order to change your reputation, you need to do ALL of these steps. Just doing one or two will not change your reputation. Also remember that changing a reputation is difficult to do and takes time, but it can be done."*

Wrap Up

Say, *"So those are the steps for changing a reputation. Tomorrow we'll continue our discussion about changing reputations and talk about which steps you can begin to take if you want to change your reputation."*

Calculate Points

Calculate the number of points earned by each teen (see Appendix E for the Daily Point Log):

- Do not publicly disclose the individual number of points
- Discourage attempts to compare number of points earned between teens

    o   Remind them that they are working as a team to earn a bigger and better graduation party

Day Three: Lesson Review and Behavioral Rehearsal

Lesson Review: Changing Reputations

- Say, *"Yesterday we learned the steps for changing a reputation. Who can tell us what the steps are for changing a reputation?"*

[Have teens generate all of the steps for **changing a reputation**. Be prepared to give prompts if necessary. Write the following bullet points and buzzwords (**bold and italicized**) on the board and do not erase until the end of the lesson.]

1. *Lay low*

    a. *Keep a low profile* and ***don't draw attention to yourself***

2. *Follow the crowd*

    a. *Try to fit in with the crowd*
    b. *Try not to stand out from the crowd*

3. *Change your look to change your rep*

4. *Own up to your previous reputation*

5. *Find a new social group*

Behavioral Rehearsal: Changing Reputations

- Present each of the following scenarios to the teens and have them come up with appropriate steps from the lesson that could be used to ***change this bad reputation***

    ○ A teen has a bad reputation for getting into physical fights, being aggressive toward others, hanging out with teens who get in trouble, and skipping school
    ○ A teen has a bad reputation for talking back to teachers and adults, getting bad grades, not doing homework, and not listening to teachers
    ○ A teen has a bad reputation for teasing or bullying other teens
    ○ A teen has a bad reputation for telling on peers, getting classmates into trouble with adults, *policing* others, and being a know-it-all
    ○ A teen has a bad reputation for wearing unusual looking clothes
    ○ A teen has a bad reputation for wearing the same clothes all the time
    ○ A teen has a bad reputation for talking excessively, barging into conversations, and being a ***conversation hog***
    ○ A teen has a bad reputation for trying to be a ***joke-teller*** all the time
    ○ A teen has a bad reputation for having bad hygiene and poor grooming
    ○ A teen has a bad reputation for having emotional outbursts and crying spells in class
    ○ A teen has a bad reputation for having behavioral outbursts, tantrums, and going into rages in class

- Go around the room and have each teen choose at least TWO things he or she could potentially do to **change his or her look**

  ○ They must pick ideas that would bring them positive attention and involve **following the crowd**

  ○ It is not important for the teen to admit wanting to **change his or her reputation**

Homework Assignments

- Briefly explain the homework for the week by saying, *"If you're interested, we're going to have you begin to take steps for changing your reputation. We're also going to have everyone continue to practice having get-togethers this week."*

- Present the homework assignments for the coming week:

  1. Practice **changing your reputation** if interested

     a. Parents and teen should discuss steps to **change a reputation**
     b. Teen should begin to take steps to **change his or her reputation** with the help of parents if interested

  2. Teens are to have a **get-together** with a friend

     a. Follow the steps for **preparing for the get-together**
     b. **Get-togethers** should be **activity-based**
     c. **Trade information** and **find common interests** at least 50 percent of the time
     d. Initial **get-togethers** with new friends should be limited to approximately two hours (depending on the activity)

  3. Practice **being a good sport**

     a. This can be done within the context of the **get-together** or anytime during the week when the teen plays games or sports

  4. Practice **handling an argument**

     a. Parents and teen should practice **handling an argument** following the steps
     b. If it comes up this week, teens should practice **handling an argument** with a friend or a sibling following the steps

        i. Parents and teen should discuss how the teen **handled the argument**

  5. **Bring outside sports equipment**

     a. Bring outside sports equipment to share with the class **Thursday and Friday of next week** (e.g., basketball, soccer ball, volleyball, football, handball, Frisbee)
     b. Do not bring solitary games or equipment (e.g., jump rope for one) or something that you are unwilling to share or are worried about damaging or losing

Wrap Up

Say, *"So those are your homework assignments for this week. Be sure to start working on these assignments right away. We'll be reviewing how they went at the beginning of next week. Tomorrow we'll continue our discussion about changing reputations, and we'll also be practicing having get-togethers and good sportsmanship."*

Calculate Points

Calculate the number of points earned by each teen (see Appendix E for the Daily Point Log):

- Do not publicly disclose the individual number of points
- Discourage attempts to compare number of points earned between teens
    - Remind them that they are working as a team to earn a bigger and better graduation party

Days Four and Five: Teen Activity—Get-Togethers and Good Sportsmanship

Lesson Review: Changing Reputations

- Say, *"This week we've been talking about how to change a reputation. Who can tell us what the steps are for changing a reputation?"*

[Have teens generate all of the steps for **changing a reputation**. Be prepared to give prompts if necessary. Write the following bullet points and buzzwords (**bold and italicized**) on the board and do not erase until the end of the lesson.]

1. *Lay low*

   a. *Keep a low profile* and *don't draw attention to yourself*

2. *Follow the crowd*

   a. *Try to fit in with the crowd*
   b. *Try not to stand out from the crowd*

3. *Change your look to change your rep*

4. *Own up to your previous reputation*

5. *Find a new social group*

Teen Activity: Get-Togethers and Good Sportsmanship

Materials Needed

- Indoor games brought by teens

- In the event that teens forget to bring indoor games, have board games and card games available to use if possible

Rules

- Notify teens they will be practicing *beginning and ending get-togethers* and *good sportsmanship*

- Break teens up into small groups (no less than three teens)

  ○ When possible, girls should be paired with girls and boys should be paired with boys

- Have teens practice *beginning a get-together*

  ○ Assign *"hosts"* and *"guests"*

    ■ One teen will be the *"host"*
    ■ One teen will be the *"arriving guest"*
    ■ The other teens will be the *"guests that have already arrived"*

- ○ Begin by having the *"host"* verbally go over the steps for ***beginning a get-together***

  1. ***Greet your guest***
  2. ***Invite them in***
  3. ***Introduce them to anyone they don't know***
  4. ***Give them a tour***
  5. ***Offer them refreshments***
  6. ***Ask them what they want to do***

  - ○ The *"arriving guest"* should step outside and knock on the door
  - ○ The *"guests that have already arrived"* should be seated somewhere near
  - ○ Have the *"host"* follow the steps for ***beginning the get-together***
  - ○ Each teen should have an opportunity to be a *"host,"* an *"arriving guest,"* and a *"guest that has already arrived"*

- Have teens practice ***good sportsmanship*** during ***get-togethers***

  - ○ Teens will play indoor games while practicing ***good sportsmanship***
  - ○ Games are chosen from appropriate ***inside games*** brought by teens and other available games provided by the instructor

    - Have teens negotiate what they will play

      - The last *"host"* should ask his or her *"guests"* what they want to play
      - They may need to compromise by playing one game for half the time and then switching games midway

  - ○ You may need to assist teens in understanding the rules for specific games

    - Try to avoid acting as a referee if disagreements occur
    - Encourage teens to work out their differences by being ***good sports***

  - ○ You may need to prompt teens to be ***good sports*** and ***praise*** their partners, saying things like:

    - *"Johnny just made a nice move, what could you say?"*
    - *"Jenny got a lucky hand, what could you say?"*
    - *"What do we say at the end of the game?"*

  - ○ Teens receive points while playing games for practicing:

    - ***Praising***
    - ***Playing by the rules***
    - ***Not refereeing***
    - ***Not coaching***
    - ***Sharing and taking turns***
    - ***Not being competitive***
    - ***Helping and showing concern if someone is injured*** (outdoor sports)
    - ***Suggesting a change if bored***
    - ***Not being a bad winner***
    - ***Not being a sore loser***
    - ***Saying "good game" at the end of the game***

- When giving points:

    - Say the teen's name first to get his or her attention
    - State what the reward is (i.e., getting a point)
    - Give the reason for the reward (i.e., being a **good sport**)

        - Examples:

            - *"Jimmy gets a point for saying 'good job'!"*
            - *"Jenny gets a point for taking turns!"*
            - *"Johnny gets a point for giving a high five!"*
            - *"Julie gets a point for saying 'good game'!"*
            - *"Joey gets a point for praising!"*

    - Speak loudly when giving out points so other teens can hear

        - The social comparison will encourage other teens to **praise** and be **good sports**

    - Be sure to keep track of points on the Good Sportsmanship Point Log (see Appendix F)

- Have teens practice **ending a get-together**

    - Assign *"hosts"* and *"guests"*

        - One teen will be the *"host"*
        - The other teens will be the *"guests"*

    - Have the *"host"* verbally go over the steps for **ending a get-together**

        1. **Wait for a pause in activities**
        2. **Give a cover story for leaving or ending the get-together**
        3. **Start walking your friend to the door**
        4. **Thank your friend for getting together**
        5. **Tell your friend you had a good time**
        6. **Say goodbye and you'll see them later**

    - The *"hosts"* and *"guests"* should be seated before they begin so that the *"host"* has to stand up and start walking the *"guests"* to the door
    - Have the *"host"* follow the steps for **ending the get-together**

        - *"Guests"* should actually leave and then come back at the end of the role-play

    - Each teen should have an opportunity to be a *"host"* and a *"guest"*

Homework Assignments

- Briefly explain the homework for the week by saying, *"If you're interested, we're going to have you begin to take steps to change your reputation. We're also going to have everyone continue to practice having get-togethers this week."*

- Present the homework assignments for the coming week:

1. Practice *changing your reputation* if interested

    a. Parents and teen should discuss steps to *change a reputation*
    b. Teen should begin to take steps to *change his or her reputation* with the help of parents if interested

2. Teens are to have a *get-together* with a friend

    a. Follow the steps for *preparing for the get-together*
    b. *Get-togethers* should be *activity-based*
    c. *Trade information* and *find common interests* at least 50 percent of the time
    d. Initial *get-togethers* with new friends should be limited to approximately two hours (depending on the activity)

3. Practice *being a good sport*

    a. This can be done within the context of the *get-together* or anytime during the week when the teen plays games or sports

4. Practice *handling an argument*

    a. Parents and teen should practice *handling an argument* following the steps
    b. If it comes up this week, teens should practice *handling an argument* with a friend or a sibling following the steps

        i. Parents and teen should discuss how the teen *handled the argument*

5. *Bring outside sports equipment*

    a. Bring outside sports equipment to share with the class **Thursday and Friday of next week** (e.g., basketball, soccer ball, volleyball, football, handball, Frisbee)
    b. Do not bring solitary games or equipment (e.g., jump rope for one) or something that you are unwilling to share or are worried about damaging or losing

Wrap Up

Say, *"So those are your homework assignments for this week. Be sure to start working on these assignments right away. We'll be reviewing how they went at the beginning of next week."*

Calculate Points

Calculate the number of points earned by each teen (see Appendix E for the Daily Point Log):

- Do not publicly disclose the individual number of points

- Discourage attempts to compare number of points earned between teens

    ○ Remind them that they are working as a team to earn a bigger and better graduation party

Parent Handout 11

PEERS® *Program for the Education and Enrichment of Relational Skills*

Changing Reputations

This week your teens will be learning the steps for *changing a reputation*. Although *changing a reputation* is never easy and takes a lot of time, it can be done. Outlined below are the steps taken by teens who have been successful at *changing their reputations*. ALL of the steps must be followed in the sequence presented. However, choosing to *change a reputation* and *follow the crowd* is a personal choice and should not be forced upon anyone.

Steps for Changing Reputations

1. *Lay low*

    a. *Keep a low profile* and *don't draw attention to yourself*
    b. *Let your reputation die down*
    c. This often takes several months (e.g., summer break is a great time to *lay low*)
    d. If you've done this correctly, people will forget all about you
    e. Be sure to find another *source of friends* that either don't know or don't care about your reputation while you're *laying low*

        i. Find extracurricular activities in the community if the bad reputation is at school

2. *Follow the crowd*

    a. *Try to fit in with the crowd*

        i. Try to fit in with the social norms of the larger peer group if you want to *change your reputation*

    b. *Try not to stand out from the crowd*

        i. Avoid doing things that may make you stand out in a negative way from the larger peer group if you want to *change your reputation*

3. *Change your look to change your rep*

    a. Do something dramatic to get the attention back on you and show that you're different (after a period of *laying low* for a while)
    b. The fastest way to let people know you're different is to *change your look*

        i. Examples: Change your clothes, hair, glasses, get in shape, wear make-up for girls

    c. By *changing your look* you're drawing positive attention to yourself and letting others know that there is something new and improved about you
    d. *Changing your look* is a physical representation that you are different
    e. A "make-over" alone will not *change your reputation*

f.   People will begin to notice that you look different and will start to investigate and ask questions

4. ***Own up to your previous reputation***

a.   When people call you out on your reputation, you need to ***own up to your previous reputation***

b.   Let people know that you've changed

c.   Don't try to deny or disprove what others thought of you before

i.   If you try to deny or disprove their beliefs about you by saying *"You just didn't know me"* or *"I was never like that"*, they are less likely to believe that you're different now

ii.   This will only make you look defensive, make it appear as if you haven't changed, and you will not get a chance to ***change your reputation***

d.   In response to someone commenting on your bad reputation you might say, *"I know people used to think that about me, but I'm different now."*

i.   This shows others that you're not defensive and that you may actually have changed

5. ***Find a new social group***

a.   Your reputation is often determined by who you hang out with

b.   Find friends that don't know or care about your previous reputation

c.   Think about which group you might fit in with and who you share ***common interests*** with and try to make friends in that group

d.   You may need to go somewhere new to find potential friends (e.g., clubs, teams, youth groups)

[Note: ALL of these steps must be followed in order to be successful at ***changing a reputation***.]

Homework Assignments

Every week your teen will have homework assignments to practice new and previously learned social skills. It is extremely helpful if parents assist teens in completing these assignments. The homework assignments for this week include the following:

1.   Practice ***changing your reputation*** if interested

a.   Parents and teen should discuss steps to ***change a reputation***

b.   Teen should begin to take steps to ***change his or her reputation*** with the help of parents if interested

2.   Teens are to have a ***get-together*** with a friend

a.   Follow the steps for ***preparing for the get-together***

b.   ***Get-togethers*** should be ***activity-based***

c.   ***Trade information*** and ***find common interests*** at least 50 percent of the time

d.   Initial ***get-togethers*** with new friends should be limited to approximately two hours (depending on the activity)

3. Practice *being a good sport*

   a. This can be done within the context of the *get-together* or anytime during the week when the teen plays games or sports

4. Practice *handling an argument*

   a. Parents and teen should practice *handling an argument* following the steps
   b. If it comes up this week, teens should practice *handling an argument* with a friend or a sibling following the steps

      i. Parents and teen should discuss how the teen *handled the argument*

5. *Bring outside sports equipment*

   a. Bring outside sports equipment to share with the class **Thursday and Friday of next week** (e.g., basketball, soccer ball, volleyball, football, handball, Frisbee)
   b. Do not bring solitary games or equipment (e.g., jump rope for one) or something that you are unwilling to share or are worried about damaging or losing

HANDLING TEASING AND EMBARRASSING FEEDBACK

Preparing for the Lesson

The focus of the lesson this week is on handling teasing and embarrassing feedback. Teasing is defined as disparaging remarks directed toward another person. Although physical bullying declines in adolescence, teasing remains frequent throughout this period of development. Teasing is frequently done in front of onlookers, perhaps as a method for gaining attention. The dominant motivation reported by perpetrators of teasing is their pleasure at the discomfort of the victim. Research suggests that those who are seen as withdrawn, physically weak, and rejected by peers are more likely to be teased by peers. While socially accepted teens tend to employ humor or assertion in response to being teased, socially rejected teens tend to get angry, upset, or physically aggressive.

The major goal of this lesson is to give teens new and more effective strategies for handling teasing. Although teasing and other forms of rejection, like physical bullying, cyber bullying, and rumors and gossip, are often intertwined, the strategies for handling verbal attacks are very different from the strategies for handling these other forms of bullying. Therefore, it is important for you and your students to think of these concepts differently in order to choose the more appropriate coping strategy.

Many of the students in your class will have a long history of being teased. Consequently, this lesson may be emotionally charged for many of the teens. You should help to limit the emotional response by not allowing teens to talk about the specific ways in which they have been teased or bullied. Teens will be more able to focus on the solutions if they are not distracted by an overwhelming emotional response. By this lesson, the teens will most likely have developed a cohesive group in which their mutual regard and support for one another will minimize much of the anxiety they may have felt in discussing this topic earlier in the program.

One issue that commonly comes up in this lesson is that teens may claim that they are "never teased" or that "no one teases" at your school. In very rare instances this may be the case, but more often these comments represent an attempt to "save face" or appear to be above this form of social rejection. It is not important to have teens confess to being teased, but it is also important not to make teens that are being teased feel embarrassed about their situation. You should normalize this experience for the other students by explaining that nearly everyone gets teased from time to time (particularly teens). Although the experience can be painful, it is not unusual.

Conversely, some teens will confess to being teased, and will want to go into lengthy stories about the ways in which they have been teased. You should not allow this discussion to go too far, as these emotionally charged confessions will make it difficult for teens to focus on the lesson.

Even if one teen is comfortable talking about his or her experiences of being teased or bullied, another teen listening to these accounts may become re-traumatized by simply listening to the story. It is helpful for you to remind teens, *"We know that teasing feels really awful and we know that it's fairly common. But we're not going to be talking about the specific ways we've been teased or bullied. Instead, we're going to focus on what we can do in these situations to make it less likely that we'll be teased in the future."* This clarification will come as a relief to many teens.

Occasionally, one of the teens may confess to teasing other teens or being a bully. You will need to briefly discuss the problems associated with being a teaser or a bully, but avoid a lengthy discussion on this topic in order to deflect the anxiety that such a disclosure may generate in other students. You might say something like, *"What could be the problem with teasing other people?"* You will open this question up to the group and not call on the person identifying him or herself as a bully. A very brief discussion of why it is bad to be a bully will send the message that this behavior is unacceptable, but avoiding a lengthy discussion will be important to minimize the anxiety this might raise in the others and maintain focus upon strategies for **handling teasing**. You will want to end this discussion with a brief moral lesson that teasing or bullying other teens is not a good way to make and keep friends, and you may want to speak privately with the confessor and his or her parents later if the issue feels unresolved.

During this lesson, you will acknowledge that some of the strategies given to teens in the past may have been ineffective for **handling teasing**. Many teens are given the advice to ignore the person, walk away, or tell an adult when being teased. Yet, the majority of teens will say that these strategies usually do not work. Acknowledging this bad advice will help you gain the trust of teens, insofar as they will be more willing to believe what you have to tell them about how to respond appropriately to teasing. If you are an adult that has given this advice in the past, try not to feel too bad about the mistake. The vast majority of well-intentioned adults give the same advice, and were probably given similar advice when they were children. The key here is to dispel the myth that ignoring, walking away, or telling an adult are useful strategies for **handling teasing**, and instead provide your students with the **ecologically valid skills** used by socially accepted teens.

After you have presented the rules for using **teasing comebacks**, a common issue that may arise is teens' eagerness to create their own **teasing comebacks**. Do not allow teens to do this, as they are rarely good at coming up with appropriate responses. In our experience, adults are also not very skilled at coming up with appropriate replies for teens, so it is best to stick to the **verbal** and **nonverbal comebacks** listed in this chapter. These comebacks represent **ecologically valid** responses used by socially accepted teens—so be safe and stick to the list.

When presenting the material about **nonverbal comebacks** to teasing (i.e., rolling eyes, shrugging shoulders, shaking head no), you will conduct a brief behavioral rehearsal to determine whether your students will be capable of performing the comebacks appropriately. Some teens with Autism Spectrum Disorder (ASD) will have trouble rolling their eyes or shrugging their shoulders appropriately. Be sure to have each teen demonstrate how they would do this during the behavioral rehearsal. In the event that they appear awkward (e.g., appear to be having a seizure when rolling their eyes, stiffly lifting their shoulders in an attempt to shrug), let them know that these nonverbal gestures are difficult to do, may not be the best option for them, and that they would be better off using **verbal comebacks** instead. To avoid embarrassment, be sure to let teens know that not everyone is good at rolling their eyes or shrugging their shoulders, so it's not a big deal. If you feel comfortable, you should make this portion of the lesson fun and playful as you and your behavioral coach act as a judge and jury determining whether the teens should use these **nonverbal comebacks**. In our experience, this portion of the lesson often includes a good deal of laughter. If you make this portion of the lesson too serious, the teens may become embarrassed by their inability to use the ***nonverbal comebacks***.

When conducting the role-play demonstration and behavioral rehearsal exercise for this lesson, it will be critical that you use benign teasing remarks. This is because avoiding emotionally charged material will be critical to enabling teens to learn and practice the strategies. If you were to use more authentic teasing comments like, *"You're a geek"* or *"You're a nerd,"* it is likely that some of your students will have difficulty concentrating. Do not make this mistake. Instead, stick to the recommended benign teasing remark, *"Your shoes are ugly."* Historically, this teasing remark has not been met with hurt or upset by the teens, and has allowed them to practice using the ***teasing comebacks*** with little discomfort.

Although it is likely that emotions will initially be elevated during this didactic lesson, this lesson should ultimately focus on the development of specific strategies for ***handling teasing*** that will lead to a lower probability of being teased in the future. When the material is presented as described in this chapter, this should actually be an enjoyable and empowering lesson for the teens.

Day One: Homework Review

Homework Review

[Start with completed homework first. If you have time, you can inquire as to why others were unable to complete the assignment and try to **troubleshoot** how they might get it done for the coming week. When reviewing homework, be sure to use the buzzwords (**bold and italicized**) and **troubleshoot** issues that come up. Spend the majority of the homework review on **handling arguments** and having **get-togethers,** as these were the most important assignments.]

[Note: Give multiple points for homework parts—not just one point per assignment.]

1. *Changing your reputation*

    a. Say, *"One of your assignments this week was to begin to take steps toward changing your reputation if interested. Raise your hand if you did anything new this week to try to change your reputation."*

        i. Have teens report what they did to **change their reputation**

            1. [Teens with **bad reputations** should be **laying low** for the moment until they can move onto the others steps.]

        ii. Have teens go over the **steps for changing a reputation**:

            1. *Lay low*
            2. *Follow the crowd*

                a. *Try to fit in with the crowd*
                b. *Try not to stand out from the crowd*

            3. *Change your look to change your rep*
            4. *Own up to your previous reputation*
            5. *Find a new social group*

2. *Get-together*

    a. Say, *"Your main homework assignment this week was to have a get-together with a friend. Raise your hand if you had a get-together this week."*

        i. Ask, *"Who did you have a get-together with?"*
        ii. Ask, *"Did you talk beforehand to figure out what you were going to do?"*
        iii. Ask, *"What did you end up doing?"*
        iv. Ask, *"Who got to pick the activities?"* (Answer: Should be the guest)
        v. Ask, *"Did you trade information?"*

            1. If yes, follow up by asking, *"What percentage of the time did you trade information?"* (Answer: Should be at least 50 percent)

        vi. Ask, *"Did you have a good time?"*
        vii. Ask, *"Did your friend have a good time?"*
        viii. Ask, *"Is this someone you might want to have a get-together with again?"*

3. ***Being a good sport***

   a. Say, *"Another assignment this week was to practice being a good sport. This may have happened during your get-together, at school during gym class, or during your extracurricular activities. Raise your hand if you practiced being a good sport this week."*

      i. Ask, *"Where did you practice being a good sport?"*

      ii. Ask, *"What did you do or say to show that you were a good sport?"*

4. ***Handling arguments***

   a. Say, *"One of your assignments was to practice handling an argument with a friend or a sibling if it came up this week. You may also have practiced with your parent during a role-play exercise. Raise your hand if you had a chance to practice handling an argument this week."*

      i. Ask, *"Who did you practice handling an argument with?"*

      ii. Ask, *"Which steps did you follow to resolve the argument?"*

      iii. If teens did not practice, have them go over the steps for handling arguments:

         1. ***Keep your cool***

         2. ***Listen to the other person***

         3. ***Repeat what they said***

         4. ***Explain your side***

         5. ***Say you're sorry***

         6. ***Try to solve the problem***

5. ***Bring outside sports equipment***

   a. Have teens identify the outside sports equipment they will bring to share with the class later in the week (e.g., basketball, soccer ball, volleyball, football, handball, Frisbee)

Wrap Up

Say, *"Good work for those of you who completed your homework assignments. Tomorrow we'll be talking about strategies for handling teasing. We won't be talking about the specific ways in which you've been teased. Instead, we'll focus on what you can do in these situations to make it less likely that you'll be teased in the future."*

Calculate Points

Calculate the number of points earned by each teen (see Appendix E for the Daily Point Log):

- Do not publicly disclose the individual number of points

- Discourage attempts to compare number of points earned between teens

   ◦ Remind them that they are working as a team to earn a bigger and better graduation party

Day Two: Didactic Lesson—Handling Teasing and Embarrassing Feedback

Didactic Lesson: Handling Teasing and Embarrassing Feedback

- Explain, *"Today we're going to be talking about teasing and what to do when someone teases us. We're not going to be talking about the specific ways we've been teased or how we feel about being teased. We all know it feels bad to be teased. Instead, we're going to focus on what we can do in these situations to make it less likely that we'll be teased again."*

[If teens try to talk about specific ways they have been teased, be sure to immediately redirect them by saying, *"We're not going to talk about the specific ways we've been teased. Instead, we're going to talk about what we can do in these situations to make it less likely we'll be teased again."*]

- Explain, *"One important way to make it less likely that we'll be teased relates to how we react when someone is teasing us. In order for us to know how to react, it's helpful to think about why people tease."*

- Ask, *"Why do people tease?"*

  ○ Answer: They're trying to get a reaction out of you, they want you to get upset, embarrassed, or tease back, they want you to put on a "show" for other teens because it's fun for them, they may even say *"Watch this!"* and get other teens in on the teasing

- Ask the questions, *"When you get upset . . ."*

  ○ *". . . are you are doing what the teaser wants?"*

    • Answer: Yes

  ○ *". . . are you are putting on a show?"*

    • Answer: Yes

  ○ *". . . are you are making the teasing fun for the teaser?"*

    • Answer: Yes

  ○ *". . . are you MORE likely or LESS likely to get teased again?"*

    • Answer: Definitely more likely

Handling Teasing

- Say, *"A lot of adults will give teens advice about what to do in response to teasing. What do most adults tell teens to do?"*

  ○ Answer: Ignore them, walk away, tell an adult

- Ask, *"Do these strategies usually work?"*

  ○ Answer: Not usually

- Explain, *"Unlike other adults, we're not going to suggest that you ignore the teaser, walk away, or tell an adult. These strategies don't usually work."*

[Present the rules for **handling teasing and embarrassing feedback** by writing the following buzzwords (**bold and italicized**) on the board. Do not erase the steps until the end of the lesson.]

- ***Don't ignore the teasing***

  ○ Ask, *"What happens when you ignore the teasing?"*

    ■ Answer: They keep teasing, you look weak, you make yourself an easy target

- ***Don't walk away***

  ○ Ask, *"What happens when you walk away?"*

    ■ Answer: They follow you, they keep teasing, you look weak, you make yourself an easy target

- ***Don't tell an adult right away***

  ○ Ask, *"What happens when you tell an adult right away?"*

    ■ Answer: You make them mad, they want to retaliate, you may get a reputation as a "snitch," "nark," or "tattletale"

  ○ Ask, *"When would it be appropriate to tell an adult?"*

    ■ Answer: If these strategies don't work and you can't handle the teasing on your own, or if you feel physically threatened

- ***Don't tease them back***

  ○ Say, *"Some people think that teasing the person back will make it less likely they'll get teased. What could be the problem with teasing back?"*

    ■ Answers: You could get into trouble, you will look like the bad guy, you might get a bad reputation, this may be the reaction they're looking for, you'll probably get teased more

- ***Don't banter***

  ○ Say, *"Some friends like to tease each other, especially boys. This kind of teasing is usually done playfully and isn't intended to be hurtful. We call this kind of teasing 'banter.' While banter is very common among teens, what could be the problem with banter?"*

    ■ Answer: It escalates, each person tries to up the ante, eventually someone could get upset

  ○ Explain, *"If our goal is to make and keep friends, we need to understand that banter is very risky. If we want to avoid the risk, we can use the strategies for handling teasing to stop the bantering."*

- *Act like what they said didn't bother you*

    ○ Say, *"Whether it's banter or not, one way you can make the teasing less fun for the teaser is by acting like it DIDN'T BOTHER YOU. Even if it hurts your feelings, you have to act like it didn't affect you. Why is it important to act like what they said DIDN'T BOTHER YOU?"*

        ▪ Answer: The teaser doesn't get the reaction they wanted, makes it less fun, they will be less likely to tease you in the future

- *Act like what they said was lame or stupid*

    ○ Say, *"Another way you can make the teasing less fun for the teaser is by acting like what they said was kind of LAME or STUPID. Why is it important to act like what they said was LAME or STUPID?"*

        ▪ Answer: This embarrasses the teaser, makes the teasing less fun, they will be less likely to tease you in the future

- *Give a short verbal comeback*

    ○ Say, *"The best way to show someone that their teasing didn't bother you and what they said was kind of lame is to give a SHORT comeback to make fun of what they said. Why is it important to keep your comebacks SHORT?"*

        ▪ Answer: If you say too much, they'll think you care

    ○ Say, *"Remember these short verbal comebacks need to give the impression that you don't care and the teasing was lame. A lot of teens will say things like . . ."*

        ▪ [Write the following examples on the board. Do not allow teens to generate their own comebacks, as they are often inappropriate]:

            - *"Whatever!"*
            - *"Yeah, and?"*
            - *"And your point is?"*
            - *"Am I supposed to care?"*
            - *"Is that supposed to be funny?"*
            - *"And why do I care?"*
            - *"Big deal!"*
            - *"So what!"*
            - *"Who cares?"*
            - *"Tell me when you get to the funny part."*
            - *"Anyway . . ."* (Good comeback to end with and walk away on)

    ○ *Sound bored*

        ▪ Explain, *"Some people sound bored or indifferent when they use these verbal comebacks. They might say "Whatever" (said casually with bored indifference)."*

    ○ *Have an attitude*

        ▪ Explain, *"Other people use these verbal comebacks with lots of attitude. They might say 'WHATEVER!' (said with lots of dramatic flair)."*

        ▪ Say, *"It's up to you to decide which way feels more comfortable for you."*

- *Give a nonverbal comeback*

  - Explain, *"In addition to giving short verbal comebacks, a lot of teens will also give a nonverbal comeback that shows they don't care. It's always better to provide a verbal comeback, but if you find it difficult to use your words in these situations, one of the nonverbal comebacks might work for you. Nonverbal comebacks include . . ."*

    - *Rolling your eyes*
    - *Shrugging your shoulders*
    - *Shaking your head no*

  - Explain, *"Not everyone is good at rolling their eyes and shrugging their shoulders. Since we don't want anyone to do something that might look weird, let's go around the room and have everyone demonstrate rolling your eyes and then separately shrugging your shoulders. If you know you can't do it, then you can pass."*

    - Have each teen demonstrate rolling their eyes
    - Have each teen demonstrate shrugging their shoulders

      - You and a coach should decide in the moment and share with the teen if he or she should use these strategies

        - Do not let the other teens weigh in

      - Keep the interaction fun and playful to avoid embarrassment
      - Normalize the fact that not everyone can or should do this

  - Say, *"Not everyone should roll their eyes or shrug their shoulders and it's not a big deal. But you should all use your short verbal comebacks no matter what. What impression do your verbal and nonverbal comebacks give the teaser?"*

    - Answer: That you don't care, that you're not bothered by what they said, that what they said was lame or stupid

- *Always be prepared with at least a few verbal comebacks*

  - Ask, *"Does the teaser usually give up after one teasing comeback?"*

    - Answer: No, they usually try a few more times

  - Explain, *"Because we know they'll probably try teasing a few times, you always need to be prepared with at least a few verbal comebacks."*

- *Remove yourself after giving teasing comebacks*

  - Say, *"After you've given a few teasing comebacks, it's a good idea to remove yourself from the situation. You can do this by casually looking away or slowly walking away. What could be the problem with standing there and looking at the person after you've used a few teasing comebacks?"*

    - Answer: It's almost an invitation or a challenge to tease more, you want to give the impression that what they said was lame and that you can't be bothered to listen anymore

- *Don't walk away without giving a teasing comeback*

  - Say, *"It's very important that you don't walk away from the teaser without showing that what they said didn't bother you. Why is it important to show the teaser that you're not bothered?"*

    - Answer: You don't want the teaser to think that you're running away, they may follow you and keep teasing

- *Teasing may get worse before it gets better*

  - Explain, *"Sometimes the teaser will be expecting a different reaction from you. Maybe in the past you got upset or teased back. When you stop doing what the teaser expects, they may try a little harder at first. That means the teasing may get worse before it gets better. You still need to stick with your teasing comebacks though."*

  - Ask, *"What could be the problem with not using teasing comebacks and going back to getting upset or putting on a show?"*

    - Answer: That's what the teasers want, you'll have proven that if they try hard enough they can get you to do what they want, this makes it more likely you'll get teased again

- *Expect the teaser to try again*

  - Explain, *"If you stick with the teasing comebacks, eventually the teasers will get bored and move on, but they may try again in the future. That means even if it seems like the teasing stopped, you should always be ready for them to try again sometime."*

  - Ask, *"Why would they try again?"*

    - Answer: They may try again to see if you'll give them the reaction they're looking for

- *Don't use teasing comebacks with physically aggressive people*

  - Explain, *"Teasing comebacks work really well because they kind of embarrass the person teasing us and make it less fun for them. Because they're embarrassing, we don't use teasing comebacks with physically aggressive people."*

  - Ask, *"How do people who get physically aggressive react when they're embarrassed?"*

    - Answer: They usually retaliate with physical aggression

  - Explain, *"Next week we'll talk about how to handle physical bullying, which is completely different from how we handle verbal bullying, or teasing. For now, just remember not to use teasing comebacks with people that have a tendency to get physically aggressive, since this might make them want to attack."*

- *Don't use teasing comebacks with adults*

  - Say, *"The last rule for using teasing comebacks is that we should never use them with adults. That includes parents, teachers, supervisors, or people in authority. What could be the problem with using teasing comebacks with adults?"*

    - Answer: It's disrespectful, you could get in trouble, you could get a bad reputation

Role-Play: Handling Teasing

[The instructor and the behavioral coach should do an APPROPRIATE role-play with the instructor *handling teasing* by using *verbal* and *nonverbal comebacks*.]

- Begin by saying, *"We're going to do a role-play. Watch this and tell me what I'm doing RIGHT in handling this teasing."*

   Example of an APPROPRIATE role-play:

   - Coach: *"Your shoes are ugly!"*
   - Instructor: (Rolls eyes) *"Whatever."* (Said with attitude, then looks away)
   - Coach: *"Seriously, those are some ugly shoes!"*
   - Instructor: *"Am I supposed to care?"* (Said with indifference, then looks away)
   - Coach: *"Well you should care because those are some nasty looking shoes!"*
   - Instructor: *"Anyway . . ."* (Shrugs shoulders, shakes head no, and casually walks away)
   - Coach: (Looks defeated)

- Say, *"Time out on that. So what did I do right in handling that teasing?"*
   - Answer: You used **verbal** and **nonverbal comebacks**, you acted like what he or she said didn't bother you and was kind of lame, you were **prepared with a few verbal comebacks**, you **removed yourself after giving teasing comebacks**

- Ask the following *Perspective Taking Questions*:
   - *"What was that like for (name of coach)?"*
      - Answers: Not fun; embarrassing; annoying
   - *"What do you think (name of coach) thought of me?"*
      - Answers: Not upset; not bothered; indifferent
   - *"Is (name of coach) going to want to tease me again?"*
      - Answer: Probably not

- Ask the behavioral coach the same *Perspective Taking Questions*:
   - *"What was that like for you?"*
   - *"What did you think of me?"*
   - *"Would you want to tease me again?"*

Handling Embarrassing Feedback

- Explain, *"Sometimes people say things that are embarrassing and may even be meant to tease us, but they may also be giving us important feedback about how people see us. This is especially true when a lot of people are giving us the same feedback or even when a few people give us the same feedback over and over. Instead of just feeling hurt, we can use this feedback to help us change the way people see us. If we think about what people are trying to tell us when they tease us, we can sometimes do things differently and make it less likely that we'll be teased in the future."*

- Go over the examples of embarrassing feedback listed in Table 13.1 and have teens come up with ideas of what they could do differently in response to this feedback

  - Present each example by saying, *"Let's say that a lot of people are giving you negative feedback about . . . (insert example of embarrassing feedback)."*
  - Ask, *"What could you do differently in response to this feedback?"*
  - Let teens come up with their own examples of what they could do differently if they are appropriate

Table 13.1 Examples of Embarrassing Feedback and How to Utilize Feedback

Examples of Embarrassing Feedback	Examples of How to Utilize Feedback
Negative feedback about clothing	Consider changing your wardrobe; try to follow the clothing norms of your peer group
Negative feedback about body odor	Use deodorant; bathe regularly using soap; wash hair regularly; wear less cologne/perfume
Negative feedback about dandruff	Use dandruff shampoo regularly
Negative feedback about oral hygiene	Brush teeth regularly; use mouthwash; floss teeth regularly; use a tongue scraper; chew gum; use breath mints; avoid certain foods; visit the dentist regularly
Negative feedback about your sense of humor	Pay attention to your humor feedback; consider telling fewer jokes; be a little more serious when first getting to know someone
Negative feedback about unusual behaviors	Consider changing or discontinuing the behavior if possible

Wrap Up

Say, *"So those are the rules for handling teasing and embarrassing feedback. Tomorrow we'll continue our discussion about teasing and practice using verbal and nonverbal comebacks."*

Calculate Points

Calculate the number of points earned by each teen (see Appendix E for the Daily Point Log):

- Do not publicly disclose the individual number of points

- Discourage attempts to compare number of points earned between teens

  - Remind them that they are working as a team to earn a bigger and better graduation party

Day Three: Lesson Review and Behavioral Rehearsal

Lesson Review: Handling Teasing and Embarrassing Feedback

- Say, *"Yesterday we worked on how to handle teasing and embarrassing feedback. Who can tell us what the rules are for handling teasing?"*

[Have teens generate all of the rules for **handling teasing**. Be prepared to give prompts if necessary. Write the following buzzwords (**bold and italicized**) on the board and do not erase until the end of the lesson.]

- ○ *Don't ignore the teasing*

- ○ *Don't walk away*

- ○ *Don't tell an adult right away*

    - ▪ Tell an adult if the others strategies don't work or you feel physically threatened

- ○ *Don't tease them back*

- ○ *Don't banter*

    - ▪ Even playful banter is risky because it can escalate

- ○ *Act like what they said didn't bother you*

- ○ *Act like what they said was lame or stupid*

- ○ *Give a short verbal comeback (sound bored or have an attitude)*

    - ▪ *"Whatever!"*
    - ▪ *"Yeah, and?"*
    - ▪ *"And your point is?"*
    - ▪ *"Am I supposed to care?"*
    - ▪ *"Is that supposed to be funny?"*
    - ▪ *"And why do I care?"*
    - ▪ *"Big deal!"*
    - ▪ *"So what!"*
    - ▪ *"Who cares?"*
    - ▪ *"Tell me when you get to the funny part."*
    - ▪ *"Anyway . . ."* (Good comeback to end with and walk away on)

- ○ *Give a nonverbal comeback*

    - ▪ Roll your eyes
    - ▪ Shrug your shoulders
    - ▪ Shake your head no

- ○ *Always be prepared with at least a few verbal comebacks*

  ○ *Remove yourself after giving teasing comebacks*

  ○ *Don't walk away without giving a teasing comeback*

  ○ *Teasing may get worse before it gets better*

  ○ *Expect the teaser to try again*

  ○ *Don't use teasing comebacks with physically aggressive people*

  ○ *Don't use teasing comebacks with adults*

- Say, *"Remember that sometimes when people tease us, they're giving us feedback about how people may see us, and there may be things we can do differently to make it less likely that we'll be teased in the future."*

Role-Play: Handling Teasing

[The instructor and the behavioral coach should do an APPROPRIATE role-play with the instructor *handling teasing* by using *verbal* and *nonverbal comebacks*.]

- Begin by saying, *"We're going to do a role-play. Watch this and tell me what I'm doing RIGHT in handling this teasing."*

  Example of an APPROPRIATE role-play:

  ■ Coach: *"Your shoes are ugly!"*
  ■ Instructor: (Rolls eyes) *"Yeah, and?"* (Said with attitude, then looks away)
  ■ Coach: *"Seriously, those are some ugly shoes!"*
  ■ Instructor: *"Am I supposed to care?"* (Said with indifference, then looks away)
  ■ Coach: *"Well you should care because those are some nasty looking shoes!"*
  ■ Instructor: *"Whatever."* (Shrugs shoulders, shakes head no, and casually walks away)
  ■ Coach: (Looks defeated)

- Say, *"Time out on that. So what did I do right in handling that teasing?"*

  ○ Answer: You used *verbal* and *nonverbal comebacks*, you acted like what he or she said didn't bother you and was kind of lame, you were *prepared with a few verbal comebacks*, you *removed yourself after giving teasing comebacks*

- Ask the following *Perspective Taking Questions*:

  ○ *"What was that like for (name of coach)?"*

   ■ Answers: Not fun; embarrassing; annoying

  ○ *"What do you think (name of coach) thought of me?"*

   ■ Answers: Not upset; not bothered; indifferent

- o   *"Is (name of coach) going to want to tease me again?"*

    - ▪   Answer: Probably not

- Ask the behavioral coach the same *Perspective Taking Questions*:

    - o   *"What was that like for you?"*
    - o   *"What did you think of me?"*
    - o   *"Would you want to tease me again?"*

Behavioral Rehearsal: Handling Teasing

- Tell the teens that they will be practicing using *teasing comebacks*

- Go around the room and have each teen individually identify THREE *verbal comebacks* they plan to practice using

    - o   Immediately conduct a behavioral rehearsal (before moving on to the next teen) to practice using these three *verbal comebacks*, otherwise the teen may forget what he or she was going to say
    - o   Discourage the teen's attempts to come up with their own *teasing comebacks*
    - o   If the teen comes up with his or her own response, be sure it fits the parameters of a good response (i.e., short, gives the impression that it didn't bother the teen and was kind of lame)

- The instructor should use the benign tease, *"Your shoes are ugly!"*

    - o   Use the same benign tease for each teen, otherwise they may take the teasing comments personally
    - o   Repeat teasing comments THREE times in succession, forcing the teen to use different *verbal comebacks* each time
    - o   Teens should reply with preapproved *verbal* and *nonverbal* (when appropriate) *comebacks*
    - o   Give performance feedback as necessary
    - o   If the teen sounds upset, sad, or angry in response to the teasing, gently point this out and have them try again until they give the impression that the teasing didn't bother them
    - o   Be sure each teen has mastered the technique before moving on

- DO NOT ALLOW TEENS TO PRACTICE TEASING EACH OTHER

    - o   It is never appropriate to have teens demonstrate or practice inappropriate social behavior

Homework Assignments

- Briefly explain the homework for the week by saying, *"We're going to continue to have you practice using teasing comebacks and organize get-togethers this week."*

- Present the homework assignments for the coming week:

    1.   Practice *handling teasing*

    a. Parents and teen should practice using **verbal** and **nonverbal teasing comebacks**

        i. Parents should use a benign tease like, *"Your shoes are ugly!"*

    b. If it comes up this week, teens should use **teasing comebacks** with peers and siblings

        i. Parents and teen should discuss how the teen **handled teasing** with peers or siblings

2. Teens are to have a **get-together** with a friend

    a. Follow the steps for **preparing for the get-together**
    b. **Get-togethers** should be **activity-based**
    c. **Trade information** and **find common interests** at least 50 percent of the time
    d. Initial **get-togethers** with new friends should be limited to approximately two hours (depending on the activity)

3. Practice **changing a reputation** if relevant

    a. Parents and teen should discuss steps to **change a reputation**
    b. Teen should begin to take steps to **change a reputation** with the help of parents if relevant

4. Practice **handling an argument**

    a. Parents and teen should practice **handling an argument** following the steps
    b. If it comes up this week, teens should practice **handling an argument** with a friend or a sibling following the steps

        i. Parents and teen should discuss how the teen **handled the argument**

5. **Bring outside sports equipment**

    a. Bring outside sports equipment to share with the class **Thursday and Friday of next week** (e.g., basketball, soccer ball, volleyball, football, handball, Frisbee)
    b. Do not bring solitary games or equipment (e.g., jump rope for one) or something that you are unwilling to share or are worried about damaging or losing

Wrap Up

Say, *"So those are your homework assignments for this week. Be sure to start working on these assignments right away. We'll be reviewing how they went at the beginning of next week. Tomorrow we'll continue our discussion about teasing and we'll be practicing having get-togethers with our classmates."*

Calculate Points

Calculate the number of points earned by each teen (see Appendix E for the Daily Point Log):

- Do not publicly disclose the individual number of points

- Discourage attempts to compare number of points earned between teens

    ○ Remind them that they are working as a team to earn a bigger and better graduation party

Days Four and Five: Teen Activity—Good Sportsmanship and Outdoor Activities

Lesson Review: Handling Teasing and Embarrassing Feedback

- Say, *"This week we've been working on how to handle teasing and embarrassing feedback. Who can tell us what the rules are for handling teasing?"*

[Have teens generate all of the rules for **handling teasing**. Be prepared to give prompts if necessary. Write the following buzzwords (**bold and italicized**) on the board and do not erase until the end of the lesson.]

- ○ *Don't ignore the teasing*

- ○ *Don't walk away*

- ○ *Don't tell an adult right away*

  - ■ Tell an adult if the others strategies don't work or you feel physically threatened

- ○ *Don't tease them back*

- ○ *Don't banter*

  - ■ Even playful banter is risky because it can escalate

- ○ *Act like what they said didn't bother you*

- ○ *Act like what they said was lame or stupid*

- ○ *Give a short verbal comeback (sound bored or have an attitude)*

  - ■ *"Whatever!"*
  - ■ *"Yeah, and?"*
  - ■ *"And your point is?"*
  - ■ *"Am I supposed to care?"*
  - ■ *"Is that supposed to be funny?"*
  - ■ *"And why do I care?"*
  - ■ *"Big deal!"*
  - ■ *"So what!"*
  - ■ *"Who cares?"*
  - ■ *"Tell me when you get to the funny part."*
  - ■ *"Anyway . . ."* (Good comeback to end with and walk away on)

- ○ *Give a nonverbal comeback*

  - ■ Roll your eyes
  - ■ Shrug your shoulders
  - ■ Shake your head no

- ○ *Always be prepared with at least a few verbal comebacks*

- ○ *Remove yourself after giving teasing comebacks*
- ○ *Don't walk away without giving a teasing comeback*
- ○ *Teasing may get worse before it gets better*
- ○ *Expect the teaser to try again*
- ○ *Don't use teasing comebacks with physically aggressive people*
- ○ *Don't use teasing comebacks with adults*

- Say, *"Remember that sometimes when people tease us, they're giving us feedback about how people may see us, and there may be things we can do differently to make it less likely that we'll be teased in the future."*

Teen Activity: Good Sportsmanship and Outdoor Activities

Materials Needed

- Outside play area or gymnasium

  - ○ If the weather is bad, there is no outside play area, or no gymnasium available, you can modify the teen activity by playing indoor games as in the previous weeks

- Outdoor sports equipment brought by teens

- In the event that teens forget to bring outdoor sports equipment, have the teens share items brought by others, and/or have sports equipment available to use if possible

Rules

- Have teens negotiate what they will play (e.g., shoot baskets with basketball, toss a football, play catch, play Frisbee, play organized sports like basketball, touch football, soccer, handball, volleyball, badminton, etc.)

- Teens can play different games and sports if there are enough people

- Do not let anyone sit out of games and sports unless for a medical reason

  - ○ Encourage any teen that has to sit out to praise the players from the sidelines

- Explain the rules for game playing:

  - ○ We have a "no contact" rule for all sports—no excessive touching, crowding, or stealing
  - ○ Must pass the ball in soccer and basketball
  - ○ Warnings will be given for *poor sportsmanship*

- You may need to assist teens in understanding the rules for specific games

  - ○ Try to avoid acting as a referee if disagreements occur
  - ○ Encourage teens to work out their differences by being *good sports*

- You may need to prompt teens to be *good sports* and *praise* their partners, saying things like:

  - *"Johnny just made a basket, what could you say?"*
  - *"Jenny just made a goal, what could you say?"*
  - *"What do we say at the end of the game?"*

- Teens receive points while playing games and sports for practicing:

  - *Praising*
  - *Playing by the rules*
  - *Not refereeing*
  - *Not coaching*
  - *Sharing and taking turns*
  - *Not being competitive*
  - *Helping and showing concern if someone is injured*
  - *Suggesting a change if bored*
  - *Not being a bad winner*
  - *Not being a sore loser*
  - *Saying "good game" at the end of the game*

- When giving points:

  - Say the teen's name first to get his or her attention
  - State what the reward is (i.e., getting a point)
  - Give the reason for the reward (i.e., being a *good sport*)

    - Examples:

      - *"Jimmy gets a point for saying 'good job'!"*
      - *"Jenny gets a point for taking turns!"*
      - *"Johnny gets a point for giving a high five!"*
      - *"Julie gets a point for saying 'good game'!"*
      - *"Joey gets a point for praising!"*

  - Speak loudly when giving out points so other teens can hear

    - The social comparison will encourage other teens to *praise* and be *good sports*

- Be sure to keep track of points on the Good Sportsmanship Point Log (see Appendix F)

Homework Assignments

- Briefly explain the homework for the week by saying, *"We're going to continue to have you practice using teasing comebacks and organize get-togethers this week."*

- Present the homework assignments for the coming week:

1. Practice **handling teasing**

   a. Parents and teen should practice using **verbal** and **nonverbal teasing comebacks**

      i.   Parents should use a benign tease like, *"Your shoes are ugly!"*

   b.   If it comes up this week, teens should use **teasing comebacks** with peers and siblings

      i.   Parents and teen should discuss how the teen **handled teasing** with peers or siblings

2.   Teens are to have a **get-together** with a friend

   a.   Follow the steps for **preparing for the get-together**
   b.   **Get-togethers** should be **activity-based**
   c.   **Trade information** and **find common interests** at least 50 percent of the time
   d.   Initial **get-togethers** with new friends should be limited to approximately two hours (depending on the activity)

3.   Practice **changing a reputation** if relevant

   a.   Parents and teen should discuss steps to **change a reputation**
   b.   Teen should begin to take steps to **change a reputation** with the help of parents if relevant

4.   Practice **handling an argument**

   a.   Parents and teen should practice **handling an argument** following the steps
   b.   If it comes up this week, teens should practice **handling an argument** with a friend or a sibling following the steps

      i.   Parents and teen should discuss how the teen **handled the argument**

5.   **Bring outside sports equipment**

   a.   Bring outside sports equipment to share with the class **Thursday and Friday of next week** (e.g., basketball, soccer ball, volleyball, football, handball, Frisbee)
   b.   Do not bring solitary games or equipment (e.g., jump rope for one) or something that you are unwilling to share or are worried about damaging or losing

Wrap Up

Say, *"So those are your homework assignments for this week. Be sure to start working on these assignments right away. We'll be reviewing how they went at the beginning of next week."*

Calculate Points

Calculate the number of points earned by each teen (see Appendix E for the Daily Point Log):

- Do not publicly disclose the individual number of points

- Discourage attempts to compare number of points earned between teens

  ○   Remind them that they are working as a team to earn a bigger and better graduation party

Parent Handout 12

PEERS® *Program for the Education and Enrichment of Relational Skills*

Handling Teasing and Embarrassing Feedback

This week your teens will be learning how to handle teasing and embarrassing feedback. Research suggests that adults often give teens the wrong advice about how to handle teasing, so be aware that the strategies taught in this lesson are those that have been shown to be effective for socially accepted teens, not simply what we think should work in these situations.

The current lesson focuses on specific strategies for handling verbal attacks. These strategies do not apply to handling physical bullying, cyber bullying, or rumors and gossip, which will be addressed in later lessons.

Handling Teasing

- *Don't ignore the teasing*

    ○ They will keep teasing, you will appear weak and an easy target, and you will probably get teased again

- *Don't walk away*

    ○ They will probably follow you and keep teasing, you will appear weak and an easy target, and you will probably get teased again

- *Don't tell an adult right away*

    ○ If you tell an adult for minor teasing, they will want to retaliate against you, you may get a bad reputation, and you will probably get teased again
    ○ Involve adults if these strategies don't work or if you feel physically threatened

- *Don't tease them back*

    ○ This may only escalate the teasing, you could get in trouble and get a bad reputation, and you will probably get teased again

- *Don't banter*

    ○ Even friendly *banter* is risky if your goal is to make and keep friends
    ○ *Banter* tends to escalate and can lead to upset feelings

- *Act like what they said didn't bother you*

- *Act like what they said was lame or stupid*

- *Give a short verbal comeback (sound bored or have an attitude)*

    ○ *"Whatever!"*

- ○ *"Yeah, and?"*
- ○ *"And your point is?"*
- ○ *"Am I supposed to care?"*
- ○ *"Is that supposed to be funny?"*
- ○ *"And why do I care?"*
- ○ *"Big deal!"*
- ○ *"So what!"*
- ○ *"Who cares?"*
- ○ *"Tell me when you get to the funny part."*
- ○ *"Anyway . . ."* (Good comeback to end with and walk away on)

- *Give a nonverbal comeback*

  - ○ Roll your eyes
  - ○ Shrug your shoulders
  - ○ Shake your head no

- *Always be prepared with at least a few verbal comebacks*

- *Remove yourself after giving teasing comebacks*

  - ○ *Don't stand there and wait to get teased more*
  - ○ *Casually look away or walk away*

- *Don't walk away without giving a teasing comeback*

- *Teasing may get worse before it gets better*

  - ○ If they expect a certain reaction from you, they may try harder before they give up

- *Expect the teaser to try again*

  - ○ Even if they stop teasing for a while, they may try again some other time

- *Don't use teasing comebacks with physically aggressive people*

  - ○ Teasing comebacks embarrass the teaser
  - ○ Physically aggressive people tend to attack when they get embarrassed

- *Don't use teasing comebacks with adults*

  - ○ This is disrespectful, could get you in trouble, and could give you a bad reputation

Handling Embarrassing Feedback

Sometimes when teens get teased, they receive *embarrassing feedback* about how others see them. There may be something your teen can do differently to make it less likely that he or she will be teased in the future. This is a personal choice.

Examples of Embarrassing Feedback	Examples of How to Utilize Feedback
Negative feedback about clothing	Consider changing your wardrobe; try to follow the clothing norms of your peer group
Negative feedback about body odor	Use deodorant; bathe regularly using soap; wash hair regularly; wear less cologne/perfume
Negative feedback about dandruff	Use dandruff shampoo regularly
Negative feedback about oral hygiene	Brush teeth regularly; use mouthwash; floss teeth regularly; use a tongue scraper; chew gum; use breath mints; avoid certain foods; visit the dentist regularly
Negative feedback about your sense of humor	Pay attention to your humor feedback; consider telling fewer jokes; be a little more serious when first getting to know someone
Negative feedback about unusual behaviors	Consider changing or discontinuing the behavior if possible

Homework Assignments

Every week your teen will have homework assignments to practice new and previously learned social skills. It is extremely helpful if parents assist teens in completing these assignments. The homework assignments for this week include the following:

1. Practice *handling teasing*

    a. Parents and teen should practice using **verbal** and **nonverbal teasing comebacks**

        i.   Parents should use a benign tease like, *"Your shoes are ugly!"*

    b. If it comes up this week, teens should use *teasing comebacks* with peers and siblings

        i.   Parents and teen should discuss how the teen *handled teasing* with peers or siblings

2. Teens are to have a *get-together* with a friend

    a. Follow the steps for *preparing for the get-together*
    b. *Get-togethers* should be *activity-based*
    c. *Trade information* and *find common interests* at least 50 percent of the time
    d. Initial *get-togethers* with new friends should be limited to approximately two hours (depending on the activity)

3. Practice *changing a reputation* if relevant

    a. Parents and teen should discuss steps to *change a reputation*
    b. Teen should begin to take steps to *change a reputation* with the help of parents if relevant

4. Practice *handling an argument*

    a. Parents and teen should practice *handling an argument* following the steps
    b. If it comes up this week, teens should practice *handling an argument* with a friend or a sibling following the steps

        i.   Parents and teen should discuss how the teen *handled the argument*

5. *Bring outside sports equipment*

   a. Bring outside sports equipment to share with the class **Thursday and Friday of next week** (e.g., basketball, soccer ball, volleyball, football, handball, Frisbee)

   b. Do not bring solitary games or equipment (e.g., jump rope for one) or something that you are unwilling to share or are worried about damaging or losing

HANDLING PHYSICAL BULLYING

Preparing for the Lesson

The didactic lesson for this week focuses on *handling physical bullying*, which includes a wide range of physical behaviors. Technically speaking, *physical bullying* involves the unprovoked systematic intimidation or physical abuse by one or more perpetrators upon a weaker victim. Within this range of behaviors, on the less threatening end of the spectrum, *physical bullying* includes throwing bits of paper at someone, tripping or shoving someone in the hall, or even putting a note on someone's back. On the more severe range of the spectrum, *physical bullying* includes hitting, kicking, pushing, or punching someone, as well as making physical threats.

Research suggests that as many as 75 percent of adolescents with Autism Spectrum Disorder (ASD) have been physically bullied. This type of bullying is generally done out of sight of adults. For example, on the way to and from school or in the school bathroom are common places where *physical bullying* occurs. Because *physical bullying* is often done out of sight, perpetrators may even be well regarded by teachers or administrators, or at least not distinguished as troublemakers themselves.

The strategies described in the last lesson on how to handle teasing are not effective against *physical bullying*, and can in fact lead to increased aggression in the form of retaliation for embarrassment of the bully. Although many teens who physically bully also engage in teasing with words, the strategies used for verbal bullying should not be used with people who have a tendency to get violent. Instructors are encouraged to help teens identify which strategies to use with which form of peer rejection (i.e., verbal attacks from non-aggressive peers should be responded to with *teasing comebacks*, while physical attacks or threats should be addressed with the strategies outlined in this chapter). Other forms of bullying include electronic bullying, also referred to as *cyber bullying*, and relational bullying, which often includes *rumors, gossip*, and social exclusion. Strategies for handling these forms of bullying will be addressed in future lessons.

One of the most challenging aspects of this lesson for school personnel is that physical acts of aggression can never be tolerated in the school setting. Consequently, the discussion of *physical bullying* is often an extremely uncomfortable topic. Your first instinct, like most adults, may be to encourage teens to report *physical bullying* immediately. While one aspect of the lesson includes the rule to *get help from adults when in danger*, the reality is that reporting *physical bullying* to adults for things like someone throwing bits of paper or putting a note on your back can actually worsen the situation rather than make it better. The reason is that some of these lower-level forms of *physical bullying*, although hurtful and upsetting to the victim, may result in very little punishment for the bully, but may make retaliation against the victim a stronger motive. Consequently, providing additional strategies like ***avoiding the bully*** and ***hanging out with other people*** may be more effective strategies for handling less severe forms of ***physical bullying***.

Although most schools have adopted "no tolerance" rules around bullying, and even occasionally claim to have "bully-free zones," the reality is that there is very little we can do to completely eradicate bullying. The implementation of anti-bullying programs in schools has shown limited to moderate success with some programs. Those that promote tolerance and acceptance and encourage students to stand up for others who are being bullied, rather than turning their backs, may be more effective. Yet very few (if any) of these programs offer strategies for how to handle bullying if you are the victim, apart from reporting the bullying to school personnel. Instead, most anti-bullying programs focus on the perpetrators of bullying, rather than the victims.

While PEERS® is by no means an anti-bullying program, the strategies taught in this curriculum focus on the victims of bullying and how they might make it less likely to be bullied in the future. Some programs may shy away from focusing on the victims, perhaps for fear that offering suggestions for how to respond may make it seem as though the victim is doing something wrong. Whatever the reason for this oversight, addressing the needs and concerns of victims of bullying by offering concrete strategies for handling these difficult and often traumatizing social situations is equally important.

Research suggests that one of the strongest predictors of later mental health problems among all youth (not just those with ASD) is peer rejection. This means that if you want to predict who will have mental health problems later in life, go to a typical middle school or high school and identify the rejected teens. These are the teens that are actively seeking out their peers but are actively being rejected—often through teasing or bullying. This type of peer rejection is also one of the strongest predictors of juvenile delinquency and early withdrawal from school. Consequently, the importance of this lesson, the previous lesson, and those to follow cannot be underestimated. Part of creating a safe environment for your students to thrive and grow in not only involves trying to promote bully-free zones, but it also includes helping them learn to make and keep friends and how to handle bullying when it does comes up.

Day One: Homework Review

Homework Review

[Start with completed homework first. If you have time, you can inquire as to why others were unable to complete the assignment and try to *troubleshoot* how they might get it done for the coming week. When reviewing homework, be sure to use the buzzwords (***bold and italicized***) and *troubleshoot* issues that come up. Spend the majority of the homework review on *handling teasing* and having *get-togethers*, as these were the most important assignments.]

[Note: Give multiple points for homework parts—not just one point per assignment.]

1. *Handling teasing*

   a. Say, *"One of your assignments this week was to practice using teasing comebacks. We know that teasing is very common for teenagers, so I expect that everyone here had an opportunity to use teasing comebacks with either a peer or a sibling, or maybe through practice with your parents. Raise your hand if you were able to practice using teasing comebacks this week."*

      i. Say, *"I don't want to know what they said to tease you. I want to know what you said and did to use teasing comebacks."*
      ii. Do not allow teens to talk about the specific ways someone teased them, instead have them focus only on their *verbal* and *nonverbal comebacks*

   b. For teens that did not use *teasing comebacks* this week, have them identify and demonstrate using THREE *teasing comebacks* before moving on

2. *Get-together*

   a. Say, *"Your main homework assignment this week was to have a get-together with a friend. Raise your hand if you had a get-together this week."*

      i. Ask, *"Who did you have a get-together with?"*
      ii. Ask, *"Did you talk beforehand to figure out what you were going to do?"*
      iii. Ask, *"What did you end up doing?"*
      iv. Ask, *"Who got to pick the activities?"* (Answer: Should be the guest)
      v. Ask, *"Did you trade information?"*

         1. If yes, follow up by asking, *"What percentage of the time did you trade information?"* (Answer: Should be at least 50 percent)

      vi. Ask, *"Did you have a good time?"*
      vii. Ask, *"Did your friend have a good time?"*
      viii. Ask, *"Is this someone you might want to have a get-together with again?"*

3. *Changing your reputation*

   a. Say, *"Another assignment this week was to begin to take steps toward changing your reputation if interested. Raise your hand if you did anything new this week to try to change your reputation."*

    i. Have teens report what they did to *change their reputation*

        1. [Teens with *bad reputations* should be *laying low* for the moment until they can move onto the others steps.]

    ii. Have teens go over the *steps for changing a reputation*:

        1. *Lay low*

        2. *Follow the crowd*

            a. *Try to fit in with the crowd*

            b. *Try not to stand out from the crowd*

        3. *Change your look to change your rep*

        4. *Own up to your previous reputation*

        5. *Find a new social group*

4. *Handling arguments*

    a. Say, *"Another one of your assignments was to practice handling an argument with a friend or a sibling if it came up this week. You may also have practiced with your parent during a role-play exercise. Raise your hand if you had a chance to practice handling an argument this week."*

        i. Ask, *"Who did you practice handling an argument with?"*

        ii. Ask, *"Which steps did you follow to resolve the argument?"*

        iii. If teens did not practice, have them go over the steps for handling arguments:

            1. *Keep your cool*

            2. *Listen to the other person*

            3. *Repeat what they said*

            4. *Explain your side*

            5. *Say you're sorry*

            6. *Try to solve the problem*

5. *Bring outside sports equipment*

    a. Have teens identify the outside sports equipment they will bring to share with the class later in the week (e.g., basketball, soccer ball, volleyball, football, handball, Frisbee)

Wrap Up

Say, *"Good work for those of you who completed your homework assignments. Tomorrow we'll be talking about strategies for handling physical bullying. We won't be talking about the specific ways you may have been bullied. Instead, we'll focus on ways to make it less likely that you'll be physically bullied in the future."*

Calculate Points

Calculate the number of points earned by each teen (see Appendix E for the Daily Point Log):

- Do not publicly disclose the individual number of points

- Discourage attempts to compare number of points earned between teens

  - Remind them that they are working as a team to earn a bigger and better graduation party

Day Two: Didactic Lesson—Handling Physical Bullying

Didactic Lesson: Handling Physical Bullying

- Explain, *"Last week we talked about how to handle teasing and verbal attacks by peers. We talked about using verbal and nonverbal comebacks in response to teasing. Today we're talking about how to handle physical bullying, which is very different from teasing. Just like last week, we're not going to be talking about the specific ways people may have bullied us or how it feels to be bullied. Instead, we're going to focus on what we can do in these situations to make it less likely that we'll be bullied again."*

- Ask the following questions and let teens come up with different explanations:

  - *"What is a bully?"*

    - Answer: Someone who gets into fights, threatens or assaults people

  - *"What do bullies do to other kids?"*

    - Answers:

      - Physically attack them (e.g., trip, shove, hit, kick, push, spit, slap, punch, etc.), get into fights, threaten to beat them up
      - Verbally attack them, tease them, make fun of them
      - Spread rumors or gossip about them
      - Cyber bully them through electronics and the Internet
      - Financially exploit them, steal from them, extort money
      - Take advantage of them, steal their homework, make them do things for them

  - *"What is the problem with being a bully?"*

    - Answer: Bullies often don't have good friends, they get into trouble, they sometimes do poorly in school

  - *"Why is it a bad idea to hang out with a bully?"*

    - Answer: You may get in trouble, people may think you're a bully, you may get a bad reputation

  - *"How do you know someone is a bully?"*

    - Answer: Sometimes they have a bad reputation

- Explain, *"There are different types of bullying. Last week we talked about teasing, which is bullying with words. There are also cyber bullies, gossips and rumor spreaders, and physical bullies, who get physically aggressive. The strategies we use for each of these bullies are COMPLETELY DIFFERENT. Today we're going to talk about how to handle PHYSICAL BULLYING."*

- Explain that **physical bullying** includes any physical act that feels threatening, violent, or exploitive:

  - Throwing bits of paper at you
  - Pushing or shoving you in the hallway

- ○ Putting a note on your back
- ○ Hitting, kicking, pushing, or punching you
- ○ Taking your money or personal possessions
- ○ Exploiting you or making you do things you don't want to do
- ○ Making physical threats
- ○ Trying to intimidate you

- Ask, *"What do most adults tell teens to do in response to physical bullying?"*

  - ○ Answer: Tell an adult

- Say, *"A lot of people will tell teens to tell an adult if someone is physically bullying you. While it's important to get help from adults if you feel threatened, are in danger, or just can't escape the bullying, what could be the problem with telling on the bully for minor offences like throwing paper at you or putting a note on your back?"*

  - ○ Answer: They won't get in much trouble, the bully will want to retaliate against you, this may make it worse for you

- Explain, *"While we want you to feel comfortable telling adults when you're having trouble handling any type of bullying, we also want to give you some strategies for handling physical bullying in place of just telling adults."*

Strategies for Handling Physical Bullying

[Present the rules for **handling physical bullying** by writing the following buzzwords (**bold and italicized**) on the board. Do not erase the rules until the end of the lesson.]

- *Avoid the bully*

  - ○ Say, *"One of the best strategies for handling physical bullying is to avoid the bully. This means we stay out of reach of the bully. For example, if the bully has a locker in a certain hallway, should you walk down that hallway?"*

    - ▪ Answer: Not if you can help it

  - ○ Ask, *"If the bully hangs out in a certain area of the lunchroom, should you go in that area of the lunchroom?"*

    - ▪ Answer: Not if you can help it

  - ○ Ask, *"Why is it important to avoid the bully?"*

    - ▪ Answer: ***If the bully can't FIND you, he can't bully you***

- *Lay low when the bully is around*

  - ○ Explain, *"Another one of the rules for handling physical bullying is to lay low. This means you need to fly under the radar, keep a low profile, and don't draw attention to yourself when the bully is around."*
  - ○ Ask, *"Why is it important to lay low when the bully is around?"*

    - ▪ Answer: ***If the bully doesn't notice you, he won't bully you***

- *Don't try to make friends with the bully*

  ○ Explain, *"It's also important not to try to talk to the bully or try to make friends with the bully. Some people think they can win the bully over, but this almost never works. Instead, it just draws attention to you."*

  ○ Ask, *"What could be the problem with trying to make friends with the bully?"*

    ▪ Answer: It probably won't work, it will just draw attention to you, they will probably bully you more, they may act like you're friends and then take advantage of you, bullies don't make good friends anyway

- *Don't use teasing comebacks with physical bullies*

  ○ Explain, *"Another rule is don't use teasing comebacks with physical bullies. This is because teasing comebacks often embarrass the bully and may only get them more agitated. We should only use teasing comebacks with people who are VERBALLY aggressive, NOT people who are PHYSICALLY aggressive."*

  ○ Ask, *"What could be the problem with using teasing comebacks with bullies who get physically aggressive?"*

    ▪ Answer: They may get more aggressive as a retaliation for being embarrassed

- *Don't provoke the bully*

  ○ Say, *"We also don't want to provoke the bully. That means we should never tease or make fun of the bully. What could be the problem with teasing a bully?"*

    ▪ Answer: They may get more aggressive as a retaliation

  ○ Say, *"We also don't want to act silly around the bully. What could be the problem with acting silly around a bully?"*

    ▪ Answer: This would draw attention to you, makes it more likely you'll get bullied

- *Don't police the bully*

  ○ Explain, *"It's also important not to police the bully or tell on the bully for minor offences. That means if the bully is passing notes in class or breaking some minor rule, we shouldn't tell on him or her."*

  ○ Ask, *"What could be the problem with telling on the bully for some minor offense?"*

    ▪ Answer: They may get more aggressive as a retaliation

  ○ Ask, *"But what should we do if the bully brings a weapon to school? Then should we tell on the bully?"*

    ▪ Answer: Yes, definitely

  ○ Say, *"We should only get involved if people are in danger, like if the bully brought a weapon to school or was threatening to beat someone up. If you do have to tell on the bully, should you do this in front of people?"*

    ▪ Answer: No, you should tell an adult privately

- ○ Explain, *"If you have to tell on the bully, be sure that you do this privately and away from people. And don't go and tell your friends, because the bully could find out and want to get back at you."*

- **Hang out with other people**

  - ○ Ask, *"Who do bullies like to pick on—people who are by themselves or in a group?"*

    - ■ Answer: People who are by themselves

  - ○ Ask, *"Why do they like to pick on people who are by themselves?"*

    - ■ Answer: Because you're an easy target when you're alone and have no one to defend you or stick up for you

  - ○ Explain, *"One of the most powerful strategies for handling physical bullying is to hang out with other people. This means you should avoid being alone. Bullies like to pick on people when they are alone and unprotected."*

  - ○ Ask, *"Why is it important to hang out with other people?"*

    - ■ Answer: Because the bully is less likely to pick on you if you have people around that might protect you

- **Stay near an adult when the bully is around**

  - ○ Ask, *"If you can't be around friends when the bully is near, who else could you hang around?"*

    - ■ Answer: Adults

  - ○ Explain, *"Bullies don't tend to pick on people when adults are there, so you can stay near an adult when the bully is around. That doesn't mean you need to hang out with the lunch monitor during lunchtime. It just means you can stay near an adult when the bully is around."*

  - ○ Ask, *"Why is it important to stay near an adult when the bully is around?"*

    - ■ Answer: Because the bully is less likely to pick on you when adults are near

- **Get help from adults when in danger**

  - ○ Say, *"Finally, if you're in danger, feel threatened, or these strategies aren't working for you, you should get help from an adult. Who can you get help from?"*

    - ■ Answer: Teachers, principal, dean, school counselor, security guard, parents

  - ○ Ask, *"Why is it important to get help from an adult?"*

    - ■ Answer: Because you shouldn't be placed in danger or feel threatened, adults can help to keep you and others safe from the bully

Wrap Up

Say, *"So those are some strategies for handling physical bullying. Tomorrow we'll continue our discussion about physical bullying and come up with strategies we might use to handle specific cases of physical bullying."*

Calculate Points

Calculate the number of points earned by each teen (see Appendix E for the Daily Point Log):

- Do not publicly disclose the individual number of points
- Discourage attempts to compare number of points earned between teens
    - Remind them that they are working as a team to earn a bigger and better graduation party

Day Three: Lesson Review and Behavioral Rehearsal

Lesson Review: Handling Physical Bullying

- Say, *"Yesterday we learned how to handle physical bullying. Who can tell us the rules for handling physical bullying?"*

[Have teens generate all of the rules for **handling physical bullying**. Be prepared to give prompts if necessary. Write the following bullet points and buzzwords (**bold and italicized**) on the board and do not erase until the end of the lesson.]

- ○ *Avoid the bully*
    - ▪ *If the bully can't FIND you, he can't bully you*
- ○ *Lay low when the bully is around*
    - ▪ *If the bully doesn't notice you, he won't bully you*
- ○ *Don't try to make friends with the bully*
- ○ *Don't use teasing comebacks with physical bullies*
- ○ *Don't provoke the bully*
- ○ *Don't police the bully*
- ○ *Hang out with other people*
- ○ *Stay near an adult when the bully is around*
- ○ *Get help from adults when in danger*

Behavioral Rehearsal: Handling Physical Bullying

- Present each of the following scenarios to the teens and have them come up with appropriate strategies from the lesson that could be used to handle these situations
    - ○ A bully continually throws bits of paper at a teen during class
    - ○ A bully keeps putting notes on a teen's back when walking through the halls
    - ○ A bully keeps pushing a teen as he walks down the hallway
    - ○ A bully shoves a teen against his locker each day between classes
    - ○ A bully teases and makes fun of a teen and occasionally pushes him around
        - ▪ (Do not use *teasing comebacks* with physical bullies)
    - ○ A bully trips a teen in the hallway each day during passing period
    - ○ A bully hits a teen whenever the teen *polices* others
    - ○ A bully cheats on an exam
        - ▪ (Do not tell on a bully for minor offences, even cheating)

- ○ A bully brings a weapon to school

  - ▪ (Tell an adult privately and don't tell other teens you told)

- ○ A bully kicks a teen when he walks by him
- ○ A bully pushes a teen whenever he tries to be a *joke-teller*
- ○ A bully punches a teen whenever he finds him alone in the bathroom
- ○ A bully takes a teen's money and personal possessions on the school bus
- ○ A bully exploits a teen by making him do his homework
- ○ A bully makes a teen do things he doesn't want to do in front of people
- ○ A bully makes physical threats toward a teen and tries to intimidate him

- Go around the room and have each teen choose at least TWO strategies he or she could potentially use to **handle physical bullying**

  - ○ They must pick from the strategies outlined in the lesson
  - ○ It is not important for the teen to admit that he or she is being bullied
  - ○ Do not allow them to mention the name of the bully or any identifying information as this may get back to that person
  - ○ Do not allow teens to talk about their experiences with bullying in the group

    - ▪ This might not be traumatizing for the teen to discuss, but it could be upsetting to other teens that are listening

  - ○ If a teen mentions being physically bullied, you should meet with him or her privately after class to discuss further and take appropriate actions if necessary

Homework Assignments

- Briefly explain the homework for the week by saying, *"We're going to have you practice handling physically bullying if it comes up and continue to practice having get-togethers this week."*

- Present the homework assignments for the coming week:

  1. Practice **handling physical bullying** if relevant

     a. Parents and teen should discuss which strategies to use to **handle physical bullying** if applicable
     b. Parents and teen should discuss how the teen **handled physical bullying**

  2. Teens are to have a **get-together** with a friend

     a. Follow the steps for **preparing for the get-together**
     b. **Get-togethers** should be **activity-based**
     c. **Trade information** and **find common interests** at least 50 percent of the time
     d. Initial **get-togethers** with new friends should be limited to approximately two hours (depending on the activity)

3. Practice *handling teasing*

    a. Parents and teen should practice using *verbal* and *nonverbal teasing comebacks*

        i. Parents should use a benign tease like, *"Your shoes are ugly!"*

    b. If it comes up this week, teens should use *teasing comebacks* with peers and siblings

        i. Parents and teen should discuss how the teen *handled teasing* with peers or siblings

4. Practice *changing a reputation* if relevant

    a. Parents and teen should discuss steps to *change a reputation*
    b. Teen should begin to take steps to *change a reputation* with the help of parents if relevant

5. *Bring outside sports equipment*

    a. Bring outside sports equipment to share with the class **Thursday and Friday of next week** (e.g., basketball, soccer ball, volleyball, football, handball, Frisbee)
    b. Do not bring solitary games or equipment (e.g., jump rope for one) or something that you are unwilling to share or are worried about damaging or losing

Wrap Up

Say, *"So those are your homework assignments for this week. Be sure to start working on these assignments right away. We'll be reviewing how they went at the beginning of next week. Tomorrow we'll continue our discussion about physical bullying and we'll be practicing good sportsmanship during outside sports activities."*

Calculate Points

Calculate the number of points earned by each teen (see Appendix E for the Daily Point Log):

*   Do not publicly disclose the individual number of points

*   Discourage attempts to compare number of points earned between teens

    o   Remind them that they are working as a team to earn a bigger and better graduation party

Days Four and Five: Teen Activity—Good Sportsmanship and Outdoor Activities

Lesson Review: Handling Physical Bullying

- Say, *"This week we've been working on how to handle physical bullying. Who can tell us the rules for handling physical bullying?"*

[Have teens generate all of the rules for **handling physical bullying**. Be prepared to give prompts if necessary. Write the following bullet points and buzzwords (**bold and italicized**) on the board and do not erase until the end of the lesson.]

- ○ *Avoid the bully*

    - ▪ *If the bully can't FIND you, he can't bully you*

- ○ *Lay low when the bully is around*

    - ▪ *If the bully doesn't notice you, he won't bully you*

- ○ *Don't try to make friends with the bully*

- ○ *Don't use teasing comebacks with physical bullies*

- ○ *Don't provoke the bully*

- ○ *Don't police the bully*

- ○ *Hang out with other people*

- ○ *Stay near an adult when the bully is around*

- ○ *Get help from adults when in danger*

Teen Activity: Good Sportsmanship and Outdoor Activities

Materials Needed

- Outside play area or gymnasium

    - ○ If the weather is bad, there is no outside play area, or no gymnasium available, you can modify the teen activity by playing indoor games as in the previous weeks

- Outdoor sports equipment brought by teens

- In the event that teens forget to bring outdoor sports equipment, have the teens share items brought by others, and/or have sports equipment available to use if possible

Rules

- Have teens negotiate what they will play (e.g., shoot baskets with basketball, toss a football, play catch, play Frisbee, play organized sports like basketball, touch football, soccer, handball, volleyball, badminton, etc.)

- Teens can play different games and sports if there are enough people

- Do not let anyone sit out of games and sports unless for a medical reason

  - Encourage any teen that has to sit out to praise the players from the sidelines

- Explain the rules for game playing:

  - We have a "no contact" rule for all sports— no excessive touching, crowding, or stealing
  - Must pass the ball in soccer and basketball
  - Warnings will be given for *poor sportsmanship*

- You may need to assist teens in understanding the rules for specific games

  - Try to avoid acting as a referee if disagreements occur
  - Encourage teens to work out their differences by being *good sports*

- You may need to prompt teens to be *good sports* and *praise* their partners, saying things like:

  - *"Johnny just made a basket, what could you say?"*
  - *"Jenny just made a goal, what could you say?"*
  - *"What do we say at the end of the game?"*

- Teens receive points while playing games and sports for practicing:

  - *Praising*
  - *Playing by the rules*
  - *Not refereeing*
  - *Not coaching*
  - *Sharing and taking turns*
  - *Not being competitive*
  - *Helping and showing concern if someone is injured*
  - *Suggesting a change if bored*
  - *Not being a bad winner*
  - *Not being a sore loser*
  - *Saying "good game" at the end of the game*

- When giving points:

  - Say the teen's name first to get his or her attention
  - State what the reward is (i.e., getting a point)
  - Give the reason for the reward (i.e., being a *good sport*)

    - Examples:

      - *"Jimmy gets a point for saying 'good job'!"*

- ○ *"Jenny gets a point for taking turns!"*
- ○ *"Johnny gets a point for giving a high five!"*
- ○ *"Julie gets a point for saying 'good game'!"*
- ○ *"Joey gets a point for praising!"*

- ○ Speak loudly when giving out points so other teens can hear

    - The social comparison will encourage other teens to **praise** and be **good sports**

- Be sure to keep track of points on the Good Sportsmanship Point Log (see Appendix F)

Homework Assignments

- Briefly explain the homework for the week by saying, *"We're going to have you practice handling physical bullying if it comes up, and continue to practice having get-togethers this week."*

- Present the homework assignments for the coming week:

1. Practice **handling physical bullying** if relevant

    a. Parents and teen should discuss which strategies to use to **handle physical bullying** if applicable
    b. Parents and teen should discuss how the teen **handled physical bullying**

2. Teens are to have a **get-together** with a friend

    a. Follow the steps for **preparing for the get-together**
    b. **Get-togethers** should be **activity-based**
    c. **Trade information** and **find common interests** at least 50 percent of the time
    d. Initial **get-togethers** with new friends should be limited to approximately two hours (depending on the activity)

3. Practice **handling teasing**

    a. Parents and teen should practice using **verbal** and **nonverbal teasing comebacks**

        i. Parents should use a benign tease like, *"Your shoes are ugly!"*

    b. If it comes up this week, teens should use **teasing comebacks** with peers and siblings

        i. Parents and teen should discuss how the teen **handled teasing** with peers or siblings

4. Practice **changing a reputation** if relevant

    a. Parents and teen should discuss steps to **change a reputation**
    b. Teen should begin to take steps to **change a reputation** with the help of parents if relevant

5. **Bring outside sports equipment**

    a. Bring outside sports equipment to share with the class **Thursday and Friday of next week** (e.g., basketball, soccer ball, volleyball, football, handball, Frisbee)

b. Do not bring solitary games or equipment (e.g., jump rope for one) or something that you are unwilling to share or are worried about damaging or losing

Wrap Up

Say, *"So those are your homework assignments for this week. Be sure to start working on these assignments right away. We'll be reviewing how they went at the beginning of next week."*

Calculate Points

Calculate the number of points earned by each teen (see Appendix E for the Daily Point Log):

- Do not publicly disclose the individual number of points

- Discourage attempts to compare number of points earned between teens

  ○ Remind them that they are working as a team to earn a bigger and better graduation party

Parent Handout 13

PEERS® *Program for the Education and Enrichment of Relational Skills*

Handling Physical Bullying

This week your teens will be learning strategies for *handling physical bullying*. Although the term "bullying" is used to describe a wide variety of behaviors like teasing, physical aggression, cyber bullying, and spreading rumors or gossip, the strategies for handling each of these situations are very different. Last week your teen learned how to *handle teasing* by using *teasing comebacks*. This week your teen is learning how to *handle physical bullying*.

Physical bullying includes a wide range of behaviors. On the less threatening end of the spectrum, *physical bullying* includes throwing bits of paper at someone, tripping or shoving someone in the hall, or even putting a note on someone's back. On the more severe range of the spectrum, *physical bullying* includes hitting, kicking, pushing, or punching someone, as well as making physical threats. The strategies for *handling physical bullying* are listed below.

Strategies for Handling Physical Bullying

- *Avoid the bully*

    ○ Stay out of reach of the bully
    ○ *If the bully can't FIND you, he can't bully you*

- *Lay low when the bully is around*

    ○ Keep a low profile when the bully is around
    ○ Don't draw attention to yourself
    ○ Try to fly under the radar when the bully is near
        ▪ If the bully doesn't notice you, he won't bully you

- *Don't try to make friends with the bully*

    ○ Don't try to talk to the bully
    ○ Trying to make friends with the bully rarely works
    ○ Bullies don't make good friends anyway

- *Don't use teasing comebacks with physical bullies*

    ○ This may embarrass the bully and only get them more agitated and aggressive
    ○ Parents may need to help teens figure out when to use *teasing comebacks*

        ▪ Use *teasing comebacks* with people that only get VERBALLY aggressive
        ▪ Do not use *teasing comebacks* with people that get PHYSICALLY aggressive

- *Don't provoke the bully*

    ○ Don't tease the bully

- ○ Don't act silly around the bully

- *Don't police the bully*

  - ○ Don't tell on the bully for minor offences
  - ○ Only tell on the bully if people are threatened or in danger

    - ▪ Do this secretly and out of the awareness of peers so the bully does not retaliate against you

- *Hang out with other people*

  - ○ Avoid being alone as this makes you an easier target
  - ○ Bullies like to pick on people when they're alone and seem unprotected

- *Stay near an adult when the bully is around*

  - ○ Bullies don't tend to pick on people when adults are near

- *Get help from adults when in danger*

  - ○ If you feel threatened, are in danger, or these strategies don't work, get help from an adult
  - ○ Get help from parents, teachers, the principal, or other school personnel

Homework Assignments

Every week your teen will have homework assignments to practice new and previously learned social skills. It is extremely helpful if parents assist teens in completing these assignments. The homework assignments for this week include the following:

1. Practice *handling physical bullying* if relevant

   a. Parents and teen should discuss which strategies to use to *handle physical bullying* if applicable
   b. Parents and teen should discuss how the teen *handled physical bullying*

2. Teens are to have a *get-together* with a friend

   a. Follow the steps for *preparing for the get-together*
   b. *Get-togethers* should be *activity-based*
   c. *Trade information* and *find common interests* at least 50 percent of the time
   d. Initial *get-togethers* with new friends should be limited to approximately two hours (depending on the activity)

3. Practice *handling teasing*

   a. Parents and teen should practice using *verbal* and *nonverbal teasing comebacks*

      i. Parents should use a benign tease like, *"Your shoes are ugly!"*

   b. If it comes up this week, teens should use *teasing comebacks* with peers and siblings

      i. Parents and teen should discuss how the teen *handled teasing* with peers or siblings

4. Practice *changing a reputation* if relevant

    a.   Parents and teen should discuss steps to *change a reputation*
    b.   Teen should begin to take steps to *change a reputation* with the help of parents if relevant

5. ***Bring outside sports equipment***

    a.   Bring outside sports equipment to share with the class **Thursday and Friday of next week** (e.g., basketball, soccer ball, volleyball, football, handball, Frisbee)
    b.   Do not bring solitary games or equipment (e.g., jump rope for one) or something that you are unwilling to share or are worried about damaging or losing

WEEK 14

HANDLING CYBER BULLYING

Preparing for the Lesson

The focus of this lesson is on *cyber bullying*, which involves the use of electronic forms of communication to hurt or harass people. The phenomenon of *cyber bullying* has become more common in the past several years, particularly among teens who frequently use the technologies associated with *cyber bullying*, like mobile phones and the Internet. Because *cyber bullying* is often done anonymously, this type of bullying can be even more aggressive and hurtful than those committed in person.

The act of *cyber bullying* may include sending harassing, threatening, or humiliating messages over cell phones, computers, or social networking sites. Six types of *cyber bullying* have been identified through research:

- **Insulting**: Posting or spreading false information, possibly causing harm to the reputation of the person targeted

- **Harassment**: Repeatedly sending malicious and harassing messages to a targeted person

- **Targeting**: Singling out a person and inviting others to attack or make fun of him or her collectively

- **Identity theft**: Pretending to be someone else to make it appear as though the targeted person said or did things he or she didn't do

- **Uploading**: Sharing emails or posting images of a person, particularly under embarrassing circumstances

- **Excluding**: Pressuring others to exclude the targeted person from membership or affiliation with a particular group

While research suggests that the incidence of *cyber bullying* is on the rise, much of the research in this area has focused on describing prevalence rates and understanding the culture of *cyber bullying*, rather than identifying effective strategies for combating *cyber bullying*. Although we are just beginning to discover new and effective strategies for *handling cyber bullying*, a few *ecologically valid* strategies have been uncovered and are presented in this chapter.

While the strategies outlined for *handling cyber bullying* are fairly straightforward and not likely to be met with resistance from students, the most common issue that comes up in this lesson is that teens will want to share stories of **cyber bullying**. You should avoid allowing teens to talk about specific ways in which they have been bullied online in order to minimize the negative effects of these disclosures. Instead, you should focus on ways to **handle cyber bullying**. You may need to redirect personal disclosures from teens by saying, *"We're not going to talk about the specific ways we or people we know have been cyber bullied. Instead, we're going to focus on what we can do in these situations to make it less likely that we'll be cyber bullied again."* If a teen appears to be particularly affected by this topic, you may want to speak with the teen at the end of the class to identify additional strategies (e.g., involving parents, notifying the principal, etc.).

Day One: Homework Review

Homework Review

[Start with completed homework first. If you have time, you can inquire as to why others were unable to complete the assignment and try to **troubleshoot** how they might get it done for the coming week. When reviewing homework, be sure to use the buzzwords (**bold and italicized**) and **troubleshoot** issues that come up. Spend the majority of the homework review on **handling physical bullying** and having **get-togethers,** as these were the most important assignments.]

[Note: Give multiple points for homework parts—not just one point per assignment.]

1. *Handling physical bullying*

    a. Say, *"One of your assignments this week was to practice handling physical bullying if it came up. Raise your hand if you used one or more of the strategies for handling physical bullying this week."*

        i.   Have teens report what they did to **handle physical bullying**
        ii. Have teens go over the rules for **handling physical bullying**:

             1. *Avoid the bully*
             2. *Lay low when the bully is around*
             3. *Don't try to make friends with the bully*
             4. *Don't use teasing comebacks with physical bullies*
             5. *Don't provoke the bully*
             6. *Don't police the bully*
             7. *Hang out with other people*
             8. *Stay near an adult when the bully is around*
             9. *Get help from adults when in danger*

2. *Get-together*

    a. Say, *"Your main homework assignment this week was to have a get-together with a friend. Raise your hand if you had a get-together this week."*

        i.   Ask, *"Who did you have a get-together with?"*
        ii.   Ask, *"Did you talk beforehand to figure out what you were going to do?"*
        iii. Ask, *"What did you end up doing?"*
        iv.   Ask, *"Who got to pick the activities?"* (Answer: Should be the guest)
        v.   Ask, *"Did you trade information?"*

              1. If yes, follow up by asking, *"What percentage of the time did you trade information?"* (Answer: Should be at least 50 percent)

        vi.   Ask, *"Did you have a good time?"*
        vii. Ask, *"Did your friend have a good time?"*
        viii. Ask, *"Is this someone you might want to have a get-together with again?"*

3. ***Handling teasing***

    a. Say, *"Another assignment this week was to practice using teasing comebacks. We know that teasing is very common for teenagers, so I expect that everyone here had an opportunity to use teasing comebacks with either a peer or a sibling, or maybe through practice with your parents. Raise your hand if you were able to practice using teasing comebacks this week."*

        i. Say, *"I don't want to know what they said to tease you. I want to know what you said and did to use teasing comebacks."*

        ii. Do not allow teens to talk about the specific ways someone teased them, instead have them focus only on their **verbal** and **nonverbal comebacks**

    b. For teens that did not use ***teasing comebacks*** this week, have them identify and demonstrate using THREE ***teasing comebacks*** before moving on

4. ***Changing your reputation***

    a. Say, *"Another assignment this week was to begin to take steps toward changing your reputation if interested. Raise your hand if you did anything new this week to try to change your reputation."*

        i. Have teens report what they did to ***change their reputation***

            1. [Teens with **bad reputations** should be **laying low** for the moment until they can move onto the others steps.]

        ii. Have teens go over the ***steps for changing a reputation***:

            1. ***Lay low***

            2. ***Follow the crowd***

                a. ***Try to fit in with the crowd***

                b. ***Try not to stand out from the crowd***

            3. ***Change your look to change your rep***

            4. ***Own up to your previous reputation***

            5. ***Find a new social group***

5. ***Bring outside sports equipment***

    a. Have teens identify the outside sports equipment they will bring to share with the class later in the week (e.g., basketball, soccer ball, volleyball, football, handball, Frisbee)

Wrap Up

Say, *"Good work for those of you who completed your homework assignments. Tomorrow we'll be talking about strategies for handling cyber bullying. We won't be talking about the specific ways you may have been cyber bullied. Instead, we'll focus on ways to make it less likely that you'll be cyber bullied in the future."*

Calculate Points

Calculate the number of points earned by each teen (see Appendix E for the Daily Point Log):

- Do not publicly disclose the individual number of points

- Discourage attempts to compare number of points earned between teens
  - Remind them that they are working as a team to earn a bigger and better graduation party

Day Two: Didactic Lesson—Handling Cyber Bullying

Didactic Lesson: Handling Cyber Bullying

- Explain, *"Over the last couple of weeks we've talked about how to handle teasing and physical bullying. Today we're going to talk about how to handle cyber bullying. The strategies for handling cyber bullying are very different from the ways we handle teasing and physical bullying. Just like before, we're not going to be talking about the specific ways people may have bullied us or how it feels to be bullied. Instead, we're going to focus on what we can do in these situations to make it less likely that we'll be cyber bullied again."*

- Ask the following questions and let teens come up with different explanations:
  - *"What is cyber bullying?"*
    - Answer: Harassing, threatening, or humiliating people over electronic forms of communication (phones, Internet, social networking sites)

  - *"What do cyber bullies do to other kids?"*
    - Answers:
      - Send or forward threatening, harassing, or hurtful email messages, text messages, or instant messages
      - Spread rumors and gossip on social networking sites
      - Create social networking pages to target a victim
      - Post photos or private information on the Internet without consent
      - Pretend to be someone else in order to humiliate someone or trick someone into revealing personal information

  - *"What do most adults tell teens to do in response to cyber bullying?"*
    - Answer: Ignore the **cyber bullying** or tell an adult

- Explain, *"A lot of people will tell teens to ignore the cyber bullying or tell an adult. While ignoring can sometimes help, and telling an adult may be a good strategy if you feel threatened or the bullying won't go away, there are other strategies for handling cyber bullying that we can also try."*

Strategies for Handling Cyber Bullying

[Present the rules for **handling cyber bullying** by writing the following buzzwords (**bold and italicized**) on the board. Do not erase the rules until the end of the lesson.]

- ***Don't feed the trolls***
  - Say, *"Some of you may have heard of 'Internet trolling.' What is a 'troll,' and what do trolls do?"*
    - Answer: **Trolls** are **cyber bullies**, they enjoy posting negative comments about people online

- ○ Explain, *"Trolling is a term used for people who bully others online by posting harassing and mean comments on social networking sites, message boards, and forums. They do this because it's fun for them and they're trying to get a reaction out of you."*
- ○ Ask, *"What kind of reaction are they trying to get?"*

    - Answer: They're hoping to upset you and get you to put on a show by defending yourself or engaging in a fight

- ○ Say, *"Trolls and cyber bullies are not so different from in-person bullies. They're always looking for a reaction. So what happens if you get upset or defend yourself and put up a fight?"*

    - Answer: You make it fun for the **cyber bully**

- ○ Ask, *"When you get upset or put up a fight, does that make it more likely or less likely that you're going to get cyber bullied again?"*

    - Answer: More likely

- ○ Explain, *"There's a saying online—'don't feed the trolls.' That means don't confront them or try to beat them at their own game. It's a losing game and you'll only feed their enjoyment and make them want to cyber bully you more. If you don't feed the trolls, they'll probably get bored, move on, and find someone else to pick on."*

- **Have friends stick up for you**

    - ○ Say, *"Just like in-person bullies, cyber bullies like to pick on people who are by themselves. Why do cyber bullies like to pick on people who are by themselves or seem unprotected?"*

        - Answer: Because when you're alone, you have no one to stick up for you or have your back, you are an easier target

    - ○ Explain, *"One of the strategies for handling cyber bullying is to have a friend stick up for you. We've already talked about how it doesn't do any good for you to defend yourself. That's what the cyber bully or the troll wants. Instead, you can have a friend or a family member around the same age defend you to show that you're not alone."*
    - ○ Ask, *"If other people come to your defense, what do you think the cyber bully will do?"*

        - Answer: They will probably move on because you no longer seem unprotected, it won't be fun for them anymore

- **Lay low online for a while**

    - ○ Explain, *"A lot of cyber bullying happens online, especially on social networking sites. If you're having trouble with people cyber bullying you, a good strategy is to lay low online for awhile."*
    - ○ Ask, *"What does it mean to lay low online?"*

        - Answer: Stay off your social networking sites for a while, don't post comments on other people's walls or in forums

    - ○ Ask, *"What happens when you lay low online for a while?"*

        - Answer: It creates distance between you and the **cyber bullying**, it gives you a chance to let the **cyber bullying** die down

- ○ Explain, *"Sometimes it can even be helpful to delete your Facebook account for a while if that's where the cyber bullying is happening."*
- ○ Explain, *"If the cyber bully can't FIND you, he can't bully you."*

- **Block the cyber bully**

  - ○ Explain, *"Since some cyber bullying happens over text messaging, instant messaging, email, and social networking sites where the bully is identifiable, one of the easiest ways to stop cyber bullying is by blocking the cyber bully."*
  - ○ Ask, *"What does it mean to block the cyber bully?"*

    - ■ Answer: That means *block* their messages from ever being delivered to your phone, email, or social networking page

  - ○ Explain, *"For example, blocking the cyber bully from Facebook will prevent them from viewing your profile, appearing in your search results or contact lists, and will break any connections you share. Blocking the bully on your phone will prevent them from calling or texting you. Although this strategy doesn't guarantee that the cyber bully won't find you in other areas of the Internet, blocking the cyber bully is a pretty good way to stop contact between you and the bully."*
  - ○ Explain, *"If the cyber bully can't CONTACT you, he can't bully you."*

- **Save the evidence**

  - ○ Say, *"Another good strategy for protecting yourself from cyber bullying is to save the evidence. What does it mean to save the evidence?"*

    - ■ Answer: Save any threatening, harassing, or humiliating communications

  - ○ Ask, *"Why is it important to save the evidence?"*

    - ■ Answer: Because if the *cyber bullying* doesn't stop, you may have to report it

  - ○ Explain, *"If someone sends you threatening or harassing messages or pictures, or posts harmful comments about you on the Internet, you need to save the evidence in case you and your parents need to report the cyber bullying."*

- **Get help from adults**

  - ○ Explain, *"Cyber bullying can be pretty upsetting. It can leave you feeling sad, frustrated, and embarrassed. When you don't know who's doing the cyber bullying, it can also leave you wondering whom you can trust. It's important to remember that you don't have to deal with this on your own. Instead, you should consider getting help from a supportive adult."*
  - ○ Ask, *"Who could you get help from if you were being cyber bullied?"*

    - ■ Answer: Your parents, family members, teachers, school counselors, the principal, etc.

  - ○ Explain, *"You should choose someone you trust and that's there to support you. Parents are usually the best choice, even if they're not involved with your school or the place where the cyber bullying is happening. Don't feel like you have to deal with this on your own. There are people who can help."*

- *Report cyber bullying to the proper authorities*

  - Explain, *"In some cases, it may be necessary for you and your parents to report the cyber bullying to the proper authorities. This might include online service providers, webmasters, schools, or in the most extreme cases, even law enforcement."*
  - Ask, *"Why would you want to get help from your parents before reporting the cyber bullying?"*

    - Answer: Knowing when and how to **report cyber bullying** can be confusing, you need to work with your parents on this strategy

  - Explain, *"Contacting the authorities is usually a last resort. You usually only do this when the other strategies aren't working. So be sure to get help from a parent if you think you need to report the cyber bullying."*

Wrap Up

Say, *"So those are some strategies for handling cyber bullying. Tomorrow we'll continue our discussion about cyber bullying and come up with strategies we might use to handle specific cases of cyber bullying."*

Calculate Points

Calculate the number of points earned by each teen (see Appendix E for the Daily Point Log):

- Do not publicly disclose the individual number of points

- Discourage attempts to compare number of points earned between teens

  - Remind them that they are working as a team to earn a bigger and better graduation party

Day Three: Lesson Review and Behavioral Rehearsal

Lesson Review: Handling Cyber Bullying

- Say, *"Yesterday we learned how to handle cyber bullying. Who can tell us some strategies for handling cyber bullying?"*

[Have teens generate all of the strategies for **handling cyber bullying**. Be prepared to give prompts if necessary. Write the following buzzwords (**bold and italicized**) on the board and do not erase until the end of the lesson.]

- ○ *Don't feed the trolls*

  - ▪ Don't get upset or try to fight back
  - ▪ Reacting to the *cyber bullying* will only make it fun for the *troll* and make it more likely that you will be *cyber bullied*

- ○ *Have friends stick up for you*

  - ▪ *Cyber bullies* like to pick on people that seem alone and unprotected
  - ▪ Have a friend or a family member around the same age defend you

- ○ *Lay low online for a while*

  - ▪ Take a break from social networking sites or online forums where *cyber bullying* is occurring
  - ▪ *If the cyber bully can't FIND you, he can't bully you*

- ○ *Block the cyber bully*

  - ▪ *Block the cyber bully* from your phone, email, or social networking page
  - ▪ *If the cyber bully can't CONTACT you, he can't bully you*

- ○ *Save the evidence*

  - ▪ Save any threatening, harassing, or humiliating communications in case you have to *report the cyber bullying*

- ○ *Get help from adults*

  - ▪ Get help from supportive adults (e.g., parents, family members, teachers, school counselors, the principal, etc.)
  - ▪ You don't have to deal with *cyber bullying* alone

- ○ *Report cyber bullying to the proper authorities*

  - ▪ You may need to *report the cyber bullying* to online service providers, webmasters, schools, or even law enforcement
  - ▪ This is a last resort if the other strategies aren't working
  - ▪ Be sure to get help from parents if you need to *report the cyber bullying*

Behavioral Rehearsal: Handling Cyber Bullying

- Present each of the following scenarios to the teens and have them come up with appropriate strategies from the lesson that could be used to handle these situations:

  - A *cyber bully* is posting lies about a teen on Facebook, causing harm to her reputation.

  - A *cyber bully* is sending harassing text messages to a teen.

  - A *cyber bully* is singling out a teen on an online school forum and inviting others to attack and make fun of her.

  - A *cyber bully* is pretending to be someone else to make it appear as though a teen said or did things he didn't do.

  - A *cyber bully* is sharing private emails from a teen that are embarrassing.

  - A *cyber bully* is anonymously spreading rumors and gossip about a teen on a social networking site.

  - A *cyber bully* is sending mean and harassing instant messages to a teen.

  - A *cyber bully* is anonymously sending graphic photos to a teen over email.

  - A *cyber bully* is pressuring others to exclude a teen from a particular group over a message forum.

  - A *cyber bully* is posting pictures on Facebook of a teen under embarrassing circumstances.

  - A *cyber bully* posted an embarrassing video of a teen on a social networking site.

  - A *cyber bully* is sharing personal voicemail messages from a teen with other people.

- Go around the room and have each teen choose at least TWO strategies he or she could potentially use to **handle cyber bullying**:

  - They must pick from the strategies outlined in the lesson

  - It is not important for the teen to admit that he or she is being *cyber bullied*

  - Do not allow teens to talk about their experiences with *cyber bullying* in the group

    - This might not be traumatizing for the teen to discuss, but it could be upsetting to other teens that are listening

Homework Assignments

- Briefly explain the homework for the week by saying, *"We're going to have you practice handling cyber bullying if it comes up and continue to practice having get-togethers this week."*

- Present the homework assignments for the coming week:

1. Practice *handling cyber bullying* if relevant

   a. Parents and teen should discuss which strategies to use to *handle cyber bullying* if applicable
   b. Parents and teen should discuss how the teen *handled cyber bullying*

2. Teens are to have a *get-together* with a friend

   a. Follow the steps for *preparing for the get-together*
   b. *Get-togethers* should be *activity-based*
   c. *Trade information* and *find common interests* at least 50 percent of the time
   d. Initial *get-togethers* with new friends should be limited to approximately two hours (depending on the activity)

3. Practice *handling physical bullying* if relevant

   a. Parents and teen should discuss which strategies to use to *handle physical bullying* if applicable
   b. Parents and teen should discuss how the teen *handled physical bullying*

4. Practice *handling teasing*

   a. Parents and teen should practice using *verbal* and *nonverbal teasing comebacks*

      i. Parents should use a benign tease like, *"Your shoes are ugly!"*

   b. If it comes up this week, teens should use *teasing comebacks* with peers and siblings

      i. Parents and teen should discuss how the teen *handled teasing* with peers or siblings

5. Practice *changing a reputation* if relevant

   a. Parents and teen should discuss steps to *change a reputation*
   b. Teen should begin to take steps to *change a reputation* with the help of parents if relevant

6. *Bring outside sports equipment*

   a. Bring outside sports equipment to share with the class **Thursday and Friday of next week** (e.g., basketball, soccer ball, volleyball, football, handball, Frisbee)
   b. Do not bring solitary games or equipment (e.g., jump rope for one) or something that you are unwilling to share or are worried about damaging or losing

Wrap Up

Say, *"So those are your homework assignments for this week. Be sure to start working on these assignments right away. We'll be reviewing how they went at the beginning of next week. Tomorrow we'll continue our discussion about cyber bullying and we'll practice good sportsmanship during outside sports activities."*

Calculate Points

Calculate the number of points earned by each teen (see Appendix E for the Daily Point Log):

- Do not publicly disclose the individual number of points

- Discourage attempts to compare number of points earned between teens
  - Remind them that they are working as a team to earn a bigger and better graduation party

Days Four and Five: Teen Activity—Good Sportsmanship and Outdoor Activities

Lesson Review: Handling Cyber Bullying

- Say, *"This week we've been talking about how to handle cyber bullying. Who can tell us the strategies for handling cyber bullying?"*

[Have teens generate all of the strategies for **handling cyber bullying**. Be prepared to give prompts if necessary. Write the following buzzwords (**bold and italicized**) on the board and do not erase until the end of the lesson.]

- ○ *Don't feed the trolls*

  - ▪ Don't get upset or try to fight back
  - ▪ Reacting to the *cyber bullying* will only make it fun for the *troll* and make it more likely that you will be *cyber bullied*

- ○ *Have friends stick up for you*

  - ▪ *Cyber bullies* like to pick on people that seem alone and unprotected
  - ▪ Have a friend or a family member around the same age defend you

- ○ *Lay low online for a while*

  - ▪ Take a break from social networking sites or online forums where *cyber bullying* is occurring
  - ▪ *If the cyber bully can't FIND you, he can't bully you*

- ○ *Block the cyber bully*

  - ▪ *Block the cyber bully* from your phone, email, or social networking page
  - ▪ *If the cyber bully can't CONTACT you, he can't bully you*

- ○ *Save the evidence*

  - ▪ Save any threatening, harassing, or humiliating communications in case you have to *report the cyber bullying*

- ○ *Get help from adults*

  - ▪ Get help from supportive adults (e.g., parents, family members, teachers, school counselors, the principal, etc.)
  - ▪ You don't have to deal with *cyber bullying* alone

- ○ *Report cyber bullying to the proper authorities*

  - ▪ You may need to *report the cyber bullying* to online service providers, webmasters, schools, or even law enforcement
  - ▪ This is a last resort if the other strategies aren't working
  - ▪ Be sure to get help from parents if you need to *report the cyber bullying*

Teen Activity: Good Sportsmanship and Outdoor Activities

Materials Needed

- Outside play area or gymnasium

  - If the weather is bad, there is no outside play area, or no gymnasium available, you can modify the teen activity by playing indoor games as in the previous weeks

- Outdoor sports equipment brought by teens

- In the event that teens forget to bring outdoor sports equipment, have the teens share items brought by others, and/or have sports equipment available to use if possible

Rules

- Have teens negotiate what they will play (e.g., shoot baskets with basketball, toss a football, play catch, play Frisbee, play organized sports like basketball, touch football, soccer, handball, volleyball, badminton, etc.)

- Teens can play different games and sports if there are enough people

- Do not let anyone sit out of games and sports unless it is for a medical reason

  - Encourage any teen that has to sit out to praise the players from the sidelines

- Explain the rules for game playing:

  - We have a "no contact" rule for all sports— no excessive touching, crowding, or stealing
  - Must pass the ball in soccer and basketball
  - Warnings will be given for *poor sportsmanship*

- You may need to assist teens in understanding the rules for specific games

  - Try to avoid acting as a referee if disagreements occur
  - Encourage teens to work out their differences by being *good sports*

- You may need to prompt teens to be *good sports* and *praise* their partners, saying things like:

  - *"Johnny just made a basket, what could you say?"*
  - *"Jenny just made a goal, what could you say?"*
  - *"What do we say at the end of the game?"*

- Teens receive points while playing games and sports for practicing:

  - *Praising*
  - *Playing by the rules*
  - *Not refereeing*
  - *Not coaching*
  - *Sharing and taking turns*
  - *Not being competitive*
  - *Helping and showing concern if someone is injured*

- ○ *Suggesting a change if bored*
- ○ *Not being a bad winner*
- ○ *Not being a sore loser*
- ○ *Saying "good game" at the end of the game*

- When giving points:

  - ○ Say the teen's name first to get his or her attention
  - ○ State what the reward is (i.e., getting a point)
  - ○ Give the reason for the reward (i.e., being a *good sport*)

    - ▪ Examples:

      - • *"Jimmy gets a point for saying 'good job'!"*
      - • *"Jenny gets a point for taking turns!"*
      - • *"Johnny gets a point for giving a high five!"*
      - • *"Julie gets a point for saying 'good game'!"*
      - • *"Joey gets a point for praising!"*

  - ○ Speak loudly when giving out points so other teens can hear

    - ▪ The social comparison will encourage other teens to *praise* and be *good sports*

- Be sure to keep track of points on the Good Sportsmanship Point Log (see Appendix F)

Homework Assignments

- Briefly explain the homework for the week by saying, *"We're going to have you practice handling cyber bullying if it comes up and continue to practice having get-togethers this week."*

- Present the homework assignments for the coming week:

  1. Practice *handling cyber bullying* if relevant

     a. Parents and teen should discuss which strategies to use to *handle cyber bullying* if applicable
     b. Parents and teen should discuss how the teen *handled cyber bullying*

  2. Teens are to have a *get-together* with a friend

     a. Follow the steps for *preparing for the get-together*
     b. *Get-togethers* should be *activity-based*
     c. *Trade information* and *find common interests* at least 50 percent of the time
     d. Initial *get-togethers* with new friends should be limited to approximately two hours (depending on the activity)

  3. Practice *handling physical bullying* if relevant

     a. Parents and teen should discuss which strategies to use to *handle physical bullying* if applicable
     b. Parents and teen should discuss how the teen *handled physical bullying*

4. Practice *handling teasing*

   a. Parents and teen should practice using *verbal* and *nonverbal teasing comebacks*

      i. Parents should use a benign tease like, *"Your shoes are ugly!"*

   b. If it comes up this week, teens should use *teasing comebacks* with peers and siblings

      i. Parents and teen should discuss how the teen *handled teasing* with peers or siblings

5. Practice *changing a reputation* if relevant

   a. Parents and teen should discuss steps to *change a reputation*
   b. Teen should begin to take steps to *change a reputation* with the help of parents if relevant

6. *Bring outside sports equipment*

   a. Bring outside sports equipment to share with the class **Thursday and Friday of next week** (e.g., basketball, soccer ball, volleyball, football, handball, Frisbee)
   b. Do not bring solitary games or equipment (e.g., jump rope for one) or something that you are unwilling to share or are worried about damaging or losing

Wrap Up

Say, *"So those are your homework assignments for this week. Be sure to start working on these assignments right away. We'll be reviewing how they went at the beginning of next week."*

Graduation Announcement

- Say, *"Your graduation party is two weeks from this Friday. That means you only have two more weeks to earn points for your graduation party and prizes, so be sure to get those assignments done."*

- You may want to explain the structure of the graduation party and graduation ceremony, which will vary according to school resources

  ○ Suggestions for the graduation party, prizes, and ceremony can be found in the lesson guide for Week 16, Day 5

Calculate Points

Calculate the number of points earned by each teen (see Appendix E for the Daily Point Log):

- Do not publicly disclose the individual number of points

- Discourage attempts to compare number of points earned between teens

  ○ Remind them that they are working as a team to earn a bigger and better graduation party

Parent Handout 14

PEERS® *Program for the Education and Enrichment of Relational Skills*

Handling Cyber Bullying

The focus of this lesson is on *cyber bullying*, which may include sending harassing, threatening, or humiliating messages over cell phones, computers, or social networking sites. Because *cyber bullying* is often done anonymously, this type of bullying can be even more aggressive and hurtful than those committed in person. The following strategies have been shown to be effective in combating cyber bullying.

Strategies for Handling Cyber Bullying

- *Don't feed the trolls*

    ○ *Trolls* are people who post negative comments online and *cyber bully* others
    ○ *Trolls* are looking for a reaction when they *cyber bully*

        ▪ They want you to get upset or fight back because it's fun for them

    ○ Reacting to the *cyber bullying* will only make it fun for the *troll* and make it more likely that you will be *cyber bullied*
    ○ Don't get upset or try to fight back if you want to avoid being *cyber bullied*

- *Have friends stick up for you*

    ○ *Cyber bullies* like to pick on people that seem alone and unprotected
    ○ Have a friend or a family member around the same age defend you
    ○ The *cyber bully* will probably back down and find someone else to pick on

- *Lay low online for a while*

    ○ Take a break from social networking sites or online forums where *cyber bullying* is occurring
    ○ *If the cyber bully can't FIND you, he can't bully you*

- *Block the cyber bully*

    ○ *Block the cyber bully* from your phone, email, or social networking page
    ○ *If the cyber bully can't CONTACT you, he can't bully you*

- *Save the evidence*

    ○ Save any threatening, harassing, or humiliating communications in case you have to *report the cyber bullying*

- *Get help from adults*

    ○ Get help from supportive adults (e.g., parents, family members, teachers, school counselors, the principal, etc.)
    ○ You don't have to deal with *cyber bullying* alone

- *Report cyber bullying to the proper authorities*

  - You may need to **report the cyber bullying** to online service providers, webmasters, schools, or even law enforcement
  - This is a last resort if the other strategies aren't working
  - Be sure to get help from parents if you need to **report the cyber bullying**

Homework Assignments

Every week your teen will have homework assignments to practice new and previously learned social skills. It is extremely helpful if parents assist teens in completing these assignments. The homework assignments for this week include the following:

1. Practice **handling cyber bullying** if relevant

   a. Parents and teen should discuss which strategies to use to **handle cyber bullying** if applicable
   b. Parents and teen should discuss how the teen **handled cyber bullying**

2. Teens are to have a **get-together** with a friend

   a. Follow the steps for **preparing for the get-together**
   b. **Get-togethers** should be **activity-based**
   c. **Trade information** and **find common interests** at least 50 percent of the time
   d. Initial **get-togethers** with new friends should be limited to approximately two hours (depending on the activity)

3. Practice **handling physical bullying** if relevant

   a. Parents and teen should discuss which strategies to use to **handle physical bullying** if applicable
   b. Parents and teen should discuss how the teen **handled physical bullying**

4. Practice **handling teasing**

   a. Parents and teen should practice using **verbal** and **nonverbal teasing comebacks**

      i. Parents should use a benign tease like, *"Your shoes are ugly!"*

   b. If it comes up this week, teens should use **teasing comebacks** with peers and siblings

      i. Parents and teen should discuss how the teen **handled teasing** with peers or siblings

5. Practice **changing a reputation** if relevant

   a. Parents and teen should discuss steps to **change a reputation**
   b. Teen should begin to take steps to **change a reputation** with the help of parents if relevant

6. **Bring outside sports equipment**

   a. Bring outside sports equipment to share with the class **Thursday and Friday of next week** (e.g., basketball, soccer ball, volleyball, football, handball, Frisbee)

b.   Do not bring solitary games or equipment (e.g., jump rope for one) or something that you are unwilling to share or are worried about damaging or losing

Graduation Announcement

PEERS® graduation is TWO WEEKS from this Friday! We thank you in advance for participating in PEERS®! We hope it has been a rewarding experience for you and your teen.

MINIMIZING RUMORS AND GOSSIP

Preparing for the Lesson

The focus of the current lesson is on how to appropriately *minimize rumors and gossip*. Spreading *rumors and gossip* is one of the more common ways people share information about the personal lives of others. *Rumors and gossip* are very common among teens, and even adults. Just consider the popularity of gossip shows and tabloid magazines.

Rumors and gossip are often thought of as mean-spirited, heartless, and unkind. Although a type of relational bullying, *rumors and gossip* may also simply represent a kind of communication that people use to connect and bond when socializing. Research suggests that gossiping may actually enhance social bonding in large groups as a form of shared communication. Whatever the case may be, it's important to understand that *rumors and gossip* are very common and unlikely to be eliminated from the social world in which we live.

Although often a way of communicating with others, spreading *rumors and gossip* is also a type of relational bullying. More common among females, the spreading of *rumors and gossip* may be mean-spirited and intended to hurt others. This type of *social weapon* may be used to retaliate against someone, get revenge on someone for something they've done, or damage the reputation of someone disliked or envied. While people who have a tendency to spread rumors or gossip, commonly referred to as *gossips*, may do this out of malicious intent, it's probably more likely that they're trying to get attention and feel important. Knowing secret details about the personal lives of others is a powerful position to be in and may even increase social standing in the larger peer group. Consequently, many teens (particularly girls) may spread *rumors and gossip* as a method of increasing their popularity.

The purpose of this lesson is to give teens the necessary tools for handling situations in which they are the target of *rumors or gossip*. Teens are taught that it is ineffective to try to *disprove the rumor, appear upset*, or *confront the person spreading the gossip*. Instead, it is best to *act amazed anyone would care or believe the gossip*, thereby indirectly denying the rumor is true and making the rumor seem silly. This will make it less "cool" for others to continue to spread the rumor. Teens are also taught to *spread the rumor about themselves* when they are the target of gossip. This involves indirectly discrediting the importance or believability of the rumor.

For teens that are socially isolated or withdrawn, this skill may be less relevant. However, for teens that have had a history of peer rejection associated with a *bad reputation*, this skill may be critical in helping to diffuse what is often a very challenging social situation.

Day One: Homework Review

Homework Review

[Start with completed homework first. If you have time, you can inquire as to why others were unable to complete the assignment and try to **troubleshoot** how they might get it done for the coming week. When reviewing homework, be sure to use the buzzwords (**bold and italicized**) and **troubleshoot** issues that come up. Spend the majority of the homework review on **handling cyber bullying** and having **get-togethers**, as these were the most important assignments.]

[Note: Give multiple points for homework parts—not just one point per assignment.]

1. *Handling cyber bullying*

    a. Say, *"One of your assignments this week was to practice handling cyber bullying if it came up. Raise your hand if you used one or more of the strategies for handling cyber bullying this week."*

    i.   Have teens report what they did to **handle cyber bullying**
    ii. Have teens go over the rules for **handling cyber bullying**:

        1. **Don't feed the trolls**
        2. **Have friends stick up for you**
        3. **Lay low online for a while**
        4. **Block the cyber bully**
        5. **Save the evidence**
        6. **Get help from adults**
        7. **Report cyber bullying to the proper authorities**

2. *Get-together*

    a. Say, *"Your main homework assignment this week was to have a get-together with a friend. Raise your hand if you had a get-together this week."*

    i.   Ask, *"Who did you have a get-together with?"*
    ii.   Ask, *"Did you talk beforehand to figure out what you were going to do?"*
    iii. Ask, *"What did you end up doing?"*
    iv.   Ask, *"Who got to pick the activities?"* (Answer: Should be the guest)
    v.   Ask, *"Did you trade information?"*

        1. If yes, follow up by asking, *"What percentage of the time did you trade information?"* (Answer: Should be at least 50 percent)

    vi.   Ask, *"Did you have a good time?"*
    vii. Ask, *"Did your friend have a good time?"*
    viii. Ask, *"Is this someone you might want to have a get-together with again?"*

3. *Handling physical bullying*

    a. Say, *"Another assignment this week was to practice handling physical bullying if it came up. Raise your hand if you used one or more of the strategies for handling physical bullying this week."*

        i. Have teens report what they did to **handle physical bullying**

        ii. Have teens go over the rules for **handling physical bullying**:

            1. *Avoid the bully*

            2. *Lay low when the bully is around*

            3. *Don't try to make friends with the bully*

            4. *Don't use teasing comebacks with physical bullies*

            5. *Don't provoke the bully*

            6. *Don't police the bully*

            7. *Hang out with other people*

            8. *Stay near an adult when the bully is around*

            9. *Get help from adults when in danger*

4. *Handling teasing*

    a. Say, *"Another assignment this week was to practice using teasing comebacks. We know that teasing is very common for teenagers, so I expect that everyone here had an opportunity to use teasing comebacks with either a peer or a sibling, or maybe through practice with your parents. Raise your hand if you were able to practice using teasing comebacks this week."*

        i. Say, *"I don't want to know what they said to tease you. I want to know what you said and did to use teasing comebacks."*

        ii. Do not allow teens to talk about the specific ways someone teased them, instead have them focus only on their **verbal** and **nonverbal comebacks**

    b. For teens that did not use **teasing comebacks** this week, have them identify and demonstrate using THREE **teasing comebacks** before moving on

5. *Changing your reputation*

    a. Say, *"Another assignment this week was to begin to take steps toward changing your reputation if interested. Raise your hand if you did anything new this week to try to change your reputation."*

        i. Have teens report what they did to **change their reputation**

            1. [Teens with **bad reputations** should be **laying low** for the moment until they can move onto the others steps.]

        ii. Have teens go over the **steps for changing a reputation**:

            1. *Lay low*

            2. *Follow the crowd*

                a. *Try to fit in with the crowd*

                b. *Try not to stand out from the crowd*

            3. *Change your look to change your rep*

4.   ***Own up to your previous reputation***
5.   ***Find a new social group***

6.   ***Bring outside sports equipment***

a.   Have teens identify the outside sports equipment they will bring to share with the class later in the week (e.g., basketball, soccer ball, volleyball, football, handball, Frisbee)

Wrap Up

Say, *"Good work for those of you who completed your homework assignments. Tomorrow we'll be talking about strategies for minimizing rumors and gossip. We won't be talking about the specific ways you may have been targeted by rumors and gossip. Instead, we'll focus on what you can do to minimize rumors and gossip in the future."*

Calculate Points

Calculate the number of points earned by each teen (see Appendix E for the Daily Point Log):

• Do not publicly disclose the individual number of points

• Discourage attempts to compare number of points earned between teens

  ◦ Remind them that they are working as a team to earn a bigger and better graduation party

Day Two: Didactic Lesson—Minimizing Rumors and Gossip

Didactic Lesson: Minimizing Rumors and Gossip

- Explain, *"Over the last few weeks we've talked about how to handle teasing, physical bullying, and cyber bullying. Today we're going to talk about how to minimize rumors and gossip. The strategies for handling rumors and gossip are very different from the ways we handle other types of bullying. Just like before, we're not going to be talking about the specific ways people may have gossiped about us. Instead, we're going to focus on what we can do in these situations to minimize the impact of rumors and gossip."*

- Say, *"Rumors and gossip are very common in middle school and high school. There's very little we can do to prevent people from gossiping. However, it can be very helpful to know why people spread rumors and gossip."*

- Ask, *"Why do people gossip?"*

  - Answers:

    - ***Rumors and gossip*** are ***social weapons***

      - They may be mean spirited and meant to hurt people
      - They may be used to damage the reputation of someone who is envied or not liked

    - ***Rumors and gossip*** may be a form of retaliation

      - They may be used to get revenge on someone for something they've done
      - They may be used to fulfill some threat (e.g., *"If you don't do what I say, I'll tell everyone . . ."*)

    - More often, ***rumors and gossip*** are just part of teenage conversation

      - Spreading gossip is a way for some teens to get attention and feel important (e.g., they know something no one else does)
      - Some people spread ***rumors and gossip*** to try to become more popular

How to Avoid Being the Target of Gossip

- Explain, *"Now that we're clear on WHY people gossip, it will be helpful to know what we can do to make it less likely that people will gossip about us. The first thing we need to think about is how we might avoid ever being the target of rumors and gossip."*

[Present the rules for ***minimizing rumors and gossip*** by writing the following buzzwords (**bold and italicized**) on the board. Do not erase the rules until the end of the lesson.]

  - ***Avoid being friends with gossips***

    - Explain, *"The first rule for avoiding being the target of rumors and gossip is to avoid being friends with gossips. 'Gossips' are people who like to tell rumors and spread gossip about other people."*

- Ask, *"What could be the problem with being friends with the gossips?"*
  - Answer: They are likely to spread rumors about you if they get mad at you, it is difficult to trust someone who is a gossip, other people may not want to be friends with you because they know you associate with the gossip

- *Don't provoke the gossips*
  - Explain, *"The next rule for avoiding being the target of rumors and gossip is not to provoke the 'gossips.' This means don't tell secrets, gossip about, or make fun of 'gossips' or their friends."*
  - Ask, *"What could be the problem with making a 'gossip' or their friends angry?"*
    - Answer: This will only provoke them to retaliate against you, you are likely to become the object of their gossip

- *Do not spread rumors about other people*
  - Say, *"Our last rule for avoiding being the target of rumors and gossip is not to spread rumors about other people. What could be the problem with spreading rumors and gossip about other people?"*
    - Answer: Because it's hurtful and people will not want to be friends with you, you may get a bad reputation, the people you gossip about may want to retaliate by gossiping about you

How to Handle Being the Target of Gossip

- Explain, *"Even though we may try our best to avoid being the target of gossip, it still may happen, so we need to know what we can do to minimize the impact of gossip when it's focused on us. The interesting thing about rumors and gossip is that most of our instincts in these situations are WRONG! Most people will try to disprove the rumor, deny the rumor, appear upset, or even confront the person spreading the rumor. But in each of those cases, we actually make the rumor stronger by adding fuel to the rumor mill."*

  - *Don't try to disprove the rumor*
    - Say, *"When you're the target of rumors and gossip, a strong instinct is to try to disprove or deny the rumor. The problem is that rumors are very difficult to disprove. You can never completely disprove a rumor once it's out there. You could have a mountain of evidence that the rumor isn't true, but if you go around trying to convince everyone that it's not true, what will the new rumor be?"*
      - Answer: ***The new rumor will be how you're freaking out trying to disprove the rumor***
    - Explain, *"If you try to disprove the rumor, you'll look defensive and guilty. The new rumor will be how you're freaking out trying to disprove the rumor. That's GOOD GOSSIP and adds fuel to the rumor mill."*
    - Ask, *"So if you try to disprove the rumor, are you making it better or worse for yourself?"*
      - Answer: Worse

  - *Don't appear upset*
    - Say, *"Another common instinct when you're the target of rumors and gossip is to get upset. What could be the problem with appearing upset?"*
      - Answer: You look defensive and guilty

- Ask, *"What if you're so upset that you stop going to school or stop talking to people. What will the new rumor be?"*

  - Answer: ***The new rumor will be how upset you are***

- Explain, *"If you appear upset and stop going to school, people may assume you have something to hide. The new rumor will be how upset you are. Again, that's GOOD GOSSIP and adds fuel to the rumor mill."*

- Ask, *"So if you appear upset, are you making it better or worse for yourself?"*

  - Answer: Worse

- Explain, *"Even though it's upsetting to be the target of rumors and gossip, you need to act like the rumors don't bother you. Privately, you can talk to family and friends, but publicly don't appear upset."*

- ○ ***Don't confront the person spreading the gossip***

  - Explain, *"Sometimes you know who's spreading the rumors about you. In this case, the instinct may be to confront the person spreading the gossip. The problem is, this will probably only escalate things and add fuel to the rumor mill."*

  - Ask, *"What could be the problem with confronting the person spreading the gossip?"*

    - Answer: The person may start spreading even more gossip about you, this may result in an argument or even a fight, the person may feel justified in spreading more gossip about you

  - Ask, *"What will the new rumor be if you confront the person spreading the gossip?"*

    - Answer: ***The new rumor will be how you freaked out and confronted the person spreading the gossip***

  - Explain, *"If you confront the person spreading the gossip, you may look defensive and guilty. The new rumor will be how you freaked out and confronted them. Again that's GOOD GOSSIP and adds fuel to the rumor mill."*

  - Ask, *"So if you confront the person spreading the rumor, are you making it better or worse for yourself?"*

    - Answer: Worse

- ○ ***Avoid the person spreading the gossip***

  - Explain, *"One of the difficult things about rumors and gossip is how much people want to talk about them and not let them go. People are always looking for new angles to the story and will be watching you to see how you react."*

  - Say, *"Imagine you know who is spreading the gossip about you. What does everyone expect you to do?"*

    - Answer: They expect you to confront the person spreading the gossip

  - Explain, *"The problem is that when you're in the same place as the person spreading the gossip, you can't win no matter what you do."*

- Ask, *"If you're in the same place and you DON'T LOOK at the person spreading the gossip, what's the new rumor going to be?"*

  - Answer: ***The new rumor will be how you couldn't even look at the person spreading the gossip***

- Ask, *"If you're in the same place and you LOOK at the person spreading the gossip, what's the new rumor going to be?"*

  - Answer: ***The new rumor will be how you gave the evil eye to the person spreading the gossip***

- Explain, *"In this case, you can't win, so it's best if you AVOID the person spreading the gossip about you."*

  o ***Act amazed anyone cares or believes the gossip***

  - Explain, *"When you're the target of rumors and gossip, people will ask you about the gossip to see your reaction. Even though your instinct may be to deny or disprove the rumor, that just makes you look guilty. Instead you should act amazed anyone CARES or BELIEVES the gossip."*
  - Ask, *"Why is it important to act amazed anyone cares or believes the gossip?"*

    - Answer: This discredits the importance or believability of the gossip

  - Explain, *"It doesn't even matter if it's true. If the rumor is true—you can't believe anyone CARES about it. If the rumor isn't true—you can't believe anyone BELIEVES it."*
  - Provide examples of what to say to ***act amazed anyone cares or believes the gossip***:

    - *"I can't believe anyone would believe that."*
    - *"Who would believe that? People are so gullible."*
    - *"Can you believe anyone cares about that?"*
    - *"Why would anyone care about that? People need to get a life."*
    - *"People seriously need to find something better to talk about."*

  - Ask, *"Why is it important to act amazed that anyone would care or believe the gossip?"*

    - Answer: Because it makes the rumor seem silly, people will be less likely to believe the rumor because you've undermined its importance or believability, people will be less likely to continue to spread the rumor because it makes them seem silly for even caring or believing it

  o ***Spread the rumor about yourself***

  - Explain, *"Even though acting amazed anyone would care or believe the gossip is a good strategy for handling questions about the gossip, you want to be even more proactive than that. You actually want to spread the rumor about yourself! That may sound crazy, but it's actually brilliant and works really well!"*
  - Explain the following:

    - Be proactive and ***spread the rumor about yourself*** to people you trust and will have your back

- *Spread the rumor about yourself* in front of people who will overhear the conversation (do this on several occasions with different people)
- *Steps for spreading the rumor about yourself:*

    1. *Acknowledge the rumor exists*

        - *"Have you heard this rumor about me . . .?"*

    2. *Discredit and make fun of the rumor*

        - *"How lame."*
        - *"That's so stupid."*
        - *"That's too ridiculous for words."*
        - *"How stupid is that one?"*

    3. *Act amazed anyone would believe or care about the rumor*

        - *"It's amazing what some people will believe."*
        - *"It's so crazy that people believe that."*
        - *"Can you believe anyone cares about that?"*
        - *"How weird that people even care about that."*
        - *"People need to seriously get a life and find something else to talk about."*
        - *"People need to get a hobby or find something interesting to talk about."*

- Ask, *"Why is it important to spread the rumor about yourself?"*

    - Answer: Because it indirectly discredits the rumor, it takes all the power out of the rumor by making it less important and less believable, few people will want to spread the old rumor because that would make them look silly

- Ask, *"What will the new rumor be?"*

    - Answer: **The new rumor will be how stupid the old rumor was**

- Explain, *"Spreading the rumor about yourself will often kill the rumor because the gossip looks stupid. People will be less likely to continue to spread the rumor because they'll look like they don't know what they're talking about. It also takes all of the shock value and power out of the rumor."*

Role-Plays: Spreading the Rumor about Yourself

[The instructor and behavioral coach should do an INAPPROPRIATE role-play with the instructor unsuccessfully *spreading a rumor about him or herself*.]

- Begin by saying, *"We're going to do a role-play. Watch this and tell me what I'm doing WRONG in spreading this rumor about myself."*

Example of an INAPPROPRIATE role-play:

- Instructor: (Sounds upset) *"Oh my God, (insert name)! You know that rumor that I have a crush on Jamie?"*
- Coach: *"Yeah, I heard that."*
- Instructor: (Sounds defensive, panicked) *"That's so not true! You know me. Jamie isn't even my type! We don't even have anything in common!"*
- Coach: (Unsure of the truth) *"I guess. If you say so."*
- Instructor: (Sounds defensive, guilty, hysterical) *"Yeah, I mean that's totally crazy! It's so not true! It's just . . . it's just crazy!"*
- Coach: (Uncertain) *"Okay."*
- Instructor: (Sounds worried, panicked) *"Seriously, it's totally made up! Don't believe it!"*
- Coach: (Uncertain, shrugs) *"Okay."*

- End by saying, *"Time out on that. So what did I do WRONG in trying to spread the rumor about myself?"*
  - Answer: You tried to disprove the rumor
- Ask the following *Perspective Taking Questions*:
  - *"What was that like for (name of coach)?"*
    - Answers: Confusing; weird; odd
  - *"What do you think (name of coach) thought of me?"*
    - Answers: Defensive; guilty; panicked; hysterical
  - *"Is (name of coach) going to believe me?"*
    - Answers: No; you look too guilty
- Ask the behavioral coach the same *Perspective Taking Questions*:
  - *"What was that like for you?"*
  - *"What did you think of me?"*
  - *"Did you believe me?"*

[The instructor and behavioral coach should do an APPROPRIATE role-play with the instructor successfully *spreading the rumor about him or herself*.]

- Begin by saying, *"We're going to do another role-play. Watch this and tell me what I'm doing RIGHT in spreading the rumor about myself."*

Example of an APPROPRIATE role-play:

- Instructor and Coach: (Standing around other people who might overhear the conversation)
- Instructor: (Calmly) *"Oh my God, (insert name). Did you hear that rumor that I have a crush on Jamie?"*
- Coach: *"Yeah, I totally heard that."*
- Instructor: (Casually) *"Who would believe that?"*
- Coach: *"I don't know who'd believe that."*
- Instructor: (Sounds amazed) *"It's so ridiculous. As if. And why would anyone care anyway?"*
- Coach: (Agreeing) *"I don't know. Who would care?"*
- Instructor: (Sounds indifferent) *"It's so lame. People need to find something better to talk about."*
- Coach: *"Absolutely.*
- Instructor: *"I mean get a hobby, right?"*
- Coach: *"Totally!"*
- Instructor: (Sounds amazed) *"It's so stupid."*
- Coach: (Agreeing) *"I know."*

- End by saying, *"Time out on that. So what did I do RIGHT in spreading the rumor about myself?"*

  - Answer: **Acted amazed anyone would care or believe the rumor, spread the rumor about yourself** to a person you trusted when there were other people around that might overhear

- Ask the following *Perspective Taking Questions*:

  - *"What was that like for (name of coach)?"*

    - Answers: Fine; normal

  - *"What do you think (name of coach) thought of me?"*

    - Answers: Fine; calm; unbothered

  - *"Is (name of coach) going to believe me?"*

    - Answers: Yes; probably

- Ask the behavioral coach the same *Perspective Taking Questions*:

  - *"What was that like for you?"*
  - *"What did you think of me?"*
  - *"Did you believe me?"*

Wrap Up

Say, *"So those are some strategies for minimizing rumors and gossip. Tomorrow we'll continue our discussion about rumors and gossip and you'll each practice spreading a rumor about yourself."*

Calculate Points

Calculate the number of points earned by each teen (see Appendix E for the Daily Point Log):

- Do not publicly disclose the individual number of points

- Discourage attempts to compare number of points earned between teens

  ○ Remind them that they are working as a team to earn a bigger and better graduation party

Day Three: Lesson Review and Behavioral Rehearsal

Lesson Review: Minimizing Rumors and Gossip

- Say, *"Yesterday we learned how to handle rumors and gossip. Who can tell us some strategies for minimizing rumors and gossip?"*

[Have teens generate all of the strategies for **minimizing rumors and gossip**. Be prepared to give prompts if necessary. Write the following bullet points and buzzwords (**bold and italicized**) on the board and do not erase until the end of the lesson.]

- ○ *Don't try to disprove the rumor*

    - ■ *The new rumor will be how you're freaking out trying to disprove the rumor*

- ○ *Don't appear upset*

    - ■ *The new rumor will be how upset you are*

- ○ *Don't confront the person spreading the gossip*

    - ■ *The new rumor will be how you freaked out and confronted the person*

- ○ *Avoid the person spreading the gossip*

    - ■ *The new rumor will be how you couldn't even look at the person spreading the gossip*
    - ■ *The new rumor will be how you gave the evil eye to the person spreading the gossip*

- ○ *Act amazed anyone cares or believes the gossip*

    - ■ *"I can't believe anyone would believe that."*
    - ■ *"Who would believe that? People are so gullible."*
    - ■ *"Can you believe anyone cares about that?"*
    - ■ *"Why would anyone care about that? People need to get a life."*
    - ■ *"People seriously need to find something better to talk about."*

- ○ *Spread the rumor about yourself*

    - ■ Don't wait for people to ask you about the rumor
    - ■ Be proactive and *spread the rumor about yourself* to people you trust and will have your back
    - ■ *Spread the rumor about yourself* in front of people who will overhear the conversation
    - ■ *Steps for spreading the rumor about yourself:*

        1. *Acknowledge the rumor exists*

            - *"Have you heard this rumor about me . . .?"*

        2. *Discredit and make fun of the rumor*

            - *"How lame."*
            - *"That's so stupid."*

- *"That's too ridiculous for words."*
- *"How stupid is that one?"*

3. **Act amazed anyone would believe or care about the rumor**

- *"It's amazing what some people will believe."*
- *"It's so crazy that people believe that."*
- *"Can you believe anyone cares about that?"*
- *"How weird that people even care about that."*
- *"People need to seriously get a life and find something else to talk about."*
- *"People need to get a hobby or find something interesting to talk about."*

Role-Play: Spreading the Rumor about Yourself

[The instructor and behavioral coach should do an APPROPRIATE role-play with the instructor successfully *spreading the rumor about him or herself*.]

- Begin by saying, *"We're going to do another role-play. Watch this and tell me what I'm doing RIGHT in spreading the rumor about myself."*

Example of an APPROPRIATE role-play:

- Instructor and Coach: (Standing around other people who might overhear the conversation)
- Instructor: (Calmly) *"Oh my God, (insert name). Did you hear that rumor that I got caught driving my parents' car without a license, and now I'm grounded for life?"*
- Coach: *"Yeah, I totally heard that."*
- Instructor: (Casually) *"Who would believe that?"*
- Coach: *"I don't know who'd believe that."*
- Instructor: (Sounds amazed) *"It's so stupid. And why would anyone care anyway?"*
- Coach: (Agreeing) *"I don't know. Who would care?"*
- Instructor: (Sounds indifferent) *"It's so lame. People need to find something better to talk about."*
- Coach: *"Absolutely."*
- Instructor: *"I mean find a hobby or something."*
- Coach: *"Exactly."*
- Instructor: (Sounds amazed) *"It's so stupid."*
- Coach: (Agreeing) *"I know."*

- End by saying, *"Time out on that. So what did I do RIGHT in spreading the rumor about myself?"*
  - Answer: **Acted amazed anyone would care or believe the rumor, spread the rumor about yourself** to a person you trusted when there were other people around that might overhear

- Ask the following *Perspective Taking Questions*:

- ○ *"What was that like for (name of coach)?"*

  - ▪ *Answers: Fine; normal*

- ○ *"What do you think (name of coach) thought of me?"*

  - ▪ Answers: Fine; calm; unbothered

- ○ *"Is (name of coach) going to believe me?"*

  - ▪ Answers: Yes; probably

- Ask the behavioral coach the same *Perspective Taking Questions*:

  - ○ *"What was that like for you?"*
  - ○ *"What did you think of me?"*
  - ○ *"Did you believe me?"*

Behavioral Rehearsal: Spreading the Rumor about Yourself

- Go around the room and have each teen practice *spreading the rumor about themselves*

- Using the list below, inform each teen that a rumor has been spread about them and that they need to *spread the rumor about themselves*

  - ○ *"The rumor is you're failing a class. Now spread the rumor about yourself."*
  - ○ *"The rumor is you got detention for talking back to a teacher. Now spread the rumor about yourself."*
  - ○ *"The rumor is you have a crush on your neighbor. Now spread the rumor about yourself."*
  - ○ *"The rumor is you got grounded for staying out late. Now spread the rumor about yourself."*
  - ○ *"The rumor is you were talking behind your friend's back. Now spread the rumor about yourself."*
  - ○ *"The rumor is you don't like your sister's boyfriend. Now spread the rumor about yourself."*
  - ○ *"The rumor is you may not graduate. Now spread the rumor about yourself."*
  - ○ *"The rumor is you got caught driving your parents' car without permission. Now spread the rumor about yourself."*
  - ○ *"The rumor is you might get kicked off the track team. Now spread the rumor about yourself."*
  - ○ *"The rumor is that you're going to ask out your best friend's ex. Now spread the rumor about yourself."*
  - ○ *"The rumor is you got into a fight with your best friend and you're not speaking to each other. Now spread the rumor about yourself."*
  - ○ *"The rumor is you skipped school and you might get suspended. Now spread the rumor about yourself."*

- Make sure each attempt at *spreading the rumor about yourself* meets the following parameters of the lesson:

  - ○ *Acknowledges the rumor exists*
  - ○ *Discredits and makes fun of the rumor*
  - ○ *Acts amazed anyone would believe or care about the rumor*

Homework Assignments

- Briefly explain the homework for the week by saying, *"We're going to have you practice handling rumors and gossip if it comes up and continue to practice having get-togethers this week."*

- Present the homework assignments for the coming week:

  1. Practice **handling rumors and gossip** if relevant

     a. Parents and teen should discuss which strategies to use to **handle rumors and gossip** if applicable

     b. Parents and teen should discuss how the teen **handled rumors and gossip**

  2. Teens are to have a **get-together** with a friend

     a. Follow the steps for **preparing for the get-together**

     b. **Get-togethers** should be **activity-based**

     c. **Trade information** and **find common interests** at least 50 percent of the time

     d. Initial **get-togethers** with new friends should be limited to approximately two hours (depending on the activity)

  3. Practice **handling cyber bullying** if relevant

     a. Parents and teen should discuss which strategies to use to **handle cyber bullying** if applicable

     b. Parents and teen should discuss how the teen **handled cyber bullying**

  4. Practice **handling physical bullying** if relevant

     a. Parents and teen should discuss which strategies to use to **handle physical bullying** if applicable

     b. Parents and teen should discuss how the teen **handled physical bullying**

        i. Parents and teen should discuss how the teen **handled teasing** with peers or siblings

  5. Practice **changing a reputation** if relevant

     a. Parents and teen should discuss steps to **change a reputation**

     b. Teen should begin to take steps to **change a reputation** with the help of parents if relevant

Wrap Up

Say, *"So those are your homework assignments for this week. Be sure to start working on these assignments right away. We'll be reviewing how they went at the beginning of next week. Tomorrow we'll continue our discussion about rumors and gossip, and we'll be practicing good sportsmanship during outside sports activities."*

Calculate Points

Calculate the number of points earned by each teen (see Appendix E for the Daily Point Log):

- Do not publicly disclose the individual number of points
- Discourage attempts to compare number of points earned between teens
  - Remind them that they are working as a team to earn a bigger and better graduation party

Days Four and Five: Teen Activity—Good Sportsmanship and Outdoor Activities

Lesson Review: Minimizing Rumors and Gossip

- Say, *"This week we've been talking about how to handle rumors and gossip. Who can tell us the strategies for minimizing rumors and gossip?"*

[Have teens generate all of the strategies for **minimizing rumors and gossip**. Be prepared to give prompts if necessary. Write the following bullet points and buzzwords (**bold and italicized**) on the board and do not erase until the end of the lesson.]

- ○ *Don't try to disprove the rumor*

  - ▪ *The new rumor will be how you're freaking out trying to disprove the rumor*

- ○ *Don't appear upset*

  - ▪ *The new rumor will be how upset you are*

- ○ *Don't confront the person spreading the gossip*

  - ▪ *The new rumor will be how you freaked out and confronted the person*

- ○ *Avoid the person spreading the gossip*

  - ▪ *The new rumor will be how you couldn't even look at the person spreading the gossip*
  - ▪ *The new rumor will be how you gave the evil eye to the person spreading the gossip*

- ○ *Act amazed anyone cares or believes the gossip*

  - ▪ *"I can't believe anyone would believe that."*
  - ▪ *"Who would believe that? People are so gullible."*
  - ▪ *"Can you believe anyone cares about that?"*
  - ▪ *"Why would anyone care about that? People need to get a life."*
  - ▪ *"People seriously need to find something better to talk about."*

- ○ *Spread the rumor about yourself*

  - ▪ Don't wait for people to ask you about the rumor
  - ▪ Be proactive and *spread the rumor about yourself* to people you trust and will have your back
  - ▪ *Spread the rumor about yourself* in front of people who will overhear the conversation
  - ▪ *Steps for spreading the rumor about yourself:*

    1. *Acknowledge the rumor exists*

       - *"Have you heard this rumor about me . . .?"*

    2. *Discredit and make fun of the rumor*

       - *"How lame."*
       - *"That's so stupid."*
       - *"That's too ridiculous for words."*
       - *"How stupid is that one?"*

3. *Act amazed anyone would believe or care about the rumor*

- *"It's amazing what some people will believe."*
- *"It's so crazy that people believe that."*
- *"Can you believe anyone cares about that?"*
- *"How weird that people even care about that."*
- *"People need to seriously get a life and find something else to talk about."*
- *"People need to get a hobby or find something interesting to talk about."*

Teen Activity: Good Sportsmanship and Outdoor Activities

Materials Needed

- Outside play area or gymnasium

  - If the weather is bad, there is no outside play area, or no gymnasium available, you can modify the teen activity by playing indoor games as in the previous weeks

- Outdoor sports equipment brought by teens

- In the event that teens forget to bring outdoor sports equipment, have the teens share items brought by others, and/or have sports equipment available to use if possible

Rules

- Have teens negotiate what they will play (e.g., shoot baskets with basketball, toss a football, play catch, play Frisbee, play organized sports like basketball, touch football, soccer, handball, volleyball, badminton, etc.)

- Teens can play different games and sports if there are enough people

- Do not let anyone sit out of games and sports unless for a medical reason

  - Encourage any teen that has to sit out to praise the players from the sidelines

- Explain the rules for game playing:

  - We have a "no contact" rule for all sports— no excessive touching, crowding, or stealing
  - Must pass the ball in soccer and basketball
  - Warnings will be given for ***poor sportsmanship***

- You may need to assist teens in understanding the rules for specific games

  - Try to avoid acting as a referee if disagreements occur
  - Encourage teens to work out their differences by being ***good sports***

- You may need to prompt teens to be ***good sports*** and ***praise*** their partners, saying things like:

  - *"Johnny just made a basket, what could you say?"*
  - *"Jenny just made a goal, what could you say?"*
  - *"What do we say at the end of the game?"*

- Teens receive points while playing games and sports for practicing:

  - *Praising*
  - *Playing by the rules*
  - *Not refereeing*
  - *Not coaching*
  - *Sharing and taking turns*
  - *Not being competitive*
  - *Helping and showing concern if someone is injured*
  - *Suggesting a change if bored*
  - *Not being a bad winner*
  - *Not being a sore loser*
  - *Saying "good game" at the end of the game*

- When giving points:

  - Say the teen's name first to get his or her attention
  - State what the reward is (i.e., getting a point)
  - Give the reason for the reward (i.e., being a *good sport*)

    - Examples:

      - *"Jimmy gets a point for saying 'good job'!"*
      - *"Jenny gets a point for taking turns!"*
      - *"Johnny gets a point for giving a high five!"*
      - *"Julie gets a point for saying 'good game'!"*
      - *"Joey gets a point for praising!"*

  - Speak loudly when giving out points so other teens can hear

    - The social comparison will encourage other teens to *praise* and be *good sports*

- Be sure to keep track of points on the Good Sportsmanship Point Log (see Appendix F)

Homework Assignments

- Briefly explain the homework for the week by saying, *"We're going to have you practice minimizing rumors and gossip if it comes up and continue to practice having get-togethers this week."*

- Present the homework assignments for the coming week:

  1. Practice **handling rumors and gossip** if relevant

     a. Parents and teen should discuss which strategies to use to **handle rumors and gossip** if applicable

     b. Parents and teen should discuss how the teen **handled rumors and gossip**

  2. Teens are to have a **get-together** with a friend

     a. Follow the steps for **preparing for the get-together**

     b. **Get-togethers** should be **activity-based**

   c. *Trade information* and *find common interests* at least 50 percent of the time

   d. Initial *get-togethers* with new friends should be limited to approximately two hours (depending on the activity)

3. Practice *handling cyber bullying* if relevant

   a. Parents and teen should discuss which strategies to use to *handle cyber bullying* if applicable

   b. Parents and teen should discuss how the teen *handled cyber bullying*

4. Practice *handling physical bullying* if relevant

   a. Parents and teen should discuss which strategies to use to *handle physical bullying* if applicable

   b. Parents and teen should discuss how the teen *handled physical bullying*

5. Practice *changing a reputation* if relevant

   a. Parents and teen should discuss steps to *change a reputation*

   b. Teen should begin to take steps to *change a reputation* with the help of parents if relevant

Wrap Up

Say, *"So those are your homework assignments for this week. Be sure to start working on these assignments right away. We'll be reviewing how they went at the beginning of next week."*

Graduation Announcement

- Say, *"Your graduation party is a week from this Friday. That means you only have one more week to earn points for your graduation party and prizes, so be sure to get those assignments done."*

- You may want to explain the structure of the graduation party and graduation ceremony, which will vary according to school resources

  o Suggestions for the graduation party, prizes, and ceremony can be found in the lesson guide for Week 16, Day Five

Calculate Points

Calculate the number of points earned by each teen (see Appendix E for the Daily Point Log):

- Do not publicly disclose the individual number of points

- Discourage attempts to compare number of points earned between teens

  o Remind them that they are working as a team to earn a bigger and better graduation party

Parent Handout 15

PEERS® Program for the Education and Enrichment of Relational Skills

Minimizing Rumors and Gossip

Strategies for Minimizing Rumors and Gossip

- *Don't try to disprove the rumor*

    o Although a natural instinct may be to disprove or deny a rumor, it's very difficult to disprove a rumor once it's out there

    o Trying to disprove or deny a rumor may make you look defensive and guilty

    o *The new rumor will be how you're freaking out trying to disprove the rumor*

- *Don't appear upset*

    o Another natural instinct may be to get upset when targeted by gossip

    o Appearing upset only *adds fuel to the rumor mill*

    o *The new rumor will be how upset you are*

- *Don't confront the person spreading the gossip*

    o Another instinct may be to confront the person spreading the gossip (if you know who it is)

    o *Confronting the person spreading the gossip* only *adds fuel to the rumor mill*

    o The person spreading the rumors may feel justified and want to spread more rumors, making it worse for you

    o *The new rumor will be how you freaked out and confronted the person*

- *Avoid the person spreading the gossip*

    o People will probably expect you to confront the person spreading the gossip (if you know who it is)

    o No matter what you do, you will *add fuel to the rumor mill* if you are around the person spreading the gossip

    o When you are in the same place as the person spreading the gossip:

        ▪ *The new rumor will be how you couldn't even look at the person spreading the gossip*

        ▪ *The new rumor will be how you gave the evil eye to the person spreading the gossip*

- *Act amazed anyone cares or believes the gossip*

    o People will bring up the gossip to see your reaction

    o If the gossip is true, *act amazed anyone would CARE about it*

        ▪ *"Can you believe anyone cares about that?"*

        ▪ *"Why would anyone care about that?"*

        ▪ *"People need to get a life."*

        ▪ *"People seriously need to find something better to talk about."*

- ○ If the gossip is not true, ***act amazed anyone would BELIEVE it***

  - ▪ *"I can't believe anyone would believe that."*
  - ▪ *"Who would believe that?"*
  - ▪ *"People are so gullible."*
  - ▪ *"Some people are so naïve."*

- ***Spread the rumor about yourself***

  - ○ Don't wait for people to ask you about the rumor
  - ○ Be proactive and ***spread the rumor about yourself*** to people you trust who will have your back
  - ○ ***Spread the rumor about yourself*** in front of people who will overhear the conversation (do this on several occasions with different people)
  - ○ ***Steps for spreading the rumor about yourself***:

    1. ***Acknowledge the rumor exists***

       - *"Have you heard this rumor about me . . .?"*

    2. ***Discredit and make fun of the rumor***

       - *"How lame."*
       - *"That's so stupid."*
       - *"That's too ridiculous for words."*
       - *"How stupid is that one?"*

    3. ***Act amazed anyone would believe or care about the rumor***

       - *"It's amazing what some people will believe."*
       - *"It's so crazy that people believe that."*
       - *"Can you believe anyone cares about that?"*
       - *"How weird that people even care about that."*
       - *"People need to seriously get a life and find something else to talk about."*
       - *"People need to get a hobby or find something interesting to talk about."*

Homework Assignments

Every week your teen will have homework assignments to practice new and previously learned social skills. It is extremely helpful if parents assist teens in completing these assignments. The homework assignments for this week include the following:

1. Practice ***handling rumors and gossip*** if relevant

   a. Parents and teen should discuss which strategies to use to ***handle rumors and gossip*** if applicable
   b. Parents and teen should discuss how the teen ***handled rumors and gossip***

2. Teens are to have a ***get-together*** with a friend

   a. Follow the steps for ***preparing for the get-together***

b. *Get-togethers* should be *activity-based*

c. *Trade information* and *find common interests* at least 50 percent of the time

d. Initial *get-togethers* with new friends should be limited to approximately two hours (depending on the activity)

3. Practice *handling cyber bullying* if relevant

a. Parents and teen should discuss which strategies to use to *handle cyber bullying* if applicable

b. Parents and teen should discuss how the teen *handled cyber bullying*

4. Practice *handling physical bullying* if relevant

a. Parents and teen should discuss which strategies to use to *handle physical bullying* if applicable

b. Parents and teen should discuss how the teen *handled physical bullying*

5. Practice *changing a reputation* if relevant

a. Parents and teen should discuss steps to *change a reputation*

b. Teen should begin to take steps to *change a reputation* with the help of parents if relevant

Graduation Announcement

PEERS® graduation is ONE WEEK from this Friday! We thank you in advance for participating in PEERS®! We hope it has been a rewarding experience for you and your teen.

FINAL REVIEW, POST-TEST ASSESSMENT, AND GRADUATION

Preparing for the Lesson

The major focus of the lesson this week is on providing a final review of the curriculum along with suggestions about where to go from here. There is no new material presented in the didactic lesson, just a brief review of some of the critical skills taught in PEERS®. Post-test assessments are recommended on Days Three and Four of this week. Even if you opted not to conduct pre-test assessments as recommended in Chapter 1 of this manual, conducting post-test assessments will provide you with a measure of the social skills knowledge and social functioning of your students, and further emphasize the structure of this curriculum as a class. Days Three and Four might be considered final exam days.

Day Five of this final week is intended to include a graduation party and ceremony. The purpose of the graduation party is to reward teens for their hard work throughout the class and to provide closure with fun and celebration. The teens have been earning points throughout the class toward the graduation party and graduation prizes by completing weekly homework assignments, participating in the class, and practicing the skills during behavioral rehearsal exercises. The purpose of the graduation ceremony is to signify the completion of the class and celebrate the students' achievements. Providing Certificates of Completion (see Appendix H) is recommended when possible. These certificates serve as a type of diploma that will be a tangible reminder of the work the students have accomplished.

Suggestions for organizing the graduation party, prizes, and ceremony are outlined in the lesson guide for Day Five of this week. Since the resources of each school will vary widely, descriptions of graduation events and rewards have been intentionally vague in the Parent Handouts and Graduation Announcements in your lesson guides. You will have to determine what is possible for your class prior to graduation. Decorating the room is highly encouraged to promote a party atmosphere. If your school is unable to provide food and beverages, you can have a potluck party and encourage students to bring snacks for the class. If you choose to have a potluck party, you might include a note to parents in the Parent Handouts at least a week prior to the party to allow for preparation time. Graduation prizes will obviously vary according to the means of the school, but should include items that require social interaction with others (e.g., games, sports equipment). When resources have been scarce, some schools have organized bake sales throughout the year to raise money for graduation prizes.

The majority of teens will be cheerful throughout the graduation party and generally in a festive mood. However, there are typically one or two teens who exhibit visible anxiety and/or sadness in response to the end of the class. While it will be important for you to empathize with this reaction, it is also helpful to focus on the progress teens have made and the pride they might feel for their accomplishments.

Some teens will also ask what comes next. They will often express an interest in taking the class again or having reunions with their fellow classmates. Although the students are free to socialize with one another after the class, and the organization of reunions by teaching staff is unlikely to do any harm, the added effectiveness of these interactions is unknown. Since there is never a one-size-fits-all, you will be the best judge for what will be helpful to your students with regard to future contact.

Day One: Homework Review

Homework Review

[Start with completed homework first. If you have time, you can inquire as to why others were unable to complete the assignment and try to **troubleshoot** how they might get it done for the coming week. When reviewing homework, be sure to use the buzzwords (**bold and italicized**) and **troubleshoot** issues that come up. Spend the majority of the homework review on **handling rumors and gossip** and having **get-togethers**, as these were the most important assignments.]

[Note: Give multiple points for homework parts—not just one point per assignment.]

1. **Handling rumors and gossip**

   a. Say, *"One of your assignments this week was to practice handling rumors and gossip if it came up. Raise your hand if you used one or more of the strategies for minimizing rumors and gossip this week."*

      i. Have teens report what they did to **handle rumors and gossip**
      ii. Have teens go over the rules for **minimizing rumors and gossip**:

         1. **Don't try to disprove the rumor**
         2. **Don't appear upset**
         3. **Don't confront the person spreading the gossip**
         4. **Avoid the person spreading the gossip**
         5. **Act amazed anyone cares or believes the gossip**
         6. **Spread the rumor about yourself**

            a. **Acknowledge the rumor exists**
            b. **Discredit and make fun of the rumor**
            c. **Act amazed anyone would believe or care about the rumor**

2. **Get-together**

   a. Say, *"Your main homework assignment this week was to have a get-together with a friend. Raise your hand if you had a get-together this week."*

      i. Ask, *"Who did you have a get-together with?"*
      ii. Ask, *"Did you talk beforehand to figure out what you were going to do?"*
      iii. Ask, *"What did you end up doing?"*
      iv. Ask, *"Who got to pick the activities?"* (Answer: Should be the guest)
      v. Ask, *"Did you trade information?"*

         1. If yes, follow up by asking, *"What percentage of the time did you trade information?"* (Answer: Should be at least 50 percent)

      vi. Ask, *"Did you have a good time?"*
      vii. Ask, *"Did your friend have a good time?"*
      viii. Ask, *"Is this someone you might want to have a get-together with again?"*

3. *Handling cyber bullying*

   a. Say, *"Another assignment this week was to practice handling cyber bullying if it came up. Raise your hand if you used one or more of the strategies for handling cyber bullying this week."*

      i. Have teens report what they did to **handle cyber bullying**

      ii. Have teens go over the rules for **handling cyber bullying**:

         1. **Don't feed the trolls**
         2. **Have friends stick up for you**
         3. **Lay low online for a while**
         4. **Block the cyber bully**
         5. **Save the evidence**
         6. **Get help from adults**
         7. **Report cyber bullying to the proper authorities**

4. **Handling physical bullying**

   a. Say, *"Another assignment this week was to practice handling physical bullying if it came up. Raise your hand if you used one or more of the strategies for handling physical bullying this week."*

      i. Have teens report what they did to **handle physical bullying**

      ii. Have teens go over the rules for **handling physical bullying**:

         1. **Avoid the bully**
         2. **Lay low when the bully is around**
         3. **Don't try to make friends with the bully**
         4. **Don't use teasing comebacks with physical bullies**
         5. **Don't provoke the bully**
         6. **Don't police the bully**
         7. **Hang out with other people**
         8. **Stay near an adult when the bully is around**
         9. **Get help from adults when in danger**

5. **Changing your reputation**

   a. Say, *"Another assignment this week was to begin to take steps toward changing your reputation if interested. Raise your hand if you did anything new this week to try to change your reputation."*

      i. Have teens report what they did to **change their reputation**

         1. [Teens with **bad reputations** should be **laying low** for the moment until they can move onto the others steps.]

      ii. Have teens go over the **steps for changing a reputation**:

         1. **Lay low**
         2. **Follow the crowd**

            a. **Try to fit in with the crowd**
            b. **Try not to stand out from the crowd**

         3. **Change your look to change your rep**

4. *Own up to your previous reputation*
5. *Find a new social group*

Wrap Up

Say, *"Good work for those of you who completed your homework assignments. Tomorrow we'll have a brief review of some of the things you've learned in PEERS® over the past 16 weeks."*

Graduation Announcement

- Say, *"Your graduation party is this Friday. That means this is your last week to earn points for your graduation party and prizes."*

- You may want to explain the structure of the graduation party and graduation ceremony, which will vary according to school resources

  ○ Suggestions for the graduation party, prizes, and ceremony can be found in the lesson guide for Day Five

Calculate Points

Calculate the number of points earned by each teen (see Appendix E for the Daily Point Log):

- Do not publicly disclose the individual number of points

- Discourage attempts to compare number of points earned between teens

  ○ Remind them that they are working as a team to earn a bigger and better graduation party

Day Two: Didactic Lesson—Final Review

Didactic Lesson: Final Review

- Explain, *"This is our last week of PEERS®, but just because the class is coming to an end doesn't mean that your work has also come to an end. Today we're going to focus on exactly what you will need to do to continue to make and keep friends."*

Where to Go From Here

- **Enroll in extracurricular activities**

    o Explain, *"It's essential that you continue to participate in extracurricular activities in order to make friends. Remember that your extracurricular activities should be focused on what you like to do so that you can meet other people with common interests."*

    o Ask, *"Why is it important to be enrolled in extracurricular activities?"*

    ■ Answer: It gives you a **source of friends** with **common interests**

    o Explain the following:

    ■ We recommend enrollment in AT LEAST ONE EXTRACURRICULAR ACTIVITY at a time focused on socializing

    • Individual music lessons, tutoring, and activities that don't involve socializing don't count

    ■ If you think you have a **bad reputation** at school, you may need to find an extracurricular activity in the community

    ■ Teens and parents should choose extracurricular activities based on your interests

    • Be sure that the extracurricular activity regularly exposes you to other accepting teens your age

    • Choose extracurricular activities that interest you since this is the best way to meet other teens with **common interests**

- **Find a social group**

    o Explain, *"Another way that you can make friends is by being a part of a social group. Remember that in every school there are different groups of people that hang out who all share some common interest."*

    o Ask, *"Why is it important to have a social group?"*

    ■ Answer: It gives you a **source of friends** with **common interests**

    o Explain the following:

    ■ We recommend that you be affiliated with AT LEAST ONE SOCIAL GROUP

    ■ Having a **social group** gives you a **source of friends** with **common interests**

    • People usually develop close friendships with people in their **social group**

- Some people are in more than one *social group*
- Floating from one *social group* to the next makes it hard to develop close friendships
- Focusing on a FEW *social groups* (at most) is more likely to lead to close friendships

■ Having a *social group* may protect you from individual teasing

- ***Bullies like to pick on teens who are by themselves***
- You are an easier target if you are alone and unprotected because no one is there to defend you
- Bullies are less likely to individually pick on teens who are in *social groups*
- Teens appear stronger and more protected when they are in a group

- **Have regular get-togethers**

  ○ Explain, *"It's also essential that you have regular get-togethers with friends. Get-togethers are the way teens form and keep close friendships. When you're first becoming friends with someone, you should try to have get-togethers to get to know them better. Even after you've developed a friendship, you need to maintain regular contact by having get-togethers if you want your friendship to be close."*

  ○ Ask, *"Why is it important to have regular get-togethers?"*

    ■ Answer: Having regular *get-togethers* is how close friendships develop, if you're not having *get-togethers* with your friends then you're probably not that close

  ○ Explain the following:

    ■ We recommend having AT LEAST ONE GET-TOGETHER PER WEEK

      - On average, most teenagers have 3–4 *get-togethers* per week, so having at least one *get-together* should be manageable
      - These *get-togethers* may include casually hanging out after school

    ■ Initial *get-togethers* with new friends should be limited to two hours (depending on the activity)

      - *Get-togethers* can be much longer as your friendship develops

    ■ *Get-togethers* should always be activity-based and focused on your *common interests*

- **Change your reputation (if interested)**

  ○ Explain, *"We've also talked about how to change your reputation if you're interested. We know that changing a reputation takes a while and probably wouldn't have been possible in the short time of our class, but we should still think about the steps we want to be following."*

  ○ Ask, *"What are the steps for changing a reputation?"*

    1. *Lay low*

       a. *Keep a low profile* and *don't draw attention to yourself*

    2. *Follow the crowd*

       a. *Try to fit in with the crowd*
       b. *Try not to stand out from the crowd*

    3. *Change your look to change your rep*

    4. ***Own up to your previous reputation***
    5. ***Find a new social group***

- ○ Explain, *"While you're waiting for your reputation to die down, be sure to be looking for other sources of friends outside of the place where you have this reputation. If you've been trying to change your reputation, you've probably been laying low. In a month or two, you may want to do something dramatic to get the attention back on you—like change your look to change your rep. Your parents might be able to help you with this step."*

- **Remember that friendship is a choice**

  - ○ Explain, *"We've also talked a lot about how friendship is a choice."*
  - ○ Ask, *"Do you get to be friends with everyone?"*

    - ■ Answer: No

  - ○ Ask, *"Does everyone get to be friends with you?"*

    - ■ Answer: No

  - ○ Explain, *"That's because friendship is a choice. There are good choices and bad choices. Do we want to choose people that are nice to us, interested in us, and share common interests with us?"*

    - ■ Answer: Yes

  - ○ Say, *"It's usually pretty easy for you to know if you want to be friends with someone, but how can you tell if someone wants to be friends with you?"*

    - ■ Answer: See Table 17.1

  - ○ Ask, *"How can you tell if they don't want to be friends with you?"*

    - ■ Answer: See Table 17.1

  - ○ Explain, *"Remember that friendship is a choice. We don't get to be friends with everyone, and everyone doesn't get to be friends with us."*

Table 17.1 Signs of Acceptance and Lack of Acceptance from Potential Friends

Signs They Want to Be Friends	*Signs They May NOT Want to Be Friends*
They seek you out to do things individually or in their group	They do not seek you out to do things
They talk to you and respond to your attempts to talk	They ignore you and/or do not respond to your attempts to talk
They give you their contact information	They do not give you their contact information
They ask for your contact information	They do not ask for your contact information
They text message, instant message, email, or call you just to talk	They do not text message, instant message, email, or call you
They respond to your text messages, instant messages, emails, or phone calls	They do not accept or return your calls or messages
They invite you to do things	They do not invite you to do things
They accept your invitations to do things	They do not accept your invitations or put off your invitations to do things
They add you to their social networking pages	They ignore your friend requests on social networking sites
They say nice things to you and give you compliments	They laugh or make fun of you

- Continue Using the PEERS® Skills

  ○ Explain, *"So those are a few of the things we've learned over the last 16 weeks. Even though this is the last week of PEERS®, that doesn't mean that just because the class is over that you should stop using these skills. These are the skills we need for making and keeping friends. These skills apply to adults too, so feel free to take them with you throughout your life and wherever you go!"*

Wrap Up

Say, *"So that concludes our final lesson for PEERS®. For the next two days we will be completing question-naires about your friendships to determine what you've learned in the class."*

Graduation Announcement

- Say, *"Remember that your graduation party is this Friday. We'll be celebrating all of your successes over the past 16 weeks."*

- You may want to explain the structure of the graduation party and graduation ceremony, which will vary according to school resources

  ○ Suggestions for the graduation party, prizes, and ceremony can be found in the lesson guide for Day Five

Calculate Points

Calculate the number of points earned by each teen (see Appendix E for the Daily Point Log):

- Do not publicly disclose the individual number of points

- Discourage attempts to compare number of points earned between teens

  ○ Remind them that they are working as a team to earn a bigger and better graduation party

Days Three and Four: Post-Test Assessment

Administer Post-Test Assessment

[Tracking progress is an essential part of determining whether your program is working. It is how a program maintains quality control. Below is a list of the tests we have used in our published research studies with PEERS®. Several standardized assessments of social functioning are included. These measures are widely available and have shown substantial change following the program.]

- Allow sufficient time to administer post-test assessments if applicable

- Instructors may want to orally administer the questionnaires if possible

- Chapter 1 of this manual provides a description of recommended post-test measures

- Suggested post-test measures include:

  o *Test of Adolescent Social Skills Knowledge* (Appendix A)
  o *Quality of Socialization Questionnaire* (Appendix B)
  o *Social Responsiveness Scale, Second Edition* (SRS–2; Constantino & Gruber, 2012)
  o *Social Skills Improvement System* (SSIS; Gresham & Elliot, 2008)
  o *Social Anxiety Scale* (SAS; La Greca & Lopez, 1998)
  o *Friendship Qualities Scale* (FQS; Bukowski, Hoza & Boivin, 1994)

Wrap Up

Say, *"Good job completing your questionnaires. These tests will help us to see how much you've learned in the class and how your friendships are going."*

Graduation Announcement

- Say, *"Remember that your graduation party is this Friday. We'll be celebrating all of the hard work you've done over the past 16 weeks."*

- You may want to explain the structure of the graduation party and graduation ceremony, which will vary according to school resources

  o Suggestions for the graduation party, prizes, and ceremony can be found in the lesson guide for Day Five

Calculate Points

If points were given, calculate the number of points earned by each teen (see Appendix E for the Daily Point Log):

- Do not publicly disclose the individual number of points

- Discourage attempts to compare number of points earned between teens

    o Remind them that they are working as a team to earn a bigger and better graduation party

Day Five: Teen Activity—Graduation Party and Ceremony

Preparing for Graduation

- Decorate the room

    ○ It is recommended that the instructor and coaches decorate the room for the graduation party in order to provide a feeling of celebration

- Display the graduation prizes

    ○ For the past 16 weeks teens have been earning points toward their graduation party and graduation prizes
    ○ To make the reward of earning graduation prizes more exciting, display the prizes on a counter or table when possible
    ○ This will give teens a chance to check-out the prizes as they enter the classroom and begin to consider what they might want

- Calculate the points

    ○ Prior to the graduation party, calculate the total earned points for each teen
    ○ Determine the order of distribution for the graduation prizes

        ■ The person with the highest number of points picks the first prize and so on

    ○ Do not calculate the points in the presence of the teens
    ○ Do not disclose the individual or group total of points publicly

Suggestions for Graduation Prizes

- Graduation prizes should be interactive in nature (e.g., not something someone could do in isolation)

    ○ Prizes typically include interactive games and sports equipment (e.g., board games, card games, basketballs, footballs, soccer balls, volleyballs, Frisbees, etc.)

- Give out graduation prizes at the beginning of the party since many teens often enjoy playing with these prizes during their graduation party

- Remind teens that they have earned graduation prizes for doing homework assignments, participating in class, and practicing the skills during behavioral rehearsal exercises

- Award the graduation prizes in order of highest number of points earned

    ○ Say, *"The first PEERS® graduation prize goes to (insert name)!"* while the teens do a drum roll
    ○ Say, *"The next PEERS® graduation prize goes to (insert name)!"* while the teens do a drum roll

- Have teens clap and cheer after each teen's name is called

- Allow teens to quickly choose their graduation prize

  o Teens will have had an opportunity to see graduation prizes in advance, so they will most likely have an idea of what they want

- Encourage teens to clap and cheer again after each teen has chosen a prize

- End by congratulating all of the teens on their hard work

- Do not mention the total number of points earned publicly

  o You may tell each teen privately what they earned if they specifically ask, but do not share the totals of other students

Suggestions for the Graduation Party

- It is recommended that pizza and beverages be provided by the school if possible

- Other snacks and desserts can be provided by teens if requested before the party

  o If you are having a potluck party, parents should have been notified at least a week prior to the party for planning purposes

- Teens should be encouraged to talk and socialize during the party, much like they would during a group *get-together*

- The instructor and coaches should give the teens space to enjoy their party with each other

- Teens often enjoy watching a movie of their choosing, playing games, listening to music, and/or talking

  o It is recommended that a selection of PG-rated movies be provided by the instructor, coaches, or students if possible

    ▪ Avoid PG-13 and R rated movies (even if all of the teens are 13 or older, as the content of PG-13 movies may be unsuitable for the school setting)
    ▪ If teens decide to watch a movie, allow them to work out the choice amongst themselves
    ▪ Teens should be allowed to narrate or joke about the movie
    ▪ Be sure teens are actually interacting with one another and talking during the movie
    ▪ The movie should be more of a background activity than the focus of attention

  o It is recommended that a selection of games be provided by the instructor, coaches, or students if possible

    ▪ Allow teens to work out the choice in games amongst themselves

  o Teens may also choose to play music during the party (usually through their mobile phones)

    ▪ If teens decide to listen to music, allow them to work out the choices in music amongst themselves

Suggestions for the Graduation Ceremony

- The instructor conducts the graduation ceremony

- The instructor and coaches should be at the front of the room with the students facing them

- The instructor begins by complimenting the teens on the hard work they've done

  ○ Comment on the progress the class has made as a whole

    ■ Avoid mentioning specific details about students since they will never be equal and feelings might get hurt

- The coaches may also want to make a few comments about the progress shown by the teens

- The instructor should then announce the start of the graduation ceremony and explain how the ceremony will work:

  ○ When teens hear their names called, they will come to the front of the room to receive a Certificate of Completion (see Appendix H for an example)
  ○ Everyone will clap and cheer for them
  ○ The instructor will shake the hand of the teen and then hand him or her the Certificate of Completion with the other hand
  ○ The teen should also shake the hand of any coaches
  ○ Everyone will continue to clap and cheer until the teen has returned to his or her seat

- Instructor presents the Certificates of Completion

  ○ Call each teen up to the front of the room and present him or her with a Certificate of Completion

    ■ Say, *"The first PEERS® Certificate of Completion goes to (insert name)!"* while the teens do a drum roll
    ■ Say, *"The next PEERS® Certificate of Completion goes to (insert name)!"* while the teens do a drum roll

  ○ Have teens clap and cheer after each name is called
  ○ Be sure the teen shakes the hand of the instructor and coaches
  ○ Encourage the teens to clap and cheer again as each teen returns to his or her seat

    ■ Say, *"Another round of applause for (insert name)!"*
    ■ Say, *"Give it up for (insert name)!"*

- After the final Certificate of Completion is awarded, make a few final comments about the wonderful progress the class has made

- Remind the teens that just because the class is over, it does not mean that they should stop using their PEERS® skills

- Encourage them to keep practicing what they've learned so that they can continue to make and keep friends

- Wish them well and end with a final round of applause

Parent Handout 16

PEERS® *Program for the Education and Enrichment of Relational Skills*

Final Review

This is the last week of PEERS®. Your teen will be receiving a brief review of the skills learned in PEERS®, along with a post-test assessment. A brief overview of where to go from here is provided below for parents.

Where to Go From Here

Enroll in Extracurricular Activities

- We recommend enrollment in AT LEAST ONE EXTRACURRICULAR ACTIVITY at a time focused on socializing

    ◦ Individual music lessons, tutoring, and activities that don't involve socializing don't count

- If you think your teen has a ***bad reputation*** at school, he or she may need to find an extracurricular activity in the community

- Teens and parents should choose extracurricular activities based on the teen's interests

    ◦ Be sure that the extracurricular activity regularly exposes your teen to other accepting teens his or her age
    ◦ Choose extracurricular activities that interest your teen since this is the best way to meet other teens with ***common interests***

Find a Social Group

- Another way that your teen can make friends is by being a part of a ***social group***

- In every school there are different groups of people that hang out who all share some ***common interest***

- We recommend that your teen be affiliated with AT LEAST ONE SOCIAL GROUP

- Having a ***social group*** gives your teen a ***source of friends*** with ***common interests***

    ◦ People usually develop close friendships with people in their ***social group***
    ◦ Some people are in more than one ***social group***
    ◦ Floating from one ***social group*** to the next makes it hard to develop close friendships
    ◦ Focusing on a FEW ***social groups*** (at most) is more likely to lead to close friendships

- Having a ***social group*** may protect your teen from individual teasing

    ◦ ***Bullies like to pick on teens who are by themselves***
    ◦ Teens are easier targets if alone and unprotected because no one is there to defend them

- Bullies are less likely to individually pick on teens who are in *social groups*
- Teens appear stronger and more protected when they are in a group

Have Regular Get-Togethers

- We recommend having AT LEAST ONE GET-TOGETHER PER WEEK

  - On average, most teenagers have 3–4 *get-togethers* per week, so having at least one *get-together* should be manageable
  - These *get-togethers* may include casually hanging out after school

- Initial *get-togethers* with new friends should be limited to two hours (depending on the activity)

  - *Get-togethers* can be much longer as your teen's friendship develops

- *Get-togethers* should always be activity-based and focused on your teen's *common interests*

Change Your Reputation (if interested)

- If your teen is interested in *changing his or her reputation*, find another *source of friends* in the community while his or her reputation dies down

- Parents will need to help with following the steps for *changing a reputation:*

  1. *Lay low*

     a. *Keep a low profile* and *don't draw attention to yourself*

  2. *Follow the crowd*

     a. *Try to fit in with the crowd*
     b. *Try not to stand out from the crowd*

  3. *Change your look to change your rep*
  4. *Own up to your previous reputation*
  5. *Find a new social group*

Remember that Friendship is a Choice

- *We don't get to be friends with everyone, and everyone doesn't get to be friends with us*

- *Friendship is a choice—there are good choices and bad choices*

- Consider whether your teen wants to be friends with someone and whether they want to be friends with him or her

Continue Using the PEERS® Skills

- Just because this is the last week of PEERS®, does not mean that your teen should stop using these skills

- These are the skills we need for making and keeping friends

- The PEERS® skills apply to adults too, so feel free to take them with you throughout your life and wherever you go!

Graduation Announcement

PEERS® graduation is this Friday! Congratulations on all of your hard work. We wish you the best of luck in the future and thank you for participating in PEERS®!

APPENDIX A

Test of Adolescent Social Skills Knowledge (TASSK)

Instructions

The following items are about making and keeping friends. After you reach each item, there will be a couple of choices to choose from. Decide which choice is the best by bubbling in the best answer. Only choose one answer per item.

1. The most important part of having a conversation is to:

   o   Trade information
   o   Make sure the other person is laughing and smiling

2. The goal of a conversation is to:

   o   Make the other person like you
   o   Find common interests

3. One of the rules for having a two-way conversation is to:

   o   Be an interviewer
   o   Don't be an interviewer

4. When you are FIRST getting to know someone, it is important to be:

   o   Funny and silly
   o   A little more serious

5. When you're calling a friend on the telephone, it is important to:

   o   Tell them your first and last name and where you go to school
   o   Have a cover story for calling

6. When you're calling a peer on the telephone:

   o   Avoid cold calling
   o   Let them do most of the talking

7. It's ALWAYS a good idea to try to make friends with someone who:

   o   Is more popular than you
   o   Likes the same things as you

8. It's a good idea to have a social group because:

   o   You're more likely to be popular
   o   It protects you from bullying

9. After you make a joke, it's a good idea to pay attention to:

   - Whether the other person is laughing
   - Your humor feedback

10. It is ALWAYS a good sign if someone laughs at your jokes:

    - True
    - False

11. When starting an individual conversation:

    - Wait for the person to notice you
    - Find a common interest

12. When you're trying to join a group conversation, the FIRST thing you should do is:

    - Watch and listen to observe the conversation
    - Make a comment about what they're saying

13. If you try to join a conversation and the people exclude you:

    - Give a cover story
    - Make sure they can hear you

14. If you try to join ten different conversations, on average how many times out of ten are you likely to be rejected:

    - 7 out of 10
    - 5 out of 10

15. Teens like to play sports with other teens who:

    - Score points and play well
    - Praise them

16. When people aren't playing by the rules:

    - Nicely remind them what the rules are
    - Don't referee them

17. When having a friend over for a get-together at your home:

    - Tell your friend what you're going to do
    - Have your friend choose the activity

18. If you're having a friend over for a get-together and someone else unexpectedly calls that you really like:

    - Invite your other friend over
    - Tell them that you're busy and will call them later

19. The FIRST thing you should do when you get into an argument with a friend is:

    - Listen and keep your cool
    - Explain your side

20. When a friend accuses you of doing something you didn't do:

    ○ Say you're sorry that this happened
    ○ Explain your side until they believe you

21. If you are trying to change your reputation at school, the FIRST thing you should do is:

    ○ Join an extracurricular activity at school
    ○ Lay low for a while

22. Which of the following is an important step for changing a reputation:

    ○ Change your look
    ○ Make sure that people get to know you better

23. If another kid teases you or calls you a name:

    ○ Give a teasing comeback
    ○ Tell an adult

24. When someone teases you, the best thing to do is:

    ○ Ignore them and walk away
    ○ Act like what they said didn't bother you

25. If someone keeps pushing you in the hallway as you pass their locker:

    ○ Gently push them back
    ○ Lay low when the bully is around

26. If someone is physically bullying you, the FIRST thing you should do is:

    ○ Get help from an adult
    ○ Avoid the bully

27. If someone is bullying you online, the FIRST thing you should do is:

    ○ Report the cyber bullying to the proper authorities
    ○ Have a friend stick up for you

28. If someone is cyber bullying you, it's a good idea to defend yourself and fight back:

    ○ True
    ○ False

29. If someone spreads a rumor about you that isn't true, you should:

    ○ Confront the person that started the rumor
    ○ Spread the rumor about yourself

30. If someone is gossiping behind your back, you should:

    ○ Let them know that the gossip hurts your feelings
    ○ Act amazed that anyone would believe the gossip

Administration of the Task

- The TASSK is intended to provide an assessment of the social skills knowledge of teens

- The TASSK can be completed by teens individually or during a group administration

  - For teens with significant language delay and/or reading impairment, it is recommended that the TASSK be administered orally

- The TASSK may be used as a pre, post, and/or follow-up assessment of treatment outcome

- The 30 items that make up the TASSK are derived from teen session content

  - Two items are taken from each of the 15 didactic lessons
  - These items are considered to be central to the social skills lessons

Scoring Key for the Task

SCORING

Items in **bold type** reflect correct answers. One point should be given per correct answer. Scores range from 0–30. Higher scores reflect better knowledge of teen social skills.

1. The most important part of having a conversation is to:
   - **Trade information**
   - Make sure the other person is laughing and smiling

2. The goal of a conversation is to:
   - Make the other person like you
   - **Find common interests**

3. One of the rules for having a two-way conversation is:
   - To be an interviewer
   - **Don't be an interviewer**

4. When you are FIRST getting to know someone, it is important to be:
   - Funny and silly
   - **A little more serious**

5. When you're calling a friend on the telephone, it is important to:
   - Tell them your first and last name and where you go to school
   - **Have a cover story for calling**

6. When you're calling a peer on the telephone:

   - **Avoid cold calling**
   - Let them do most of the talking

7. It's ALWAYS a good idea to try to make friends with someone who:

   - Is more popular than you
   - **Likes the same things as you**

8. It's a good idea to have a social group because:

   - You're more likely to be popular
   - **It protects you from bullying**

9. After you make a joke, it's a good idea to pay attention to:

   - Whether the other person is laughing
   - **Your humor feedback**

10. It is ALWAYS a good sign if someone laughs at your jokes:

    - True
    - **False**

11. When starting an individual conversation:

    - Wait for the person to notice you
    - **Find a common interest**

12. When you're trying to join a group conversation, the FIRST thing you should do is:

    - **Watch and listen to observe the conversation**
    - Make a comment about what they're saying

13. If you try to join a conversation and the people exclude you:

    - **Give a cover story**
    - Make sure they can hear you

14. If you try to join ten different conversations, on average how many times out of ten are you likely to be rejected:

    - 7 out of 10
    - **5 out of 10**

15. Teens like to play sports with other teens who:

    - Score points and play well
    - **Praise them**

16. When people aren't playing by the rules:

    - Nicely remind them what the rules are
    - **Don't referee them**

17. When having a friend over for a get-together at your home:

    ○ Tell your friend what you're going to do
    • **Have your friend choose the activity**

18. If you're having a friend over for a get-together and someone else unexpectedly calls that you really like:

    ○ Invite your other friend over
    • **Tell them that you're busy and will call them later**

19. The FIRST thing you should do when you get into an argument with a friend is:

    • **Listen and keep your cool**
    ○ Explain your side

20. When a friend accuses you of doing something you didn't do:

    • **Say you're sorry that this happened**
    ○ Explain your side until they believe you

21. If you are trying to change your reputation at school, the FIRST thing you should do is:

    ○ Join an extracurricular activity at school
    • **Lay low for a while**

22. Which of the following is an important step for changing a reputation:

    • **Change your look**
    ○ Make sure that people get to know you better

23. If another kid teases you or calls you a name:

    • **Give a teasing comeback**
    ○ Tell an adult

24. When someone teases you, the best thing to do is:

    ○ Ignore them and walk away
    • **Act like what they said didn't bother you**

25. If someone keeps pushing you in the hallway as you pass their locker:

    ○ Gently push them back
    • **Lay low when the bully is around**

26. If someone is physically bullying you, the FIRST thing you should do is:

    ○ Get help from an adult
    • **Avoid the bully**

27. If someone is bullying you online, the FIRST thing you should do is:

    ○ Report the cyber bullying to the proper authorities
    • **Have a friend stick up for you**

28. If someone is cyber bullying you, it's a good idea to defend yourself and fight back:

    ○ True
    • **False**

29. If someone spreads a rumor about you that isn't true, you should:

    ○ Confront the person that started the rumor
    • **Spread the rumor about yourself**

30. If someone is gossiping behind your back, you should:

    ○ Let them know that the gossip hurts your feelings
    • **Act amazed that anyone would believe the gossip**

APPENDIX B

Quality of Socialization Questionnaire—Adolescent (QSQ-A)

We are interested in the number of get-togethers you have had in the last month. A get-together is any time that teens follow through with a plan to spend time together.

- It may be a planned activity like going to the movies, playing videogames, or hanging out.
- It may be organized well in advance or spontaneously for later the same day.
- It may be with one other teen or a group of teens.

How many get-togethers did you organize in the last month?　　　_____

Please list the **first names** of all of the friends who came to your get-togethers **in the last month**. If you did not organize a get-together with another teen or other teens in the past month, leave the section below blank.

Friend's first name _____　　　Friend's first name _____

Friend's first name _____　　　Friend's first name _____

Friend's first name _____　　　Friend's first name _____

Friend's first name _____　　　Friend's first name _____

How did you and your friends get along at your LAST get-together?

Circle the number below that describes how true each sentence is.

	Not at all true	Just a little true	Pretty much true	Very much true
We didn't share games or personal items	0	1	2	3
We got along well	3	2	1	0
We got upset at each other	0	1	2	3
We had fun	3	2	1	0
We argued with each other	0	1	2	3
We enjoyed each other	3	2	1	0
We criticized or teased each other	0	1	2	3
We shared conversation	3	2	1	0
We were bossy with each other	0	1	2	3
We needed a parent to solve problems	0	1	2	3
We didn't hang out with each other	0	1	2	3
We annoyed each other	0	1	2	3

How many get-togethers were you invited to by other teens in the last month? _____

Fill in the **first names** of your friends who invited you to their get-togethers **in the last month**. If you were not invited to a get-together in the last month, leave the section below blank.

Friend's first name _____　　　Friend's first name _____

Friend's first name _____　　　Friend's first name _____

Friend's first name _____　　　Friend's first name _____

Friend's first name _____　　　Friend's first name _____

Quality of Socialization Questionnaire—Parent (QSQ-P)

We are interested in the number of get-togethers your teen has had in the last month. A get-together is any time that teens follow through with a plan to spend time together.

- It may be a planned activity like going to the movies, playing videogames, or hanging out.
- It may be organized well in advance or spontaneously for later the same day.
- It may be with one other teen or a group of teens.

How many get-togethers did your teen organize in the last month? _____
Please list the **first names** of all of the friends who came to your teen's get-togethers **in the last month**. If your teen did not organize a get-together with another teen or other teens in the past month, leave the section below blank.

Friend's first name _____   Friend's first name _____

Friend's first name _____   Friend's first name _____

Friend's first name _____   Friend's first name _____

Friend's first name _____   Friend's first name _____

At the last get-together your teen organized, when you could see or hear what was happening, how did the teens get along? Circle the number below that describes how true each sentence is.

	Not at all true	Just a little true	Pretty much true	Very much true
They didn't share games or personal items	0	1	2	3
They got along well	3	2	1	0
They got upset at each other	0	1	2	3
They had fun	3	2	1	0
They argued with each other	0	1	2	3
They enjoyed each other	3	2	1	0
They criticized or teased each other	0	1	2	3
They shared conversation	3	2	1	0
They were bossy with each other	0	1	2	3
They needed a parent to solve problems	0	1	2	3
They didn't hang out with each other	0	1	2	3
They annoyed each other	0	1	2	3

How many get-togethers was your teen invited to by other teens in the last month? ____
Fill in the **first names** of the friends who invited your teen to their get-togethers **in the last month**. If your teen was not invited to a get-together in the last month, leave the section below blank.

Friend's first name _____   Friend's first name _____

Friend's first name _____   Friend's first name _____

Friend's first name _____   Friend's first name _____

Friend's first name _____   Friend's first name _____

Administration of the QSQ

- The QSQ-A takes approximately five minutes to complete. Most teens can complete this measure independently. However, it should be orally administered to teens with reading or comprehension difficulties.

- The QSQ-P takes approximately five minutes to complete and should be completed independently by the parent.

Scoring Key for the QSQ

- Important scores to use as outcome measures:
  - The number of HOSTED get-togethers in the last month
  - The number of different friends that the teen HOSTED during get-togethers in the last month
  - The number of INVITED get-togethers in the last month
  - The number of different friends who INVITED the teen over for get-togethers in the last month

- Calculate the total Conflict Scale score by summing the scores from the items in the box.
  - Scores greater than 3.5 indicate significant conflict.

APPENDIX C

Phone Roster

This phone roster is to be used to complete the IN-CLASS CALLS. Please use this table to keep track of the person you are assigned to call each week and note the day and time of the scheduled call. If you would prefer that a different number be used than the one listed below, please let us know.

Teen Name	Phone Number	Week 1 Day/Time	Week 2 Day/Time	Week 3 Day/Time	Week 4 Day/Time	Week 5 Day/Time	Week 6 Day/Time

APPENDIX D

In-Class Call Assignment Log

Week 1

Caller _____ Receiver _____
Caller _____ Receiver _____
Caller _____ Receiver _____
Caller _____ Receiver _____
Caller _____ Receiver _____
Caller _____ Receiver _____

Week 2

Caller _____ Receiver _____
Caller _____ Receiver _____
Caller _____ Receiver _____
Caller _____ Receiver _____
Caller _____ Receiver _____
Caller _____ Receiver _____

Week 3

Caller _____ Receiver _____
Caller _____ Receiver _____
Caller _____ Receiver _____
Caller _____ Receiver _____
Caller _____ Receiver _____
Caller _____ Receiver _____

Week 4

Caller _____ Receiver _____
Caller _____ Receiver _____
Caller _____ Receiver _____
Caller _____ Receiver _____
Caller _____ Receiver _____
Caller _____ Receiver _____

Week 5

Caller _____ Receiver _____
Caller _____ Receiver _____
Caller _____ Receiver _____
Caller _____ Receiver _____
Caller _____ Receiver _____
Caller _____ Receiver _____

Week 6

Caller _____ Receiver _____
Caller _____ Receiver _____
Caller _____ Receiver _____
Caller _____ Receiver _____
Caller _____ Receiver _____
Caller _____ Receiver _____

APPENDIX E

Daily Point Log

Week _____

Name	Day 1	Day 2	Day 3	Day 4	Day 5	Total
Totals						

APPENDIX F

Good Sportsmanship Point Log

Week _____

Name	Day 3 (Week 8 only)	Day 4	Day 5	Total
Totals				

APPENDIX G

See page 444

Homework Compliance Sheet

Week	1	2	3	4	5	6	7	8	9	10	11	12	13	14	15	16
Date																

C = Complete   P = Partially Complete   I = Incomplete

Teen Name	Personal Item	Trading Info w/ Parent	In-Class Call	Out-Class Call	Extra-curricular Activity	Humor Feed-back	Enter & Exit Convo	Good Sport	Get-Together	Arguments	Change Rep	Teasing	Physical Bullying	Cyber Bullying	Rumors & Gossip

APPENDIX H

See page 446

PEERS®

Program for the Education & Enrichment of Relational Skills

Certificate of Completion

Presented to

(Name of teen)

For the successful completion of PEERS®

(Date including year)

_____

(Coach Name and Signature)

_____

(Instructor Name and Signature)

BIBLIOGRAPHY

Altman, I. & Taylor, D. (1973). *Social Penetration: The Development of Interpersonal Relationships*. New York: Holt, Rinehart & Winston.

Anckarsäter, H., Stahlberg, O., Larson, T., Hakansson, C., Jutblad, S. B., Niklasson, L., & Rastam, M. (2006). The impact of ADHD and autism spectrum disorders on temperament, character, and personality development. *American Journal of Psychiatry, 163*, 1239–44.

Attwood, T. (2000). Strategies for improving the social integration of children with Asperger syndrome. *Autism, 4*, 85–100.

Attwood, T. (2003). Frameworks for behavioral interventions. *Child and Adolescent Psychiatric Clinics of North America, 12*, 65–86.

Azmitia, M. (2002). Self, self-esteem, conflicts, and best friendships in early adolescence. In T. M. Brinthaupt (ed.), *Understanding Early Adolescent Self and Identity: Applications and Interventions* (pp. 167–92). Albany: State University of New York Press.

Barnhill, G. P. (2007). Outcomes in adults with Asperger syndrome. *Focus on Autism and Other Developmental Disabilities, 22*, 116–26.

Barnhill, G. P., Cook, K. T., Tebbenkanmp, K., & Myles, B. S. (2002). The effectiveness of social skills intervention targeting nonverbal communication for adolescents with Asperger syndrome and related pervasive developmental delays. *Focus on Autism and Other Developmental Disabilities, 17*, 112–18.

Baron-Cohen, S. (1995). *Mindblindness: An Essay on Autism and Theory of Mind*. Cambridge, MA: MIT Press.

Baron-Cohen, S., Leslie, A., & Frith, U. (1985). Does the autistic child have a "theory of mind"? *Cognition, 21*, 37–46.

Barry, T. D., Klinger, L. G., Lee, J. M., Palardy, N., Gilmore, T., & Bodin, S. D. (2003). Examining the effectiveness of an outpatient clinic-based social skills group for high-functioning children with autism. *Journal of Autism and Developmental Disorders, 33*, 685–701.

Baumeister, R. F., Zhang, L., & Vohs, K. D. (2004). Gossip as cultural learning. *Review of General Psychology, 8*, 111–21.

Bauminger, N., & Kasari, C. (2000). Loneliness and friendship in high-functioning children with autism. *Child Development, 71*, 447–56.

Bauminger, N., Shulman, C., & Agam, G. (2003). Peer interaction and loneliness in high-functioning children with autism. *Journal of Autism and Developmental Disorders, 33*, 489–507.

Bauminger, N., Solomon, M., Aciezer, A., Heung, K., Gazit, L., Brown, J., & Rogers, S. J. (2008). Children with autism and their friends: A multidimensional study in high functioning autism spectrum disorders. *Journal of Abnormal Child Psychology, 36*, 135–50.

Baxter, A. (1997). The power of friendship. *Journal on Developmental Disabilities, 5*(2), 112–17.

Beaumont, R., & Sofronoff, K. (2008). A multi-component social skills intervention for children with Asperger syndrome: The Junior Detective Training Program. *Journal of Child Psychology and Psychiatry, 49*, 743–53.

Berndt, T. J., Hawkins, J. A., & Jiao, Z. (1999). Influences of friends and friendships on adjustment to junior high school. *Merrill-Palmer Quarterly, 45*, 13–41.

Bock, M. A. (2007). The impact of social-behavioral learning strategy training on the social interaction skills of four students with Asperger syndrome. *Focus on Autism and Other Developmental Disabilities, 22*, 88–95.

Bordia, P., DiFonzo, N., Haines, R., & Chaseling, E. (2005). Rumors denials as persuasive messages: Effects of personal relevance, source, and message characteristics. *Journal of Applied Social Psychology, 35*, 1301–31.

Boulton, M. J., & Underwood, K. (1992). Bully/victim problems among middle school children. *British Journal of Educational Psychology, 62*, 73–87.

Bowler, D. M., Gaigg, S. B., & Gardiner, J. M. (2008). Subjective organization in the free recall learning of adults with Asperger's syndrome. *Journal of Autism and Developmental Disorders, 38*, 104–13.

Brown, B. B., & Lohr, M. J. (1987). Peer-group affiliation and adolescent self-esteem: An integration of ego-identity and symbolic-interaction theories. *Journal of Personality and Social Psychology, 52*, 47–55.

Buhrmester, D. (1990). Intimacy of friendship, interpersonal competence, and adjustment during preadolescence and adolescence. *Child Development, 61*, 1101–11.

Buhrmester, D., & Furman, W. (1987). The development of companionship and intimacy. *Child Development, 58*, 1101–13.

Bukowski, W. M., Hoza, B., & Boivin, M. (1993). Popularity, friendship, and emotional adjustment during early adolescence. In W. Damon (series ed.) & B. Laursen (vol. ed.), *New Directions for Child Development: Vol. 60. Close Friendships in Adolescence* (pp. 23–37). San Francisco: Jossey-Bass.

Bukowski, W. M., Hoza B., & Boivin, M. (1994). Measuring friendship quality during pre- and early adolescence: The development and psychometric properties of the Friendship Qualities Scale. *Journal of Social and Personal Relationships, 11*(3), 471–84.

Burack, J. A., Root, R., & Zigler, E. (1997). Inclusive education for students with autism: Reviewing ideological, empirical, and community considerations. In D. J. Cohen & F. Volkmar (eds.), *Handbook of Autism and Pervasive Developmental Disorders* (pp. 796–807) New York: Wiley.

Capps, L., Sigman, M., & Yirmija, N. (1996). Self-competence and emotional understanding in high-functioning children with autism. *Annual Progress in Child Psychiatry & Child Development*, 260–79.

Carter, A. S., Davis, N. O., Klin, A., & Volkmar, F. R. (2005). Social development in autism. In F. R. Volkmar, R. Paul, A. Klin, & D. Cohen (eds.), *Handbook of Autism and Pervasive Developmental Disorders* (pp. 312–34). Hoboken, NJ: John Wiley & Sons.

Castorina, L. L., & Negri, L. M. (2011). The inclusion of siblings in social skills training groups for boys with Asperger syndrome. *Journal of Autism and Developmental Disorders, 41*, 73–81.

Cederlund, M., Hagberg, B., & Gillberg, C. (2010). Asperger syndrome in adolescent and young adult males. Interview, self- and parent assessment of social, emotional, and cognitive problems. *Research in Developmental Disabilities, 31*, 287–98.

Chang, Y. C., Laugeson, E. A., Gantman, A., Dillon, A. R., Ellingsen, R., & Frankel, F. (in press). Predicting treatment success in social skills training for adolescents with autism spectrum disorders: The UCLA PEERS® program. *Autism: The International Journal of Research and Practice*.

Church, C., Alisanski, S., & Amanullah, S. (2000). The social, behavioral, and academic experiences of children with Asperger syndrome. *Focus on Autism and Other Developmental Disabilities, 15*, 12–20.

Coie, J. D., Dodge, K. A., & Kupersmidt, J. B. (1990). Peer group behavior and social status. In, S. R. Asher & J. D. Coie (eds.), *Peer Rejection in Childhood* (pp. 17–59). New York: Cambridge University Press.

Coie, J. D. & Kupersmidt, J. B. (1983). A behavioral analysis of emerging social status. *Child Development, 54*, 1400–16.

Coie, J., Terry, R., Lenox, K., Lochman, J., & Hyman, C. (1995). Childhood peer rejection and aggression as predictors of stable patterns of adolescent disorder. *Development and Psychopathology, 7*, 697–713.

Collins, W. A., & Madsen, S. D. (2006). Personal relationships in adolescence and early adulthood. In A. L. Vangelisti & D. Perlman (eds.), *The Cambridge Handbook of Personal Relationships* (pp. 191–209). New York: Cambridge University Press.

Constantino, J. N., & Gruber, C. P. (2012). *Social Responsiveness Scale, Second Edition.* Torrance, CA: Western Psychological Services.

Constantino, J. N., & Todd, R. D. (2005). Intergenerational transmission of subthreshold autistic traits in the general population. *Biological Psychiatry, 57,* 655–60.

Crick, N. R. & Grotpeter, J. K. (1996). Children's treatment by peers: Victims of relational and overt aggression. *Development and Psychopathology, 8,* 367–80.

Crick, N. R. & Ladd, G. W. (1990). Children's perceptions of the outcomes of social strategies: Do the ends justify being mean? *Developmental Psychology, 26,* 612–20.

Croen, L. A., Grether, J. K., Hoogstrate, J., & Selvin, S. (2002). The changing prevalence of autism in California. *Journal of Autism and Developmental Disorders, 32,* 207–15.

DeRosier, M. E., & Marcus, S. R. (2005). Building friendships and combating bullying: Effectiveness of S.S.GRIN at one-year follow-up. *Journal of Clinical Child and Adolescent Psychology, 24,* 140–50.

Dodge, K. A., Schlundt, D. C., Schocken, I., & Delugach, J. D. (1983). Social competence and children's sociometric status: The role of peer group entry strategies. *Merrill-Palmer Quarterly, 29,* 309–36.

Elder, L. M., Caterino, L. C., Chao, J., Shacknai, D., & De Simone, G. (2006). The efficacy of social skills treatment for children with Asperger syndrome. *Education & Treatment of Children, 29,* 635–63.

Emerich, D. M., Creaghead, N. A., Grether, S. M., Murray, D., & Grasha, C. (2003). The comprehension of humorous materials by adolescents with high-functioning autism and Asperger's syndrome. *Journal of Autism and Developmental Disorders, 33,* 253–57.

Fraley, R., & Davis, K. E. (1997). Attachment formation and transfer in young adults' close friendships and romantic relationships. *Personal Relationships, 4,* 131–44.

Frankel, F. (1996). *Good Friends are Hard to Find: Help Your Child Find, Make, and Keep Friends.* Los Angeles, CA: Perspective Publishing.

Frankel, F., & Mintz, J. (2011). Maternal reports of play dates of clinic referred and community children. *Journal of Child and Family Studies, 20*(5), 623–30.

Frankel, F., & Myatt, R. (2003). *Children's Friendship Training.* New York: Brunner-Routledge.

Frankel, F., Myatt, R., Whitham, C., Gorospe, C., & Laugeson, E. A. (2010). A controlled study of parent-assisted Children's Friendship Training with children having Autism Spectrum Disorders. *Journal of Autism and Developmental Disorders, 40,* 827–42.

Frith, U. (2004). Emanuel Miller lecture: Confusions and controversies about Asperger syndrome. *Journal of Child Psychology and Psychiatry, 45,* 672–86.

Gantman, A., Kapp, S. K., Orenski, K, & Laugeson, E. A. (2011). Social skills training for young adults with high-functioning autism spectrum disorders: A randomized controlled pilot study. *Journal of Autism and Developmental Disorders, 42*(6), 1094–103.

Gauze, C., Bukowski, W. M., Aquan-Assee, J., & Sippola, L. K. (1996). Interactions between family environment and friendship and associations with self-perceived well-being during early adolescence. *Child Development, 67,* 2201–16.

George, T. P., & Hartmann, D. P. (1996). Friendship networks of unpopular, average, and popular children. *Child Development, 67,* 2301–16.

Gerhardt, P. F. & Lainer, I. (2011). Addressing the needs of adolescents and adults with autism: A crisis on the horizon. *Journal of Contemporary Psychotherapy, 41,* 37–45.

Goldstein, A. P., & McGinnis, E. (2000). *Skill Streaming the Adolescent: New Strategies and Perspectives for Teaching Prosocial Skills.* Champaign, IL: Research Press.

Gralinski, J. H. & Kopp, C. (1993). Everyday rules for behavior: Mothers' requests to young children. *Developmental Psychology, 29,* 573–84.

Gresham, F. M., & Elliot, S. (2008). *Social Skills Improvement System-Intervention Guide.* Bloomington, MN: Pearson Assessments.

Gresham, F. M., Sugai, G., & Horner, R. H. (2001). Interpreting outcomes of social skills training for students with high-incidence disabilities. *Exceptional Children, 67,* 331–45.

Griffin, H. C., Griffin, L. W., Fitch, C. W., Albera, V., & Gingras, H. G. (2006). Educational interventions for individuals with Asperger syndrome. *Intervention in School and Clinic, 41*, 150–55.

Hartup, W. W. (1993). Adolescents and their friends. In, B. Laursen (ed.), *Close Friendships in Adolescence. Series: New Directions for Child Development* (W. Damon, series editor in chief). Number 60, pp. 3–22.

Hill, E. L. (2004). Executive dysfunction in autism. *Trends in Cognitive Sciences, 8*, 26–32.

Hillier, A., Fish, T., Coppert, P., & Beversdorf, D. Q. (2007). Outcomes of a social and vocational skills support group for adolescents and young adults on the autism spectrum. *Focus on Autism and Other Developmental Disabilities, 22*, 107–15.

Hodgdon, L. Q. (1995). Solving social-behavioral problems through the use of visually supported communication. In K. A. Quill (ed.), *Teaching Children with Autism: Strategies to Enhance Communication and Socialization* (pp. 265–86). New York: Delmar.

Hodges, E., Boivin, M., Vitaro, F., & Bukowski, W. M. (1999). The power of friendship: Protection against an escalating cycle of peer victimization. *Developmental Psychology, 35*, 94–101.

Hodges, E., Malone, M. J., & Perry, D. G. (1997). Individual risk and social risk as interacting determinants of victimization in the peer group. *Developmental Psychology, 33*, 1032–9.

Hodges, E. V. E. & Perry, D. G. (1999). Personal and interpersonal antecedents and consequences of victimization by peers. *Journal of Personality & Social Psychology, 76*, 677–85.

Hollingshead, A. B. (1975). *Four Factor Index of Social Status.* (Available from P.O. Box 1965, Yale Station, New Haven, CT 06520, USA.)

Howlin, P., & Goode, S. (1998). Outcome in adult life for people with autism, Asperger syndrome. In F. R. Volkmar (ed.), *Autism and Pervasive Developmental Disorders* (pp. 209–41). New York: Cambridge University Press.

Hume, K., Loftin, R., & Lantz, J. (2009). Increasing independence in autism spectrum disorders: A review of three focused interventions. *Journal of Autism and Developmental Disorders, 39*, 1329–38.

Humphrey, N. & Symes, W. (2010). Perceptions of social support and experience of bullying among pupils with autistic spectrum disorders in mainstream secondary schools. *European Journal of Special Needs Education, 25*, 77–91.

Johnson, S. A., Blaha, L. M., Houpt, J. W., & Townsend, J. T. (2010). Systems factorial technology provides new insights on global-local information processing in autism spectrum disorders. *Journal of Mathematical Psychology, 54*, 53–72.

Kapp, S. K., Gantman, A., & Laugeson, E. A. (2011). Transition to adulthood for high-functioning individuals with autism spectrum disorders. In M.R. Mohammadi (series ed.), *A Comprehensive Book on Autism Spectrum Disorders* (pp. 451–78). New York: InTech.

Kasari, C., & Locke, J. (2011). Social skills interventions for children with autism spectrum disorders. In D. G. Amaral, G. Dawson and D. H. Geschwind (eds.), *Autism Spectrum Disorders* (pp. 1156–66). New York: Oxford University Press.

Kerbel, D. & Grunwell, P. (1998). A study of idiom comprehension in children with semantic-pragmatic difficulties. Part I: Task effects on the assessment of idiom comprehension in children. *International Journal of Language & Communication Disorders, 33*, 1–22.

Klin, A. (2011). From Asperger to modern day. In D. G. Amaral, G. Dawson, and D. H. Geschwind (eds.), *Autism Spectrum Disorders* (pp. 44–59). New York: Oxford University Press.

Klin, A. & Volkmar, F. R. (2003). Asperger syndrome: Diagnosis and external validity. *Child and Adolescent Psychiatric Clinics of North America, 12*, 1–13.

Klin, A., Volkmar, F. R., & Sparrow, S. S. (2000). *Asperger Syndrome.* New York: Guilford Press.

Koegel, L. K., Koegel, R. L., Hurley, C., & Frea, W. D. (1992). Improving social skills and disruptive behavior in children with autism through self-management. *Journal of Applied Behavior Analysis, 25*, 341–53.

Koning, C., & Magill-Evans, J. (2001). Social and language skills in adolescent boys with Asperger syndrome. *Autism, 5*, 23–36.

Krasny, L., Williams, B. J., Provencal, S., & Ozonoff, S. (2003). Social skills interventions for the autism spectrum: Essential ingredients and a model curriculum. *Child and Adolescent Psychiatry Clinics of North America, 12*, 107–22.

La Greca, A. M., & Lopez, N. (1998). Social anxiety among adolescents: Linkages with peer relations and friendships. *Journal of Abnormal Child Psychology, 26*(2), 83–94.

Larson, R., & Richards, M. H. (1991). Daily companionship in late childhood and early adolescence: Changing developmental contexts. *Child Development, 62*, 284–300.

Lasgaard, M., Nielsen, A., Eriksen, M. E., & Goossens, L. (2009). Loneliness and social support in adolescent boys with autism spectrum disorders. *Journal of Autism and Developmental Disorders, 40*, 218–26.

Laugeson, E. A., Ellingsen, R., Sanderson, J., Tucci, L., & Bates, S. (2012). *The ABC's of Teaching Social Skills to Adolescents with Autism Spectrum Disorders in the Classroom: The UCLA PEERS® Program.* Manuscript submitted for publication.

Laugeson, E. A., & Frankel, F. (2010). *Social Skills for Teenagers with Developmental and Autism Spectrum Disorders: The PEERS Treatment Manual.* New York: Routledge.

Laugeson, E. A., Frankel, F., Gantman, A., Dillon, A. R., & Mogil, C. (2012). Evidence-based social skills training for adolescents with autism spectrum disorders: The UCLA PEERS® program. *Journal of Autism and Developmental Disorders, 42*(6), 1025–36.

Laugeson, E. A., Frankel, F., Mogil, C., & Dillon, A. R. (2009). Parent-assisted social skills training to improve friendships in teens with autism spectrum disorders. *Journal of Autism and Developmental Disorders, 39*, 596–606.

Laugeson, E. A., Paley, B., Frankel, F., & O'Connor, M. (2011). *Project Good Buddies Trainer Workbook.* Atlanta, GA: U.S. Department of Health and Human Services, Centers for Disease Control and Prevention.

Laugeson, E. A., Paley, B., Schonfeld, A., Frankel, F., Carpenter, E. M., & O'Connor, M. (2007). Adaptation of the Children's Friendship Training program for children with fetal alcohol spectrum disorders. *Child & Family Behavior Therapy, 29*(3), 57–69.

Laursen, B. & Koplas, A. L. (1995). What's important about important conflicts? Adolescents' perceptions of daily disagreements. *Merrill-Palmer Quarterly, 41*, 536–53.

Little, L. (2001). Peer victimization of children with Asperger spectrum disorders. *Journal of the American Academy of Child & Adolescent Psychiatry, 40*, 995

Mandelberg, J., Frankel, F., Gorospe, C., Cunningham, T. D., & Laugeson, E. A. (in press). Long term outcomes of parent-assisted Children's Friendship Training for children with autism spectrum disorders. *Journal of Mental Health Research in Intellectual Disabilities.*

Mandelberg, J., Laugeson, E. A., Cunningham, T. D., Ellingsen, R., Bates, S., & Frankel, F. (in press). Long term treatment outcomes for parent-assisted social skills training for adolescents with autism spectrum disorders: The UCLA PEERS® program. *Autism: The International Journal of Research and Practice, Special Issue on Evidence-Based Treatments for Autism Spectrum Disorders.*

Marriage, K. J., Gordon, V., & Brand, L. (1995). A social skills group for boys with Asperger's syndrome. *Australian & New Zealand Journal of Psychiatry, 29*, 58–62.

Matson, J. L. (2007). Determining treatment outcome in early intervention programs for autism spectrum disorders: A critical analysis of measurement issues in learning based interventions. *Research in Developmental Disabilities, 28*, 207–18.

Matson, J. L., Matson, M. L., & Rivet, T. T. (2007). Social-skills treatments for children with autism spectrum disorders: An overview. *Behavior Modification, 31*, 682–707.

McGuire, K. D., & Weisz, J. R. (1982). Social cognition and behavior correlates of preadolescent chumship. *Child Development, 53*, 1478–84.

McKenzie, R., Evans, J. S. B. T., & Handley, S. J. (2010). Conditional reasoning in autism: Activation and integration of knowledge and belief. *Developmental Psychology, 46*, 391–403.

Mesibov, G. B. (1984). Social skills training with verbal autistic adolescents and adults: A program model. *Journal of Autism and Developmental Disorders, 14*, 395–404.

Mesibov, G. B., & Stephens, J. (1990). Perceptions of popularity among a group of high-functioning adults with autism. *Journal of Autism and Developmental Disorders, 20*, 33–43.

Miller, P. M., & Ingham, J. G. (1976). Friends, confidants and symptoms. *Social Psychiatry, 11*, 51–8.

Morrison, L., Kamps, D., Garcia, J., & Parker, D. (2001). Peer mediation and monitoring strategies to improve initiations and social skills for students with autism. *Journal of Positive Behavior Interventions, 3*, 237–50.

Müller, E., Schuler, A., & Yates, G. B. (2008). Social challenges and supports from the perspective of individuals with Asperger syndrome and other autism spectrum disabilities. *Autism, 12*, 173–90.

Murray, D. S., Ruble, L. A., Willis, H., & Molloy, C. A. (2009). Parent and teacher report of social skills in children with autism spectrum disorders. *Language, Speech and Hearing Services in Schools, 40*, 109–15.

Nelson, J., & Aboud, F. E. (1985). The resolution of social conflict between friends. *Child Development, 56*, 1009–17.

Newcomb, A. F., & Bagwell, C. L. (1995). Children's friendship relations: A meta-analytic review. *Psychological Bulletin, 117*, 306–47.

Newcomb, A. F., Bukowski, W. M., & Pattee, L. (1993). Children's peer relations: A meta-analytic review of popular, rejected, neglected, controversial, and average sociometric status. *Psychological Bulletin, 113*, 99–128.

Newman, B., Reinecke, D. R., & Meinberg, D. L. (2000). Self-management of varied responding in three students with autism. *Behavioral Interventions, 15*, 145–51.

O'Connor, A. B., & Healy, O. (2010). Long-term post-intensive behavioral intervention outcomes for five children with autism spectrum disorder. *Research in Autism Spectrum Disorders, 4*, 594–604.

O'Connor, M. J., Frankel, F., Paley, B., Schonfeld, A. M., Carpenter, E., Laugeson, E., & Marquardt, R. (2006). A controlled social skills training for children with fetal alcohol spectrum disorders. *Journal of Consulting and Clinical Psychology, 74*(4), 639–48.

O'Connor, M. J., Laugeson, E. A., Mogil, C., Lowe, E., Welch-Torres, K., Keil, V., & Paley, B. (2012). Translation of an evidence-based social skills intervention for children with prenatal alcohol exposure in a community mental health setting. *Alcoholism: Clinical and Experimental Research, 36*(1), 141–52.

Olweus, D. (1993). Bullies on the playground: The role of victimization. In C. H. Hart (ed.), *Children on Playgrounds* (pp. 45–128). Albany, NY: State University of New York Press.

Orsmond, G. L., Krauss, M. W., & Selzter, M. M. (2004). Peer relationships and social and recreational activities among adolescents and adults with autism. *Journal of Autism and Developmental Disorders, 34*, 245–56.

Ozonoff, S., & Miller, J. N. (1995). Teaching theory of mind: A new approach to social skills training for individuals with autism. *Journal of Autism and Developmental Disorders, 25*, 415–33.

Parker, J. G., & Asher, S. R. (1993). Friendship and friendship quality in middle childhood: Links with peer group acceptance and feelings of loneliness and social dissatisfaction. *Developmental Psychology, 29*, 611–21.

Parker, J., Rubin, K., Price, J., & de Rosier, M. (1995). Peer relationships, child development, and adjustment. In D. Cicchetti, & D. Cohen (eds.), *Developmental Psychopathology: Vol 2. Risk, Disorder, and Adaptation* (pp. 96–161). New York: Wiley.

Perry, D. G., Kusel, S. J., & Perry, L. C. (1988). Victims of aggression. *Developmental Psychology, 24*, 807–14.

Perry, D. G., Williard, J. C., & Perry, L. C. (1990). Peer perceptions of the consequences that victimized children provide aggressors. *Child Development, 61*, 1310–25.

Phillips, C. A., Rolls, S., Rouse, A., & Griffiths, M. D. (1995). Home video game playing in schoolchildren: A study of incidence and patterns of play. *Journal of Adolescence, 18*, 687–91.

Putallaz, M. & Gottman, J. M. (1981). An interactional model of children's entry into peer groups. *Child Development, 52*, 986–94.

Rao, P. A., Beidel, D. C., & Murray, M. J. (2008). Social skills interventions for children with Asperger's syndrome or high-functioning autism: A review and recommendations. *Journal of Autism and Developmental Disorders, 38*, 353–61.

Rapin, I. (1999). Appropriate investigations for clinical care versus research in children with autism. *Brain & Development, 21*, 152–6.

Reichow, B., & Volkmar, F. R. (2010). Social skills interventions for individuals with autism: Evaluation for evidence-based practices within a best evidence synthesis framework. *Journal of Autism and Developmental Disorders, 40,* 149–66.

Remington, A., Swettenham, J., Campbell, R., & Coleman, M. (2009). Selective attention and perceptual load in autism spectrum disorder. *Psychological Science, 20,* 1388–93.

Riggio, R. (1989). Assessment of basic social skills. *Journal of Personality and Social Psychology, 51,* 649–60.

Rubin, Z. & Sloman, J. (1984). How parents influence their children's friendships. In M. Lewis (ed.), *Beyond the Dyad* (pp. 223–50). New York: Plenum.

Sansosti, F. J., & Powell-Smith, K. A. (2006). Using social stories to improve the social behavior of children with Asperger syndrome. *Journal of Positive Behavior Interventions, 8,* 43–57.

Schopler, E., Mesibov, G. B., Kunce, L. J. (1998). *Asperger's Syndrome or High Functioning Autism?* New York: Plenum Press.

Shantz, D. W. (1986). Conflict, aggression and peer status: An observational study. *Child Development, 57,* 1322–32.

Shattuck, P., Seltzer, M., Greenberg, M. M., Orsmond, G. I., Bolt, D., Kring, S., et al. (2007). Change in autism symptoms and maladaptive behaviors in adolescents and adults with an autism spectrum disorder. *Journal of Autism and Developmental Disorders, 37,* 1735–47.

Shtayermann, O. (2007). Peer victimization in adolescents and young adults diagnosed with Asperger's syndrome: A link to depressive symptomatology, anxiety symptomatology and suicidal ideation. *Issues in Comprehensive Pediatric Nursing, 30,* 87–107.

Sigman, M., & Ruskin, E. (1999). Continuity and change in the social competence of children with autism, Down syndrome, and developmental delays. *Monographs of the Society for Research in Child Development, 64,* 114.

Smith T., Scahill, L., Dawson, G., Guthrie, D., Lord, C., & Odom, S., et al. (2007). Designing research studies on psychosocial interventions in autism. *Journal of Autism and Developmental Disorders, 37,* 354–66.

Solomon, M., Goodlin-Jones, B., & Anders, T. F. (2004). A social adjustment enhancement intervention for high-functioning autism, Asperger's syndrome, and pervasive developmental disorder NOS. *Journal of Autism & Developmental Disabilities, 34*(6), 649–68.

Starr, E., Szatmari, P., Bryson, S., & Zwaigenbaum, L. (2003). Stability and change among high-functioning children with pervasive developmental disorders: A 2-year outcome study. *Journal of Autism and Developmental Disorders, 33,* 15–22.

Tantam, D. (2003). The challenge of adolescents and adults with Asperger syndrome. *Child and Adolescent Psychiatric Clinics of North America, 12,* 143–63.

Taylor, J. L., & Seltzner, M. M. (2010). Changes in autism behavioral phenotype during the transition to adulthood. *Journal of Autism and Developmental Disorders, 40,* 1431–46.

Thurlow, C., & McKay, S. (2003). Profiling "new" communication technologies in adolescence. *Journal of Language and Social Psychology, 22,* 94–103.

Travis, L. L., & Sigman, M. (1998). Social deficits and interpersonal relationships in autism. *Mental Retardation and Developmental Disabilities Research Reviews, 4,* 65–72.

Tse, J., Strulovitch, J., Tagalakis, V., Meng, L., & Fombonne, E. (2007). Social skills training for adolescents with Asperger syndrome and high functioning autism. *Journal of Autism and Developmental Disorders, 37,* 1960–8.

Van Bourgondien, M. E. & Mesibov, G. B. (1987). Humor in high-functioning autistic adults. *Journal of Autism and Developmental Disorders, 17,* 417–24.

Volkmar, F. R., & Klin, A. (1998). Asperger syndrome and nonverbal learning disabilities. In E. Schopler, G. B. Mesibov, & L. J. Kunce (eds.), *Asperger Syndrome or High Functioning Autism?* (pp. 107–21). New York: Plenum Press.

Warm, T. R. (1997). The role of teasing in development and vice versa. *Journal of Developmental & Behavioral Pediatrics, 18,* 97–101.

Webb, B. J., Miller, S. P., Pierce, T. B., Strawser, S., & Jones, P. (2004). Effects of social skills instruction for high-functioning adolescents with autism spectrum disorders. *Focus on Autism and Other Developmental Disabilities, 19*, 53–62.

Weiss, M. J., & Harris, S. L. (2001). Teaching social skills to people with autism. *Behavior Modification, 25*(5), 785–802.

Wentzel, K. R., Barry, C. M., & Caldwell, K. A. (2004). Friendships in middle school: Influences on motivation and school adjustment. *Journal of Educational Psychology, 96*, 195–203.

White, S. W. (2011). *Social Skills Training for Children with Asperger Syndrome and High-Functioning Autism*. New York: Guilford Press.

White, S. W., Keonig, K., & Scahill, L. (2007). Social skills development in children with autism spectrum disorders: A review of the intervention research. *Journal of Autism and Developmental Disorders, 37*, 1858–68.

White, S. W., Koenig, K., & Scahill, L. (2010). Group social skills instruction for adolescents with high-functioning autism spectrum disorders. *Focus on Autism and Other Developmental Disabilities, 25*, 209–19.

White, S. W., & Robertson-Nay, R. (2009). Anxiety, social deficits, and loneliness in youth with autism spectrum disorders. *Journal of Autism and Developmental Disorders, 39*, 1006–13.

Whitehouse, A. J., Durkin, K., Jaquet, E., & Ziatas, K. (2009). Friendship, loneliness and depression in adolescents with Asperger's syndrome. *Journal of Adolescence, 32*, 309–22.

Wing, L. (1983). Social and interpersonal needs. In E. Schopler & G. Mesibov (eds.), *Autism in Adolescents and Adults* (pp. 337–354). New York: Plenum Press.

Winter, M. (2003). *Asperger Syndrome: What Teachers Need to Know*. London: Jessica Kingsley Publishers.

Wood, J. J., Drahota, A., Sze, K., Har, K., Chiu, A., & Langer, D. A. (2009). Cognitive behavioral therapy for anxiety in children with autism spectrum disorders: A randomized, controlled trial. *Journal of Child Psychology and Psychiatry, 50*, 224–34.

Wood, J. J., Drahota, A., Sze, K., Van Dyke, M., Decker, K., Fujii, C., Bahng, C., Renno, P., Hwang, W., & Spiker, M. (2009). Effects of cognitive behavioral therapy on parent-reported autism symptoms in school-aged children with high-functioning autism. *Journal of Autism & Developmental Disabilities, 39*, 1608–12.

Woodward, L. J., & Fergusson, D. M. (2000). Childhood peer relationship problems and later risks of educational under-achievement and unemployment. *Journal of Child Psychology and Psychiatry, 41*, 191–201.

INDEX

Note: Page numbers in *italics* are for tables.